British Monetary Policy
1945–51

British Monetary Policy 1945–51

SUSAN HOWSON

CLARENDON PRESS · OXFORD

1993

Oxford University Press, Walton Street, Oxford OX2 6DP
Oxford New York Toronto
Delhi Bombay Calcutta Madras Karachi
Kuala Lumpur Singapore Hong Kong Tokyo
Nairobi Dar es Salaam Cape Town
Melbourne Auckland Madrid
and associated companies in
Berlin Ibadan

Oxford is a trade mark of Oxford University Press

Published in the United States
by Oxford University Press Inc., New York

British Library Cataloguing in Publication Data
Data available

Library of Congress Cataloging in Publication Data
Howson, Susan, 1945–
British monetary policy, 1945–51/Susan Howson.
Includes bibliographical references.
1. Monetary policy—Great Britain—History. I. Title.
HG939.5.H648   1993   332.4'941—dc20   93–18831
ISBN 0–19–828656–2

1 3 5 7 9 10 8 6 4 2

Typeset by Create Publishing Services Ltd., Bath, Avon
Printed in Great Britain
on acid-free paper by
Biddles Ltd.,
Guildford & King's Lynn

Acknowledgements

I SHOULD like to thank several friends and colleagues for their encouragement, advice, and criticism over the period that I have been working on the monetary policy of the first post-war Labour governments in Britain. I am especially indebted to those who read and commented on the complete or almost complete drafts of this book: Donald Moggridge (twice), David Laidler, Christopher Dow, Peter Clarke, Leslie Pressnell, and Forrest Capie. I am also grateful to those who read earlier versions of parts of it: Elizabeth Durbin, James Meade, Sir Alec Cairncross, Ian Drummond, Ron Shearer, Brian Tew, Geoff Wood, and Jeremy Wormell. They are not, of course, to be blamed for the errors, omissions, and infelicities which remain.

I much appreciate the helpful suggestions and information I have received from James Meade, Marjorie Durbin, Kenneth Morgan, Leslie Pressnell, Sir Alec Cairncross, Lady Trend and the late Lord Trend, Lord Jay, Lord Mayhew, and the late Lord Roberthall. I specially wish to thank Dr Angela Raspin of the British Library of Political and Economic Science for her invaluable assistance in using the Crosland, Dalton, Durbin, Meade, and Piercy Papers. Henry Gillett of the Bank of England and Dr Stephen Bird of the Labour Party were also generous in their help with the archives of the Bank of England and the Labour Party.

For permission to cite unpublished material I have to thank Dr Raspin, James Meade, Elizabeth Durbin, J. L. Piercy, Susan Crosland, the late Colin Clark, Leslie Pressnell, Brian Tew, the British Library of Political and Economic Science, the Labour Party, the Fabian Society, the Provost and Scholars of King's College, Cambridge, J. S. Fforde and the Bank of England, and, last but not least, the Controller of Her Majesty's Stationery Office.

I should also like to acknowledge the financial assistance of the Social Sciences and Humanities Research Council of Canada and the Humanities and Social Sciences Committee of the Research Board of the University of Toronto, and the generous hospitality of the Warden and Fellows of Nuffield College, Oxford and the President and Fellows of Wolfson College, Cambridge, which enabled me to commence and to complete the research and writing of this book.

Contents

Abbreviations

AER	*American Economic Review*
BEQB	*Bank of England Quarterly Bulletin*
BLPES	British Library of Political and Economic Science
BOE	Bank of England Archives
CEEC	Committee on European Economic Cooperation
CEPS	Central Economic Planning Staff
CIC	Capital Issues Committee
CLCB	Committee of London Clearing Bankers
CSO	Central Statistical Office
EEA	Exchange Equalization Account
EHR	*Economic History Review*
EJ	*Economic Journal*
ECA	Economic Cooperation Administration
EPT	Excess Profits Tax
EPU	European Payments Union
ERP	European Recovery Programme
FCI	Finance Corporation for Industry Ltd.
fob	free on board
FT	*Financial Times*
GATT	General Agreement on Tariffs and Trade
GDFCF	Gross domestic fixed capital formation
GDP	Gross domestic product
GNP	Gross national product
HF	Home Finance Division (of Treasury)
HMG	Her/His Majesty's Government
HMSO	Her/His Majesty's Stationery Office
HOPE	*History of Political Economy*
IBRD	International Bank for Reconstruction and Development
ICFC	Industrial and Commercial Finance Corporation
IEPS	Intra-European Payments Scheme
IMF	International Monetary Fund
JEEH	*Journal of European Economic History*
JEL	*Journal of Economic Literature*
JMK	*The Collected Writings of John Maynard Keynes*
JRSS	*Journal of the Royal Statistical Society*
LSE	London School of Economics and Political Science
MEW	Ministry of Economic Warfare

MP	Member of Parliament
n.d.	not dated
NDC	National Debt Commissioners
NEC	National Executive Committee (of Labour Party)
NFRB	New Fabian Research Bureau
NIB	National Investment Board
NIC	National Investment Council
OEEC	Organization for European Economic Cooperation
OEP	*Oxford Economic Papers*
OF	Overseas Finance Division (of Treasury)
PPS	Parliamentary Private Secretary
PRO	Public Record Office
QJE	*Quarterly Journal of Economics*
TDRs	Treasury deposit receipts
TRCs	Tax reserve certificates
TUC	Trades Union Congress

List of Tables

Introduction

> Everyone ... anticipated a better future after the enemy's
> defeat but what they had really hoped for was an improved
> past which the socialists ... failed to deliver.[1]

THE first post-war Labour government under Prime Minister
Clement Attlee was elected by a landslide in July 1945, two
months after the Allied defeat of Hitler's Germany—and, as it
turned out, three weeks before the end of the war with Japan.
The third Labour government in Britain, it was the first to command a majority in the House of Commons. It remained in
office—with a greatly reduced majority after a general election in
February 1950—until October 1951. Labour came to power
pledged to maintain full employment, to reform the UK financial
system, to nationalize major industries, and to improve the social
services. The plans for financial reform included the nationalization of the Bank of England in order to provide greater government control over the banking system and the establishment of a
'National Investment Board' to plan and to help finance public
and private investment.

The sudden final end of the war in August 1945, and the
immediate ending of American Lend-Lease, faced the new
government with unexpectedly acute external economic problems, most immediately the financing of a massive current
account balance-of-payments deficit which at £1,600m amounted
to 16 per cent of GNP. UK merchandise exports had been drastically cut back during the war and overseas assets had been sold off
to pay for supplies; it would take several years to build up exports
again and to raise them sufficiently above their pre-war volume
(by 50–75 per cent on official estimates) to make up for the
permanent loss of invisible earnings. In the meantime essential
imports had to be paid for and Britain's existing external
indebtedness was enormous. Net liabilities totalled £3,600m (of

---

[1] Michael Moorcock, *Mother London* (Harmondsworth, 1989), 60.

which £2,500m was to the rest of the sterling area) or 37 per cent of national income. UK official international reserves at £610m amounted to only 30 per cent of a year's imports.[2]

At the time of victory in Europe the war in the Far East was expected to last another eighteen months. During this period—known as Stage II—reconversion and the export drive could begin gradually in advance of full peace, Stage III. As it was, the Stage II and Stage III problems had to be faced simultaneously: the balance-of-payments problem; the transfer of manpower out of the armed forces and munitions production into peacetime occupations and the reconversion of British industry to produce more capital equipment, consumer goods, and exports; and the potential post-war inflation. Reconstruction and reconversion and the drive to increase exports would all mean heavy demands on scarce resources throughout the transitional period. The pressure of demand threatened serious domestic inflation which could make reconstruction more expensive and provoke resentment among consumers and workers. Similar conditions in the rest of the world also threatened to increase import prices.

The threat of domestic inflation in Britain, as in other countries, was increased by the legacy of wartime monetary policy. During the war the Treasury and the Bank of England (the UK monetary authorities) had deliberately kept nominal interest rates on government debt down to 3 per cent for long-term borrowing and greatly increased the quantities of money and liquid assets in the hands of the banks and the non-bank public. The money stock (measured as M3, the sum of currency in circulation and the total deposits of all UK banks) doubled from 1939 to 1945, growing at an average rate of 13 per cent a year. Since UK prices rose only about 50 per cent in the course of the war, the real value of the money balances held by the private sector was some 50 per cent higher at the end of the war than at the beginning. On the other

---

[2] R. S. Sayers, *Financial Policy 1939–45* (London, 1956), appendix I; C. H. Feinstein, *National Income, Expenditure and Output of the United Kingdom 1855–1965* (Cambridge, 1972), table 2. On wartime estimates of the post-war balance-of-payments problem see L. S. Pressnell, *External Economic Policy since the War, Volume I: The Post-War Financial Settlement* (London, 1987), appendix 27, and Austin Robinson, 'The economic problems of the transition from war to peace: 1945–49', *Cambridge Journal of Economics* 10 (1986), esp. 169–71.

hand real income (GDP) in 1945 was only 12.5 per cent higher than in 1939.[3]

Although economists in the Labour Party recognized that inflation and the balance of payments were the more *immediate* post-war problems,[4] the Party's plans were dominated by the desire to avoid the chronic unemployment that had dogged the British economy before the war. After the First World War a vigorous and highly inflationary reconstruction boom in 1919 collapsed early in 1920 at a time of tightening monetary policy. An equally severe but longer-lived slump followed. Unemployment, which reached 18 per cent as officially measured by December 1921, remained high throughout the interwar years. The officially recorded unemployment percentage fell below 10 per cent only in 1927 and rose above 30 per cent in the early 1930s under the impact of the world depression. The British economy then recovered quite rapidly compared with other countries but not sufficiently to remove the problem of a million unemployed (in a workforce of 23.6m) before the Second World War.[5]

Many in the Labour Party blamed Britain's economic ills on monetary mismanagement, especially Britain's return to the gold standard at pre-First World War parity with the US dollar in 1925, which dictated a tight monetary policy involving historically high nominal interest rates throughout the 1920s.[6] The party's plans for financial reform were developed in the 1930s after the 1931 financial crisis had brought down the second Labour government under Ramsay MacDonald and pushed Britain off the gold standard. Hugh Dalton, a professional economist who became the first Chancellor of the Exchequer in Attlee's government, took the initiative, enlisting the help of several younger economists

[3] Feinstein, *National Income*, tables 5 and 61; Forrest Capie and Alan Webber, *A Monetary History of the United Kingdom 1870–1982, Volume 1: Data, Sources, Methods* (London, 1985), table I(3).

[4] Labour Party, *Full Employment and Financial Policy*, Apr. 1944; Evan F. M. Durbin, 'The economic problems facing the Labour government', in Donald Munro (ed.), *Socialism: the British Way* (London, 1948), 3–29.

[5] Feinstein, *National Income*, tables 57 and 58.

[6] On the contribution of monetary policy to Britain's interwar economic performance see D. E. Moggridge, *British Monetary Policy 1924–1931* (Cambridge, 1972) and Susan Howson, *Domestic Monetary Management in Britain 1919–38* (Cambridge, 1975), and for a recent assessment Barry Eichengreen, 'The interwar economy in a European perspective', paper presented to the conference on Recent Research on Economic History in Britain, St Catharine's College, Cambridge, April 1991.

and Labour sympathizers in the City of London, in preparing a practical programme of economic and financial policy for a future majority Labour government. The main items in the post-war Labour government's economic policy proposals were adopted at the 1937 party conference.[7] During the war Dalton and some of his 'young economists' produced the party's policy statement, *Full Employment and Financial Policy*, published in April 1944. This anticipated the 'full employment' white paper of the wartime coalition government under Winston Churchill by six weeks and, once adopted by the party conference later that year, marked the official acceptance by the Labour Party of 'Keynesian' ideas on macroeconomic policy.

The coalition government's white paper on *Employment Policy* also originated in fears of a post-war slump, which were widespread on both sides of the Atlantic after the experience of the interwar years. In the circumstances of war it was morally and politically necessary to plan for a post-war world without the blight of heavy unemployment.[8] The white paper also reflected the belief of many economists and officials in wartime Whitehall that governments could take effective action to maintain employment in peace as well as in war.

The theory of output and employment developed by J. M. Keynes and his younger colleagues and disciples in the 1930s held out the prospect that *cyclical* unemployment could be prevented or at least reduced by the management of aggregate demand. Keynesian economists in wartime government service, especially James Meade in the Economic Section of the Cabinet Offices and Keynes himself in the Treasury, saw to it that planning for the post-war world built upon these ideas. (Since Keynesian economists such as Meade, Colin Clark, and Joan Robinson advised the Labour Party in the 1930s the convergence of views in the two 'white papers' on employment policy in 1944 was not coincidental.) Developments in economic *policy* in the 1930s also helped to persuade permanent civil servants and politicians that a macroeconomic employment policy was poss-

[7] Hugh Dalton, *The Fateful Years: Memoirs 1931–1945* (London, 1957), 23–4, 115–30; Ben Pimlott, *Hugh Dalton* (London, 1985), ch. XIV; and Elizabeth Durbin, *New Jerusalems: The Labour Party and the Economics of Democratic Socialism* (London, 1985).

[8] *Employment Policy*, Cmd. 6527, May 1944; Paul Addison, *The Road to 1945: British Politics and the Second World War* (London, 1975).

ible. The abandonment of the gold standard in 1931 and the adoption of a managed floating exchange rate from 1932 freed monetary policy for domestic objectives and increased the power of the Treasury over monetary policy. A policy of 'cheap money' had been maintained from 1932 through Britain's recovery from the depression, rearmament in 1938–9, and into the war. Bank rate was kept at 2 per cent, except for a short-lived rise in August–October 1939. In the later 1930s, under the pressure of rearmament, the Treasury's commitment to balancing the government's budget was also weakening. The Keynesian 'stabilization' budget' of April 1941 was for many years regarded as the culmination of that process—although the conventional view has been under attack for the last decade.[9]

The Labour Party statement and the government White Paper both envisaged the use of countercyclical budgetary policy to stabilize aggregate demand and maintain high employment in the longer run, that is after the inflationary transitional period. In the shorter run both documents argued for the retention of wartime economic controls to suppress immediate post-war inflation. They also recommended the continuation of the wartime cheap money policy in order to keep nominal interest rates low during the transitional period. This would require the continuation of wartime exchange controls to insulate the domestic capital market and of restrictions on bank lending as well as government controls over investment and the allocation of raw materials. For the Party economists these would be the beginning of *permanent* government control over the UK financial system.

In the event the monetary policy of the post-war Labour government in 1945–51 was neither cautious nor radical. The Bank of England was taken into public ownership by March 1946, but the National Investment Board never materialized. Wartime financial controls were continued but instead of using them to maintain the wartime 3 per cent level for nominal long-term

[9] On the evolution of UK monetary and fiscal policy in the 1930s see Howson, *Domestic Monetary Management*, chs. 5 and 6; Susan Howson and Donald Winch, *The Economic Advisory Council 1930–1939: A Study in Economic Advice during Depression and Recovery* (Cambridge, 1977), ch. 5; G. C. Peden, *British Rearmament and the Treasury 1932–1939* (Edinburgh, 1979); Roger Middleton, *Towards the Managed Economy* (London, 1985); Alan Booth, *British Economic Policy, 1931–49: Was There a Keynesian Revolution?* (1989), ch. 2. On wartime developments see Sayers, *Financial Policy*, ch. 3; Jim Tomlinson, *Employment Policy: The Crucial Years 1939–1955* (Oxford, 1987); and Booth, *British Economic Policy, 1931–49*, chs. 3–7.

interest rates, Dalton tried to *lower* interest rates to 2½ per cent—an unusual objective at a time of severe inflationary pressure. He began by reducing short-term interest rates on the government's floating debt in October 1945. In 1946 he tried, at first successfully, to reduce nominal yields on long-term government securities by ½ per cent. When he tried to sell irredeemable government bonds yielding 2½ per cent at par, he ran into difficulties which appear, at least with hindsight, inevitable. The immediate consequence was to prolong the rapid monetary expansion of the war for two years into the peace. Dalton's 'cheaper money policy' was effectively abandoned early in 1947, a year of domestic and external economic crises.

The fuel and convertibility crises of 1947 had major and longlasting effects on economic policy in the remaining four years of the Labour administration.[10] In August 1945 the Attlee government's first attempt to deal with the immediate balance-of-payments problem had been to send Lord Keynes, who remained in the Treasury as an adviser to Dalton until his death in April 1946, to Washington to negotiate for American financial assistance. The Anglo-American Financial Agreement of 6 December 1945 provided for a line of credit of $3,750m from the effective date of the agreement, which came to be 15 July 1946, to 31 December 1951. The conditions attached to the agreement included that one year from the effective date of the agreement the UK would make sterling freely convertible into US dollars and other currencies for current transactions. The British government also borrowed a further $1,250m from the Canadian government in March 1946.[11] In 1947 the UK balance of payments deteriorated markedly on both current and capital accounts, the American loan was drawn on at an unexpectedly rapid rate, and when convertibility was duly restored on 15 July 1947 the further loss of reserves forced its suspension five weeks later, on 20 August.

These events brought home to government ministers as well as to already worried officials the international context in which domestic economic policy had to be made and hence the need to

[10] On the development of the crises see Alec Cairncross, *Years of Recovery: British Economic Policy 1945–51* (London, 1985), chs. 6 and 13, and Alex J. Robertson, *The Bleak Midwinter 1947* (Manchester, 1987).

[11] On the loans see Pressnell, *External Economic Policy since the War, Volume I: The Post-War Financial Settlement*, and R. N. Gardner, *Sterling-Dollar Diplomacy* (London, 1956).

reduce inflationary pressure rather than attempt to suppress it by physical and price controls remaining from wartime. The controls were proving inadequate to the task and although attempts were made to strengthen them, especially on investment, budget surpluses were now to be the main weapon against inflation.[12] Monetary policy was not, however, called in to assist in an anti-inflation policy.

Dalton resigned as Chancellor of the Exchequer in November 1947, after carelessly 'leaking' details of a supplementary budget before presenting it to the House of Commons. His austere successor, Sir Stafford Cripps, continued the 'disinflationary' budgetary policy initiated by Dalton for another three years. He also continued 'cheap money'. Bank rate remained at 2 per cent and the fixed low interest rates on the floating debt at about ½ per cent, while nominal yields on long-term government bonds, which had returned to 3 per cent during 1947, were allowed to drift slowly upwards to around 3¾ per cent by 1950. The money supply (M3) grew slowly, at about 2 per cent a year instead of the double-digit rates of wartime and Dalton's cheaper money policy, so that with prices rising slightly faster real money balances were declining. Since rising bank lending tended to offset the effect of government budget surpluses on the money supply, the London clearing banks were from time to time 're-quested' by the Chancellor of the Exchequer through the Governor of the Bank of England to moderate the growth of their advances. Although this was the only visible sign of concern to control monetary growth or to adjust domestic monetary policy to external realities, it in fact masked prolonged discussions in the Treasury and the Bank of England over the problem of monetary policy.[13]

Britain had a fixed exchange rate for the pound against the US dollar from 1939 until 1972. The devaluation of the pound, from US $4.03 to US $2.80, on 18 September 1949, was a major step in the transition from war to peace in the world economy, prompting similar or smaller devaluations of several other currencies.

[12] J. C. R. Dow, *The Management of the British Economy 1945-60* (Cambridge, 1964), chs. 2, 6–8; Cairncross, *Years of Recovery*, chs. 15, 17.
[13] Howson, 'The problem of monetary control in Britain, 1948–51', *JEEH* 20 (Spring, 1991), 59–92; J. S. Fforde, *The Bank of England and Public Policy, 1941–1958* (Cambridge, 1992), ch. 5(*g*); see also Cairncross, 'Prelude to Radcliffe: Monetary policy in the United Kingdom 1948–57', *Rivista di Storia Economica*, 4 (1987), 1–20.

The 1947 balance-of-payments crisis had resulted from both an increasing current account deficit and capital outflows, in spite of the fact that the convertibility required under the Loan Agreement was for current not capital transactions and that exchange controls had been in force up until July. The deterioration of the balance of payments again two years later was also on both current and capital accounts even though the pound was inconvertible. When the current account returned to overall balance in 1948, a sizeable deficit with the dollar area remained while the countries with which Britain enjoyed a surplus had currencies which were not convertible into dollars. Economists including those in government such as Robert Hall and Marcus Fleming in the Economic Section began to argue for devaluation. The change took place once speculation had built up sufficiently to make it inevitable and once economists in government—most notably three young ministers, Hugh Gaitskell, Douglas Jay, and Harold Wilson (then, respectively, the Minister of Fuel and Power, Economic Secretary at the Treasury, and the President of the Board of Trade)—had managed to persuade a reluctant Cripps that it was both inevitable and desirable.[14]

In 1950 further progress was made in the transition from a war to a peace economy. Domestically direct controls were being relaxed—except in the monetary field. Externally import and exchange controls were beginning to be reduced with the establishment of the European Payments Union. But the outbreak of the Korean War in June 1950 and the 1950–1 commodity price boom brought new problems of rearmament and renewed problems of inflation and the balance of payments. These faced a new Chancellor of the Exchequer, Hugh Gaitskell, who took over when Cripps resigned because of ill-health in October 1950. He had been Minister of State for Economic Affairs at the Treasury since February. He followed his predecessor in using 'disinflationary' budgetary policy as his main weapon against inflation. As in 1949 there was considerable agreement among economists—including those actively involved in the Labour Party—that use should also be made of monetary instruments. There was also pressure from the Bank of England to raise short-term interest rates, as has long been suspected and as the published

---

[14] Cairncross, *Years of Recovery*, ch. 7.

diaries of some of the policymakers make clear.[15] This pressure was part of a long-drawn-out campaign by C. F. Cobbold, Governor of the Bank since March 1949, to restore the Bank's pre-war position in the UK financial system in spite of its nationalization by the Labour Government. Although Gaitskell paid more attention to monetary conditions than Cripps had, he did not make any dramatic changes in monetary policy in his year at the Treasury.

Cobbold brought his campaign to a successful conclusion after the defeat of the Labour goverment and the election of a Conservative government in October 1951. The new Chancellor of the Exchequer, R. A. Butler, readily agreed to the request of the Bank and the strong advice of his Treasury officials to raise Bank rate to 2½ per cent and to 'return to the pre-war use of a flexible monetary policy'.[16] The monetary measures included the rise in Bank rate on 7 November; a change in the relation between Bank rate and money market rates of interest; and the replacement of nearly one-third of outstanding Treasury bills by special short-term bonds with a higher interest rate. These were followed by the introduction of restrictions on hire purchase finance early in the new year and a further rise in Bank rate to 4 per cent, announced in the budget on 11 March 1952.[17] In this way monetary policy was 'revived' after twenty years of cheap money. With the Bank of England in firm control again of UK monetary policy, it ended the hopes of Dalton's 'young economists' for major reform of the financial system.

From the perspective of a monetary economist forty years later the monetary policies of the first post-war Labour governments raise several puzzles, which are the starting point and motivation for this book. The availability of official records for the period since the early 1980s and of improved statistical series enables them to be looked at with new evidence, which is discussed below.

First, just what was the 'cheaper money policy' of 1945–7 and

---

[15] Dow, *Management of the British Economy*, 60, 230; Philip M. Williams (ed.), *The Diary of Hugh Gaitskell 1945–1956* (London, 1983), 227; Alec Cairncross (ed.), *The Robert Hall Diaries 1947–53* (London, 1989), 134, 143, 157, 152.

[16] R. A. Butler, *The Art of the Possible* (London, 1971), 158.

[17] Committee on the Working of the Monetary System, *Report*, Cmnd. 827, 1959, paras. 406–8; Fforde, *Bank*, ch. 6(a).

what was it intended to achieve? Why did Dalton try to lower nominal interest rates on government debt at a time of severe inflationary pressure? What was the relation of his policy to the wartime 'cheap money' whose continuance was recommended in the *Employment Policy* white paper and the party's own *Full Employment and Financial Policy*?

Secondly, what were the consequences of 'cheaper money'? It has often been argued that Dalton's policy, even if inapproriate to the immediate post-war situation, could have had little effect on the British economy at the time. As C. M. Kennedy pointed out, 'inflationary pressures were in any case to be expected in all sectors of the economy, and whether these pressures were aggravated to any appreciable extent by Cheaper Money remains ... a matter of doubt'. In the 1960s Christopher Dow also thought that 'it must remain doubtful whether cheap money was seriously harmful'. More recently Sir Alec Cairncross argued that cheap money was '*à la mode*'—other countries had low nominal interest rates, in some cases lower than Britain's—and that open inflation was not a problem in Britain in the first two post-war years.[18]

The conventional view of the (limited) effects of cheaper money plays down, even if it does not entirely ignore, the potential impact of monetary expansion on private consumption expenditure, reflecting a Keynesian view of the transmission mechanism of monetary policy which sees monetary policy as operating mainly through the effects of interest-rate changes on investment. More 'monetarist' theories stress the real balance effects of monetary policy on consumption demand and also allow for significant lags in the effects of monetary policy. Also, theories of the balance of payments of a small open economy under fixed exchange rates imply that if monetary expansion does boost aggregate demand the impact will be seen in the balance of payments rather than on the rate of inflation at home. There is a case for reassessing the contribution of cheaper money to Britain's economic difficulties in the later 1940s in the light of more recent economic theory.

A third question relates to the abandonment of cheaper money:

[18] C. M. Kennedy, 'Monetary policy', in G. D. N. Worswick and P. H. Ady (eds.), *The British Economy 1945–1950* (Oxford, 1952), 195; Dow, *Management of the British Economy*, 21–2; Cairncross, *Years of Recovery*, 428–9.

what induced Dalton to retreat when he did and was the 'failure' of his policy inevitable? As Dow remarked, 'The fact that it failed gives an air of inevitability to the failure; but it constitutes no proof.'[19] The implied counterfactual becomes easier to judge once one has looked again at the extent of monetary expansion in 1946–7 and considered the authorities' aims and objectives at that time as they appear from the official records.

After the retreat from cheaper money the authorities apparently pursued a 'neutral money' policy during Stafford Cripps's (and Hugh Gaitskell's) time at the Exchequer. Here again one would like to know just what the policy was and what was its official rationale? Why did the authorities revert to cheap money rather than use monetary policy more actively to back up the deflationary budgetary policy either before or after the 1949 devaluation? As I have already indicated, this was not just a reaction against the activist policy of the previous two years, but the outcome of a lengthy and unresolved (under the Labour governments) dispute between ministers, Treasury officials, and government economists, and the Bank of England over the role of monetary policy. The positions of the major players in the dispute go far to explain why there was no change in monetary stance to accompany the 1949 devaluation and also why Gaitskell chose to maintain (insofar as he did) the stance of monetary policy set by his predecessor.

By the time Gaitskell became Chancellor of the Exchequer outside opinion on the utility of monetary policy, in Britain as in many other countries on both sides of the Atlantic, had swung away from the attachment to cheap money of the immediate post-war years. Several other countries made major changes in their conduct of monetary policy at the beginning of the 1950s. Gaitskell was a professional economist (the second to become Chancellor of the Exchequer, Dalton having been the first); one wonders whether and to what extent his views on macroeconomic policy in an inflationary world had changed in the same direction as those of other British economists including his friends and colleagues in the Labour Party. Since the return to a

---

[19] *Management of the British Economy*, 227; see also his evidence to the Radcliffe Committee: 'The economic effect of monetary policy 1945–57', in Committee on the Working of the Monetary System, *Principal Memoranda of Evidence*, vol. 3 (London, 1960), 78.

'flexible' monetary policy took place immediately after the 1951 general election, would it have taken place anyway if Labour had been re-elected? Other countries had made similar moves somewhat earlier; to what extent was the British move simply the following of a fashion in the conduct of economic policy? Was it a (belated) recognition that the UK was now a small open economy whose domestic monetary policy under a fixed exchange rate would have to conform to the requirements of external balance?

There is in principle no independent role for monetary policy in a small open economy with a fixed exchange rate. When a balance-of-payments deficit is financed by the running down of official international reserves, this will reduce the domestic money stock unless the monetary authorities can sterilize the effects of the reserve losses by buying domestic-currency securities from the private sector. Since reserve losses cannot continue indefinitely and since an inflationary monetary policy would tend to worsen the balance-of-payments deficit, monetary policy must sooner or later conform to the requirements of external balance. Similarly, a balance-of-payments surplus and accumulation of reserves should lead ultimately to an increase in the domestic money supply (or its rate of growth). In consequence, nominal interest rates on domestic securities—and the domestic rate of price inflation for that matter—will not be able to diverge for long from the level prevailing in the rest of the world. Exchange controls and import controls can provide some insulation by reducing imports of goods and services or outflows of capital, and hence a balance-of-payments deficit, below what they would have been in the absence of the controls, but in peacetime at least, cannot *close* an economy completely. The extent of the UK authorities' control over capital flows and imports was declining—though not at all steadily—after the war, especially from 1947 onwards.

Before accepting the increasing openness of the UK economy as *the* explanation of the development of the 1945–51 Labour governments' monetary policies, it is, however, necessary to consider the links between Britain's balance of payments, official international reserves, and the money supply. As I explain in Chapter 1 below, the nature of the wartime exchange control and the existence of the 'sterling area' to which this control applied, meant that the links were not straightforward either during or after the war. In 1945 and 1946 the UK current account balance of payments was not a major influence on the money supply. At the same time UK reserves (and money supply) were not insulated from external shocks in the form of capital movements in spite of exchange control on capital account transactions. The degree of international capital mobility was low (since capital flows could not respond freely to interest rate differentials) but it cannot be assumed to be zero. The usual Mundell–Fleming type assumption that with capital controls and a fixed exchange rate a current account deficit would require sterilization of reserve changes by the central bank is thus not appropriate.[20] On the one hand the current account of the overseas sterling area might be in surplus while Britain's was in (smaller) deficit; on the other there were capital movements between the dollar and sterling areas. However, these factors might point in the same direction as the UK current account, and an increasing UK deficit on current account might also provoke a speculative capital outflow from sterling, making an indirect link between the UK deficit and the reserves. The premature attempt at making the pound freely convertible into dollars for current transactions in 1947, and the swift return to inconvertibility, further complicated Britain's external financial arrangements, with significant implications (not all running in the same direction) for the degree of openness (on both capital and current account) of the UK economy in the later 1940s. The behaviour of Britain's reserves did not always follow the behaviour of her balance-of-payments deficit—or consistently dictate the behaviour of the money supply.

The relations between Britain's balance-of-payments position and domestic monetary variables are a recurrent theme in the chapters which follow. But the major international financial events which formed the backdrop to domestic monetary policy are not the main focus of this book. Other authors have already told a large part of the story of economic policymaking in connection with these events, including the convertibility crisis, the Marshall Plan and the European Recovery Programme, the 1949 devaluation, the formation of the European Payments Union, Korean war rearmament, and the balance-of-payments crisis of

---

[20] On financially closed and financially open economies see R. I. McKinnon, 'The exchange rate and macroeconomic policy: changing postwar perspectives', *JEL* 19 (1981), 531–57.

1951.[21] The recently published official history of the Bank of England 1941–58 by J. S. Fforde and the forthcoming official history of Britain's external economic policy 1945–58 by L. S. Pressnell both provide much fuller accounts of the formulation of Britain's international monetary policy, especially since the relevant official documents have not yet all been released. What this book does attempt to show is how the *domestic* financial policy of the Labour governments was shaped in the context of international monetary developments and the balance-of-payments problems of the UK. My perspective is different from J. S. Fforde's account of monetary policy in the 1940s and 1950s from the Bank of England point of view, even though partly based on the same archival documents.

It follows from what I have just said that another concern of this book is the 'socialist' element in Labour monetary policy, both as planned and as it turned out. According to its election manifesto, *Let Us Face the Future*, the 1945 Attlee government was explicitly and proudly socialist in planning to nationalize the major industries in Britain. The pre-war plans in the party for monetary policy and financial reform were intended to facilitate this transformation of the British economy as well as to provide full employment. In spite of the forward planning in the party before 1945, by 1951 control of the banking system and other financial institutions in Britain was little changed from what it had been before the Second World War, except that the Bank of England was no longer a private company.

The sources used for this study are both statistical and archival. In 1985 the publication of the first volume of *A Monetary History of the United Kingdom 1870–1982* by Forrest Capie and Alan Webber provided for the first time estimates of the total UK money stock for years before 1963, including monthly figures from the 1920s. Previously monthly data were available only for the components of the monetary base (currency in circulation plus bank reserves) and the balance sheets of the London clearing banks. Although the incomplete data could indicate the main trends in UK monetary growth because the deposits of the London clearing banks

---

[21] Alan Milward, *The Reconstruction of Western Europe 1945–51* (London, 1984); Cairncross, *Years of Recovery*, chs. 4–10; Michael J. Hogan, *The Marshall Plan: America, Britain and the Reconstruction of Western Europe, 1947–52* (Cambridge, 1987); Jacob J. Kaplan and Günther Schleiminger, *The European Payments Union: Financial Diplomacy in the 1950s* (Oxford, 1989); and Fforde, *Bank*, ch. 4.

constituted nearly 85 per cent of total UK bank deposits in 1945–51, the advantage of the *Monetary History* series is not only their coverage of other UK banks but that they comprise consistent series for several monetary aggregates (M1, M3, and one measure of the monetary base) and their components. The discussion in this book of the behaviour of monetary variables is based mainly on their data.

The official papers of the 1945–51 Labour governments have been generally available in the Public Record Office since January 1982. I have utilized mainly the Treasury records, which include those of the Economic Section since the Section was moved from the Cabinet Offices to the Treasury in 1953. I have used Cabinet records to a lesser extent since the day-to-day problems of monetary policy rarely reached the Cabinet. An indispensable source of information on those problems has been the papers on monetary policy and debt management of the Chief Cashier of the Bank of England in the Bank of England Archives, which are still in the process of being opened. The Bank generously allowed me access to Bank files for the 1945–51 period while J. S. Fforde was working on his official history of the Bank.

The private papers of Hugh Dalton, James Meade, and Lord Piercy, in the British Library of Political and Economic Science (BLPES) at LSE have proved invaluable. I have also consulted the papers of Colin Clark (Brasenose College, Oxford), Anthony Crosland and Evan Durbin (BLPES), Joan Robinson (King's College, Cambridge), and Lord Butler and Lord Pethick-Lawrence (Trinity College, Cambridge). Unfortunately the Cripps Papers in Nuffield College, Oxford are sparse and the Gaitskell Papers (University College, London) are still closed. Fortunately, as already mentioned above, the published diaries of Gaitskell and Robert Hall both shed much light on the monetary policies of Cripps and Gaitskell. Last but not least, I have used the archives of the Labour Party (at Labour Party Headquarters) and the Fabian Society (Nuffield College, Oxford), especially in investigating the sources of ideas in the Party on 'socialist' monetary policy in the 1930s and 1940s.

Chapter 1 describes the theoretical and practical background to post-war monetary policy. It begins with an outline of Keynesian monetary theory as it had developed by the outbreak of the

Second World War, before describing British wartime financial policy and monetary arrangements, including their legacy for the post-war national debt and the money stock. It then considers wartime official plans for post-war monetary policy and debt management, which had been clearly spelled out under the coalition government in a 'National Debt Enquiry' early in 1945. I look at these before considering wartime planning for post-war in the Labour Party, because they followed logically from the wartime cheap money policy. I also consider the plans of the Bank of England which differed considerably in their aims and presuppositions about the post-war world and post-war monetary problems.

The nature and extent of the plans in the Labour Party for the economic and financial policy of a majority Labour government have already been indicated. The plans, and their development by Dalton's 'young economists' in the later 1930s and early 1940s, are the subject of Chapter 2, which also covers the role of party economists in post-war planning within the Churchill coalition government as well as in the policy committees of the party.

Chapter 3 relates the monetary and financial policies pursued by Dalton as Chancellor of the Exchequer in 1945–6: his 1945 and 1946 budgets, his attempts at financial reform and the nationalization of the Bank of England, and his 'cheaper money policy'. I consider why Dalton's financial reforms were so limited relative to the party's plans formulated by his colleagues and protegés and why he pursued cheaper money which was *not* in those plans and a dangerous policy to pursue in immediate post-war circumstances. The narrative covers the deliberations of the policymakers behind each step in the policy and the details of debt management. After indicating the consequences of cheaper money for the behaviour of the money supply the chapter concludes with an assessment of Dalton's reasons for his policy and the acceptance or at least acquiescence in it of his advisers.

Chapter 4 is devoted to the failure of the cheaper money experiment. This has four aspects which I consider in turn. First, there is the external background to the abandonment of cheaper money—the economic crises of 1947 and the reorientation of budgetary policy in response to the balance-of-payments problem. Second is the authorities' gradual retreat from cheaper money during 1947. Thirdly, there are the adverse effects of the policy on the British economy, which have been played down in most previous analyses. Finally, there is the question whether the policy did or could achieve Dalton's aims. His aims included the inexpensive financing of the nationalization of the major industries, which is treated in an appendix to this chapter. Having argued in the third section that the inflationary impact of the cheaper money policy was likely to be far-reaching, I conclude that the policy was both inappropriate and bound to fail.

The problem of monetary control left by Dalton's (and wartime) monetary policy for his successors as Chancellor of the Exchequer is the subject of Chapter 5. After outlining the behaviour of the balance of payments in 1948–51 and the disinflationary policy pursued under Cripps, the chapter recounts the recurring and often confused discussions over the role of monetary policy among the monetary authorities during Cripps's time at the Exchequer. It also looks at the relation between monetary policy under Cripps and the devaluation of the pound in September 1949, and the behaviour of monetary variables in 1948–51.

Chapter 6 discusses the continuation and intensification of the dispute over monetary policy in 1950–1 after the general election in February 1950 between Gaitskell and the Governor of the Bank. It first briefly describes the new problems faced by Gaitskell and his budget of April 1951. It also indicates some of the changes of opinion in 1950–1 among official and party economists on future economic prospects and on the role of monetary policy. The chapter concludes with the end of the monetary dispute between Bank and Treasury in the winter of 1951–2, after the defeat of the Labour government in the October 1951 election, and indicates the (limited) extent to which the 'revival' of monetary policy in Britain in 1951 was influenced by similar earlier developments in other countries.

A short final chapter summarizes my conclusions.

1

Cheap Money

> For some time after the war it will be necessary ... to maintain a policy of cheap money. Thereafter, the possibility of influencing capital expenditure by the variation of interest rates will be kept in view.[1]

THE meaning of 'cheap money' has changed over the years. It used to mean low money market rates of interest, at which commercial bills could be discounted, and since these rates were strongly infuenced by Bank rate, a 3 per cent Bank rate was regarded as the upper limit of cheap money. By the 1940s it included low *long-term* nominal interest rates, thought to be relevant to firms' investment decisions. Since then in a more inflationary world it has come to mean low *real* interest rates. The purpose of this chapter is to describe the policy of cheap money adopted in Britain for the duration of the Second World War and to explain why it was generally expected to be continued for at least the 'transitional period' from war to peace. The discussion is in three parts: I first outline some salient features of monetary theory in the 1940s before describing UK wartime financial policy and its limited role for monetary policy; I then turn to wartime official plans for post-war financial policy, especially monetary policy and debt management. Chapter 2 will discuss the plans of the Labour Party for post-war financial policy, whose origins go back to the early 1930s and the aftermath of the downfall of the last Labour government in 1931.

Monetary theory in the early 1940s

When Sir Richard Hopkins, just retired as Permanent Secretary to the Treasury, was asked in the spring of 1945 to draft the report of an official committee on post-war monetary policy and debt

[1] *Employment Policy*, Cmd. 6527, May 1944, para. 59.

management, he read Keynes's *General Theory of Employment, Interest and Money* (1936) twice and D. H. Robertson's *Essays in Monetary Theory* (1940).[2] Robertson was a major critic of Keynes's monetary theory, and Keynes and Robertson had both provided advice to the Treasury in 1939 on the appropriate monetary policy for the war.

In the late 1930s monetary economics had been dominated by reaction and response to Keynes's *General Theory*, with its effective demand theory of output and employment, marginal efficiency of capital theory of investment, and liquidity preference theory of interest. At the same time, after the worldwide depression of the early 1930s and only partial recovery from it in many countries, there had been growing concern that a new slump would sooner or later occur, possibly even 'secular stagnation' if the opportunities for large-scale capital investments dried up in mature high-saving economies. Rearmament and war postponed the date of the anticipated slump to the later 1940s. The fear of a major post-war slump combined with academic monetary theory to downgrade the potential of monetary policy in the views of many economists on both sides of the Atlantic.

According to the classical economic theory of interest, the equilibrium level of interest rates was determined by the 'real forces of productivity and thrift': that is, it was the level which equated aggregate desired capital investment, which depended on the marginal productivity of capital and the rate of interest, with desired aggregate savings (dependent on people's thriftiness as well as on interest rates). The equilibrium would involve the full employment of available resources (capital and labour) as long as there were no rigidities in prices and wage rates to interfere with the movement towards equilibrium. Keynes attacked this view on the grounds that saving was a function of income rather than of interest rates, that investment was dominated by entrepreneurs' expectations and their 'animal spirits', and that discrepancies between desired saving and desired investment were resolved by changes in income, not interest rates. Interest rates were instead determined by the demand for money

---

[2] *The Collected Papers of James Meade, Volume IV: The Cabinet Office Diary 1944–46*, eds. Susan Howson and Donald Moggridge (London, 1990), 70. The committee was the National Debt Enquiry, whose deliberations are discussed later in this chapter.

to hold (liquidity preference) and the supply of money determined by the banking system (including the central bank).[3] The rate of interest was therefore a *monetary* phenomenon:

the rate of interest at any time, being the reward for parting with liquidity, is a measure of the unwillingness of those who possess money to part with their liquid control over it. The rate of interest is not the 'price' which brings into equilibrium the demand for resources to invest with the readiness to abstain from present consumption. It is the 'price' which equilibrates the desire to hold wealth in the form of cash with the available quantity of cash . . . .[4]

According to the *General Theory*, the demand for money arose for three reasons, which Keynes summarized as: '(i) the transactions-motive, i.e. the need of cash for the current transaction of personal and business exchanges; (ii) the precautionary-motive, i.e. the desire for security as to the future cash equivalent of a certain proportion of total resources; and (iii) the speculative-motive, i.e the object of securing profit from knowing better than the market what the future will bring forth.'[5] The last was the most volatile, depending on assetholders' expectations of future interest rates, so that although short-term money-market interest rates were easily controlled by the monetary authorities, long-term nominal interest rates were determined largely by those expectations. Keynes drew the implication, which Hopkins was to fasten on in writing his report:

Thus a monetary policy which strikes public opinion as being experimental in character or easily liable to change may fail in its objective of greatly reducing the long-term rate of interest, because M_2 [the amount of money held for speculative reasons] may tend to increase almost without limit in response to a reduction of r [the rate of interest] below a certain figure. The same policy, on the other hand, may prove easily successful if it appeals to public opinion as being reasonable and practicable and in the public interest, rooted in strong conviction, and promoted by an authority unlikely to be superseded.

It might be more accurate, perhaps, to say that the rate of interest is a highly conventional, rather than a highly psychological, phenomenon. For its actual value is largely governed by the prevailing view as to what

---

[3] The classical theory therefore determined the real rate of interest in the first instance, the Keynesian theory the nominal rate. On either theory the nominal rate would differ from the real rate by the expected rate of inflation, which was usually assumed implicitly or explicitly to be zero.

[4] *General Theory*, 167.   [5] Ibid. 170.

its value is expected to be. *Any* level of interest which is accepted with sufficient conviction as *likely* to be durable *will* be durable; subject, of course, in a changing society to fluctuations for all kinds of reasons round the expected normal.'[6]

Keynes's critics took him to task for neglecting in his liquidity preference theory the real forces of productivity and thrift, which must after all play some role in the determination of interest rates in anything other than the shortest run. Even on the Keynesian assumption that individuals' decisions to save and consume do not depend significantly on interest rates, real or nominal, an increase in investment or a reduction in saving will raise income and the transactions demand for money; this would raise interest rates if the money supply were not also increased.[7] Robertson and the Swedish economist Bertil Ohlin both developed an alternative theory to encompass both real and monetary forces in the determination of interest rates, according to which interest rates are determined by the demand and supply of credit or 'loanable funds'. The supply of loanable funds includes current savings, past savings previously used for investment in fixed or working capital and now available for reinvestment, past savings previously held as idle money balances, and new bank loans; the demand for loanable funds reflects both the demand for borrowed funds to invest in real capital or to consume in excess of current income and the demand for money to hold idle. Thus nominal (and real) interest rates are determined in practice by the supply and demand for the whole range of securities other than money and hence reflect all the factors, including the real forces of productivity and thrift, that determine the stock of securities in existence and the prices that assetholders are willing to pay for them.[8]

The resulting debate between Keynes and Robertson (with contributions from Ohlin, J. R. Hicks, R. G. Hawtrey, and others) is perhaps best summed up in Robertson's epigraph to his *Essays*: 'And so she [Alice] went on, taking first one side and then

[6] Ibid. 203; below p. 52.

[7] This point was made by Robertson in his *Essays on Monetary Theory* (11–12 and 134–5, for instance) and by Meade in the National Debt Enquiry (below).

[8] Robertson, 'Mr. Keynes and the rate of interest', *Essays in Monetary Theory*, 2–4; see also Robertson, 'Some notes on Mr Keynes' theory of employment', *QJE* 51 (Nov. 1936), 188–91 and Ohlin, 'Some notes on the Stockholm theory of savings and investment', *EJ* 47 (June and Sept. 1937), 53–69, 221–40.

the other, and making quite a conversation of it altogether.' None the less by the end of the 1930s it had become clear that with appropriate definitions the 'alternative' theories were consistent with one another. To put it most briefly, general equilibrium requires that the demands and supplies of securities other than money must be equal to each other and that the demand for money must be equal to its supply. Interest rates can be equally well said to be determined in the market for loanable funds or in the market for money.[9] In Robertson's words, 'when we have picked our way through these verbal tangles we are left . . . in no doubt about the relation between the two methods of approach. Essentially they are two different ways of saying the same thing'.[10]

With the adoption of the Keynesian theory of output and employment, especially by younger economists, liquidity preference became the fashionable theory of money and interest. By the time that the war took most economists away from academic life there had been a considerable amount of empirical work to develop and test the liquidity preference theory.[11] There had also been empirical studies of the interest-elasticity of investment expenditures, the most influential being the famous survey by the Oxford Economists' Research Group of firms' views on the role of interest rates in their investment decisions. The replies received were generally negative on the direct effect of interest rates on investment plans but they were not unambiguous as to the indirect effects especially of changes in long-term interest rates.[12] Although one Oxford economist, James Meade, did not

[9] J. R. Hicks, *Value and Capital* (Oxford, 1939), ch. XII; see also Bernard F. Haley, 'Value and Distribution', and Henry H. Villard, 'Monetary theory', both in Howard S. Ellis (ed.), *A Survey of Contemporary Economics* (American Economic Association, 1948), esp. 39–42 and 331–6.

[10] Robertson, *Essays in Monetary Theory*, 9.

[11] For example, A. J. Brown, 'The liquidity-preference schedules of the London Clearing Banks', *OEP*, no. 1 (Oct. 1938), 49–82, and 'Interest, prices and the demand schedule for idle money', *OEP*, no. 2 (May 1939), 46–69, and M. Kalecki, 'The short-term rate and the long-term rate', *OEP*, no. 4 (Sept. 1940), 15–22. For a fascinating and informative personal account of the impact of the *General Theory* on research and teaching in Oxford in the late 1930s see Arthur Brown, 'A worm's eye view of the Keynesian Revolution', in John Hillard (ed.), *J. M. Keynes in Retrospect* (Aldershot, 1988), 18–44.

[12] J. E. Meade and P. W. S. Andrews, 'Summary of replies to questions on effects of interest rates', *OEP*, no. 1 (Oct. 1938), 14–31, and Andrews, 'A further inquiry into the effects of rates of interest', *OEP*, no. 3 (March 1940), 33–73. The two articles were reprinted in abridged form in T. Wilson and P. W. S. Andrews,

conclude that investment was insensitive to interest-rate changes, most agreed with Richard Sayers:

that 'the potency of that weapon [the rate of interest] in a constantly changing world must, I think, be described as very low' ... In general, ... 'the evidence warns us not to expect the instruments of banking policy—particularly the rate of interest—to do more than help us in the right direction. Banking policy is not enough.'[13]

Thus, although sharply rising interest rates might help to check investment in a boom, in a slump the government would have to supplement or substitute for expansionary monetary policy other macroeconomic policy measures, especially budgetary policy, in order to prevent large-scale unemployment.

Keynes's and Robertson's views on the role of monetary policy in the business cycle were rather different. Keynes himself did not share the belief that investment was interest-inelastic but because of his emphasis on the role of expectations in entrepreneurs' and assetholders' decisions he believed that there was limited scope for using interest-rate variations to control investment. The cyclical fluctuations in entrepreneurs' estimates of the marginal efficiency of capital could require large swings in long-term interest rates to offset their effects on capital investment, while assetholders' interest-rate expectations could make it very difficult for the monetary authorities to engineer such swings. Long-term nominal interest rates would have to be kept fairly low throughout the business cycle, because if the central bank raised them in order to check investment in a boom it could find it difficult to lower them again in the slump.[14] As he put it in his 'Notes on the trade cycle' in the *General Theory*:

The boom which is destined to end in a slump is caused ... by the combination of a rate of interest, which in a correct state of expectation would be too high for full employment, with a misguided state of expec-

Oxford Studies in the Price Mechanism (Oxford, 1951), 27–30, 51–67. On the origins of the inquiry see H. D. Henderson, 'The significance of the rate of interest', *OEP*, no. 1 (Oct. 1938), 1–13 (also in Wilson and Andrews, *Oxford Studies in the Price Mechanism*, 16–27).

[13] R. S. Sayers, 'The rate of interest as a weapon of economic policy', in Wilson and Andrews, *Oxford Studies in the Price Mechanism*, 5. Sayers is quoting his own 'Business men and the terms of borrowing', *OEP*, no. 3 (Mar. 1940), 23–31 (Wilson and Andrews, *Oxford Studies in the Price Mechanism*, 67–74).

[14] *General Theory*, 161–4, 202–4, 315–20; D. E. Moggridge and S. Howson, 'Keynes on monetary policy, 1910–1946', *OEP* 26 (July 1974), 239–40.

tation which, so long as it lasts, prevents this rate of interest from being deterrent. A boom is a situation in which over-optimism triumphs over a rate of interest which, in a cooler light, would be seen to be excessive.

Thus the remedy for the boom is not a higher rate of interest but a lower rate of interest! For that may enable the so-called boom to last. The right remedy for the trade cycle is not to be found in abolishing booms and thus keeping us permanently in a semi-slump; but in abolishing slumps and thus keeping us permanently in a quasi-boom.[15]

To such extravagant remarks Robertson took strong objection. In addition to his suspicion that Keynes overestimated the contribution of monetary as opposed to real factors in determining long-term real and nominal interest rates, he had serious doubts whether monetary forces were important in causing cyclical fluctuations: 'if I have a personal heresy in these matters, it is that in recent years, alike in academic financial and political circles, we have heard rather too much about . . . [interest rates] in connection with the processes of trade recovery and recession.' To him 'the phenomena of boom and slump are not primarily a matter of interest rates at all, but of something much more deep-seated, namely, of the inevitable discontinuity which attends the efforts of man to achieve material progress', in other words the bunching of new inventions and technological innovations. On this view, it 'seems doubtful how much the most skilful monetary policy can be expected to do, either in flattening out the precipitous peaks of activity into long continuous tablelands, or in filling up the ravines which lie between'.[16] To try to prolong a boom indefinitely by means of cheap money might merely result in inflation without maintaining full employment; it would be better to allow nominal interest rates to rise in a boom to discourage speculative or otherwise undesirable investment and plan to use expansionary fiscal policy along with cheaper money to prevent a severe fall in employment in the slump. He did not share Keynes's concern that cheaper money might be hard to achieve after a spell of dear money, since he was 'less sanguine . . . about the power of the monetary authority to make the rate of interest what it pleases . . . [and] also less apprehensive . . . about the

---

[15] *General Theory*, 322, where the two paragraphs appear in the reverse order and where Keynes makes it clear that the policy conclusion only holds if there are in force alternative methods of checking investment in a boom.

[16] *Essays in Monetary Theory*, 147, 126–7.

power of the hoarding instinct to oppose a chronic resistance to such a secular fall in the rate of interest as the forces of thrift and productivity may dictate'.[17] When giving advice to the British government in 1937 on 'the maintenance of trade activity' in the slump expected in the near future he disagreed with Keynes's recommendation to maintain low nominal long-term interest rates in face of a boom and strongly supported proposals for the advance planning of countercyclical public works.[18]

As the end of the Second World War approached the fears of a major slump resurfaced. The general expectation was that it would be only two or three years after the war ended when unemployment would threaten to become a problem again. In his appendix to William Beveridge's *Full Employment in a Free Society* (1944) on 'The quantitative aspects of the full employment problem in Britain', Nicholas Kaldor explicitly assumed the transition from war to peace would last 2½ years, so that if the war in Europe ended in the middle of 1945, 1948 would be the 'first normal post-war year'.[19] It was anticipated on both sides of the Atlantic that the slump would begin in the United States. Although academic criticisms and the wartime experience of full employment had reduced fears of 'secular stagnation' in the USA, they had not completely banished them. Many American economists viewed the first post-war slump with considerable apprehension. Some also feared that the countercyclical measures that would be taken in response might not be sufficient to prevent the slump spreading to the rest of the world through declining US demand for imports.[20]

There was also considerable support in the United States for the idea that interest rates were ineffective in influencing investment. The Oxford study was often cited as was a comparable

[17] Ibid. 152.

[18] Howson and Winch, *The Economic Advisory Council 1930–1939*, 140–1, 343–53.

[19] William H. Beveridge, *Full Employment in a Free Society* (London, 1944), appendix C, 367. On the views of the economists who assisted Beveridge see also Ch. 2 below.

[20] Herbert Stein, *The Fiscal Revolution in America* (Chicago, 1969), 175–6; Benjamin Higgins, 'Concepts and criteria of secular stagnation', in *Income, Employment and Public Policy, Essays in Honor of Alvin H. Hansen* (New York, 1948), 82–107; League of Nations, *Economic Stability in the Post-War World: Report of the Delegation on Economic Depressions, Part II* (Geneva, 1945), chapter 16; and, for the views in early 1945 on post-war prospects of economists working for the Roosevelt administration, Meade, *Cabinet Office Diary*, 37, 44, 54.

study by J. F. Ebersole at Harvard and F. A. Lutz's article on 'The interest rate and investment in a dynamic economy', which sought to provide a theoretical basis for the apparently negative findings of the empirical studies on the influence of interest rates on investment. As Henry Wallich of the Federal Reserve Bank of New York put it, there had been a 'Great Disillusionment' with monetary policy as a regulator of economic activity after the US experience of the 1930s. He argued that the interest rate was now less important as a countercyclical policy instrument than as a factor influencing income distribution, largely because of the increase in the size of the US national debt.[21] This increase was one legacy of wartime financial policy, to which I shall now turn.

Wartime financial policy

In war the assignment of economic policy instruments to policy targets is necessarily dominated by the single major objective of channelling all available resources to the war effort. Subsidiary objectives are to achieve this in ways which minimize the associated costs of inflation during the war and the post-war debt burden. In Britain during the Second World War fiscal policy and direct controls were jointly assigned to the tasks of making the maximum amount of domestic resources available for war purposes and keeping the rate of inflation down to some 'acceptable' level. It was decided in October 1939 that nominal interest rates would be fixed so as to keep down the cost of wartime government borrowing and of servicing the post-war debt. In this decision the desire to avoid the high interest rates of the First World War, academic advice on the possibilities of controlling nominal interest rates, and the experience of cheap money since 1932 all played a part.[22] With the exchange rate of sterling against the dollar pegged for the duration, a prerequisite for the maintenance of cheap money was exchange controls, which were imposed in

[21] J. Franklin Ebersole, 'The influence of interest rates upon entrepreneurial decisions in business—a case study', *Harvard Business Review* 17 (Autumn 1938), 35–9; Friedrich A. Lutz, 'The interest rate and investment in a dynamic economy', *AER*, 35 (Dec. 1945), 811–30; Villard, 'Monetary theory', in Ellis (ed.), *A Survey of Contemporary Economics*, 345–51; Henry C. Wallich, 'The changing significance of the interest rate', *AER*, 36 (Dec. 1946), 761–87; see also Wallich, 'Debt management as an instrument of economic policy', *AER*, 36 (June 1946), 292–310.

[22] Sayers, *Financial Policy*, ch. 5; and below.

September 1939. Monetary policy was not assigned any of its usual roles, such as the preservation of external balance, the control of inflation, or the distribution of resources between consumption and investment.

Before the war the pound had been floating in principle, managed in practice by the Exchange Equalization Account (EEA) introduced in 1932. It had been fairly steady around $4.95 from late 1933 until mid–1938. During these years Bank rate had been unchanged at 2 per cent and nominal yields on long-term government debt averaged just over 3 per cent. The threat of war induced large capital flows from Europe to America; the UK authorities allowed the pound to fall in 1938 before pegging it at $4.68 in January 1939. On 24 August they again abandoned support, and raised Bank rate from 2 to 4 per cent. On the outbreak of war ten days later they introduced exchange controls and pegged the exchange rate at $4.03. The rate chosen, on the recommendation of the Bank of England, was not seriously questioned during the war; the only proposal to alter it was in 1943–4 to simplify it to $4.00, which did not seem worth the disruption.[23]

The basic decision on wartime interest rates was also taken in 1939 for the duration. The academic advice came from Keynes and Robertson. They were both members of the government's Committee on Economic Information which produced its last report, on the problems of financing defence expenditure in a near-war situation, in July 1939. Reflecting mainly Keynes's ideas, the report advocated the rationing of investment expenditure through controls, limitation of firms' dividends and the investment of their undistributed profits in government securities, and measures to stimulate exports, in order to reduce inflationary pressure and the balance-of-payments problem caused by increased defence expenditure. The direct control of investment was needed because the 'classical remedy' of dear money would have little immediate impact on firms which financed investment out of undistributed profits, would have its main impact on the building industries and hence release few

---

[23] S. Howson, *Sterling's Managed Float: The Operations of the Exchange Equalisation Account, 1932–39,* Princeton Studies in International Finance No. 46, Nov. 1980, 31–2; Sayers, *Bank of England,* 561–7, 571–5, and *Financial Policy,* 460–4; Pressnell, *External Economic Policy since the War,* vol. 1, 161.

resources for exports, and would be expensive to the 'greatest borrower in the market to-day', the government.[24]

At the same time Treasury officials, in a Committee on the Control of Savings and Investment chaired by Sir Frederick Phillips (Joint Third Secretary), which they asked Dennis Robertson to join, were discussng ways of maximizing the flow of funds into government securities. They considered the views on wartime government borrowing of both the Bank of England and of Keynes, which converged in recommending the maintenance of low nominal interest rates throughout the war. In April 1939 the Governor of the Bank (Montagu Norman) had told the Chancellor of the Exchequer that 'maximum rates of interest for medium and long issues by H.M.G. [should be set] at the outset and adhered to for all subsequent issues'.[25] Keynes made his views known in letters to the Chancellor and the Governor and in letters and articles in *The Times* as well as through the Committee on Economic Information. In line with his liquidity preference theory he argued that the government could and should finance its rapidly increasing expenditure at low interest rates by supplying short- or long-term securities to match assetholders' preferences, if necessary borrowing from the banks and allowing the money supply to expand if liquidity preference was high. The Treasury could set the interest rates it chose on government borrowing by

attending to three simple principles: by giving the market the increased amount of liquidity which it demands in present circumstances, by waiting until the market is ready [before making any new issues of gilt-edged securities], and by promoting a sense of confidence in what the future borrowing policy of the Treasury is going to be,

thus making sure assetholders had no expectation of higher future interest rates. The level of nominal interest rates he suggested was the average of those prevailing in 1935-7.[26]

Senior Treasury officials were at first doubtful whether the

[24] EAC(SC)34, Committee on Economic Information, 27th Report, Defence expenditure and the economic and financial problems connected therewith, 20 July 1939, CAB58/30, PRO; Howson and Winch, *Economic Advisory Council*, 148-50.
[25] Norman to Chancellor, 26 Apr. 1939, and Bank of England, 'Borrowing in War-time', T160/1289/F19426/1, PRO; see also Sayers, *Bank of England*, 583-4.
[26] 'Borrowing by the state', *The Times*, 24 and 25 July 1939, *JMK*, vol. 21, 558-9: see also 533-46.

authorities could set nominal interest rates on long-term government debt and sustain them during a long war.[27] At the committee's second meeting, however, it considered a note by Robertson restating, critically, Keynes's thesis. As Sayers noted, Robertson was critical of Keynes's proposals for the *pre-war* period. He thought that a ' "repressive" policy' should include five ingredients: direct control of public investment, rationing of structural materials, capital issues control, government borrowing of undistributed profits, and 'hardening of interest rates'. He continued: 'I still feel some surprise at the warmth with which many of those who accept 1 to 4 . . . repudiate (5) as unthinkable. But I am not wedded to (5) on any grounds of principle if it can be avoided.' With physical and financial controls, as there would be in wartime, interest rates could be kept down. According to the minutes the Treasury committee 'discussed the questions of economic theory involved, and their relation to Treasury policy in borrowing on short- and long-term'.[28] The committee's report in August considered and rejected the idea of compelling building societies and insurance companies to increase their holdings of British government securities, recommended the control of all new private capital issues, and pointed out the authorities could increase the demands for government securities as a whole by offering a wide range of securities with different conditions and maturities to suit different types of investors with their different attitudes to risk and return. The report did not specify the level of interest rates to be offered but it did assume a considerable amount of borrowing would be on Treasury bills. When the Treasury consulted the Governor of the Bank, they agreed that the the key rate (for moderately long-term government securities) should be 3 per cent.[29] The methods subsequently used to maintain this level were the same as those favoured by Keynes and the Bank (see below).

The imposition of exchange control had long been regarded as

[27] 'Borrowing in war-time, comments by Sir F. Phillips on the note by the Bank of England', 17 May 1939, and 'Note by Sir F. Phillips on the matters before the committee', T160/1289/F19426/1, PRO.

[28] Robertson, 'The problem of "pre-war" finance', 7 July, and Committee on Control of Savings and Investment, Second Meeting, 10 July 1939, T160/1289/F19426/1; Sayers, *Financial Policy*, 155–6.

[29] Report of Committee on Control of Savings and Investment, 11 Aug. 1939, T160/1289/F19426/3; Sayers, *Financial Policy*, 161, *Bank of England*, 583–4.

inevitable if war came. The Bank had, with the Treasury, been planning for it since 1937.[30] The wide ranging controls applied to the foreign assets of UK residents, the sterling assets of those living outside the sterling area, and all monetary transactions between the UK and countries outside the sterling area. The sterling area included the Dominions and colonies of the British Empire, except Canada and Newfoundland (which were in the dollar area) and Hong Kong, plus Egypt, the Sudan, Iraq, and Ireland. These countries had held their foreign exchange reserves in sterling in London before the war but the sterling area as such was formally created by the UK controls. The first steps in 1939 were to enable the Treasury to requisition foreign-currency securities from UK residents, who were prohibited from disposing of them without the authorities' permission; to require UK residents to sell all gold and foreign exchange held or received to the authorities; to permit UK residents to obtain foreign currency only for specified purposes from the banks who were authorized to act as the authorities' agents; and to restrict payments in *sterling* by UK residents to non-residents.[31] The 'foreign currencies' and 'non-residents' of the regulations did not include those of certain Commonwealth countries, thus legally defining the sterling area; these Commonwealth countries introduced similar exchange controls of their own and other countries were added as and when they instituted effective exchange control.

The controls did not at first extend to non-residents' holdings of sterling, which could be freely transferred between non-residents, used to pay for imports from sterling area countries, or converted into hard currencies. It therefore became necessary in 1940 to reduce the availability and usability of such balances, by further limiting the purposes for which residents could make payments to non-residents, by requiring UK exports of important commodities to be invoiced in dollars, and by making bilateral payments agreements with the monetary authorities of countries outside the sterling area. These measures also successfully enforced a single official exchange rate for all transactions

---

[30] Sayers, *Bank of England*, 567–71.

[31] For details of the regulations, orders and exemptions see Sayers, *Financial Policy*, ch. 8, and 'The U.K. exchange control: a short history', *BEQB* 7 (Sept. 1967), 246–51.

between the sterling area and the rest of the world, by drying up the free market for sterling.

During the war the countries of the overseas sterling area generally sold the gold and foreign exchange they earned to the Bank of England for sterling, as well as receiving sterling in payment for UK imports. (An exception was the retention of some newly mined gold by South Africa.) The resulting 'dollar pool' (of gold, dollars, and a very small quantity of other foreign currencies) could be drawn on for all sterling area payments for imports from the dollar area. In order to conserve the centralized reserves it was necessary to supplement exchange control with import controls, which were gradually introduced in the relevant countries over 1940–1.[32] Since UK exports were restricted during the war (by the need to produce guns rather than butter and by conditions attached to US Lend-Lease), the amount of imports permitted by the controls became the major determinant of the current account of the balance of payments.

Britain's wartime balance of payments is shown in Table 1.1. The current account deficit increased during the course of the war from £250m in 1939 (4 per cent of a GDP of just under £6,000m) to over £1,600m (16 per cent of GDP) in 1945. It was financed first by the running down of reserves and the sale of overseas assets and then by US Lend-Lease and Canadian mutual aid as well as by the accumulation of liabilities in sterling to the rest of the sterling area. On 31 August 1939 Britain's gold and foreign currency reserves (predominantly US and Canadian dollars) were £503m.[33] They fell below £70m in 1941 before the introduction of Lend-Lease enabled Britain and the rest of the sterling area to procure military and other supplies from the USA without immediate payment or a monetary debt but for some 'consideration' to be negotiated. (President Roosevelt made the offer of Lend-Lease on 17 December 1940 and signed the Lend-Lease Act on 11 March 1941 but it was some more months before existing contracts on a cash-and-carry basis were completed and British-owned American assets sold for dollars as required by the US Administration.) Over 1942–4 these reserves, which were for the whole sterling area, were built up at the same time as Britain's

[32] Kenneth M. Wright, 'Dollar pooling in the sterling area, 1939–1952', *AER*, 44 (Sept. 1954), 559–76.
[33] *Reserves and Liabilities 1931 to 1945*, Cmd. 8354, 1951.

TABLE 1.1 *UK Balance of Payments, Annual, 1939–45, £m*

	1939	1940	1941	1942	1943	1944	1945
Exports of goods[1]							
Cash	500	400	400	300	240	270	450
Reciprocal aid				100	700	800	500
Imports of goods[1]							
Cash	800	1,000	1,100	800	800	900	700
Lend-Lease			300	1,200	2,100	1,600	1,300
Trade balance	−300	−600	−1,000	−1,600	−1,960	−2,430	−1,050
Net invisibles[2,3] (a)	+50	−200	−120	−160	−120	−50	−620
(b)		−200	−200	−300	−300	−300	−600
(c) Government		−300	−300	−400	−300	−100	−400
(d) Shipping		0	−100	−100	−100	−200	−100
(e) Interest and other invisibles		100	200	200	100	0	−100
Current balance excluding grants	−250	−800	−1,120	−1760	−2080	−2480	−1670
Grants			300	1,100	1,400	1,600	800
Current account	−250	−800	−820	−660	−680	−680	−870
Net long-term capital flows		200	300	200	200	100	100
Changes in overseas sterling holdings[4]		200	600	500	700	700	700
Changes in official international reserves[5]		−437	−133	+113	+203	+144	+9

Notes

[1] fob

[2] Includes private and government transfers *except* major grants of aid.

[3] (a) = Feinstein's figures; (b)–(e) = Sayers's estimates.

[4] Includes sterling and dollar liabilities.

[5] With respect to reserve figures, + = increase, − = decrease.

Sources

Sayers, *Financial Policy 1939–45* (London, 1956), Appendix I, tables 7 and 10; Feinstein, *National Income, Expenditure and Output of the United Kingdom 1855–1965* (Cambridge, 1972), 112–13 and table 37.

liabilities to the overseas sterling area and to other countries mounted to over £3,000m by the end of the war. Lend-Lease and the sterling balances took care of the balance-of-payments problem until August 1945 when, in line with the provisions of the Lend-Lease Acts, President Truman terminated Lend-Lease after VJ day.

On the domestic front the Keynesian analysis of the 'inflationary gap' between total desired expenditure and available output was employed from the 1941 budget on to ascertain how far *fiscal policy* could be used to 'close the gap' and thus finance government expenditure without inflation.[34] In terms of the national income identity

$$Y = C + I + G + X - M$$

if expenditure (the sum of items on the right hand side) threatens to exceed output (Y), then the gap will be closed by inflation. Since exports (X) were deliberately cut back to release resources for war production and imports (M) controlled, and government expenditure (G) was in effect to be maximized, private consumption and investment (C and I) had to be reduced if inflation were to be avoided. Equivalently, writing the identity as

$$G - T + X + R - M = S - I$$

where T = revenue from taxation and R = international transfer payments (so that $X + R - M$ = the current account of the balance of payments), the current account was balanced by Lend-Lease etc. and the problem of fiscal policy was to raise taxation so as to make $G - T$ equal to estimated voluntary private saving (net of private investment which was small and subject to direct controls). By August 1945 the standard rate of income tax had reached 50 per cent and the highest marginal rate 97.5 per cent, while tax allowances had been reduced. Part of the income tax paid, specifically that resulting from the reduction of allowances in the 1941 budget, was a deferred credit payable after the war— the 'post-war credits'—an innovation loosely based on Keynes's proposal in his *How to Pay for the War* (1940).[35]

In addition to high taxation *direct controls* were used to restrict inessential consumption and to confine investment to that needed for war production, as well as to allocate resources among competing government uses. By the end of the war the controls included the rationing of consumer goods and price controls; the control of investment by machinery and building licences; allocation of raw materials; the direction of labour in accordance with a 'manpower budget'; and import controls.[36]

[34] Sayers, *Financial Policy*, chs. 3 and 4; see also Richard Stone, 'The use and development of national income and expenditure estimates', in D. N. Chester (ed.), *Lessons of the British War Economy* (Cambridge, 1951), 89–94.

[35] For details of wartime tax rates and allowances see B. E. V. Sabine, *British Budgets in Peace and War, 1932–1945* (London, 1970).

[36] W. K. Hancock and M. M. Gowing, *British War Economy* (London, 1949), chs. 11, 12, and 15.

An important part of the attempt to use budgetary policy to control wartime inflation was the provision of subsidies to major items in the official cost-of-living index, beginning with food subsidies in December 1939. In his 1941 'stabilization budget' the Chancellor of the Exchequer (Sir Kingsley Wood) made the commitment to 'endeavour to prevent any further rise in the cost-of-living index number, apart from minor seasonal changes, above the present range of 125–130 in terms of the pre-war level'.[37] The main reason for the policy was to remove excuses for wartime wage increases. By August 1945 the cost-of-living index stood at 132 (September 1939 = 100), while money wages had risen by 50 per cent over the same period, implying annual average rates of price and wage inflation of 5.3 and 8.3 per cent.[38]

Table 1.2 shows the outcome for real macroeconomic variables. By 1945 consumption and imports of goods and services had both been reduced to 86 per cent of their pre-war levels, fixed invest-

TABLE 1.2 *Gross Domestic Product and Gross National Product, 1939–45, £m at 1938 Market Prices*

	1939	1940	1941	1942	1943	1944	1945
C	4,416	3,999	3,837	3,796	3,751	3,864	4,108
G	1,134	2,646	3,317	3,478	3,594	3,364	2,733
I	530	460	370	320	220	170	190
S	+100	+150	+60	−50	+60	−120	−120
X	700	480	410	370	410	520	420
M	1,090	1,110	970	820	810	900	860
GDP	5,790	6,625	7,024	7,094	7,225	6,898	6,471
PI	158	114	88	61	49	42	40
GNP	5,948	6,739	7,112	7,155	7,274	6,940	6,511

Notes
C = consumers' expenditure, G = government current expenditure on goods and services, I = gross domestic fixed capital formation, S = value of change in stocks, X = exports of goods and services, M = imports of goods and services, GDP = gross domestic product, PI = net property income from abroad, and GNP = gross national product.

Source
Feinstein, *National Income, Expenditure and Output of the United Kingdom 1855–1965*, table 5.

[37] *House of Commons Debates*, vol. 370, 7 Apr. 1941, cols. 1322–3, quoted in Sayers, *Financial Policy*, 66.
[38] Calculated from Feinstein, *National Income*, table 61.

ment to less than one-third and exports to little over half their pre-war levels, while government current expenditure had more than trebled. Consumers' expenditure took up 63 per cent, rather than the pre-war 79 per cent, of real national income, government current expenditure 42 per cent (instead of 17 per cent) and gross fixed investment only 3 per cent (compared with 11 per cent in 1939).

Taxation covered about 50 per cent of wartime government expenditure. The wartime role of monetary policy and debt management was to facilitate government borrowing at low nominal interest rates, as far as possible by attracting the savings of the non-bank private sector into government bond issues, and if that could not be done without raising interest rates, by borrowing from the banking system. The '3 per cent war' began with the lowering of Bank rate in October 1939 to 2 per cent—from 3 per cent to which it had been lowered on 28 September after its rise to 4 per cent in August—and with the fixing of the Treasury bill rate at 1 per cent. From the summer of 1940 it involved the continuous supply of a range of maturities of government securities so as to maintain their nominal yields around 2½ per cent for medium-term and 3 per cent for long-term government bonds. With their prices thus fixed the quantities of the different assets outstanding including the nominal money stock were determined by the private sector's demand for the different maturities, and the extent to which the debt was monetized depended on assetholders' 'liquidity preference'.

Treasury bills were as in peacetime issued to the money market by weekly tender and to government departments on tap. In the First World War Treasury bills had been offered on 'tap' at fixed rates to the private sector as well as to public departments. In the Second World War the authorities retained the weekly tender and provided an additional instrument, Treasury deposit receipts (TDRs), for borrowing from the banking system. The rate of interest on Treasury bills was fixed at 1 per cent for the duration by the Bank of England standing ready to buy in Treasury bills from the discount houses at that rate rather than Bank rate.

TDRs were suggested by the Bank of England after the 'dismal failure' of the first wartime bond issue in March 1940. The state of the war in the spring of 1940 also threatened heavy reliance on floating debt.[39] From July the major banks operating in the London money market—the London clearing banks and the Scottish banks plus the Commonwealth Bank of Australia and the National Bank of Egypt—were instructed each Friday to lend to the government whatever total amount was required to cover the difference between its current expenditure and revenue from all other sources. TDRs were of six months' maturity, compared with the three months of Treasury bills, and bore interest at 1⅛ per cent, compared with 1 per cent on Treasury bills. (On their customers' deposits which the banks were thus transferring to the Exchequer the banks had already agreed not to pay more than 1 per cent interest.) Although the innovation was seen in some quarters as revolutionary (see Chapter 2), it was intended to preserve existing arrangements, whereby the discount houses covered the weekly tender of Treasury bills and the the Bank did not deal directly with the commercial banks. The authorities continued to supply Treasury bills to the discount houses, from whom the domestic banks bought them, to other central banks and to UK government departments: of the £4,000m Treasury bills outstanding at the end of the war (compared with £1,000m at the beginning) approximately one-third was held by each of UK banks, overseas official holders, and public departments.

The first wartime bond issue for cash was a conventional issue (£300m 3% War Loan 1955/59) offered for sale on 12 and 13 March 1940. Private sector subscriptions were meagre and a high proportion of the stock was bought in by the authorities, who thereafter tried a different tack.[40] They offered each bond issue on tap for several months at a time, successfully encouraging private demand by making it clear at the outset that later issues would be offered on worse terms. The first tap issue in June 1940 of 2½% National War Bonds was of 5–7 years' maturity; the first issue of 3% Savings Bonds at the beginning of 1941 was for 14–21 years. The terms of subsequent issues were worsened by maintaining these coupon rates and slightly lengthening the maturities, so that the 2½ per cent and 3 per cent bonds on tap in August 1945 were for 9–11 years and 20–30 years respectively. Each tap was closed once sales had reached a respectable size so as to avoid a bunching of maturities in post-war years, although this could not prevent a high volume of maturing stocks to be repaid or replaced

[39] Sayers, *Financial Policy*, 218–25.   [40] Ibid. 198–207.

after the war. The total amount of longer-term gilt-edged stocks sold was £2,984m for the 2½% National War Bonds and £2,781m for 3% Savings Bonds (by December 1945) but some of these were held by public departments and the Issue Department of the Bank of England.

It had become standard practice before the war for the authorities to 'underwrite' new government issues, by purchasing some of the new stock for the Issue Department of the Bank of England, who would gradually sell it as private demand arose. The Commissioners for the Reduction of the National Debt, more commonly known as the National Debt Commissioners (NDC), also bought long-term government issues for the funds they administered such as the deposits of the Trustee Savings Banks and the Post Office Savings Bank (the savings bank funds, for short). Both the NDC and the Issue Department also bought up stocks nearing maturity in order to convert them when a conversion offer of replacement stock was duly made and to reduce the amount repaid in cash if there was no conversion.[41] Under the wartime cheap money policy the NDC bought long-term securities only from the tap, so as not to take up securities that would otherwise be held in private sector portfolios. In order to allow an adequate return on their investments (necessary to pay interest on the savings bank funds, for instance), from October 1941 they were issued with special stocks, at first tranches of existing marketable issues. In March 1943 the Treasury decided to provide a special non-marketable security, 3 per cent terminable annuities, of which £120m were issued to the NDC on 12 April 1943 and again on seven subsequent occasions up to and including 10 July 1945.[42] The annuities did not constitute net government borrowing but their existence was to complicate post-war debt management policy in 1945–6.

The government also controlled new private capital issues, mainly in order to avoid competition with government issues

[41] Ibid. 150–1; Howson, *Domestic Monetary Management*, app. 2. The National Debt Commissioners are formally the Speaker of the House of Commons, the Chancellor of the Exchequer, the Master of the Rolls, the Accountant-General, the Governor and the Deputy Governor of the Bank of England, and the Lord Chief Justice. With a quorum of three, the 'active' commissioners are the Chancellor and the Governors, more accurately, their senior officials.

[42] This followed a precedent set by W. E. Gladstone when he was Chancellor of the Exchequer in 1863: Brittain to Eady, 24 and 25 Mar. 1943, T160/1379/F18445/1, PRO; E. L. Hargreaves, *The National Debt* (London, 1930), 177–82.

rather than as a check on real investment. The Capital Issues Committee (CIC) worked under a Treasury Memorandum of Guidance issued in September 1939. This essentially ruled out domestic issues for purposes not related to the war effort or for renewal of old issues, and permitted conversion issues by local authorities and Dominion governments only when the Bank of England agreed to the amounts and the timing. At the same time the banks were asked by the Governor of the Bank at the request of the Chancellor of the Exchequer to restrict their lending to loans for defence production, exports, coal-mining, and agriculture. In May 1945, with the end of war in Europe, the Treasury issued a new Memorandum to the CIC and sent a new request on bank advances to the Governor. New issues would now be allowed for reconstruction as well as defence purposes, especially in connection with exports, the development areas and the repair of war damage. The Chancellor's letter to the Governor asked that the banks should be informed that 'unduly large advances should not be made for personal needs'; that 'no facilities should be given for the speculative buying or holding either of securities or stocks of commodities'; that they should be guided by the criteria in the revised memorandum to the CIC in considering other loans and 'in particular, that they would give special consideration to advances for any form of export business'.[43]

Throughout the war the authorities tried to encourage 'small savings', offering special non-marketable securities with relatively generous interest rates, tax-free in the case of national savings certificates, and with limits on the amounts that could be held by the individual holders. National savings certificates had been introduced in 1916; defence bonds, which were available in larger units, were added in November 1939.[44] Wartime

---

[43] Sayers, *Financial Policy*, ch. 6; *Capital Issues Control: Memorandum of Guidance to the Capital Issues Committee*, Cmd. 6645, May 1945; Sir John Anderson to Lord Catto, 24 May 1945, C40/685, BOE.

[44] The seventh issue of savings certificates, on sale from 22 Nov. 1939 to 31 Mar. 1947, each cost 15s. 0d., could be cashed at any time, and were repayable at £1 0s. 6d. after ten years, thus yielding 3.17 per cent if held to maturity. There was also a £1 issue, on sale from 11 Jan. 1943 to 31 Mar. 1947, with a slightly lower yield. Defence bonds could be bought in multiples of £5, bore annual interest at 3 per cent, and were redeemable at a 1 per cent premium on maturity; four issues were made, the first with a seven-year term, the other three with a ten-year term. Individuals could hold a maximum of 500 savings certificates, plus 250 of the £1

borrowing by 'small savings' amounted to over £2,000m and constituted almost 10 per cent of total government debt in March 1945.[45]

Government borrowing under the wartime cheap money policy markedly changed the structure of the national debt. In the 1930s marketable gilt-edged debt had constituted almost three-quarters of the total debt; in 1945 it was only a half. Before the war floating debt had been less than 10 per cent of total national debt, and *long-term* gilt-edged debt (with a term to maturity of at least 15 years) over 60 per cent; at the end of the war these proportions were 26 and 30 per cent respectively.[46] Table 1.3 provides estimates of the maturity structure of *private sector* holdings of government debt. It shows that nearly 20 per cent of the private sector portfolio of government debt in 1945 consisted of floating debt, compared with just over 3 per cent in 1939, and a further 8 per cent was in gilt-edged with short maturities (under 5 years) (1 per cent in 1939). The proportion in long-term gilt-edged had fallen by more than half, while that of 'small savings' had more than doubled.

The wartime assignment of macroeconomic policy instruments to the policy targets implied a simple pattern of causality in the economic system. In terms of a simple (augmented IS–LM) model,

$$Y = C(Y, \bar{T}) + \bar{I} + \bar{G} + \bar{X} - \bar{M}$$
$$P = P(Y)$$
$$M^S/P = M^D(Y, \bar{\imath})$$

issue, and £1000 of Defence Bonds. Pember and Boyle, *British Government Securities in the Twentieth Century* (2nd edn., London, 1950), 302–11, 316–17; '"National savings": types and trends', *Midland Bank Review*, (Oct. 1949), 4–5.

[45] Another non-marketable debt instrument, tax reserve certificates (TRCs), similar to US tax anticipation notes, was also a wartime innovation. TRCs were introduced on 23 Dec. 1941 for firms and individuals wishing to set aside sums for the later payment of accruing taxes. They could be held for periods from two months to two years, used in payment for taxes (except death duties and Schedule E income tax) when they earned interest at 1 per cent per annum tax-free, or cashed earlier without interest. An intended consequence of their issue on the monetary statistics was to reduce bank deposits and TDRs (by the amounts that taxpayers would otherwise have held as bank deposits in anticipation of tax payments): Sayers, *Financial Policy*, 210–18. They continued to be available until 1973.

[46] Calculated from Pember and Boyle, *British Government Securities in the Twentieth Century*, 427, 435, 447.

TABLE 1.3   *Private Sector Holdings of National Debt, by Maturity Class, 31 March 1935, 1939, 1945, 1952, % of Total*

	Floating debt[1]	Marketable securities[2] With a maximum life of:			Small savings[4]	TRCs	Total private sector[5]
		Less than 5 years	5–15 years	Over 15 years[3]			
1935	6.2	2.4	9.9	74.9	6.6	—	100.0
1939	3.2	1.1	13.8	76.0	6.0	—	100.0
1945	19.2	8.3	17.0	36.5	14.6	4.4	100.0
1952	7.7	16.5	11.7	47.3	14.8	2.1	100.0

Notes

[1] 1935 figure = 'market Treasury bills', i.e. total outstanding less holdings of Issue Department of Bank of England, National Debt Commissioners, Exchange Equalization Account and other government departments. 1939, 1945, and 1952 figures = 'market Treasury bills' *less* holdings of Banking Department of Bank of England and overseas holders, *plus* Treasury deposit receipts (1945 only).

[2] Includes government-guaranteed securities.

[3] Includes undated.

[4] National savings certificates and Defence Bonds.

[5] Some small items have been omitted because there is no breakdown between official and non-official holdings.

Sources

1935: Calculated from Committee on the Working of the Monetary System, *Principal Memoranda of Evidence*, Vol. I, 110 and 125.

1939: Calculated from ibid. 111, Pember and Boyle, *British Government Securities in the Twentieth Century*, 435 and 503, and Issue Department statements, HM Treasury.

1945: Calculated from 'Exchequer financing and national debt 1945–51', *Economic Trends* (Dec. 1961), tables 2(b), 3, and 4, and Pember and Boyle, *British Government Securities in the Twentieth Century*, 447.

1952: Calculated from Committee on the Working of the Monetary System, *Principal Memoranda of Evidence*, vol. 1, 56, 110, and 125.

(where bars indicate variables controlled by the authorities), fiscal policy (G and T) determined real income (Y) and prices (P), and with fixed nominal interest rates (i) the resulting demand for money (M^d) determined the money stock (M^s). Replacing the last equation with a set of portfolio balance equations would show that the private sector's financial assets (which were accumulating rapidly during the war) would be distributed among the different assets according to the current (fixed) relative rates of return and expectations of future relative rates of return, but it would still be the case that these portfolio choices would not, as

TABLE 1.4 *Growth Rates of Monetary Aggregates and Other Variables, Annual, 1939–45, % p.a.*

Year to December	C	R	H	D	M1	M3	P	Money GDP	Real GDP
1939	9.5	5.5	8.0	5.6	9.6	9.7	4.4	6.9	3.9
1940	8.2	20.4	12.7	12.1	21.2	11.8	8.6	26.2	14.4
1941	36.3	−5.5	20.0	17.7	24.6	20.0	9.0	17.4	6.0
1942	22.9	10.2	19.0	9.6	14.7	11.3	7.2	8.6	1.0
1943	17.0	11.4	15.4	11.4	13.6	12.4	4.5	6.4	1.8
1944	12.2	22.1	14.9	13.3	12.0	12.9	6.0	0.6	−4.5
1945	10.7	11.2	10.8	7.7	8.6	8.2	3.0	−4.3	−6.2

Notes
C = currency in circulation outside banks
R = reserves of UK commercial banks
H = C + R
D = net deposits of UK commercial banks
M1 = currency in circulation + demand deposits of UK commercial banks
M3 = C + D
P = GDP deflator

Sources
C and R: Calculated from data on currency in circulation in *Bank of England Statistical Summary*, January 1942, table I, and subsequent issues 1942–6, and F. Capie and A. Webber, *A Monetary History of the United Kingdom 1870–1982*, vol. I, table II(2), cols. V and VI.
D, M1 and M3: F. Capie and A. Webber, *A Monetary History of the United Kingdom 1870–1982*, vol. I, tables I(2) and I(3).
Money GDP, real GDP, GDP deflator: Feinstein, *National Income, Expenditure and Output of the United Kingdom 1855–1965*, tables 3, 5, and 61.

they would in peacetime, feed back on real economic activity. However, although with fixed nominal interest rates, causality would run from money income to money stock rather than the other way round, a change in administered interest rates could affect expenditure and income, other things being equal. Further, changing private sector portfolio choices (prompted by, say, changed expectations of future rates of interest or inflation) would affect expenditure and income unless either private expenditure or the behaviour of financial institutions was strictly controlled.

Tables 1.4 and 1.5 show what happened to the money stock in 1939–45. Table 1.4 gives the wartime growth rates of two measures of the money supply and their components, of prices, and of money and real output. Table 1.5 looks at the broad money stock (M3) in terms of its 'proximate determinants', the

TABLE 1.5 *The Money Stock (M3) and its Proximate Determinants, Annual, 1939–45*

December	M3, £m	H, £m	D/C	D/R
1939	3,394.8	731.2	6.23	10.82
1940	3,793.4	823.8	6.45	10.07
1941	4,551.5	988.2	5.57	12.54
1942	5,065.5	1,175.9	4.97	12.47
1943	5,692.6	1,357.2	5.73	12.47
1944	6,427.0	1,559.2	4.77	11.57
1945	6,955.3	1,728.1	4.65	11.20

Notes

$$M3 = H \cdot \frac{D/R \, (1 + D/C)}{D/R + D/C}$$

where M3 = currency in circulation plus net deposits of UK commercial banks, C = currency in circulation outside banks, R = reserves of UK commercial banks, D = net deposits of UK commercial banks, and H = C + R

Sources
As for table 1.4

monetary base (currency and bank reserves) and the ratios of bank deposits to currency in the hands of the non-bank public and of bank deposits to bank reserves.[47] Real output grew substantially, by nearly 15 per cent, in 1940 as the economy moved from the 'phoney war' to full mobilization; its growth slowed to 1–2 per cent in 1942–3, and became negative in 1944–5. Money income and prices followed the same pattern with rapid increases in 1940 and 1941, slower rates of rise for the rest of the war, and for money income but not for prices, a decline in 1945. The monetary aggregates (M1, M3, and the monetary base) all grew at double digit rates throughout the war, reaching 20 per cent or more in 1941. The public's currency holdings grew faster than their bank deposits in 1941–3 and M1 grew faster than M3 in 1940–3. The deposit-currency ratio did not decline much in 1940–1, fell steadily through 1942–3, and then levelled off. (It did

[47] The series for the monetary aggregates come from Capie and Webber, *Monetary History*, except that the monetary base series has been recalculated (from their data plus the primary sources) on the conventional definition of the base as currency in circulation plus the cash reserves of the UK commercial banks. Their series for the base includes the reserve of notes and coin in the Banking Department of the Bank of England. (On the definitions of the monetary base see Capie and Webber, *Monetary History*, 12–13, and 'The monetary base—a statistical note', *BEQB*, 21 (Mar. 1981), 59–65.) The bank reserve figures used here also exclude the Banking Department's reserve.

not start to rise again until late 1947.) The deposit-reserve ratio rose only slightly from an 1939 average of 10.76 to 11.46 for 1945. The monetary authorities in effect supplied the quantity of base money needed for the monetary expansion required by the rise in money incomes and the maintenance of low nominal interest rates. The result was to raise the real value of the money stock (M3 divided by the GDP deflator) by 36 per cent over six years of war. This left the private sector with real money balances around 70 per cent of income for M3 and 50 per cent for M1, compared with averages of 60 per cent (M3) and 35 per cent (M1) in the 1930s.

The continuation of cheap money

If cheap money of the wartime variety was to be continued into the peace that presumed that the conditions for which it was appropriate were going to persist. In one major sense that could not be true: there would no longer be the single overriding objective of macroeconomic policy to which all others were subordinate. On the other hand the problem of inflation would remain for at least a short post-war transitional period, and the official plans for post-war policy assumed that almost all the wartime economic and financial controls would remain in order to repress that inflation and prevent a boom like that of 1919–20. As Keynes put it in 1942:

all controls—rationing control, raw material control, new issue control, bank credit control and high taxation control must be retained in principle for a period of at least two years and only gradually relaxed as and when consumer goods become available in greater quantities.

If the vast bulk of purchasing power which must necessarily exist at the end of the war, is released in psychological conditions necessarily surrounding the end of the war, the result cannot be different from what it was in 1919 to 1921.[48]

In this context there was a strong case for maintaining low nominal interest rates through the reconstruction period—especially since the post-reconstruction period was widely expected to be one of high unemployment. Inflation would then be

[48] Note by Keynes, 7 Jan. 1942, T172/1384, PRO, quoted in S. Howson, ‘‘‘A dear money man’’?: Keynes on monetary policy, 1920’, *EJ* 83 (June 1973), 462.

no longer a problem and low *real* interest rates would be needed to encourage investment: with stable or falling prices that would require low *nominal* interest rates again.

As Dow has said, 'The White Paper on *Employment Policy* is its own evidence of how seriously the likelihood of deflation was taken.[49] According to the white paper (para. 19), the post-war transitional period of high demand and supply shortages might not last long and then 'the first aim of employment policy—the maintenance of an adequate level of expenditure on goods and services—will no longer be realized automatically, as a by-product of the war effort or of reconstruction'. In the period of shortages, controls would be necessary to prevent open inflation and cheap money would be maintained in order to keep down the cost of capital investment (para. 16). The white paper outlined several ways in which *fiscal* policy should be used to achieve internal balance after the transition but was deliberately vague on subsequent monetary policy. It also expressed some scepticism of the efficacy of monetary policy in a depression, which could be taken to suggest that the end of the cheap money policy might mean higher nominal interest rates, although earlier drafts had explicitly contemplated lower interest rates after the transitional period.[50]

The ambiguity over monetary policy in the white paper reflected a conflict in wartime official opinion between the desirability of low and stable long-term interest rates, which would be helpful for long-term public and private investment as well as keeping down the cost of the national debt, and the use of interest rates, short- and long-term, for varying the amount of investment in the short term. (Since inflation was not generally expected to be a permanent problem the distinction between nominal and real interest rates was not usually drawn.) In 1939 Keynes and Robertson had been able to advise the Treasury to set wartime interest rates at low levels because the authorities could influence one way and another the determining variables in wartime cir-

[49] *Management of the British Economy*, 10.

[50] *Employment Policy*, paras. 59–60; Brittain, 'Interest rate policy', 9 Aug. 1944, T273/389, PRO. The view that since 'cheap credit is not enough' fiscal instruments would have to be used to maintain employment in a post-war slump was even to be found in the Conservative Party's contribution to the reconstruction debate, a report on *Work: the Future of British Industry*, issued in Jan. 1944, although its support of public works in a depression was distinctly lukewarm.

cumstances. In 1944, with the end of the European war in sight, the authorities had to consider not only the role of monetary policy in the longer term but also the methods by which cheap money would be sustained in the early post-war years, when assetholders' preferences might not be so easily manipulated as in wartime to suit the authorities' intentions.

The issues were thrashed out in a special committee set up under the coalition government at the beginning of 1945. Chaired by the Permanent Secretary to the Treasury, the *National Debt Enquiry* was composed of officials and economists from the Treasury, the Economic Section of the War Cabinet Offices and the Board of Inland Revenue. In the summer of 1944 Clement Attlee, then Deputy Prime Minister, had asked the Economic Section for a note on a post-war capital levy—a method of reducing the debt popular in the Labour Party. James Meade in the Section proposed a wider-ranging document on the post-war debt problem and consulted the Permanent Secretary to the Treasury, Sir Richard Hopkins, who had long been interested in such issues.[51] Although at first sceptical of the need to 'attempt a very difficult study in the midst of all our present pre-occupations', Hopkins was soon persuaded that there was a case for an early inquiry by a committee of officials and economists, which would also consider the future of the cheap money policy. On that last subject, Hopkins noted, 'Lord Keynes has promised to produce ... some far-reaching proposals'.[52] Hopkins proposed himself as chairman, and as members Meade and Lionel Robbins from the Economic Section, Keynes, Sir Herbert Brittain and Sir

[51] Note by Meade, 18 July 1944, T230/94, PRO. Hopkins had moved from the Board of Inland Revenue to become Controller of Finance at the Treasury in 1927 and had been Permanent Secretary since 1942. As Robbins put it, he was 'by common consent ... one of the best minds in the public service' and 'on the subject of governmental finance ... an intellectual match for anyone in his generation', including Keynes. He had also taken the lead in picking up the proposals of the Economic Section for post-war macroeconomic policy and setting in train the preparation of the white paper on *Employment Policy*: Lord Robbins, *Autobiography of an Economist* (London, 1971), 186–7. On Hopkins's career see also 'Sir Richard Hopkins', *Public Administration* 34 (Summer 1956), 115–23 and G. C. Peden, 'Sir Richard Hopkins and the "Keynesian revolution" in employment policy, 1929–45', *EHR* 36 (1983), 281–96.

[52] Hopkins to Chancellor, 18 July, Hopkins to Padmore, n.d., and 14 Aug., Hopkins to Eady, 18 and 21 Aug. 1944, T273/389; see also Hopkins to Brittain, 17 Jan. 1945, T233/158, and an unsigned note probably also by Hopkins on T233/159, PRO.

Wilfrid Eady from the Treasury, and Sir Cornelius Gregg and Paul Chambers from the Inland Revenue. (Robbins and Meade were then the Director and Deputy Director of the Economic Section; Eady was Joint Second Secretary, Brittain Third Secretary, at the Treasury; Gregg was Chairman of the Board of Inland Revenue and Paul Chambers its Director of Statistics and Intelligence.) When Hopkins officially retired from the Treasury at the end of February 1945 his successor, Sir Edward Bridges, took the chair but Hopkins remained on the committee and wrote its first report on post-war monetary policy. The Enquiry also produced a report on a capital levy.

When the Enquiry first met, on 19 February 1945, it agreed that Meade would complete a memorandum on a capital levy, the Inland Revenue would provide statistical and historical papers on the same subject, and in the meantime Keynes would open the discussion on the cheap money policy.[53] Before it ended with the general election in July 1945 it also discussed, more briefly, the control of capital issues, the problem of post-war inflation, and some of the longer-term problems of budgetary policy.

One strand in the 1940s arguments about monetary policy in and out of Whitehall which has been emphasized in the past is scepticism among economists of the influence of interest rates on investment. This was not much in evidence in the National Debt Enquiry, except that insofar as a low value was placed on the responsiveness of investment to monetary policy it encouraged the adoption of a fixed nominal interest-rate policy: the argument (which Meade and Robbins put forward) that such a policy could be inappropriate in an inflationary situation could be met with the counterargument that conventional monetary policy was too weak an instrument to be relied upon to prevent inflation so that other instruments would have to be used anyway.[54] Keynes's views dominated the meetings and first report. As explained above he did not think that investment was interest-inelastic but

[53] The minutes of the Enquiry's meetings are on T230/94 and T233/158, its memoranda on T230/95 and T233/159. Keynes's notes for the meetings and his summary of his proposals are in *JMK*, vol. 27, 388–404.

[54] This can be seen as an application of the principle of comparative advantage in the assignment of instruments to targets which Mundell has made well known, and which is open to criticism on control-theoretic grounds: Robert A. Mundell, 'The appropriate use of monetary and fiscal policy for internal and external stability', *IMF Staff Papers*, 9 (1962), 70–7.

he did believe that it could be difficult for the authorities to set long-term interest rates at appropriate levels to encourage investment and economic growth in the longer term if variations in interest rates were used as an instrument of short-run demand management.

Keynes gave three long 'lectures' to the committee. He began by outlining his *General Theory* analysis of the relation between savings and investment and of interest rates. According to Meade, he 'goes out of his way to give the maximum stress to the difference between his theory and old-fashioned orthodoxy'.[55] He argued that the government could determine both the level and structure of nominal interest rates as long as it did not also try to determine the maturity composition of the debt. According to the minutes (22 March),

The authorities in his view can control the rate of interest, but only if the State decides only the amount of borrowing and allows the public to decide the degree of liquidity which it desires. In other words, the method of borrowing should be that of the [wartime] tap issue rather than the fixed offer.

The authorities should not try to fund the debt, that is lengthen its average term to maturity by converting short-term, especially floating, debt into longer-term bonds. As for the nominal rates to be chosen, his criteria were the desired volume of investment and the rate of return on private saving. To the committee Keynes stressed the latter:

The modern theory was to encourage investment by cheap money, thereby incidentally promoting savings, and to make the volume of desirable investment the prime consideration in determining the rate of interest.

[But] he personally had turned to the conservative view that one must also consider the socially desirable reward of saving, with its implications regarding the provision for families, the working of charitable institutions, and other aspects of social life.

These provided 'valid reasons for keeping some of the Government debt at round about a 3% basis'. There would also be a need to maintain savings for internal balance in the transitional period but after that a reduction in interest rates might be required to discourage saving. There was no need to raise interest rates in the

[55] Meade, *Cabinet Office Diary*, 48.

TABLE 1.6   *Wartime Borrowing and Keynes's National Debt Enquiry Proposals*

Outcome of wartime borrowing 31 March 1945			Keynes's proposals for post-war borrowing	
Security	Amount outstanding £m	Nominal yield % p.a	Security	Yield % p.a.
Treasury bills	3,681	1.0	Treasury bills (except overseas holders	0.5 1.0)
TDRs	1,859	1.125	TDRs	0.625
TRCs	682	1.0	TRCs	1.0
1¾% Exchequer bonds 1950	202	1.75	5 year Exchequer bonds	1.5
2½% National War bonds				
1945/47	444	2.49	10 year bonds	2.0
1946/48	493	2.48		
1949/51	714	2.48		
1951/53	522	2.48		
1952/54	810	2.49		
Total	2,983			
3% Savings bonds			Savings bonds	
1955/65	713	2.98	redeemable after 10	
1960/70	1,009	2.95	years but with no	
1965/75	194	3.0	final redemption date	3.0
Total	1,916			
Savings certs.	1,511	3.17	Savings certificates	3.17
Defence bonds	762	3.0	Defence bonds	3.0

Sources
Pember and Boyle, *British Government Securities in the Twentieth Century* (London, 1950), 447; *The Economist*, 7 Apr. 1945; *JMK*, vol. 27, 399.

transitional period because the continuation of wartime controls on domestic investment and on bank advances would be needed to prevent inflation.[56]

Keynes's detailed suggestions are given along with the current structure of borrowing in Table 1.6. They were intended to maintain current nominal long-term interest rates for the transitional period without committing the authorities beyond it. He proposed annual tap issues of 3% Savings Bonds with an early optional redemption date, only ten years hence, and a distant or

[56] Minutes of 2nd, 3rd, and 4th meetings of National Debt Enquiry, 8, 22 and 27 Mar. 1945. Keynes suggested the committee read E. V. Morgan's recent article on 'The future of interest rates' (*EJ* 54 (Dec. 1944), 340–51), which argued the case against raising interest rates after the war on Keynesian liquidity-preference grounds.

(preferably) no final redemption date. His 'ideal security' would, like 2½% Consols, be repayable only at the Treasury's option (a so-called 'irredeemable' or 'undated' stock). At the other end of the debt, short-term rates on floating debt should be reduced by ½ per cent, so as to reduce interest payments to the public departments, overseas central banks, and domestic banks who were the major holders. This would improve the balance of payments on current account and there was no economic or social reason to pay more to the banks (or public departments). In between five-year bonds could be offered at 1½ per cent and ten-year bonds at 2 per cent. Bank rate should be reduced to 1 per cent. After a meeting in which the other economists and the Treasury officials expressed their views, the Enquiry agreed that Keynes, Eady, and Brittain should draw up a statement of Keynes's proposals. At the next meeting it discussed the timing of the introduction of the measures and agreed Hopkins should draft a report.[57]

Meade and Robbins disliked the idea of giving up the possibility of short-run variations in interest rates. They tried 'to counter some of Keynes' more extreme remarks ... such that "productivity of capital and thrift have got nothing to do with the rate of interest" and his view that the rate of interest should no longer be used to control inflation or deflation'.[58] They were not successful, judging from the minutes (and Hopkins's report). At the fifth meeting Robbins 'confirmed that the doctrinal analysis was one with which he (in common with most professional economists at the present time) agreed' and that cheap money was generally desirable on grounds of employment policy. 'But he felt that there should be a certain flexibility.' It might prove necessary to raise interest rates in the transitional period to help to avoid inflation and to lower them subsequently to prevent heavy unemployment. Although 'emphatically in agreement' with Keynes on funding policy he was uncertain about the proposals for reducing short-term rates.[59]

[57] *JMK*, vol. 27, 396–404; minutes of 4th, 5th, and 6th meetings, 27 Mar., 5 and 10 Apr. 1945. Keynes also suggested, in line with his desire to encourage thrift, that the 3 per cent yield on national savings certificates should be maintained although that of defence bonds might be reduced to 2½ per cent.

[58] Meade, *Cabinet Office Diary*, 61.

[59] Minutes of 5th meeting, 5 Apr. 1945; see also Robbins's note, 'Financial Policy, Statement on Keynes's Exposition', T230/94, PRO.

Meade also sharply disagreed with Keynes's views on the appropriate reward to saving:

The more I examine the problem, the more certain it seems to me that the proper radical solution is get interest rates down to or towards zero, thereby killing two birds with one stone: avoiding economic stagnation and removing the burden of debt interest on the budget. The only argument against this would be if it led to inflation; but within reason such a development could be counteracted by running a budgetary surplus.

If interest rates could be reduced (and kept down) it would 'remov[e] the rentier without disturbing either the entrepreneur or the man who wished to hoard money'.[60] He told the Enquiry that he 'preferred to lay more emphasis [than Keynes] on the importance of keeping interest rates down when we are entering a period of possible stagnation, with a view to lowering the cost of socially desirable public and semi-public investment'. In Keynes's *General Theory* productivity and thrift could affect the rate of interest via the effect of changing income on the transactions demand for money, if the nominal money stock were not increased, and since many forms of investment were significantly interest-elastic internal balance should be sought by a combination of monetary and fiscal policy and direct controls. But he 'entirely agreed' with Keynes's practical proposals, because they provided for a later reduction in long-term interest rates and by reducing short-term interest rates an immediate improvement in the balance of payments.[61]

The Treasury officials generally supported Keynes's proposals for maintaining cheap money and, with reservations, his arguments against funding. They were concerned whether short-term interest rates could be reduced on overseas holdings of sterling balances, but Keynes claimed it would be possible to provide a higher rate on these balances than for domestic holders of Treasury bills. Hopkins raised the broader question of main-

---

[60] *Cabinet Office Diary*, 46, 48–9.

[61] Minutes of 2nd and 5th meetings, 8 Mar. and 5 Apr. 1945; see also Meade, *Cabinet Office Diary*, 61, and his manuscript notes on T230/95, PRO. The notes make clear that he did not believe investment was interest-inelastic and that he feared a severe post-war depression: 'As to its [the rate of interest's] effect on investment, . . . the present fashion is, in my opinion, to give it too little weight'; with respect to longer-term policy, '*Probability* of stagnation because of capital satiety. This coming soon in USA, & rather later here. In such cases great case for further reduction of interest rates to stimulate investment' (emphasis in original).

taining full employment and cheap money in the face of an external depression, prompting considerable argument between Keynes, Eady, and Meade over the possibility and desirability of changing the exchange rate in such a situation. On the details of Keynes's proposals it was decided not to recommend a reduction in Bank rate and that the reduction in short-term rates should take place before the new tap bond issues were introduced.[62]

Hopkins's first draft of a report, for which he read Keynes's *General Theory* and Robertson's *Essays in Monetary Theory*, claimed more unanimity than existed in the committee. He suggested all the members agreed that 'the desirable ideal for this country, as far ahead as can reasonably be envisaged, is not merely the maintenance but even the reduction of existing levels [of interest rates], both for long term and for short', and that although there was 'less certainty and less unanimity' about permitting interest rate variations in the short run they also agreed that variations should be confined to short-term rates and regarded as secondary to the control of bank advances. Meade and Robbins succeeded in altering these passages but not in preventing later drafts implying that controls were the best defence against post-war inflation.[63] In his first draft Hopkins gave two grounds for the continuance of a cheap money policy, which were elaborated in the final version of the report: the encouragement of investment in the longer term and the saving on interest payments in the budget. These implied the lowest possible long-term interest rates and the 'desirable low limit might then be governed ... by social and psychological considerations concerning the need to foster the habit of thrift'. This passage was both moderated and expanded by the rest of the committee, reflecting Meade's and Robbins's desire not to rule out interest-rate flexibility and Keynes's views on the reward to saving by individuals and charitable institutions.[64] Hence nominal interest rates should be

[62] Minutes of 6th and 7th meetings, 10 and 19 Apr. 1945.
[63] NDE Paper 9, 'Draft prepared by Sir R. Hopkins of an interim report for the Chancellor's eye only', paras. 6–8; Meade, *Cabinet Office Diary*, 70, 73; NDE Paper 11, 'Revised draft prepared by Sir R. Hopkins of an interim report for the Chancellor's eye only', and National Debt Enquiry, First Report, 'The question of future gilt-edged interest rates', 15 May 1945, paras. 6, 11–13.
[64] NDE Paper 9, paras. 9–10; First Report, paras. 7–10.

fixed from time to time in the light of experience and should pay attention primarily (*a*) to the effects of Government policy on the market for borrowing by private institutions, companies and individuals and on the problem of controlling and maintaining the desired rate of investment at home and abroad, (*b*) to social considerations in the wider sense and (*c*) perhaps especially to the burden of interest charges on the Exchequer and other State funds and on Local Authorities. (First Report, para. 25)

The rest of the report dealt with the technical methods of pursuing cheap money, basing them explicitly on the *General Theory*, assuming control over international capital movements, and recommending Keynes's detailed proposals. On the ability of the authorities to dictate nominal long-term interest rates Hopkins invoked the *General Theory*, quoting the passage quoted above (p. 20) as one which 'would now command a wide measure of agreement among economists' (para. 18). He claimed that 'the Committee feel justified on the evidence before them in taking the passage as a working guide ... both because it appears to have been consistent with recent experience in varying conditions and because they know of no other general theory which begins to hold out the same prospect of achiveing a very important objective' (para. 19). Hopkins also followed Keynes in justifying the 3% Savings Bonds on the grounds that it would be premature to lower long-term interest rates during the transitional period, that the interest burden was low with current high rates of direct taxation and that the provision for possible early redemption left the authorities' options open (para. 34). Hopkins' report went to the Chancellor of the Exchequer (Sir John Anderson) in May 1945.

Meanwhile a subcommittee—Hopkins, Gregg, Robbins, and Meade—turned Meade's memorandum on a capital levy into a report for the Chancellor. Meade had favoured a post-war capital levy in principle as a 'once-for-all surgical operation' which would allow the government to redeem a large proportion of the national debt without a prolonged period of high taxation. Having considered the probable very low yield from a levy when interest rates were low and income taxes high, he concluded that in the circumstances of 1945 the practical alternative to 'the capital levy earthquake' was a post-war low interest-rate policy, which would have the same distributional effects.[65] The report which went to the Chancellor in June 1945 argued that although the problems of equity, administration, and effects on the capital market were not insuperable, the current high rates of taxation and low rates of interest would reduce the net saving to the budget of a feasible levy to a negligible magnitude—permitting only a 1¼ per cent cut in the standard rate of income tax. 'The question, therefore, arises whether the game is worth the candle.' This echoed the report of the Colwyn Committee twenty years earlier, which had also argued that the yield of a feasible levy would not be sufficient to justify the disruption involved, but the latter's estimate of yield was higher with 1920s tax and interest rates and the Committee had been more worried about a levy's effects on business confidence.[66] The National Debt Enquiry report was, however, reconsidered in late 1947 (see Chapter 5 below).

In May and June 1945 the National Debt Enquiry also finally discussed wider issues relating to post-war fiscal policy, such as the possible consequences for the national debt of maintaining full employment by budget deficits and the possibility (which it rejected) of a separate 'capital budget'.[67] It also devoted a meeting to the problem of inflation, prompted by Meade's and Robbins's concern. Meade and Robbins were still uneasy about the reliance on controls to prevent inflation in the transitional period; they argued strongly, in a joint memorandum and at the meeting on it on 24 May, that high wartime taxation should not be reduced until the danger of inflation was clearly past. According to Meade, 'Keynes opposed us vigorously. He wants to see a considerable reduction in taxation in an autumn Budget and to rely

[65] NDE Paper 5, 'The capital levy, Note by the Economic Section', repr. in S. Howson (ed.), *The Collected Papers of James Meade, Volume II: Value, Distribution and Growth* (London, 1988), 262–79; see also Meade, *Cabinet Office Diary*, 48–9, 65. On the reaction of the subcommittee to his memorandum, Meade wrote that 'Hoppy [Sir Richard Hopkins] would simply love to be in charge of a Capital Levy. . . . As an artist in financial administration he is as disappointed as I am that the arithmetic of the yield of a levy shows it not really to be worthwhile.'

[66] 'The Capital Levy' (printed proof), T230/95; Committee on National Debt and Taxation, *Report*, Cmd. 2800, 1927, Part II, Sect. I, 'The Capital Levy'.

[67] Minutes of 11th and 15th meetings, 18 May and 28 June 1945; NDE Papers 4 and 6, Meade, 'The fiscal problem set by the debt' and 'Debt repayment and employment policy' (repr. in *The Collected Papers of James Meade*, vol. 2, 251–62, 279–84); NDE Papers 12 and 14, 'Proposals for a Capital Budget, Memorandum by Sir Herbert Brittain' and 'The Concept of a Capital Budget (Memorandum by Lord Keynes)'; Meade, *Cabinet Office Diary*, 81–2. 101–2.

almost solely on the direct controls to prevent inflation.'[68] The discussion also revealed that the general expectation (though probably not Keynes's)[69] was that post-war inflationary pressures would last two years.

The Bank of England was not represented on the National Debt Enquiry—Hopkins had 'doubt[ed] whether it would be wise'—and it did not see the Enquiry's first report until October 1945.[70] During the war it had also been considering post-war monetary policy, setting up two internal committees, one on post-war exchange control in August 1941 and the other on domestic finance in March 1943. Their preoccupations—and views— were rather different from those of the Treasury or the Economic Section.

The Post-war Exchange Policy Committee, whose members were H. A. Siepmann, Henry Clay, and G. K. Bolton (advisers to the Governors), and Lucius Thompson-McCausland (who was to become an adviser in 1949), produced an interim report in June 1942 that assumed the post-war international economy would comprise several currency areas rather than a full multilateral system of trade and payments. In order to avoid a return to the floating exchange rates of the 1930s, it

envisage[d] a continuation and even extension of exchange control not merely as a pis aller to be dropped as soon as conditions improve but as a deliberate and constructive policy calculated to prevent a recurrence of the mass capital movements of the pre-war period and to build up a system which will fit into a world in which exchange control will have become the almost universal rule.

Any moves toward multilateralism would take the form of payments agreements between different currency areas, agreements which would provide for fixed exchange rates and *de facto* convertibility for current account transactions.[71]

[68] NDE Paper 10, 'The control of inflation: the three alternatives, Note by the Economic Section', 3 May 1945; Minutes of 12th meeting, 24 May 1945; and Meade, *Cabinet Office Diary*, 83–4.

[69] Keynes was more optimistic than the majority of the committee about post-war employment: in 1943 he had suggested that the transitional period 'might last five years,—but it is anybody's guess' and that a further five or ten years might elapse before an excess of savings became a problem ('The long-term problem of full employment', *JMK*, vol. 27, pp. 320–4).

[70] Hopkins to Eady, 18 Aug. 1944, T273/389, PRO; Fforde, *Bank*, 335.

[71] O'Brien, 'Summary of Interim Report of Post War Committee', 15 July 1942, G15/255, BOE (emphasis in original).

By the time of this report, the government was committed by Article VII of the Lend-Lease agreement with the United States to work toward multilateralism after the war and had adopted Keynes's plan for an international 'clearing union' as a basis for discussion on the post-war international monetary system with the Americans. Commenting on Keynes's proposals in the winter of 1941/2 the Bank had made it clear that its view of the post-war future was very different from Keynes's.[72] It is not surprising that the Bank did not intend its internal report to go to the Treasury. The one senior Treasury official (Sir Frederick Phillips) to whom C. F. Cobbold (then an executive director, later Deputy Governor 1945–9 and Governor 1949–61) had shown it ' "ad personam" ', found it 'terribly depressing'.[73]

When the Bank committee redrafted its report in the spring of 1943 Cobbold sent a memorandum based on it to the Treasury. This was 'concerned with the underlying and technical measures to be adopted [by the UK] as the "foreground" for any international organisation which may come into existence ...' The starting point for the Bank was again the sterling area and the continuation of exchange controls, in order to reduce capital mobility while freely permitting current payments at a fixed exchange rate. Behind the proposals was the Bank's desire to preserve sterling as an international currency:

it is evidently in our interest, and we may perhaps claim in the general interest, that sterling should resume its place as an international currency and should not leave the whole field to the dollar. Our first concern therefore in ... the international monetary field will be to make sterling as stable and serviceable a currency as possible whilst preventing its use as a medium of ... undesirable capital movements.

To this end it was thought essential to work toward free convertibility of all sterling held by nonresidents (in principle only for current transactions, but the payments agreements envisaged in

[72] See *JMK*, vol. 25, pp. 40-1, 66, Pressnell, *External Economic Policy*, vol. 1, pp. 68–9, 71–2, and Fforde, *Bank*, ch. 2(b).
[73] Cobbold to Governors, 1 July 1942, and Phillips to Cobbold, 26 June 1942, G15/255, BOE; see also Fforde, *Bank*, 50–1. Phillips was the head of the Treasury mission in Washington from 1940 to his death in 1943. Cobbold had entered the Bank as an adviser on the overseas side in 1933, after a few years in the City, 'quickly established a reputation for administrative ability, power of command, tenacity of purpose, and capacity for hard work', and became an Executive Director, aged only 34, in 1938 (ibid. 38).

the memorandum did not include *strict* controls on capital transfers not involving resident holders of sterling).[74] The document also assumed that capital issues control for all borrowers would be continued in peacetime, so that with exchange control on residents the UK *domestic* capital market would be both insulated and controlled.

The Committee on Post-War Domestic Finance, consisting of Sir Otto Niemeyer and Edward Holland-Martin (directors of the Bank), the Chief Cashier Sir Kenneth Peppiatt, Henry Clay, and R. N. Kershaw (another adviser), was asked 'to suggest the best means of securing in the immediate post-war period effective co-operation between H.M. Government and the City in providing short and long-term finance' for both government and private borrowers while avoiding both inflation and unemployment. It also assumed that post-war exchange control and capital issues control would insulate the domestic capital market, and also that wartime physical and price controls would be temporarily retained to prevent inflation in the transitional period. At the same time the report expressed doubts whether it would be possible for long to retain cheap money along with price stability, because the money stock in the hands of the public was very large and wartime controls on consumption and raw materials would not be continued indefinitely. It might become necessary to allow some rise in interest rates in order to increase saving and hence finance the desired level of investment without inflation. In the immediate post-war period the government would remain a heavy borrower, at the least to replace maturing wartime debts: the Bank should continue as in wartime to support the market for government bonds and might have to allow the floating debt to increase in the transitional period. The major practical proposal of the report was, however, the establishment of an 'Industrial Development Corporation', to provide finance to small firms who could have difficulty in raising funds on the new issue market. The corporation's capital would be provided by the Bank, the clearing banks and some other financial institutions. Such an institution, which was also advocated in other

---

[74] 'Sterling after the War', 7 Apr. 1943, G15/255, BOE. See also Fforde, *Bank*, 52–3, and Pressnell, *External Economic Policy*, vol. 1, 96–7, and, on the Bank's resulting opposition to the Anglo-American plans for an international monetary fund, ibid. 137–44, 147–50, and Fforde, *Bank*, 53–61.

quarters in 1943–4 (see Chapter 2), was established in the summer of 1945 as the Industrial and Commercial Finance Corporation (ICFC), together with a sister institution for larger loans, Finance Corporation for Industry Ltd. (FCI).[75]

The Bank was thus less convinced than the Treasury of the desirability, and the feasibility, of low post-war interest rates. Sir Otto Niemeyer, commenting in November 1945 on the first report of the National Debt Enquiry, thought the Treasury was 'still obsessed with pre-war fears of "underinvestment"' and 'gravely underestimate[d]'post-war demands for both consumption and capital goods. It also seemed to him 'never to have looked at all at the actual structure and market standing of the existing medium and long term debt'. The issue of an 'irredeemable' government bond with an early optional redemption date recommended by Keynes and the Enquiry would represent only a fraction of the at least £7,400m existing non-floating debt due to mature before 1960 and there were plenty of existing stocks callable in ten years and yielding around 3 per cent. If there was a need to lower interest rates after the post-war transitional period, the authorities would have plenty of opportunities.[76]

The Bank's immediate aim was to continue the wartime practice of debt management into the post-war period, by issuing medium- and long-term bonds at 2½ per cent and 3 per cent respectively, with the maximum possible maturities. When in November 1944 the authorities had closed the current tap issue of 2½ per cent ten-year bonds and offered instead a five-year bond with a 1¾ per cent coupon, the Bank had not seen this as a move toward lower interest rates. As the Chief Cashier had recorded after a discussion with the Treasury:

no such idea was contemplated and ... our joint aim was to do no more than maintain the present rate structure, having particularly in mind the heavy borrowing programme which lies before the

---

[75] Report of Committee on Post-war Domestic Finance, 19 Oct. 1943, C40/775 and ADM14/8, BOE; Sayers, *Bank of England*, 559–60; see also Fforde, *Bank*, 320–1 and 704–27. ICFC and FCI were merged in 1974 to form Finance for Industry Ltd., later renamed Investment in Industry (3i).

[76] Niemeyer to Governor, 20 Nov. 1945, G18/3 and C40/450, BOE. Niemeyer's remarks are quoted extensively in Fforde, *Bank*, 335–7. Before Niemeyer joined the Bank as an adviser in 1927 he had been Controller of Finance at the Treasury and much concerned with debt management (Howson, *Domestic Monetary Management*, ch. 3).

Government both during the remainder of the war and in the transitional period beyond.[77]

In the spring of 1945 Keynes suggested lengthening the term of the 1¾% Exchequer Bonds to seven years, as a step toward his suggested 1½ per cent for five years, but the Bank was already planning to resume the sale of 2½% National War Bonds with a maturity of 10–11 years.[78] The Treasury (including Keynes) would have preferred to withdraw the Exchequer Bonds without replacing them for the time being but the Bank believed the weakness of the gilt-edged market was a reason for offering the 2½ per cent bonds. 1¾% Exchequer Bonds were withdrawn on 12 June and 2½% National War Bonds 1954/56 offered the following day.[79]

In June 1945 the Bank considered the immediate future of Bank rate. An increase was 'uncalled for and indeed out of the question politically'. A reduction to 1 per cent could have some useful consequences—the clearing banks might stop paying interest on deposits, and the annual cost of short-term government borrowing would be reduced by about £20m—but it might also reduce demand for government securities and it could make it difficult to increase Bank rate again. The ability to raise the rate was important for two reasons: the threat of domestic inflation and the maintenance of the sterling exchange rate.[80]

An important point about the Bank's attitude to Bank rate in 1945 is that it had had no experience of using it for monetary control in a post-gold standard world. Apart from the short-lived increase in Bank rate in August 1939, there had been no changes in Bank rate since June 1932. In 1944 Lucius Thompson-McCausland recorded that the Deputy Governor (B. G. Catterns)

[77] Peppiatt, '2½% Conversion Loan 1944/49', 22 Dec. 1944, C40/450, BOE. (Peppiatt had been consulted on a suggestion of Keynes's to repay the Conversion Loan in order to boost sales of the new bonds, which were not much in demand.) At the time of issue of the 1¾% Exchequer Bonds the Bank had advised 2 per cent but the Treasury preferred the lower coupon rate: Sayers, *Financial Policy*, 209–10, Fforde, *Bank*, 331–2.

[78] Minutes of 4th meeting of National Debt Enquiry, 27 Mar. 1945; Peppiatt to Governors, 'Successor to 1¾% Exchequer Bonds 1950', 27 Mar. 1945, C40/447, BOE.

[79] Eady to Brittain, '1¾%'s', 5 May, Keynes to Eady, Eady to Bridges, and Bridges to Chancellor, 14 May, Brittain to Eady, 'New Issue of National War Bonds', 30 May 1945, T233/148, PRO.

[80] Peppiatt, 'Bank Rate', 21 June 1945, C42/1; see also Bolton to Peppiatt, 20 June 1945, G18/3, BOE.

is uneasy at the prospect of our entering the post-war period without having any clear idea of what dials to watch in determining bank policy. Under the Gold Standard there were well understood indicators. . . . [Since then] we have proceeded on a hand to mouth basis, learning much, lucky in not having suffered much, but not yet in possession of anything which could be called a system. If money is needed we see that it is there.[81]

In answering Catterns's request for some thought on the matter Thompson-McCausland produced arguments which were to reappear in the disputes between the Bank and the Treasury over monetary control in 1948–9. He pointed out that since the gold standard had been abandoned the Bank '[had] had to give relatively little thought to limiting the amount of money in existence'. Neither, he said, had the economists who were arguing for low and stable interest rates to prevent unemployment. He was concerned, however, that if the money supply had been expanded to prevent interest rates from rising in response to a rise in the demand for idle money balances, there would be an excess supply of money when the demand for money fell again—what he called 'flabby money'. Although he claimed that an increase in short-term bank loans to business would not cause such problems, echoing the long-discredited nineteenth-century 'real bills' doctrine, he recognized that money would not stay 'taut' when there had been an expansion of the banks' holdings of gilt-edged securities as there had been since 1932. The problem was to eliminate the 'flabby money' by a funding issue or other open-market operations in gilt-edged securities.[82]

A year later he elaborated his ideas in a memorandum on Keynes's liquidity preference theory of interest rates which he sent to James Meade. Anticipating some of the criticisms of the Bank of England line that Meade's successor as the senior economist in Whitehall, Robert Hall, would make three and a half years later, Meade wrote to Thompson-McCausland that he did not

[81] 'Note of a conversation with the Deputy Governor on 14th February 1944', ADM14/4, BOE. Thompson-McCausland, 'an Anglo-Irishman of considerable intellectual power and persuasive talent' as Fforde (*Bank*, 322) put it, had joined the Bank in 1939, after some experience in merchant banking and financial journalism, having been 'rescued from the Ministry of Information' by Cobbold, who had been his contemporary at King's College, Cambridge (King's College, *Annual Report*, (1984), 77). Cobbold had gone down after only one year, Thompson-McCausland left with a double first in classics. He was a self-taught economist.

[82] 'Money after the gold standard', 24 Mar. 1944, ADM14/4, BOE.

'make it sufficiently clear by what criterion you would judge whether "flabby" money exists, or whether there is a "superfluity" of money'. In his letter and in subsequent conversation over luncheon at the Reform Club Meade also

> tried hard to persuade him that the correct criterion for an expansionist or restrictionist monetary policy was whether the total national expenditure was showing signs of declining or rising too rapidly. . . . But Lucius persists in thinking in terms of what he calls 'flabby' money which rushes from commodity to commodity causing speculative booms and slumps, undermining confidence and thus leading to a general slump. He wishes to drain away such stagnant pools, keeping money what he calls 'taut'. But the danger is, of course, that the general process of keeping money 'taut' will maintain the rate of interest at an unduly high level so that there is a more or less permanent deficiency of total national expenditure.'[83]

In the summer of 1945 the UK monetary authorities had clear ideas of the monetary policy they wanted to pursue after the war. The Treasury officials essentially wished to continue the wartime cheap money policy through the transitional period from war to peace, but lowering the fixed short-term interest rates on floating debt while maintaining 3 per cent nominal for long-term gilt-edged securities. They favoured this policy both because low nominal interest rates reduced government expenditure on interest payments and because they shared the widespread fears of a post-war depression on the 1930s scale; hence they accepted the Keynesian arguments that interest rates could and should be kept down during the transition. The Bank of England did not think that wartime controls, or low nominal interest rates, could be long maintained in peacetime, but it also envisaged the continuation of the wartime system of tap bond issues at low nominal interest rates with the longest possible maturities while the government budget remained in deficit and there were maturing

[83] Thompson-McCausland, 'Cheap Money, A Criticism of Lord Keynes' Theory, and an alternative view', Mar. 1945, and Meade to Thompson-McCausland, 23 Apr. 1945, ADM14/16, BOE, T230/70, PRO, and Meade Papers 1/9, BLPES; Meade, *Cabinet Office Diary*, 74. Thompson-McCausland had met and become friends with Meade when he went to North America with the 'Law Mission' (which included Keynes, Robbins, and Meade) to discuss post-war economic policy with the US administration: *The Wartime Diaries of Lionel Robbins and James Meade, 1943–45*, eds. S. Howson and D. Moggridge (London, 1990), 92, 150. On his memoranda see also Fforde, *Bank*, 322–3.

wartime issues to be replaced. While the official National Debt Enquiry wanted to allow for the possibility of lowering long-term interest rates, the Bank, expecting higher rather than lower nominal rates after the immediate post-war period, was concerned to preserve the *status quo* on rates for as long as possible. As Fforde has emphasized, it was particularly important not to lower Bank rate.[84]

Cheap money for the immediate post-war period was adopted for similar reasons in several other countries. Although some continental European countries, including France, Belgium, and somewhat later West Germany, resorted to a drastic 'monetary reform' in order to eliminate an excess supply of money,[85] those countries which had successfully maintained cheap money and (relatively) low inflation through the war period held on to cheap money for some more years after the end of the war. In America, soon after the United States entered the war the Federal Reserve Board had announced in April 1942 that it would peg the Treasury bill rate at ⅜ per cent by buying or selling any amount offered or demanded at that rate. Although there was no rigid commitment for other US government securities their yields were effectively maintained at 1½ per cent for short-term notes and 2½ per cent for long-term bonds. The pattern largely reflected prevailing market yields in early 1942, except for pegging the Treasury bill rate slightly higher than its current market rate. The discount rate was also lowered in late 1942 to ½ per cent. At the end of the war, although there were differences of opinion between the Treasury and the Federal Reserve (and within the Federal Reserve), the pegging of the Treasury bill rate was continued until 1947. As in Britain, the differences between the central bank and the Treasury were not resolved until 1951.[86]

In Canada, '[t]he fear that Canadian economists shared with most of their colleagues throughout the Western world was that the end of the war might bring a quick and sharp decline in the pace of economic activity, which might then merge into a con-

---

[84] Ibid. 323–5.

[85] Charles P. Kindleberger, *A Financial History of Western Europe* (London, 1984), 409–19.

[86] M. Friedman and A. J. Schwartz, *A Monetary History of the United States, 1867–1960* (Princeton NJ, 1963), 562–3, 578–9; Herbert Stein, *The Fiscal Revolution in America* (Chicago, 1969), ch. 10; Fforde, *The Federal Reserve System 1945–1949* (Oxford, 1954). Fforde and Stein both discuss the authorities' views at length.

tinuation of the stagnation of the 1930s'. The Bank of Canada signalled its intention to maintain a post-war low interest-rate policy by reducing its Bank rate to 1½ per cent in February 1944 and maintained its wartime policy of stabilizing government bond prices until 1948. It did not raise its discount rate to 2 per cent until the Canadian dollar was floated in face of massive capital inflows in 1950, although it had to resort to moral suasion on the chartered banks to try to restrain the growth of bank lending in 1948-9 and again in 1951.[87]

In neutral Sweden the stabilization of the interest rate at a low level, about 3 per cent for long-term government securities, was the 'main goal' of monetary policy in the 1940s, because of the '"undesirable" side effects of higher interest rates' on distribution and the burden of the national debt. The government and central bank persisted with low interest rates until the mid-1950s, trying like the Canadian authorities to restrain bank lending and hence the money supply by quantitative controls and moral suasion before finally resorting to higher interest rates. Australian monetary policy was complicated by conflict between the private banks and the central bank, but 'the ideology of "cheap money" . . . long had deep roots in Australia' and a post-war low interest policy was pursued even longer than in other countries.[88]

Thus at the end of the Second World War monetary policy was not generally accorded an important role in the policy assignment of economic weapons; reflecting these attitudes the continuance of wartime cheap money was officially accepted policy for at least the immediate post-war period.

[87] H. Scott Gordon, 'A twenty year perspective: some reflections on the Keynesian revolution in Canada', in S. F. Kaliski (ed.), *Canadian Economic Policy since the War*, ch. 2 (Ottawa: Canadian Trade Committee, 1965), 28–9; Gordon R. Sparks, 'The theory and practice of monetary policy in Canada: 1945–83', in John Sargent (ed.), *Fiscal and Monetary Policy* (Toronto, 1986), 126–7; Graham F. Towers, 'Review of post-war monetary policy', in E. P. Neufeld (ed.), *Money and Banking in Canada* (Toronto, 1964), 266–70.

[88] Assar Lindbeck, 'Theories and problems in Swedish economic policy in the post-war period', *AER*, 58 (Suppl. June 1968), 47–51, and E. Lundberg, 'The rise and fall of the Swedish model', *JEL*, 23 (Mar. 1985), 12–16; W. M. Corden, 'Australian economic policy discussion in the post-war period: a survey', *AER*, 58 (Suppl. June 1968), 110–13.

2

'Socialist' Monetary Policy

> Finance must be the servant, and the intelligent servant, of
> the community and productive industry; not their stupid
> master.[1]

THE overwhelming victory of the Labour Party in the general
election of July 1945 was unexpected but the party was not
unprepared to take power. After the resignation of the second
Labour government during the 1931 financial crisis, a 'national'
government under Ramsay MacDonald had taken Britain off the
gold standard on 21 September and won a landslide victory in a
general election a month later. Over 200 Labour MPs lost their
seats. Out of Parliament 1931-5, Hugh Dalton became a member
of the new Policy Committee of the party's National Executive
Committee (NEC) and chaired its Finance and Trade Commmit-
tee. He took the lead in organizing a practical programme of
financial and economic policy for a future majority Labour
government, with the assistance of XYZ, a group of Labour sympathizers in the City of London, and several younger economists.[2]

XYZ was formed by H. V. Berry of the Union Discount Co. at
the beginning of 1932 'to discuss financial problems from a
socialist point of view, and [to] be ready to offer its help to the
Labour Party'.[3] Most of the 'young economists', who included
Colin Clark, Evan Durbin, Hugh Gaitskell, Douglas Jay, and
James Meade, were members of the New Fabian Research
Bureau (NFRB) founded by the Oxford economist G. D. H. Cole
in March 1931 but several, notably Durbin, Gaitskell, and Jay in

---

[1] Labour Party, *Full Employment and Financial Policy*, (1944), 3.
[2] Dalton had been on the academic staff at LSE since 1919 (Cassel Reader in
Commerce since 1920), part-time after he entered Parliament in 1924. He returned
to the School full-time in 1931-5. He had been a junior minister at the Foreign
Office in the second Labour government.
[3] Berry, 'XYZ: The Early Days', quoted in Durbin, *New Jerusalems*, 82.

1934, joined XYZ later.[4] They came eventually to dominate XYZ, especially after the 1945 general election when, with several of them in Parliament, their meetings moved to the House of Commons. In its early years XYZ, in memoranda Dalton passed on to the Finance and Trade Committee, concentrated on the possibilities of reforming and controlling the financial system so as to avoid a repeat of 1931. The NFRB, in meetings and conferences and pamphlets worked more on employment policy which included monetary and fiscal policy and more direct control of investment.

Elizabeth Durbin has told the story of the contribution up to 1939 of the 'young economists' and 'XYZ' to the party's economic plans, which included the nationalization of the Bank of England and of the major industries and the establishment of a National Investment Board. The young economists also made detailed recommendations for the conduct of financial policy by a future Labour government.[5] The increasing threat of war with Germany and then the financial innovations of the Second World War led Dalton's advisers to make further plans and new proposals, first for the finance of a war and then for the conduct of monetary and fiscal policy by a peacetime Labour government. This chapter describes the attempts of Dalton and his advisers in the 1930s and early 1940s to develop a monetary policy appropriate for a future majority Labour government—a government which would have the power to reform Britain's economic and financial system and the conduct of monetary and fiscal policy. After outlining the ideas of the Labour economists in the 1930s it focuses on the

[4] Most of the young economists had been undergraduates at Oxford. In the 1930s Clark, Durbin, and Gaitskell were lecturing at Cambridge, LSE, and University College London respectively. Meade was a fellow of Hertford College, Oxford, after a year in Cambridge in 1930-1. Jay was a financial journalist for *The Economist* from 1933, having been a sub-editor on *The Times* and a fellow of All Souls' College 1930-2; he became City Editor of the *Daily Herald* in 1937, taking over from Francis Williams (an early member of XYZ).

[5] Elizabeth Durbin, *New Jerusalems*. On Dalton, XYZ and the 'young economists' see also Dalton, *The Fateful Years: Memoirs 1931-1945* (London, 1957), ch. 1; Ben Pimlott, *Labour and the Left in the 1930s* (Cambridge, 1977), chs. 2-4, and *Hugh Dalton*, ch. 14; Francis Williams, *Nothing So Strange* (London, 1970); Nicholas Davenport, *Memoirs of a City Radical* (London, 1974), ch. 4; Douglas Jay, *Change and Fortune: A Political Record* (London, 1980); and Durbin, 'Keynes, the British Labour Party and the economics of democratic socialism', in O. F. Hamouda and J. N. Smithin (eds.), *Keynes and Public Policy after Fifty Years* (Aldershot, 1988), vol. I, 29-42.

evolution of their plans from 1938 to 1945. It concentrates, though not exclusively, on their ideas on monetary policy and debt management. The origins of Dalton's 'cheaper money policy' in 1945–7 lie in some of these ideas, although most of his advisers did not advise him to pursue it. The wartime ideas and experience also shed light on why the post-war Labour governments did not significantly reform the UK financial system after 1945, a topic to be taken up again in Chapter 3.[6]

The plans of the 1930s

The first fruits of Dalton's initiative appeared as a policy report for the 1932 party conference on *Currency, Banking and Finance* prepared with the assistance of XYZ. Dalton later drew heavily on it in his *Practical Socialism for Britain* (1935). The 1932 conference passed the report, which thus became party policy. It also passed an amendment by the left-wing Socialist League to nationalize the major commercial banks as well as the Bank of England, but the 1937 party conference omitted this from *Labour's Immediate Programme*.

The main resolution of *Currency Banking and Finance* began by assuming that 'the British trade depression and its resulting unemployment have been considerably aggravated by the deflationary monetary policy pursued in recent years' and that 'the enormous power exercised by the financial system cannot continue to be left in private control'. It proposed that with the end of the gold standard the aim of monetary policy should be domestic price stability and, if it was possible through international co-operation, some stability of exchange rates. The Bank of England should be nationalized and its Governor appointed by the government. A National Investment Board should control all new capital issues. And 'all necessary emergency powers should be taken to deal with any attempt by private financial institutions to obstruct a Labour Government, damage national credit, or create a financial panic'.[7]

The first work of the NFRB for Dalton's Finance and Trade

---

[6] The perspective is somewhat broader than in my '"Socialist" monetary policy: monetary thought in the Labour Party in the 1940s', *HOPE*, 20 (Winter 1988), 543–64.

[7] Labour Party, *Currency Banking and Finance*, (July 1932), 3.

Committee was on the last of these recommendations.[8] A 'financial panic' on the election of a Labour government would most likely take the form of a capital outflow, which would cause reserve losses or exchange-rate depreciation (depending on whether exchange rates were initially fixed or not), a rise in short-term interest rates and a fall in security prices. Since internal stability was more important than exchange-rate stability, a Labour government should not attempt to maintain a fixed exchange rate (and should suspend the gold standard if the UK was on it). Since the inflationary effects of a severe exchange-rate depreciation had also to be avoided, the 'Oxford economists', who included James Meade, Roy Harrod, and Redvers Opie, recommended 'some measure of exchange control without fixed [exchange] rates'. Exchange control over at least capital flows thus became a presumption of Labour monetary policy, the proposal being elaborated in several later memoranda by Dalton's advisers.[9] A collapse in Stock Exchange prices should be met with an easing of monetary policy by the Bank of England. Other less likely forms of 'internal panic'—a run on the banks or hoarding of goods—would also require a temporary easing of monetary policy.

In 1932 Meade had written a pamphlet for the NFRB on *Public Works in their International Aspect*, published in January 1933, in which he used the concept of the multiplier to advocate counter-cyclical government expenditure on public works, which should accompany the appropriate monetary policy.[10] He subsequently produced a memorandum for Dalton's committee on the 'Financial Policy of a Socialist Government during the Transition to

[8] 'Proposals on the control of a financial panic, prepared by a group of Oxford Economists who are members of the Party', Policy No. 113, Mar. 1933, Dalton Papers 2/1, BLPES, and Fabian Society Papers J25/2, Nuffield College Oxford.
[9] 'Measures to combat foreign exchange panic', Policy No. 296, May 1935, and 'Financial panic and how to meet it', Policy No. 309, Sept. 1935, Dalton Papers 2/2; 'Labour policy and the foreign exchange market', Finance Policy No. 1, Nov. 1938, Dalton Papers 2/3; see also Hugh Gaitskell, 'Financial Policy in the Transitional Period' in G. E. G. Catlin (ed.), *New Trends in Socialism* (London, 1935), 169–200. Elizabeth Durbin has suggested that the Oxford economists' proposal was 'contrary to Labour's official policy of maintaining stable prices and exchange rates', but as described in *Currency Banking and Finance* that policy gave price stability priority over exchange-rate stability.
[10] Repr. in Howson (ed.), *The Collected Papers of James Meade, Volume I: Employment and Inflation* (London, 1988), 6–25.

Socialism' (that is, while the major industries were being nationalized). Here he advocated the countercyclical use of three sets of policy instruments to prevent unemployment in a slump and inflation in a boom: the control of interest rates and the stock of money by the Bank of England; the control of public and private investment by a National Investment Board; and the management of the government's budget which should be divided into an income account and a capital account. The government should cover its current expenditure by taxation and the income from nationalized industries, but vary the balance on capital account over the cycle. In a slump the government should increase capital expenditure and borrowing, while reducing taxation (in excess of that needed to finance current expenditure) and debt redemption. In a boom it should do the opposite. (Booms were undesirable because they usually led to slumps and because they tended to reduce real wages and the share of national income going to wage-earners.) Since it was more important to change the way financial institutions were operated than to change their ownership Meade advocated the socialization of the Bank of England rather than the banking system as a whole and saw the main role of the National Investment Board as arranging for the flotation of loans to finance approved investment projects. He also pointed out that during the transition it would be necessary to pay full compensation to the expropriated owners of nationalized industries in order to maintain investment and employment in private industry. Later, 'once ... the main body of capitalists are rentiers the Government can make drastic use of the instrument of taxation to buy them out', particularly by inheritance taxes and possibly a capital levy. Commenting on Meade's first draft, Dalton wanted to discuss the division of the budget, which he 'doubt[ed] whether ... [it] is important', compensation, on which he agreed with Meade against many of his party colleagues, and exchange controls.[11] Meade elaborated his views on monetary and fiscal policy, exchange policy, compensation and nationalization in further work for both Dalton and the NFRB and in his textbook *Economic*

[11] Policy No. 189, Dec. 1933, Dalton Papers 2/1; Dalton to Meade, 9 October 1933, Meade Papers 2/7, BLPES. For other views on compensation see 'Industrial compensation, Memorandum submitted by a committee of the New Fabian Research Bureau', Policy No. 194, Dec. 1933, Fabian Society Papers J20/4.

Analysis and Policy (1936).[12] On international economic policy he was a firm believer in the removal of barriers to trade, flexible (but managed) exchange rates, and the use of exchange controls to control the capital account of the balance of payments, in order to permit the adoption of a Keynesian domestic macroeconomic policy by a Labour government.

Meade in Oxford and Colin Clark, who organized an NFRB group in Cambridge, both brought Keynesian ideas into Labour Party planning well before the publication of the *General Theory* in 1936. By the late 1930s most of the younger economists in the party were 'Keynesians'.[13] Durbin alone remained sceptical whether Keynesian macroeconomic policy could solve the problems of economic growth and cycles.[14] Dalton utilized some Keynesian ideas on budgetary policy in his writings, citing Clark's work on the control of investment and Keynes's *The Means to Prosperity* (1933). He asked Clark for assistance with the sections on investment in the NEC's 1933 policy report and subsequently for a memorandum on budgetary policy for a Labour government. Clark's 'socialist budget' included increased expenditure on social services and 'a national development programme' of public investment (to be financed mainly by borrowing) to reduce unemployment by 1 million persons. On the revenue side it included a shift from indirect taxation toward direct taxation and the reform of surtax and death duties. The budget, which would be divided into separate capital and income accounts, would thus be used for both macroeconomic control

[12] See Dalton to Meade, 24 Nov. 1933, and Meade, 'Compensation', Policy No. 196, Dec. 1933, Meade Papers 2/7; 'The exchange policy of a socialist government', 19 June 1934, on the same file, repr. in Howson (ed.), *The Collected Papers of James Meade, Volume III: International Economics* (London, 1988), ch. 2; 'Outline of economic policy for a Labour government', 1935, Meade Papers 2/9, reprinted in his *Collected Papers*, vol. I, ch. 4; *An Introduction to Economic Analysis and Policy* (Oxford, 1936).

[13] The clearest example is Douglas Jay, *The Socialist Case* (London, 1937); on its origins see his *Change and Fortune*, 62–3.

[14] For Durbin's 'Hayekian' views see his *Purchasing Power and Trade Depression* (London, 1933), 'Money and prices', in G. D. H. Cole (ed.), *What Everybody Wants to Know about Money* (London, 1933), ch. 7, *Socialist Credit Policy*, NFRB pamphlet No. 15 (London, December 1933), and *The Problem of Credit Policy* (London, 1935). In February 1938, writing to compliment Joan Robinson on her 'brilliantly lucid' *Introduction to the Theory of Employment* (London, 1937), he told her: 'I am sure you will understand that I do not pretend to be a convert to these views. . . . But it was a real intellectual pleasure to find a perfect statement, even of views with which one does not agree' (Joan Robinson Papers vii, King's College Cambridge).

and income redistribution.[15] Clark had explained on Keynesian lines the need for a capital development programme in an earlier NFRB pamphlet which also dealt with the objectives and functions of a National Investment Board.

Clark's proposals for a National Investment Board differed considerably from those of XYZ. Nicholas Davenport (a stockbroker and a journalist) and other members of the 'City group' envisaged the Board as a licensing agency for all capital issues including foreign issues. The Stock Exchange would not be able to give 'leave to deal' in a stock unless the issue had been approved by the Board. The Board would also have a 'planning' function in that its full-time staff, including economists and statisticians, would collate all proposed investment projects, public and private, and draw up a scheme of national investment for consideration by the government. The Board need not have the power to raise finance for investment by issuing its own bonds: Davenport believed it should not because it was 'absolutely imperative that the next Labour Government should preserve the Government credit and refrain from bestowing Government guarantees on every piece of capital expenditure which happens to be of national importance', although Berry thought that it might be able to after the first years of a Labour government.[16] Clark and other Labour economists, however, followed the original idea of a National Investment Board in the Liberal Party's 1928 'Yellow Book', which had been a means of financing public investment and large-scale private investment projects, with power to control overseas issues in Britain in times of emergency or balance-of-payments difficulties. The Board he proposed would both raise capital by issuing government-guaranteed bonds, using the proceeds to make or guarantee loans to approved private investment projects as well for public invest-

[15] Dalton, *Practical Socialism for Britain*, ch. 25; Dalton to Clark, 18 May 1933 and 24 Nov. 1934, Colin Clark Papers MPP 76 A1, Brasenose College Oxford; Clark, 'Memorandum on budgetary considerations', Policy No. 276, Feb. 1935, Meade Papers 2/7, and *A Socialist Budget*, NFRB Pamphlet No. 22, (London, 1935).

[16] Davenport, *Memoirs of a City Radical*, appendix; [Davenport], 'The national control of investment', Policy No. 145, May 1933, and Berry, 'Further notes on the stock exchange', Policy No. 220, Dalton Papers 2/1; [Davenport], 'Supplement to Report No. 145 . . . on the National Control of Investment', Policy No. 204, Jan. 1934, Dalton Papers 2/2. In his 1933 memorandum Davenport used Colin Clark's estimates of UK national income in 1927–31 to illustrate the need for government control of national investment.

ment, and control by licensing all new issues, domestic as well as foreign.[17] The more limited XYZ proposal appeared in the party's annual Policy Reports from 1932 onwards,[18] but debate continued among Dalton's advisers, although it took second place to methods of nationalizing the banking system until that was omitted from *Labour's Immediate Programme* in 1937. When Christopher Mayhew, employed to undertake research for the NFRB for a year in 1938–9, surveyed the memoranda prepared since 1931 on the Party's financial policy, he drew attention to the disagreement over the Board's functions. In the report which he subsequently wrote on the control of investment he advocated a Board with three functions: the planning of investment, licensing of new issues, and the financing of investment.[19] Such a Board eventually appeared in the party's statement on *Full Employment and Financial Policy* in 1944, but in 1938–9 XYZ was still working on a draft bill to establish the more limited institution.[20]

Up to 1939 XYZ concentrated on institutional reform of the financial system and on the ways to achieve greater government control over the various types of financial institutions: the banks, the discount and acceptance houses, the Stock Exchange, and large institutional investors such as insurance companies. A main objective was to be able to control aggregate investment and hence maintain employment in a depression. Other objectives were: to reduce the amount of short-term overseas borrowing and lending and hence the possibility of disruptive speculative capital outflows, which had contributed to the 1931 financial crisis; to increase the amount of medium- and long-term finance provided to British industry instead of to overseas borrowers; and to reduce socially useless stock-market speculation. Some of these concerns consciously echoed those of the Macmillan Com-

[17] Liberal Industrial Inquiry, *Britain's Industrial Future* (London, 1928), 111–15; Clark, *The Control of Investment*, NFRB Pamphlet No. 8 (London, 1933), pt. II.

[18] Keynes criticized the party for not being more ambitious in 'The monetary policy of the Labour Party', *New Statesman and Nation*, 17 and 24 Sept. 1932 (*JMK*, vol. 21, pp. 128–37).

[19] Mayhew, 'Financial Policy Committee: Memorandum on the official and unofficial material dealing with the Labour Party's financial policy', Fabian Society Papers J26/7, and 'The national control of investment', ibid., J26/6. The latter was published by the Fabian Society in 1939 as *Planned Investment: The Case for a National Investment Board*. (The NFRB amalgamated with the Fabian Society in 1939.)

[20] Berry to Piercy, 18 Mar. 1938, and 'Draft bill for a National Investment Board', Piercy Papers 5/72, BLPES.

mittee in 1930–1.[21] Although XYZ included the nationalization of the joint-stock banks in its plans while that was official party policy, the City members doubted its necessity. By 1935 or 1936 Durbin and Gaitskell came to share their doubts.[22] Berry, who worked for a discount house, believed a nationalized Bank of England could sufficiently control the discount and acceptance houses; Davenport, a stockbroker, claimed a National Investment Board set up on his lines would reduce the role of the Stock Exchange. Some minor Stock Exchange reforms were proposed (such as to make all settlements for cash, to restrict bank advances for stock purchases by imposing margin requirements, to place a turnover tax on transactions, and to reduce stockbrokers' commissions), but they were not regarded as urgent.[23]

The centrepiece of XYZ proposals was the nationalization of the Bank, in order to make it 'to an even greater degree than it is now, the pivot of the British financial system. It is through the Bank of England that control of other financial institutions can most effectively be operated.'[24] XYZ drew up a series of draft bills, of which the December 1938 version was approved by the NEC Policy Committee in February 1939.[25] This provided for: the transfer of ownership of the Bank from the shareholders to the Crown; full compensation of the shareholders in cash or government securities; and the appointment of the Governor, Deputy Governor, up to five Assistant Deputy Governors, and ten other members of

[21] Berry, 'London money market', Policy No. 29, April 1932, Davenport, 'The national control of investment', Policy No. 145, May 1933, Dalton Papers 2/1; Davenport, 'Supplement to Report No.145 . . . ', Policy No. 204, Jan. 1934, 'Stock exchange reform', Policy No. 219, and 'Further notes on the stock exchange', Policy No. 220, Feb. 1934, Francis Williams, 'Memorandum on the organisation of the stock exchange', Policy No. 245, May 1934, Dalton Papers 2/2; Commitee on Finance and Industry, *Report*, Cmd. 3897, 1931.

[22] 'Further notes on financial policy: banks', Policy No. 149, May 1933, Dalton Papers 2/1; Berry and Durbin, 'Memorandum on the nationalisation of the English banking system', Policy No. 297, June 1935, Dalton Papers 2/2; Philip M. Williams, *Hugh Gaitskell* (Oxford, 1982), 71; Durbin, *New Jerusalems*, 155.

[23] According to Berry, XYZ also discussed nationalization of insurance companies 'until someone realized that the companies had 10,000 door-to-door salesmen whom it would be electoral folly to antagonize' (Durbin, *New Jerusalems*, 165). The same argument was used in the NEC in 1949: Kenneth O. Morgan, *Labour in Power 1945–1951* (Oxford, 1984), 125–7.

[24] Labour Party, *Currency, Banking and Finance*, para. 25.

[25] 'Heads of a Bill on Finance', Finance Policy No. 3, Dec. 1938, Dalton Papers 2/3; Minutes of the 12th meeting of the Policy Committee, 21 Feb. 1939, Research Department Volume 2, Labour Party Archives.

the Court of the Bank for specified terms by the Chancellor of the Exchequer, who would have the power to 'give [legally binding] instructions' to the Governor or the Deputy Governor. Although it also provided for the amalgamation of the weekly returns of the Issue and Banking Departments of the Bank, the publication of an annual report, and the determination of the Bank's note issue, it contained fewer and less detailed provisions than the 1935 version which had incorporated provisions relating to the clearing banks. Like the 1935 bill it covered the setting up of a National Investment Board.

By 1938 the role of monetary policy under a nationalized Bank envisaged by Labour economists reflected the practical development of British monetary policy since 1931. As XYZ had not failed to point out, the abandonment of the gold standard had increased the Treasury's role in monetary management.[26] The Bank had lost its traditional role of maintaining a fixed exchange rate and the Treasury had taken advantage of the newly gained monetary independence to introduce cheap money in 1932. The government, with the assistance of the Bank, established the Exchange Equalization Account (EEA) to manage the exchange rate and provide some automatic sterilization of capital flows, instituted some control of capital issues, and converted a large block of First World War debt from a 5 per cent to a 3½ per cent coupon. Nominal yields on long-term government debt had fallen below 3 per cent in the middle of the decade and were still below 3½ per cent in early 1939. Yet in spite of a housebuilding boom and increasing prosperity for those in work, unemployment, although falling, remained above its 1920s levels until the impact of rearmament began to make itself felt in 1938. In that year large-scale capital outflows due to fears of a European war and a fall in security prices reminded Dalton's advisers again of the problems of financial 'confidence' (earlier brought home to them by the experience of the Popular Front in France in 1936).[27]

In the Labour economists' plans, the role of the Bank on the external side would be to continue to manage the EEA under the

[26] The strongest statement appears in Berry's anonymous pamphlet, *The City Today* (by 'A Citizen'), NFRB pamphlet No. 38 (1938). On Berry's views see also below.

[27] 'Labour policy and the foreign exchange market', Finance Policy No. 1, 11 Nov., and 'Labour's financial policy', Finance Policy No. 2, 22 Nov. 1938, Dalton Papers 2/3.

Treasury's direction and also administer the exchange controls which a Labour government would introduce. On the domestic side, the Bank would continue to carry out conventional monetary policy by means of open-market operations and Bank rate changes, aided by some 'technical improvements' intended to make monetary policy more effective in influencing bank lending and investment. The improvements included the power to fix and vary banks' reserve ratios as recommended by the Macmillan Committee; the provision of more statistical and other information by the banks to the Bank (also recommended by the Macmillan Committee); and the creation of a co-ordinating committee under the Governor of the Bank of representatives of the five largest clearing banks plus the Treasury and the Board of Trade. Berry and Durbin also suggested that banks could be encouraged to lend in a depression by providing government guarantees.[28]

With respect to employment policy in a slump the weapons of a Labour government were to include: an expansionary monetary policy, with nominal long-term interest rates on private bonds forced down to 2½ or 3 per cent by large-scale open-market purchases by the Bank; additional encouragement of private investment through government loan guarantees or subsidies; increased public investment; deficit budgeting; and perhaps also special measures to tackle 'special' unemployment in the depressed areas. In the circumstances of the 1930s less consideration was given to economic policy in a boom, but it was not ignored, the general recommendation being the reversal of expansionary measures.[29]

How to pay for the war

By 1938, when XYZ was helping to prepare up-to-date plans for exchange control, Bank nationalization, and a National Investment Board for the party's Finance and Trade Committee, it was

[28] Berry and Durbin, 'Memorandum on the nationalisation of the English banking system', Policy No. 297, June 1935, Dalton Papers 2/2, and 'Memorandum on the nationalisation of the English banking system', Finance Policy No. 5, January 1939 [revised version of their earlier memorandum], Dalton Papers 2/3.

[29] Ibid.; Clark, Durbin, Gaitskell, and Jay, 'Memorandum by the Economic Group', Research No. 311, June 1936, Colin Clark Papers MPP 76 A4; Mayhew, 'Memorandum on the official and unofficial material dealing with the Labour Party's financial policy', Fabian Society Papers J26/7.

also contemplating methods for financing war against Germany. A 'War Finance Group' consisting of Berry, Durbin, Gaitskell, Jay, Bill Piercy, and George Wansbrough (an early City member of XYZ) began meeting in April 1938 and published its proposals under Durbin's name as *How to Pay for the War* in 1939. Piercy, an LSE-trained economic historian turned stockbroker (after government service in the First World War), was a new recruit to XYZ joining both the War Finance Group and a 'Stock Exchange Committee' under Gaitskell in the spring of 1938. The committee's task was to revise the part of a 1935 memorandum by Gaitskell on financial panic dealing with a fall in security prices, and then to redraft a bill for a National Investment Board.[30] It is fortunate for this study that Piercy joined XYZ at this point, for his secretary, Miss Bradshaw, took on the typing and circulating of minutes and correspondence, which are preserved in his papers. This section describes XYZ's proposals for wartime finance, and the implications it drew for future peacetime monetary policy, largely on the basis of those papers.

At its first meeting the War Finance Group agreed its objects to be:

(a) that the war should be financed with as little addition to the real burden of the national debt as was compatible with the rapid and efficient financing of the war itself.

(b) the economic burden of the war should be distributed as justly as possible between different classes—i.e. as progressively as possible between income groups—during the actual progress of the war.

(c) that the method of financing should lead to the creation of a wide and efficient machinery of industrial control.'

In subsequent meetings it would discuss, on the basis of memoranda by Durbin, Gaitskell, and Berry, the magnitude and mistakes of war finance in 1914–18; 'the historically normal method

---

[30] Piercy to Durbin, 12 Apr. 1938, Berry to Piercy, 18 May 1938, Piercy Papers 5/72; 'II. Labour policy and security prices', Finance Policy No. 1, 11 Nov. 1938, Dalton Papers 2/3. The other members of the 'Stock Exchange Committee' were Davenport and Wansbrough. When Dalton first met Wansbrough in October 1931, he described him as 'an Etonian Bolshevik who . . . is now in Bensons (merchant bankers) [and who] thinks we ought to nationalise the Stock Exchange': Ben Pimlott (ed.), *The Political Diary of Hugh Dalton 1918–40, 1945–60* (London, 1986), 157. For the details of Piercy's varied career see the obituary in *Journal of Royal Statistical Society*, Ser. A, 1967 pt. 2, 274–6.

of war finance ... inflation and borrowing'; the possibility of increasing financing by taxation; and wartime control of industry.[31] The group communicated its detailed recommendations to Dalton and F. W. Pethick-Lawrence (a senior Labour MP and a former Financial Secretary to the Treasury) and completed the book shortly after the outbreak of war.[32]

The argument of the book was simple and followed logically from the group's objects. The main economic problem of war was to switch resources (equal to some 40 per cent of national income, Durbin estimated on the basis of statistics for 1914–18) from peacetime uses to war-related purposes (chapter 1). There were three ways to do this: (i) direct state control of industries; (ii) taxation; (iii) borrowing. To finance the whole cost of the war by taxation would be desirable because it would be equitable and non-inflationary and add nothing to the national debt, thus satisfying objects (a) and (b), but too unpopular to be practicable. Similarly, direct control of the necessary industries would not increase the burden of the national debt and would obviously satisfy object (c), but it could not be brought about quickly enough. Thus borrowing, 'the most familiar, the most speedy, and ... the least unpopular method' (p. 47), which apparently did not satisfy any of the group's objects, was inevitable (chapter 2). The group found the way out of this dilemma in government borrowing from the banking system. Since this would increase the money supply it would be inflationary but inflation would have certain advantages—increasing the profits and hence the output of the war industries, increasing monetary savings when consumption was restricted and reducing the real burden of the debt. Hence 'a moderate and controlled inflation of expenditure is excellently desirable in a period of war finance ... [although] an uncontrolled inflation is a terrible disaster at any time' (pp. 58–9, Durbin's

[31] 'Minutes of the first meeting of the War Finance Group', (Apr. 1938), Piercy Papers 5/72.

[32] Piercy Papers 5/72 includes minutes of several meetings, notices of others, and a run of memoranda by Durbin ('Memorandum on the financing of a major war', 10 Nov. 1938, and several undated papers), Gaitskell ('The conscription of wealth', 3, 12, and 24 Apr. 1939), and Berry ('Draft memo. by Mr Berry on interest rates and control of banking', June 1939, and 'Notes on banking control', Oct. 1939). Gaitskell's proposals for an annual capital tax appeared as an appendix to the book: E. F. M. Durbin, *How to Pay for the War, An Essay on the Financing of War* (London, 1939), 109–13. Pethick-Lawrence became Lord Pethick-Lawrence in 1945 and the party's economic and financial spokesman in the House of Lords.

italics). The desirable amount of inflation could be achieved by government borrowing at very low interest rates directly from the banks, whose other lending should be strictly controlled (chapter 3). Thus the recommended programme of war finance was to increase both taxation and direct control of industry as rapidly as possible; to allow 'a moderate and strictly limited' inflation, by government borrowing, accompanied by rationing, other restrictions on consumption, and a savings campaign (to induce the non-bank public to place their inflated money balances in low interest government loans); and to make sure that borrowing was at low interest rates—with Treasury bill rates down to their pre-war levels (½ per cent) and long-term rates as low as 2½ per cent—by borrowing from the banks and controlling their other lending (chapter 4). A quantitative estimate of the effects of such a policy assumed that voluntary savings could be trebled and that the price level would double if the war lasted five years. The burden of the post-war debt would then be tolerable and could also be further reduced by a capital levy at the end of the war (pp. 84–90). The whole argument assumed (implicitly in the book, explicitly in the earlier memoranda) the existence of exchange control, which had been introduced by the time the book came out. The group had also recommended the reduction of Bank rate to 2 per cent (which had also been carried out by November 1939).[33]

XYZ's discussions of war finance, which continued in the Fabian Society's War Economics Committee in the winter of 1939–40, are of interest here chiefly because of the implications drawn for a peacetime Labour monetary policy. In June 1939 Berry pointed out that the necessity of preventing high wartime interest rates could lead to closer control of the banking system. Assuming the introduction of exchange control to prevent capital outflows, the authorities could determine the Treasury bill rate and thus longer-term interest rates. Since the discount houses were dependent on the the supply of Treasury bills for their very existence and the banks held large amounts of government bonds, they were in no position to refuse to co-operate by, for

[33] Durbin made two other points in the book. First, assuming that the USA would be reluctant to make large loans to Britain and France, it would be necessary to maintain UK exports as well as use gold and overseas assets to pay for imports (ch. 5). Secondly, a post-war deflation must be avoided by maintaining a high level of government expenditure during the reconstruction period (pp. 100–7).

instance, refusing to take up Treasury bills at the weekly tender, if the authorities made it clear they would not allow interest rates to rise.[34] Once the war began, the City's 'general willingness to co-operate ... [which] is a natural result of the growth of Treasury power since 1931' implied a low interest-rate policy could control the banks as effectively as nationalization (as long as the Bank of England was nationalized in due course).

The banks understand the necessity; for this end they will accept a good deal of persuasion, which in the last resort means control. Therefore, by every possible means we should tie the Government down to this point. ... We should extort from the Government a declaration that 2½ [per cent] will be the maximum war loan interest. ... The lower the rate of interest which can be secured, the more of each war loan will have to be forced on banks and financial houses [since private investors would be unwilling to take up the issues]. The more that can be forced on them, the more dependent they become on the government.

Moreover, if their advances to other borrowers were limited:

it would ... mean that at the end of the war the banks would be tied hand and foot to the government by their huge holdings of government securities, short or long, and the credit of the government would be their chief concern.

Berry also suggested government control over bank advances might be strengthened by adding one or two government representatives to the Committee of London Clearing Bankers, but noted: 'The disadvantage of mere changes in machinery is that they might be dropped immediately the war ended.' In another paper which outlined for discussion the methods of government borrowing from the banks, Berry went further:

My own feeling is that the right policy, and the easiest one, to pursue, is just an extension of [Neville] Chamberlain's policy [as Chancellor of the Exchequer 1932–7]—i.e. to make money capital excessively cheap, to use every banking weapon to drive interest rates down to as near vanishing point as possible and keep them there.[35]

[34] 'Draft Memo by Mr. Berry on Interest Rates and Control of Banking', June 1939, Piercy Papers 5/72.
[35] Berry, 'Notes on Banking Control', 16 Oct. 1939, and 'Finance by Bank Credits', Piercy Papers 5/72. The first of these was discussed at a meeting with Dalton, the second at a meeting with other XYZ members in February 1940: Dalton to Berry, 25 Oct. 1939, and Berry to Piercy, 15 Feb. 1940, on same file.

As far as wartime finance was concerned Berry's colleagues generally agreed with him. In November 1939 they recorded they had agreed to the strengthening of the London Clearing Banks Committee and to the shortening of maturities of government loans (in order to permit lower interest rates on them). In April 1940 Durbin was emphasizing the need to direct the banks to take up government securities at low interest rates and to limit their other lending.[36]

Meanwhile Keynes had published his proposals on *How to Pay for the War*, first in two articles in *The Times* in November 1939 and then as a booklet in February 1940. XYZ and the young economists were enthusiastic.[37] Dalton's advisers also generally approved of the wartime monetary policy adopted from the summer of 1940. When discussion resumed in the party on post-war financial policy later in the war, it took the wartime system as its starting point. Dalton told the party's Reconstruction Committee in December 1942 that

the Bank of England has now become a mere branch of the Treasury, and the Joint Stock Banks mere collecting agencies for Government finance. The Treasury Deposit Receipt is a wartime invention of great value, and we must seek, after the war, to be most conservative as regards financial institutions, and to hold fast what we have won.'[38]

Post-war planning

When the National Government under Neville Chamberlain fell on 10 May 1940, Winston Churchill formed a coalition

---

[36] 'Minute, 13th November 1939', Piercy Papers 5/72; Durbin, 'Monetary Expansion and the Cost of Borrowing', 9 Apr. 1940, Fabian Society Papers K18/1. Other subjects discussed in the Fabian Society's War Economics Committee in the winter of 1939–40 were exchange controls and wartime economic planning.

[37] For instance, Piercy wrote to Berry on 22 February 1940: 'I wonder if you went to the Keynes lunch yesterday. . . . I heard it went off very well. I have had a proof of Keynes's new pamphlet in my hand; I was not able, naturally, to read it through but it is exceedingly good. It will be out next week' (Piercy Papers 5/72).
The lunch with the Fabian Society was one of Keynes's many 'exercises in persuasion' for his proposals at this time: see *JMK*, vol. 22, pp. 86–90, 97–8, 102, for reactions of Jay, Dalton, Wilmot, and others. Gaitskell had also heard Keynes on his proposals at the Tuesday Club in December. (Durbin, Gaitskell and Jay had all on occasion attended the informal dining club founded by Keynes and others in 1917, and Gaitskell had been elected a member in January 1939: information from D. E. Moggridge.)

[38] Dalton Diary, vol. 27, 20 Dec. 1942, BLPES.

government for the duration. As partners in the coalition Labour ministers played an important role in the government's post-war planning, especially on the domestic front. Clement Attlee, Ernest Bevin, and Herbert Morrison were members of the War Cabinet (Attlee and Bevin from 1940, Morrison from November 1942) and of the powerful Lord President's Committee which Attlee came to chair when he succeeded Sir John Anderson as Lord President of the Council in September 1943. Dalton was first Minister of Economic Warfare and then, from February 1942, President of the Board of Trade. They all took part in the ministerial discussions surrounding the preparation and publication of the *Employment Policy* white paper in 1944.

The 'young economists' also worked for the coalition as wartime civil servants. Gaitskell joined the Ministry of Economic Warfare (MEW) in September 1939, becoming Dalton's principal private secretary when Dalton arrived at MEW in May 1940, and moving with him to the Board of Trade. Evan Durbin joined the Economic Section of the Cabinet Offices in August 1940; in 1942 he became personal assistant to Attlee after Attlee became Deputy Prime Minister. Jay served in the Ministry of Supply until Dalton had him transferred to the Board of Trade in October 1943 as his personal assistant to work on reconstruction especially in the Development Areas. Piercy served in the Ministries of Supply and Production before joining Durbin as an adviser to Attlee in 1943. Since it is therefore not possible to separate the Labour economists' work for the party from their involvement in wartime government, this section indicates their contributions to post-war planning in the government as well as within the party committees.

The composition of the group of economists advising the Labour Party in the early 1940s was somewhat different from that of the 1930s. Colin Clark had emigrated to Australia in 1937. Mayhew was in the Army, although after serving in France in 1939–40 he joined the Intelligence Corps and worked for Dalton in MEW before returning to active service in 1942. Meade went to work for the League of Nations in Geneva in 1937; when he returned to England in the summer of 1940 to join what soon became the Economic Section of the Cabinet Offices he 'decided to behave exactly as a Civil Servant without engaging in political activity'.[39] Joan Robinson, earlier a member of Clark's NFRB group in Cambridge, served on some of the party's reconstruction committees, as did John Wilmot, a member of XYZ and a Member of Parliament (in 1933–5 and since 1939), who was Dalton's Parliamentary Private Secretary at both MEW and the Board of Trade. Joan Robinson, as an 'eminent economist ... known to be in sympathy with the aims of the Trade Union Movement', also advised the Trades Union Congress in preparing their reconstruction plans.[40]

The Labour Party appointed a Reconstruction Committee with several subcommittees, including one on post-war finance chaired by Dalton, in July 1941, but it was early 1943 before discussions on post-war financial policy began in earnest. By then the Beveridge Report on *Social Insurance and Allied Services* (Cmd. 6404) had been published on 1 December 1942, and the Economic Section—in the person of James Meade—was taking the initiative in pressing for a white paper on post-war employment policy. Keynes's plan for an international 'clearing union' to provide international liquidity and balance-of-payments adjustment in a multilateral post-war trade and payments system had received Cabinet approval as a basis for discussions with the US administration in April 1942. It was subsequently published as a white paper (Cmd. 6437) simultaneously with the American Treasury plan for a stabilization fund, in April 1943. In July 1942 Meade had drafted a complementary plan for a 'commercial union' for post-war commercial policy, which had been enthusiastically endorsed by the Board of Trade.[41]

As President of the Board of Trade Dalton was encouraged by Gaitskell to support the clearing union and actively to promote the commercial union. When Bevin denounced the former in the ministerial reconstruction committee as a return to the gold stan-

[39] Meade to Howson, 12 May 1986. Meade began to advise the Labour Party again, and joined XYZ, after he resigned from government service in 1947.

[40] TUC, *Interim Report on Post-war Reconstruction* (1944), para. 6; below. John Wilmot was the author of *Labour's Way to Control Banking and Finance* (London, 1935) which expounded party policy on financial reform at that time (including the nationalization of the joint-stock banks as well as of the Bank of England, a National Investment Board, and reform of company law).

[41] See Addison, *Road to 1945*, ch. VIII; *JMK*, vol. 27, chs. 4 and 5, and vol. 25, chs. 1 and 2; Tomlinson, *Employment Policy*, ch. 3. Meade's 'A proposal for an international commercial union', 25 July 1942, T230/125, PRO, is reproduced in his *Collected Papers*, vol. 3, ch. 3.

dard and 'an Anglo-American bankers' conspiracy against the
working class', Dalton thought 'the proposals were most enlight-
ened and reasonable—or so Gaitskell had explained to me at
lunch, I not having had time to read them'.[42] Dalton did read
Meade's proposals—in an August 1942 draft prepared in
collaboration with Gaitskell—agreed to circulate them as a Board
of Trade official paper, and arranged for Meade to be seconded
part-time to the Board (in which capacity Meade was to represent
the Board in interdepartmental committees in Whitehall and in
Anglo-American discussions on his commercial union in Washington in September–October 1943).[43]

Dalton had been a believer in free trade since he was an undergraduate reading economics at Cambridge. In the Second World
War he was also strongly in favour of Anglo-American collaboration in shaping the post-war world economy. In October 1941 he
had emphasized to his party colleagues, in a reconstruction subcommittee on international relationships, both his belief in the
need for such co-operation, especially in 'monetary and investment policy', in order to secure full employment after the war
and his preference for multilateralism rather than bilateral
arrangements in international trade. On exchange rates he
favoured managed flexible rates with some controls over capital
movements.[44] The attraction of the clearing union to Dalton and
Gaitskell was that it provided a compromise between exchange-
rate stability, which was conducive to international trade and
hence Britain's exports, and exchange-rate flexibility, which was
desirable for the maintenance of domestic full employment

[42] Ben Pimlott (ed.), *The Second World War Diary of Hugh Dalton, 1940–45* (London, 1986), 406. The clearing union proposals being discussed are reproduced in
JMK, vol. 25, pp. 108–39; the ministerial meeting was on 31 March 1942: EP(42) 1st
meeting, CAB87/2, PRO. For Gaitskell's views see his comments to Leith-Ross on
T230/37, PRO, where his one major criticism was that the scheme did not allow
sufficient scope for exchange-rate adjustments.

[43] Pimlott (ed.) *Second World War Diary of Hugh Dalton*, 476, 501, 515–16, 541–2,
576–9; 'A proposal for an international commercial union', 17 Aug. 1942, and
subsequent memoranda on T230/125, PRO; 'Post-war commercial policy, A proposal for a commercial union', 24 Aug. 1942, and subsequent memoranda in
Dalton Papers 7/4.

[44] Hugh Dalton, *Call Back Yesterday, Memoirs 1887–1931* (London, 1953), ch. III;
'Notes on international economic policy in the post-war world', attached to
RDR4, [Durbin?], 'Note and preliminary questions on post-war international
economic policy', Oct. 1941, Reconstruction Committee Papers, Labour Party
Archives.

policies; the attraction of the commercial union a similar compromise between freer trade and the ability to use import restrictions for balance-of-payments adjustment in certain circumstances.

This concern to promote international trade after the war is also evident in Durbin's contributions to the Labour Party's reconstruction discussions. He argued in June 1943 that there were three main tasks to be undertaken in order to increase post-war trade in goods and services: to prevent cyclical depressions, to reduce trade barriers, and to restore the flow of international lending—these three factors having all reduced world trade in the interwar years. He therefore supported an international stabilization fund, on the lines of the Keynes and White plans, which should allow exchange-rate changes or import restrictions as means of balance-of-payments adjustment for a country maintaining domestic full employment. There should also be an international investment programme, administered by the International Bank or Fund to lend the surpluses of surplus countries, especially to less developed countries. The Labour Party should strongly support international agreements to reduce tariffs and quantitative restrictions.[45] A few months later when he tried his hand at a few paragraphs on international economic policy for a party policy pamphlet on post-war employment policy, he included three 'essential' points: (i) There should be no return to the gold standard or rigidly fixed exchange rates; this did not preclude international co-operation 'to make sensible international arrangements for the management of the exchanges. Far from it.' (ii) This co-operation should include an 'International Development (or Investment) Board'. (iii) Since 'it [is] obvious that the barriers to trade had grown too high in the capitalist world before the war', the international agreement should provide for the progressive reduction of tariffs and other trade barriers, even though 'As Socialists we believe in the planning of imports and exports' and would wish to maintain some of the wartime arrangements for bulk purchases, etc. A fourth point was the need to increase Britain's exports after the war by organizing an 'export drive'.[46]

[45] 'International economic policy', RDR22l, June 1943, Labour Party Archives. An earlier draft of the paper, initialled by Durbin, is in Piercy Papers 8/74.

[46] Durbin to 'Comrades', 18 Jan. 1944, 'Employment and Prosperity, Draft section on foreign finance and trade', Piercy Papers 8/24.

Dalton was to make use of these paragraphs in writing the party's 'white paper' on *Full Employment and Financial Policy* (see below).

On domestic policy Dalton made clear his priorities for the contribution of the Board of Trade to post-war planning in the House of Commons debate on economic policy on 3 February 1943. The Chancellor of the Exchequer, Sir Kingsley Wood, had focused on the problems of the post-war transition, which would require a continuance of some wartime controls and of heavy taxation until the danger of an inflationary post-war boom like that of 1919–20 had passed, on the need to restore the balance of payments, and on the need for international economic co-operation as envisaged in Article VII of the Mutual Aid Agreement. Dalton fastened on Wood's acknowledgment of the need for controls to prevent a recurrence of the 1919–20 experience, and elaborated on that experience by treating the House to a run of dramatic statistics. After relating the discussions his department was undertaking with various industries about their post-war problems and plans including the export problem, he emphasized the necessity to provide full employment—'to secure that we will come as near as we can to a state of affairs in which every man or woman who is fit and able to work and desirous to work is able to get work under suitable conditions regarding wages and the like'—and to tackle the special problems of the 'distressed areas' where unemployment had been continuously heavy between the wars.[47]

An official Steering Committee on Post-war Employment was appointed in July 1943 in response to the circulation of the Economic Section paper on 'The maintenance of full employment' in May. In its submission to this committee the Board of Trade argued both that budgetary measures could and should be used to maintain aggregate demand and that aggregate demand management and microeconomic measures to deal with 'structural' unemployment were complementary, not alternative, policies. It took issue with the Treasury's arguments against budget deficits, since such a policy 'though admittedly somewhat crude, appears to be the simplest instrument at the disposal of the Government for stimulating an increase in con-

[47] *House of Commons Debates*, vol. 386, 2 Feb. 1943, cols. 812–27 (Wood), 3 Feb. 1943, cols. 978–95 (Dalton).

sumption' in a slump.[48] With characteristic vigour, 'bullying his own civil servants', Dalton saw to it that the white paper included a chapter on 'The Balanced Distribution of Industry'. This 'describe[d] the measures which the Government will take to check the development of localised unemployment in particular industries and areas', namely to take work to the workers in the 'development areas' as well as to promote occupational and geographic labour mobility. He followed this up with legislation for the planning and control of the location of industry in his Distribution of Industry Bill, which was passed after Dalton and his Labour colleagues withdrew from the coalition government immediately before the dissolution of Parliament for the 1945 general election. He was determined to incorporate as many as possible of his own and his party's ideas on reconstruction into the coalition government's post-war plans, for he expected the Conservative party led by Churchill would win a general election held soon after victory in Europe.[49]

Dalton was also concerned that the reconstruction efforts should include a government institution to provide finance for small and new businesses, an idea which also appeared in the report of the Steering Committee on Post-war Employment. The Bank of England preferred a private institution, as in the report of its committee on post-war domestic finance (see Chapter 1). When Lord Catto succeeded Lord Norman as Governor in 1944 he persuaded the London and Scottish bankers to set up ICFC (Industrial and Commercial Finance Corporation) to preempt the government. Dalton deputed Jay to keep an eye on the resulting negotiations between Whitehall (the Treasury and the Board of Trade) and the City (the Bank and the clearing bankers). When ICFC came into existence in 1945, Bill Piercy was its first chairman and James Lawrie, another member of XYZ and formerly with the London office of the Bank of New Zealand, general manager.[50]

[48] EC(43)12, 'Maintenance of Employment, Board of Trade Observations on Prefatory Note by the Treasury', 20 Oct. 1943, CAB87/63, PRO; see also Tomlinson, *Employment Policy*, 56.

[49] Pimlott, *Hugh Dalton*, 363–7, 402–3, and *Second World War Diary of Hugh Dalton*, xxx-xxxiv; Jay, *Change and Fortune*, ch. 6; *Employment Policy*, Cmd. 6527, ch. 3.

[50] Eady to Hopkins, 'Finance for industry', 5 Feb., and 'Steering Committee— Lord Keynes' note on finance for industry', 25 Feb. 1944, and subsequent memoranda on T160/1381/F18757, PRO; Fforde, *Bank*, 715–22; John Kinross, *Fifty Years in*

Gaitskell also assisted Dalton in his reconstruction campaigns at the Board of Trade, participating on occasion as the Board's representative in the official discussions on the preparation of the *Employment Policy* white paper.[51] By this time Durbin was working as Attlee's personal assistant. In the Economic Section he had commented favourably on the first of Meade's long series of memoranda on post-war employment policy, finding himself 'in general agreement' but wanting it to go further in its recommendations for countercyclical budgetary policy—to emphasize more strongly the possibility of using subsidies and tax changes to influence consumption, and to raise the possibility of financing the deficits by 'borrowing from the Banks at a zero Rate of Interest'.[52] When the 'public' version of Meade's 1943 memorandum on 'The maintenance of full employment' was circulated outside the Section, Durbin urged Attlee to read it.

1. The main Report is, I think you will agree, beautifully written and it bears out my contention, with which I fear I may have wearied you in the past, that economists are now able to agree on interesting and important propositions. The Economic Section contains economists of almost every persuasion, from extreme faith in capitalism to membership of the Fabian Society and the Labour Party. Yet they have been able to produce an agreed document of great interest.

His criticisms were 'small in comparison with the main grounds of agreement'. What was now needed was that 'some one man of ability and vigour is appointed—in the Treasury I would suggest' to ensure its implementation.[53] The man was certainly Keynes: in another memorandum to Attlee Durbin (or Piercy) proposed a 'Keynes report' on employment policy—as Meade had to Keynes

---

the City: Financing Small Business (London, 1982), ch. 11; see also Dalton, 'The finance of industrial re-organisation', 14 Apr. 1944, Dalton Papers 7/6, and Piercy, 'The Macmillan gap and the shortage of risk capital', *JRSS*, ser. A, 118 (1955), 1–7.

[51] Williams, *Hugh Gaitskell*, 100-l.

[52] EC(S)(41)24, 'The Prevention of General Unemployment, Note by Mr. Durbin', 27 Mar. 1941, T230/13, PRO. Meade's major wartime memoranda on full employment are in his *Collected Papers*, vol. 1, chs. 11–14.

[53] Durbin to Deputy Prime Minister, 'Maintenance of Employment PR(43)26', 24 May 1943, Piercy Papers 8/24. The number of Fabian economists in the wartime Economic Section was in fact quite high judging from the minutes of meetings of the Economics Committee of the Society in 1943: Fabian Society Papers K18/2. For an attempt to categorize the views of Section economists see EC(S)(41)51, 'The future economic functions of the state, Note by Mr. Durbin', 22 Dec. 1941, T230/13, PRO.

himself—and once a white paper was in prospect he 'repeat[ed], as you will expect me to do, that there is only one person who should be asked to do it—Keynes'.[54]

Meanwhile Dalton, with the assistance of John Wilmot, had galvanized the party's Post-war Finance Subcommittee into action in late 1942. The third meeting, on 14 January 1943, was 'attended by all our tribe of experts', including Berry, Durbin, Jay, Piercy and, for the first time, Joan Robinson.[55] It had before it papers on wartime exchange controls, post-war monetary policy and post-war financial policy, by Mayhew, Durbin, and Jay respectively. Mayhew's paper described the wartime exchange control system and recommended its post-war continuation. The committee readily agreed that 'control should be continued permanently and not only in the transitional post-war period'. The papers by Durbin and Jay were 'discussed in general terms'. After some discussion on 'the scope of our plans', the committee appointed a subcommittee, of Berry, Durbin, Gaitskell, Jay and Piercy, to consider the papers and to prepare a report on 'things which should be done'.[56] The subcommittee subsequently prepared four memoranda for Dalton's committee, covering international economic policy and post-war taxation as well as employment policy and control of the financial system. Most of their ideas were included in the draft report on employment policy that Dalton arranged for Durbin, Gaitskell, and Jay to prepare after the subcommittee's memoranda had been discussed by his committee.

Durbin's first paper for the Post-war Finance Committee echoed his arguments of the later 1930s and his comments on Meade's 1941 memorandum. In order to maintain full employment expansionary monetary policy was necessary but not sufficient. It could be reinforced by public works, and both policies could be made effective if carried to 'a logical extreme' (such as a

[54] Unsigned undated note to Deputy Prime Minister, 'Post-war employment policy', and Durbin to Deputy Prime Minister, 'Full Employment, Minutes R(44) 8th meeting', 25 Jan. 1944, Piercy Papers 8/24. For Meade's request to Keynes, on 8 Jan. 1943, see *JMK*, vol. 27, pp. 314–15.

[55] Dalton Diary, vol. 27, 4 Aug. and 20 Dec. 1942 and 14 Jan. 1943, BLPES; see also Pimlott, *Hugh Dalton*, 392–3, and *Second World War Diary of Hugh Dalton*, 548.

[56] RDR172, 'Exchange Control', Jan. 1943, and Minutes of Third Meeting of Post-war Finance Subcommittee, Labour Party Archives; see also Durbin, 'Programme of work', 26 Jan. 1943, Piercy Papers 8/74.

zero rate of interest). A more powerful method of maintaining consumers' incomes would be to reduce taxation and finance the resulting budget deficit by borrowing at low or zero interest rates from the banking system, to which the only objections were 'purely practical', i.e. administrative and political. The release of the post-war tax credits introduced in the 1941 budget could also be used to influence consumption. Since the authorities already had the power to carry out these policies if they chose to do so, 'it seems to follow that the changes of machinery that are absolutely necessary are comparatively small': the Bank of England should be nationalized, wartime controls over financial institutions should be maintained in peacetime, plans for public investment programmes should be drawn up well in advance, and a National Investment Board should provide additional control over investment by regulating new capital issues and by making loans to private borrowers. In order to prevent a post-war slump, the party should be urging these proposals on the coalition government rather than preparing ambitious plans for 'socialization of finance', if only because a victorious Churchill coalition government was likely immediately after the war.[57]

Durbin and Jay in his two papers both distinguished between the immediate post-war transition, which would last at least two years and require an overall policy stance similar to wartime in order to assist reconstruction and repress inflation, and the subsequent deflationary period. For the latter Jay's proposals were similar to Durbin's: to maintain both consumption and investment expenditures, by reduced taxation and the release of post-war credits, increased government expenditures on the social services, large-scale public investment, low interest rates which should be ensured by formal Treasury control over the Bank of England and the clearing banks, 'some form of National Investment Board' to encourage investment as well as to control private capital issues, and, as a last resort, a budget deficit financed by increasing the money supply. Jay was, however, concerned about the distributive consequences of an increasing national debt and proposed the introduction of an annual capital tax as an alternative to a capital levy. Gaitskell, on the other hand, in his discussion of tax reform in the post-transitional period on the assumption that full employment was achieved, rejected both a

[57] RDR173, 'Post-war monetary policy', Jan. 1943, Labour Party Archives.

capital levy and an annual capital tax as not worth their political and administrative problems when tax rates were high and interest rates low.[58]

Berry wrote a memorandum on the 'machinery of financial control'. He advocated the consolidation of the wartime system: retaining exchange control, advances control, and capital issues control, converting the last, together with the Public Works Loan Board, into a National Investment Board, and formalizing the *de facto* nationalization of the Bank of England. The proposed National Investment Board was now to have the power to borrow and lend money, not just to license new issues as in pre-war XYZ memoranda.[59]

When Jay's and Berry's papers came before Dalton's committee in March 1943, they were circulated along with a paper written a few months earlier by Joan Robinson on wartime control of interest rates, as a result of discussions she had had with Jay on his second paper. She argued that the wartime innovations of tap bond issues and Treasury deposit receipts could be used to pursue a permanent low interest-rate policy, in order to encourage long-term investment and to reduce rentier incomes.

The most important feature of this development is not so much the technique that has been evolved for controlling the rate of interest (though that is a very remarkable achievement) as the fact that the Treasury has assumed responsibility for fixing the gilt-edged rate of interest, which was formerly regarded as something quite outside its control. The actual rates fixed upon are somewhat arbitrary, and there is no reason in principle why they should not be further reduced. Probably 1% is unnecessarily generous to the banks. They survived the cheap money epoch of '33 and '34 on ½%, when their volume of business was less than at present. An abrupt reduction in the bond rate would probably lead to dangerous reactions, but a gradual fall should be possible. Once the rentier class have been broken in to 3%, and have come to regard 3% as the *upper* limit to the gilt-edged rate, they will be glad enough to take up bonds of longer date than those at present offered

[58] RDR175, 'Post-war financial policy', Jan. 1943, RDR200, 'Post-war employment policy', RDR200, Mar. 1943, and RDR 222, 'Notes on post-war taxation policy', June 1943, Labour Party Archives. The authorship of these papers can be ascertained from Durbin's 'Programme of work' and subsequent notes in Piercy Papers 8/74.

[59] RDR201, 'Notes on machinery of financial control', Mar. 1943, Labour Party Archives.

at 2½%. When 2½% has become established as a 'normal' rate they will take up bonds at 2% and so on.

Such a policy would require the maintenance of exchange controls to prevent capital flows. It would also involve 'abandoning altogether the traditional use of the rate of interest as a check to inflation', but 'the rate of interest would be much too weak a defence to use against inflation in the post-war situation' when rationing and controls would be needed anyway.[60]

The idea of a *long-term* policy of cheap money was, of course, more purely Keynesian than the anti-cyclical monetary policy espoused by other Labour party economists. It depended on both the liquidity preference theory of interest and the assumption that full employment in the long run would require continuous direct intervention to maintain the volume of investment as well as to bring about the 'euthanasia of the rentier'. It was a more ambitious version of the proposal Keynes was to put to the National Debt Enquiry two years later (Chapter 1 above). Robinson's proposal made a more public appearance in an appendix to Beveridge's *Full Employment in a Free Society*, which was prepared with the help of Nicholas Kaldor, Joan Robinson, and E. F. Schumacher, and in the TUC *Interim Report on Post-War Reconstruction*.[61] In the former she answered a question which Durbin might have asked her: 'why the Government should not decide right away that the best rate of interest is a zero rate and proceed to finance all its deficits by the "creation" of new cash or bank money'? She gave two reasons: the sudden windfall appreciation in capitalists' wealth and the difficulties that the disappearance of relatively riskless long-term bonds would cause for institutional investors such as insurance companies, pension funds, and charitable foundations. 'These two objections lose their force when applied to a gradual and long-term policy of reducing the

[60] RDR133, 'War-time control of the rate of interest', Sept. 1942, Labour Party Archives and Piercy Papers 8/12. There is a longer version of the same paper, with corrections made in or after April 1943 to take account of the Keynes and White plans, in Joan Robinson Papers ii/4, King's College, Cambridge. For the discussions with Jay see 'Notes by Mrs. Joan Robinson on Memorandum by Mr. Douglas Jay', Piercy Papers 8/12.

[61] *Full Employment in a Free Society*, app. B, note 4, 337–341; Trades Union Congress, *Interim Report on Post-War Reconstruction*, (1944), 35–8. For Robinson's statement of the Keynesian theory on which her proposals were based see her 'The rate of interest', *Econometrica* 19 (Apr. 1951), 92–111, reprinted in *The Rate of Interest and other Essays* (London, 1952), 1–30.

rate of interest; but they would appear to have considerable weight against a policy of sudden changes.'

Her views dominated the discussion of the fourth meeting of the party committee. Asked to provide 'a few additional notes on the actual powers to be taken to control the rate of interest', she specifically recommended:

The powers at present enjoyed by the authorities over the banking system, especially the power to demand Treasury Deposits, should not be relaxed after the war.

These powers should be used to maintain continuous low interest. The present short rates . . . are unnecessarily generous to the banks, having regard to the great increase in the volume of business, and should be reduced. The present mechanism for maintaining the gilt-edged rate of interest by selling bonds on tap should be continued even when the budget is balanced. Any tendency for the rate to rise should be counteracted by using Treasury Deposits to buy in bonds from the market.

The policy of reducing the gilt-edged rate should be continued. Only experience can show how low it is possible to force it, but the first objective should be to get 2½% Consols to par.

She therefore expressed 'some disagreement' with Jay's paper on post-war employment policy: in a slump the government should first expand consumption by budgetary measures, second increase public investment in the nationalized industries, and 'in the third place only' encourage private investment. 'There must be direct Government control over sufficient sectors of investment.'[62]

The meeting also considered the memorandum by Berry and agreed that 'what we want is the substance of control, not merely formal control over the Bank of England'. The Bank should be given powers of control over the commercial banks—'The question was, how do we give the Bank of England those powers?' There was also general agreement on the functions of a National Investment Board as described by Berry. Dalton was pleased with the meeting: he thought that the committee had '[done] some more good work. They are an outstanding lot, though most of the men don't like Mrs. Robinson, who,

[62] 'Note to be appended to RDR133—Wartime Control of the Rate of Interest', Piercy Papers 8/12; Minutes of the fourth meeting of the Post-war Finance Sub-committee, 25 Mar. 1943, Labour Party Archives and Piercy Papers 8/12.

however, seems to be extremely able and to have the right approach.'[63]

The two other memoranda prepared by Durbin's committee came with several other papers before the next meeting of Dalton's committee in October 1943, at which Joan Robinson was not present. The other papers included one on 'Long term employment policy', which may have been written by Robinson since it incorporates her proposals on investment and budgetary policy. Dalton's purpose at this meeting was to arrange that Durbin, Gaitskell and Jay would begin the drafting of a report on post-war financial policy for the NEC and the party conference. He got the committee to agree that Gaitskell and Jay should prepare a report on 'Post-war Employment and Finance' and Durbin one on international economic policy.[64] Gaitskell and Jay's memorandum was discussed by Dalton with Berry, Durbin, Gaitskell, Jay, Piercy, and Wilmot in January, and then drastically redrafted by Dalton, incorporating a few paragraphs on international economic policy drafted by Durbin (above), before it was unanimously approved by his committee in April 1944.[65]

The most obvious difference between the early drafts and the final version is in the order of their recommendations. Dalton placed more emphasis on the need to maintain controls and cheap money in the transitional period than on the budgetary measures required to maintain aggregate demand and employment in the longer term. The drafts explicitly focused on general

[63] Ibid.; Dalton Diary, vol. 28, 25 Mar. 1943. Dalton asked Robinson to 'elaborate further her proposals for the division of the budget into ordinary, Social Security and Capital Budgets'. She was also asked to prepare a paper on price control.

[64] RDR206, 'Long term employment policy', Apr. 1943, and Agenda and Minutes of Fifth Meeting of Post-war Finance Subcommittee, 20 Oct. 1943, Labour Party Archives; Dalton Diary, vol. 29, 20 Oct. 1943.

[65] For its preparation see 'Outline for a draft on Employment Policy', 'Points that are generally agreed', 'Draft outline for memorandum on employment', and 'Policies for Maintaining Employment', Piercy Papers 8/24. The last two papers usefully indicate the source of some of the ideas, including Joan Robinson's. For the redraftng see Durbin to 'Comrades', 18 Jan. 1944, Piercy Papers 8/24, and Second World War Diary of Hugh Dalton, 698, 718, 723 (ll Jan., 4–5 Mar. and 18–19 Mar. 1944). According to his diary Dalton found 'the draft by D. J. and H. G. so frightful I just can't do anything with it', and even after asking Durbin to redraft, 'it [was] extraordinary how little use most of the drafts made by other people are'. The minutes of the sixth meeting of the Post-war Finance Subcommittee, 5 Apr. 1944, are in the Labour Party Archives.

unemployment as distinct from structural unemployment and pointed out that aggregate demand could be maintained equally by policies to influence consumption and investment. These policies would include increased expenditure on social services, tax reductions, releases of post-war income tax credits—financing a deficit by borrowing from the banking system if necessary—in order to maintain consumption; and long-term planning of public investment plus the indirect control of private investment (by licensing, monetary policy, and government loan guarantees or similar measures to reduce the cost or increase the supply of credit) in order to maintain total investment. On the international side, Britain's exports could be permanently encouraged by the reduction of trade barriers and multilateral trading arrangements, international co-operation in full employment policies, international institutions like the Clearing Union, international buffer stock schemes for primary commodities, and the resumption of international lending. Within international agreements short-term balance-of-payments adjustment should be allowed when necessary by means of exchange-rate changes, temporary import restrictions and control over capital movements. The administrative measures needed included the continuation of exchange control and wartime financial controls (including, of course, the formalization of the wartime relationship between the Treasury and the Bank of England), central planning of investment, and a National Investment Board.[66]

Dalton's argument ran as follows: We can and must have full employment after the war, as we have had during the war. Since unemployment has financial causes, we must keep the wartime financial arrangements including Treasury deposit receipts, capital issues control, and exchange controls. Exchange control was 'vital if we are to maintain cheap money, as we must, . . . [and] for the control of exchange rates'. In this context the 'central point' in Labour's full employment policy was the maintenance of aggregate demand to prevent both inflation and deflation. In the transitional period, inflation would be held in check by price control, rationing, cost-of-living subsidies, etc.; thereafter, when deflation threatened, budgetary policy—increased expenditure and reduced taxation—would be used to increase consumption and investment, especially public investment. Investment had to

[66] 'Draft outline for memorandum on employment', Piercy Papers 8/24.

be planned well in advance, which provided 'one of the the strongest reasons' for nationalizing major industries. By thus ensuring total investment equalled savings at full employment, general unemployment could be prevented. However, special measures, including control of the location of industry would also be essential to reduce regional unemployment in the North of England and Scotland and Wales. The national investment plan should pay special regard to these areas, and should be administered by a National Investment Board with the three functions of forecasting, licensing, and financing investment. Finally, we needed international monetary and trade arrangements which would permit the maintenance of full employment at home and abroad. Here Dalton closely followed the paragraphs Durbin had drafted.[67]

Dalton's draft of *Full Employment and Financial Policy* was passed with few amendments by the Post-war Finance committee, by the Policy Committee of the NEC and by the NEC, and published a few weeks before the white paper on *Employment Policy*. Dalton later described his document as 'largely Keynesian ... [with] some socialist additions', identifying the Keynesian elements as aggregate demand management and the proposed international monetary arrangements, the socialist additions as direct control over the banking system, the nationalization of major industries and control of industrial location.[68] The adoption of the report at the party conference in December 1944 marked the formal acceptance by the party of Keynesian ideas; its recommendations on employment policy appeared again in the manifesto for the 1945 election.

At the party conference many speakers were more attracted by the 'socialist additions' than by the 'Keynesian' elements in the document, and pressed for more socialism, that is more nationalization (including of banking and of the iron and steel industry). The resolution welcoming the report 'and the re-statement of the Party's Socialist faith contained therein' drew attention to the recommendations for controls, especially over the banking system and investment, for the location of industry, and for international monetary and trade agreements. Moving the resolution,

[67] RDR265, 'Full employment and financial policy', Mar. 1944, Piercy Papers 15/90.
[68] Dalton, *The Fateful Years*, 422–3.

Emanuel Shinwell claimed that it dealt with 'three inter-related subjects—full employment; the establishment of sound, efficient and effective economic controls; and public ownership'. The report went further than the government white paper in seeking not just a 'high and stable level of employment' but *full employment*, which he defined as 'a situation in which there are more jobs available than there are men and women to fill them'. Closing the debate, Philip Noel-Baker argued that since 1931 'everybody' had come to recognize the utility of loan-financed public works to maintain employment and also that the Bretton Woods Agreements of July 1944 were necessary to enable individual countries to maintain full employment. Both the NEC resolution and that of its left-wing critics were carried.[69]

The TUC shared the desire for 'full employment' rather than just a 'high and stable level of employment'.[70] It also wanted more nationalization. Most of the *Interim Report on Post-war Reconstruction* adopted at the 1944 Congress was devoted to detailed recommendations for public ownership and public control of industry. It also included, a statement on finance and investment policy, which stressed the need to avoid both inflation and deflation after the war and clearly reflected Joan Robinson's views. The major cause of instability in prices and employment was the instability of private investment expenditure which must therefore be controlled. In the immediate post-war period controls would also be needed to prevent open inflation. Interest rates were 'a weak instrument for regulating the flow of private investment', but once it was recognized that more direct controls would be needed 'the way is opened for the pursuit of a permanent policy of "cheap money"' as long as capital movements and bank lending were also controlled. The permanent planning and control of investment should be exercised by a National Investment Board with the power to provide finance for approved investment plans.[71] Although such a Board was now part of Labour

---

[69] Labour Party, *Report of the 43rd Annual Conference held in Central Hall, Westminster, December 11th to December 15th, 1944*, 160–8. Noel-Baker's second point had been suggested to him by James Meade: Meade, *Cabinet Office Diary*, 15.

[70] *Interim Report*, paras. 145 and 147–64.

[71] Ibid. para. 146; see also 'Summary of interim report on post-war reconstruction adopted at the 1944 Congress', paras. 29–43, in *Four TUC Documents Approved by the Blackpool Congress 1945*, 61–3. The four documents were statements

Party plans as well it was to fall by the wayside as soon as the party came to power.

Well before the end of hostilities in Europe the Labour Party had adopted a fairly specific programme for post-war financial policy. First developed in the mid–1930s and modified at the end of the decade and during the war, this combined wartime financial controls and monetary arrangements with Keynesian budgetary policy and older party proposals such as the nationalization of the Bank of England and the planning and control of investment through a National Investment Board. In the light of later developments it is interesting to note that it did not explicitly include a cheaper money policy such as Dalton pursued in 1945-6, although Dalton had noted with approval Joan Robinson's proposals for a permanent low interest-rate policy to encourage long-term investment and reduce rentier incomes. Dalton and his 'young economists' had also made direct contributions to the development of the wartime official consensus on post-war economic policy, in order to ensure any post-war government would seek to maintain a high level of employment. The practical proposals recommended in the party policy document, *Full Employment and Financial Policy* could also be adopted wholeheartedly by a Labour government or pressed upon the Churchill government that was widely expected in the summer of 1945.

on fiscal policy, transport, the financial aspects of nationalization, and trusts and cartels; the first of these was concerned with the redistributive effects of the tax structure.

3

Dalton at the Treasury

The chief problems of which I was conscious, when I went to
the Treasury in 1945, were these. First, reconversion . . .;
second, . . . a smooth transition, maintaining full employment and avoiding strikes and lock-outs and any sharp rise
in the cost of living; third, our pledge to extend the social
services . . .; fourth, the reshaping of taxation so as to reduce
the total and to narrow from both ends the gap between the
richest and the poorest; fifth, our pledge to nationalise the
Bank of England, the coal industry, and other key industries
and services; sixth, more immediate and more difficult than
all the rest, how for the next few years to pay for [our]
imports . . . .[1]

IN July 1945 the new Prime Minister, Clement Attlee, appointed
Hugh Dalton Chancellor of the Exchequer, Ernest Bevin Foreign
Secretary, Stafford Cripps President of the Board of Trade, and
Herbert Morrison Lord President of the Council with overall
responsibility for domestic economic policy. Although Dalton
had expected to go to the Foreign Office (and Bevin to the
Treasury),[2] he was not short of ideas for his new job. According
to *Full Employment and Financial Policy*, the first majority Labour
government would maintain exchange control and other wartime
financial controls, nationalize the Bank of England, continue government borrowing at low interest rates from the banking system through the system of Treasury deposit receipts, and set up a
National Investment Board. It would use the budget and public
investment to maintain aggregate demand and employment after
the transitional period. As Chancellor Dalton also wished to use
his fiscal and monetary policy for redistributive purposes and to
finance the nationalization of key industries as cheaply as poss-

---

[1] H. Dalton, *Principles of Public Finance*, 4th edn. (London, 1954), 229.
[2] Pimlott, *Hugh Dalton*, 410–11; Alan Bullock, *Ernest Bevin, Foreign Secretary*
(Oxford, 1985), 3.

ible. At the same time, however, the post-war balance-of-payments problem 'hung over Britain like a black thundercloud'.[3]

Dalton immediately took steps to prepare legislation to nationalize the Bank and to maintain exchange and capital issues controls permanently. He did not set up a National Investment Board, however, contenting himself with a purely advisory National Investment Council. He then attempted to utilize wartime monetary arrangements to drive down long-term nominal interest rates on government debt. He also introduced four budgets: an interim budget in October 1945, annual budgets in April 1946 and April 1947, and a supplementary budget in November 1947 after the convertibility crisis. This chapter has two main aims: to outline the steps Dalton took to implement the Labour party's plans for financial reform and indicate why they were so limited; and to describe the pursuit of 'cheaper money' in 1945–6. It also describes briefly the balance-of-payments problem and its temporary solution in the Anglo-American Financial Agreement of December 1945, and the main lines of Dalton's first two budgets. The chapter explains the consequences of the cheaper money policy for the monetary aggregates but the further consequences are discussed along with the reasons for its abandonment in 1947 in the next chapter. The last section of this chapter analyses Dalton's (and his official advisers') reasons for the pursuit of a monetary policy so different from that planned in the Labour Party as well as indicating the reaction of his former advisers to the policy.

Dalton's responsibilities as Chancellor of the Exchequer only covered *financial policy*. Other aspects of macroeconomic policy were the purview of the Lord President of the Council, who chaired the Lord President's Committee and was the minister to whom the Economic Section (as under the wartime coalition government) reported. As in wartime the machinery for economic planning was largely interdepartmental and the Treasury did not fully recover its pre-war pre-eminence within Whitehall until 1947. This did not mean that Treasury officials were not heavily involved in, for instance, the setting up and running of the interdepartmental committees on the planning and control of investment in 1945–6. It did mean that the Chancellor contributed

[3] Dalton, *Public Finance*, 228–9, 234.

very little to this process, which was set in motion by Sir Edward Bridges (Permanent Secretary to the Treasury), Norman Brook (Deputy Secretary to the Cabinet) and James Meade in the Economic Section.[4] The division of responsibilities also restricted the contribution of the economists in the Section to monetary and budgetary policy, even though Meade, on agreeing to become Director, had insisted on being a member of the top secret Budget Committee, which was composed of senior officials from the Treasury and the Inland Revenue. In preparing his budgets Dalton took heed of Meade's advice on occasion. But he resisted the Section's attempt to integrate economic 'planning' and the budget by preparing the annual Economic Survey for the financial year rather than the calendar year; the surveys prepared under Meade's direction served as one among several background papers in the budget discussions. In the making of monetary policy the Section made no direct contribution during Dalton's period of office.[5] In addition to his official Treasury and Bank of England advisers Dalton relied on two semi-official advisers: Lord Keynes, who remained in the Treasury until his death in April 1946, and the recently retired Permanent Secretary, Sir Richard Hopkins.

The July 1945 general election brought several of Dalton's former advisers into Parliament, including Durbin, Gaitskell, and Mayhew. Dalton made Durbin his Parliamentary Private Secretary, while Mayhew became PPS to Herbert Morrison as Lord President of the Council. Gaitskell was appointed Parliamentary Secretary at the Ministry of Fuel and Power. Jay served as the Prime Minister's personal assistant until he too was elected

[4] On these developments see Meade, *Cabinet Office Diary*, and Tomlinson, *Employment Policy*, ch. 5. Meade was appointed in November 1944 to succeed Lionel Robbins as Director at the end of the war; he formally took over on 1 January 1946 and remained Director of the Section until he resigned from government service in the spring of 1947. Bridges was Secretary to the Cabinet 1938–46 and Permanent Secretary of the Treasury 1945–56; Brook, in addition to being Deputy Secretary to the Cabinet, was Permament Secretary of the Ministry of Reconstruction 1943–5; he followed Bridges in becoming Secretary to the Cabinet (1947–62) and Permanent Secretary of the Treasury (1956–62).

[5] On the work of the Section in these years see Alec Cairncross and Nita Watts, *The Economic Section 1939–1961: A Study in Economic Advising* (London, 1989), especially ch. 8, as well as Meade's diary. The first two economic surveys prepared under Meade's direction were not published; the third was completely rewritten outside the Section before it was published as the *Economic Survey for 1947* (Cmd. 7046) in February 1947.

TABLE 3.1 *UK Balance of Payments, Annual, 1945–8, £m*

	1945	1946	1947	1948
Exports of goods[1]	950	960	1,180	1,639
Imports of goods[1]	2,000	1,063	1,541	1,790
Trade balance	−1,050[2]	−103	−361	−151
Net invisibles[3,4] (a)	−620	−127	−20	177
(b)	−600	−133	−28	197
(c) Government	−400	−323	−149	−76
(d) Shipping	−100	29	36	80
(e) Interest	−100 {	80	93	91
(f) Other invisibles[5]	{	81	−8	102
Current balance excluding grants	−1,670	−230	−381	26
Grants[6]	800	—	30	138
Current account	−870	−230	−351	164
Intergovernmental loans (net)[6]	—	214	307	304
Net long-term capital flows[7]	100	99	−301	−167
Changes in overseas sterling holdings[8]	700	69	250	−336
Changes in official international reserves[9]	+9	+54	−152	−55

Notes
[1] fob
[2] Includes Lend-Lease and reciprocal aid.
[3] Includes private and government transfers *except* major grants of aid.
[4] (a) = Feinstein's figures for 1945–8; (b)–(f) Sayers's estimate for 1940, CSO estimates for 1946–8.
[5] Travel, private transfers and other.
[6] Lend-Lease and mutual aid (net), Marshall Aid, etc.
[7] Includes UK government subscriptions to IMF and IBRD.
[8] For 1946–8 includes balancing item.
[9] For 1945 includes sterling and dollar liabilities.
[10] With respect to reserve figures, + = increase, − = decrease.

Sources
Table 1.1; Feinstein, *National Income, Expenditure and Output of the United Kingdom 1855–1965* (Cambridge, 1972), table 37; *United Kingdom Balance of Payments, 1946–1957* (HMSO, 1959), table 1.

a Member of Parliament in July 1946. With one exception none was involved in financial policy while Dalton was Chancellor. They were also generally critical, as was Meade, of his cheaper money policy.

The breathing space

Attlee's government had only been in office for two weeks when, with the surrender of Japan after the bombing of Hiroshima and Nagasaki, the Second World War suddenly ended.

This brought an equally sudden end to Lend-Lease which had been covering almost half of the UK's current account balance-of-payments deficit of £1,670m (see Table 3.1). A large component was a £620m deficit on invisible trade, of which government expenditure overseas (net of other governments' expenditure in the UK) accounted for £400m. The invisibles deficit remained negative until 1948. The trade deficit, at £250m for cash trans-actions, was, however, smaller in 1945 than it had been in 1940-4, and it was halved in 1946 before rising again in 1947.

The government's response to the ending of Lend-Lease was to seek further American aid to tide the country over until exports could be raised to cover imports. On 23 August the new Cabinet decided to send Lord Keynes to Washington to lead (with Lord Halifax, the British Ambassador to the USA) a small team to negotiate for financial assistance, preferably in the form of a grant. After three months of bitter and protracted negotiations the American government agreed to lend $3.75bn, with interest at 2 per cent for 50 years beginning in 1951. It also lent $650m on the same terms in a final settlement of Lend-Lease. The Canadian government agreed to lend a further $1.25bn in March 1946. The strings attached to the US loan included the requirements that the UK make the pound convertible into dollars for current trans-actions one year from the effective date of the agreement, give up discriminating in trade against US imports at the same time, and make agreements with overseas sterling area countries to make their accumulated sterling balances convertible gradually over a number of years.[6] Having reluctantly agreed to the agreement, the government put it before Parliament in mid-December along with the Bretton Woods bill to approve Britain's joining the International Monetary Fund and the International Bank for Reconstruction and Development. After several more months of uncertainty, the agreement passed the US Congress and came into force on 15 July 1946. Whereas the IMF Articles of Agree-

---

[6] *Financial Agreement between the Governments of the United States and the United Kingdom*, Cmd. 6708, 6 Dec. 1945, paras. 8 and 10. The purposes of the loan were stated as 'to facilitate purchases by the United Kingdom of goods and services in the United States, to assist the United Kingdom to meet transitional post-war deficits in its current balance of payments, to help the United Kingdom to maintain adequate reserves of gold and dollars and to assist the Government of the United Kingdom to assume the obligations of multilateral trade as defined in this and other agreements' (para. 3).

ment adopted at the Bretton Woods conference in July 1944 allowed exchange controls on payments for current trans-actions to remain for five years, the loan agreement required current account convertibility of sterling by 15 July 1947. Al-though Dalton harboured doubts as to whether Britain would be able to keep to the conditions,[7] he none the less thought that the existence of the loan *plus exchange control* allowed him to formulate and conduct domestic monetary and fiscal policy without any need to consider the effects on the balance of payments.

In August 1945 the Labour government had extended exchange control and other wartime controls with the Supplies and Ser-vices (Transitional Powers) Act, 1945, which enabled it to retain all the measures introduced under the Emergency Powers Acts and the Defence (Finance) Regulations for five years.[8] Under the wartime exchange control Britain had bilateral payments agree-ments with a large number of countries, including by the end of the war those liberated from German occupation from the summer of 1944 onwards. The European monetary agreements generally allowed for credit balances to be run up in both cur-rencies to specified limits (beyond which settlement had to be made in gold or convertible currency) and for sterling held by the other country to be transferred to a third country if the UK authorities agreed. This 'administrative transferability' meant that these payments agreements were less strictly bilateral than earlier wartime ones. In 1946-7 the Treasury and the Bank of England sought to prepare for early convertibility of sterling by increasing the possibility under existing bilateral agreements with administrative transferability of transferring sterling to third countries and by setting up 'transferable accounts' under supple-mentary monetary agreements, the first of which was made with

[7] Dalton Diary, 14 Dec. 1945, quoted in Dalton, *High Tide and After: Memoirs 1945-1960* (London, 1962), 89, Cairncross, *Years of Recovery*, 110, and Pressnell, *External Economic Policy*, 329.

[8] Churchill's caretaker government had introduced a similar bill, not passed before the general election, to maintain controls for two years. The Labour Cabinet decided to increase its life and to extend it to cover the exchange and capital issues controls, in order to 'give more time for legislation of a permanent character on that subject': Cabinet 23(45), 16 Aug. 1945, CAB128/1; CP(45)11, Supplies and Services Bill, Memorandum by the Home Secretary, 14 Aug. 1945, CAB129/1, PRO.

Argentina on 3 October 1946.[9] Sterling held in the transferable accounts of one country could be used to make payments for current transactions not just to the sterling area but to another country's transferable account or to an American account—and sterling in the latter was already convertible into dollars or gold. In return the monetary authorities of the transferable account countries agreed to accept and hold sterling from any other country, usually without limit, the intention being to help sterling become an international currency again. In spite of the continuation of wartime exchange controls freedom to use sterling outside the sterling area was being given to an increasing number of countries; sterling was effectively convertible for both American account and transferable account countries before 15 July 1947. At the same time limited progress was made in regulating the use of the accumulated sterling balances of the sterling area countries.[10] However, although the UK economy was not financially closed by the early post-war exchange control, this did not become obvious to the government before 1947.

During the breathing space provided by the American loan the balance of payments at first improved significantly (Table 3.1). On current account there was a very encouraging near-doubling in exports of goods for cash in 1946, which kept total merchandise exports up to what they had been including reciprocal aid in 1945. The export growth continued in 1947–8, with a 23 per cent rise in 1947 and a 39 per cent rise in 1948. With the ending of the war and of Lend-Lease, total imports of goods fell by nearly half, permitting a reduction in the trade deficit in 1946. There was a large fall in the invisibles deficit, which reflected a renewed income from shipping and interest and owed little to a reduction in government overseas expenditure. Since government overseas expenditure *was* reduced in 1947, the invisibles position continued to improve but the improvement in visible trade did not: imports of goods rose by 45 per cent and the trade deficit trebled. The current account deficits of 1946 and 1947 were covered by overseas loans and in 1946 a net long-term

[9] Brian Tew, *International Monetary Co-operation 1945–52* (London, 1952), 131–5; 'The U.K. exchange control: a short history', *BEQB* 7 (Sept. 1967), 251–2; Sir Hugh Ellis-Rees, 'The convertibility crisis of 1947', T276/3, PRO, paras. 10–50; Cairncross, *Years of Recovery*, 123–8; Fforde, *Bank*, 124–41, 103–8.

[10] See Pressnell, *External Economic Policy*, ch. 9, Ellis-Rees, 'The convertibility crisis', paras. 51–68, and Fforde, *Bank*, ch. 3(*a*) and (*d*).

TABLE 3.2 *Gross Domestic Product, by Category of Expenditure, 1945–8, £m at 1938 Market Prices*

	1945	1946	1947	1948
Consumers' expenditure	4,108	4,533	4,675	4,719
Government current expenditure on goods and services	2,733	1,500	1,058	1,017
Gross domestic fixed capital formation	190	480	560	603
Value of change in stocks	−120	+70	+140	+80
Exports of goods and services	420	710	710	865
Less Imports of goods and services	860	860	865	845
Gross domestic product at market prices	6,471	6,433	6,278	6,439

Source
Feinstein, *National Income, Expenditure and Output of the United Kingdom 1855–1965*, tables 3 and 5.

capital inflow, which was dramatically reversed the following year.

The rise in merchandise exports and the fall in imports in 1946 were both larger than expected. The estimates used in the loan negotiations assumed exports of £650m (rather than £960m) and imports of £1,150m (£1,063m).[11] Real gross domestic product was sustained in the face of the halving of government current expenditure on goods and services (Table 3.2), thanks to the rise in exports and to substantial gross investment which increased 2½ times in both nominal and real terms. Consumers' expenditure rose by about 10 per cent in real terms (14 per cent in nominal terms). With both retail prices and average weekly earnings rising at a little over 4 per cent in 1946, for the first eighteen months the post-war transition appeared to be going fairly smoothly. As the *Economic Survey for 1947* put it, 'the general balance has not been unsatisfactory. ... By the end of the year [1946], the change-over to civil production was well on the way to completion ... [and] a high level of industrial activity had been achieved' (Cmd. 7046, para. 58).

Dalton's four budgets are summarized in Table 3.3. In his first two he reduced heavy wartime taxation as war-related government expenditure fell, relying on the continued controls and cost-of-living subsidies to prevent open inflation. His last two budgets were designed to produce substantial surpluses to combat infla-

[11] Pressnell, *External Economic Policy*, vol. 1, app. 27, table 3(*b*).

tion and reduce the pressure on the balance of payments. As a professional economist who had specialized in public finance and as a Labour politician, Dalton had strong views on the appropriate structure of taxation, which he also tried to put into practice. In making post-war tax reductions he preferred income tax changes which would increase incentives especially for the lower income-earners while making taxes on higher incomes more progressive. He wished to maintain a fairly high level of indirect taxation because it had less effect on incentives. In his redistributive efforts he was especially keen to reform the death duties.[12]

With the end of the European war in May the Treasury had been preparing for an autumn budget since the summer. The Budget Committee (which included Bridges, Hopkins, Keynes, Brittain, and Padmore from the Treasury, Sir Cornelius Gregg of the Inland Revenue, and Robbins and Meade from the Economic Section), had concentrated on income tax rates and allowances after the abolition of the post-war tax credits. Reporting to Dalton in September the committee proposed the restoration of the allowances that had been cut when post-war credits were introduced in the 1941 budget. It also recommended a cut in the standard rate of income tax (from 50 to 45 per cent), with new reduced rates for small incomes, to come into effect in the 1946/7 financial year.[13] Dalton insisted that the proposed income tax reductions were accompanied by an increase in surtax rates, so that the tax reductions for higher incomes were not larger than those on smaller incomes. Although he would have preferred a new form of profits taxation to replace the wartime Excess Profits Tax (EPT), he agreed to his officials' recommendation of a reduction of EPT from 100 to 60 per cent from 1 January 1946.[14]

Before making his taxation decisions, Dalton had asked for 'a

[12] On his academic career see *Call Back Yesterday*, ch. 6. His major research was on the measurement and determination of income inequality ('The measurement of the inequality of incomes', *EJ* 30 (Sept. 1920), 348–61; *Some Aspects of the Inequality of Incomes in Modern Communities* (London, 1920)), his bestselling textbook *Principles of Public Finance* (London, 1922, 1929, 1936, 1954). For his views on direct and indirect taxation see *Public Finance* 1935 edn., chs. 10 and 11, and 1954 edn., 230–3, and *High Tide and After*, 25–8, 113–14.

[13] 'Budget Committee Report', T171/372, PRO; for the earlier discussions see the same file and Meade, *Cabinet Office Diary*, 107–8.

[14] Dalton, 'Income Tax & Surtax' and 'EPT', 9 Sept., Trend, 'Budget', 17 Sept. 1945, T171/372; see also Dalton, *High Tide and After*, ch. 4. Burke Trend was Dalton's principal private secretary.

TABLE 3.3 *Dalton's Budgets, 1945–7*

	Expected surplus £m	Realized surplus £m	Total change in taxation £m[1]	Major tax changes
1945–6	–2,300[2]	–2,207	–385	*Income tax* (from April 1946): increase in personal allowances and in exemption limit to 1940–1 levels; reduction in standard rate to 9s 0d in £; reduced rates on small incomes; increase in surtax on large incomes. *Purchase tax* removed from domestic cooking and heating appliances. *Excess profits tax* reduced from 100% to 60% (from 1 Jan. 1946).
1946–7	–694	–586	–146	*Income tax*: increase in married women's earned income allowances and in earned income relief; repayment of some post-war credits to old age pensioners. Reductions in *purchase tax*, mainly on household items. *Excess profits tax* repealed (from 31 Dec. 1946) *Death duties*: increase for large estates and in exemption limit for small estates.
1947–8[3]	270		+54	*Income tax*: increase in earned income relief and in children's allowance. *Purchase tax* reimposed on domestic heating and cooking appliances. *Tobacco duty* doubled. *Profits tax* increased on distributed profits. *Death duties*: Increase in legacy and succession duties.
1947–8[4]	318	636	+197	Ceiling on *cost-of-living subsidies* at existing level. *Purchase tax* rates raised. *Beer, wine and spirits duties* increased. *Profits tax* doubled. *Betting tax* introduced.

Notes
[1] In full financial year.
[2] Before changes in Dalton's supplementary budget of 23 Oct. 1945.
[3] In Apr. 1947 budget.   [4] In Nov. 1947 budget.

Sources
Alec Cairncross, *Years of Recovery: British Economic Policy 1945–51*, 421; J. C. R. Dow, *The Management of the British Economy 1945–60*, 198–9; budget speeches of 23 Oct. 1945, 9 Apr. 1946, 15 Apr. and 12 Nov. 1947.

broad picture of probable expenditure in next four years'. The Treasury responded with a national income and budget forecast for 1948, as 'a typical year of "full peace"', assuming the restoration of the pre–1941 tax allowances and unchanged tax rates. Meade produced estimates of personal income and the supplies of consumer goods in 1946, in order to indicate the amount of personal savings needed to prevent inflation and hence the total tax reductions possible without increasing inflationary pressure. The estimated revenue loss in 1946/7 from Dalton's tax changes fell toward the upper end of Meade's £300–400m. It was not as 'Keynesian' an exercise in budget-making as that for the wartime budgets but, as Dow pointed out, 'Exact calculations of the inflationary gap would hardly have been relevant in the circumstances.'[15] (They would also have been difficult if not impossible to produce in a hurry in those early days of national income forecasting.)

On the overall budget balance Dalton's views were only halfway to Keynesian ideas. In his budget speech he suggested that

we should aim at balancing the Budget, not necessarily each year, but over a period of years, deliberately planning Budget surpluses when trade is firmly good and equally deliberately planning Budget deficits when trade is bad or ... threatening to go bad; but balancing, over a period, surpluses against deficits.[16]

This had been his position in the mid–1930s, when he added a chapter on 'Balancing the Budget' to his *Public Finance*. There he criticized the old-fashioned 'puritanical' preference for an annually balanced (or surplus) budget and advocated countercyclical budgeting. But the deficits had to be temporary, otherwise they would permanently increase the national debt, which would be 'an economic evil'. To Dalton the burden of the internal debt depended on whether the transfers from taxpayers to debtholders increased or decreased the inequality of incomes. As he put it in *Public Finance*, 'If the British debt consisted exclusively of Savings Certificates held by wage earners, and if British taxation consisted exclusively of income tax and death duties on the wealthy, the British debt transactions would involve a large direct

[15] Note by Dalton, 9 Sept., Brittain, 'National Income and Budget Forecast for 1948', 27 Sept., and Meade to Brittain, 24 Sept. 1945, T171/371; Dow, *Management of the British Economy*, 19.

[16] *House of Commons Debates*, vol. 414, 23 Oct. 1945, col. 1886

real benefit to the community.' The actual transfers, however, were 'from the poorer to the richer members of the community . . . [and] also transfers, on balance, from the younger to the older generations, and from the active to the passive elements in the economic life of the community'. Furthermore, the taxation required to service the debt could reduce incentives to work and save, and the existence of the debt service constrain more desirable forms of public expenditure. The burden would also be increased by falling prices especially after a war.[17]

When Dalton revised his textbook again, in the early 1950s, he allowed that the maintenance of full employment might require chronic deficits. The 'Keynesian revolution' meant that: 'We may now free ourselves from the old and narrow conception of balancing the budget, no matter over what period, and move towards the new and wider conception of the budget balancing the whole economy.' The budget was now 'a powerful instrument' for achieving full employment, a high level of investment, avoidance of inflation and deflation, and an improved distribution, although these aims could often conflict. The conflict between employment and distributional objectives could perhaps be mitigated by a combination of capital taxes—death duties, capital levies, and capital gains taxation—and cheap money.[18]

In his budget speech in October 1945 Dalton emphasized the danger of post-war inflation and the need to maintain a high level of personal savings. He claimed, justifiably, that his tax reductions were the most that could be made without increasing the risk of inflation. His main weapons against inflation were, however, the continuation of price controls and of subsidies on food and other items in the cost-of-living index. He committed himself to maintaining the index at its current level of 31 per cent above pre-war, admitting this could increase the size of the subsidies, especially with the ending of Lend-Lease. He also announced his cheaper money policy (see below) as a way of reducing the cost of borrowing by government and industry.[19]

Dalton was particularly pleased with his second budget in April

---

[17] *Public Finance*, 1935 edn., chs. 26 and 22. This view of the debt burden was the basis of his advocacy of a capital levy after the First World War.

[18] *Public Finance* (1954 edn.), ch. 27.

[19] *House of Commons Debates*, vol. 414, 23 Oct. 1945, cols. 1876–82, 1902.

1946. He was able to announce a significant increase in expenditure—on education, housing, family allowances, old age pensions, the development areas, civil aviation, and forestry (Dalton was very fond of trees). At the same time, with the fall in war-related expenditure, the estimated deficit of £694m for 1946/7 was well below the previous year's in spite of the tax reductions announced in October. He also introduced some of his desired innovations in taxation.[20]

The budget was framed on the assumption that the loan agreement would pass Congress. In the spring of 1946 Dalton also thought that the risk of inflation was abating and could be kept at bay by maintaining the cost-of-living subsidies and going slow with post-war tax reductions. Others were not so sanguine, Meade arguing to Dalton that 1946/7 would be a year of 'extreme inflationary pressure in the markets for consumption goods' so that tax reductions should be 'kept to a very minimum'.[21] His Treasury advisers, especially Keynes, were worried about the increasing cost of the food subsidies as world food prices rose rapidly in 1946. They wanted some flexibility in the interpretation of the commitment to hold the cost-of-living index steady, although they did not then go as far as the Economic Section in arguing for a ceiling on the food subsidies. Dalton at first strongly disagreed but was persuaded to admit in his speech that there could be seasonal and other small fluctuations in the index and that the policy might be reconsidered if there were large rises in import prices.[22]

On the revenue side Dalton told his officials his inclinations: 'To do no more about Income Tax & Surtax'; to reduce purchase tax, mainly on household items; 'Not to do much more in reducing indirect taxation—particularly in view of high & uncertain cost of food, etc. subsidies'; to abolish EPT 'only on condition that . . . I can get a substitute tax'; 'a development of the Death Duties': and the creation of a 'National Estates Fund' to help to create or expand national parks.[23] He did make some income tax concessions on

[20] *Public Finance* (1954 edn), 233–4, *High Tide and After*, ch. 10.

[21] Dalton, *Public Finance* (1954 edition), 233; Meade, *Cabinet Office Diary*, 196, see also p. 258.

[22] Trend, 'Budget', 20 Feb., Proctor to Gilbert, 'Cost-of-Living Index and Subsidies', and Gilbert to Bridges, 22 Feb., and Keynes to Chancellor, 'Budget speech', 31 Mar. 1946, T171/386; *House of Commons Debates*, vol. 421, 9 Apr. 1946, cols. 1803–40.

[23] Dalton to Bridges, 'Next Year's Budget', 17 Nov. 1945, T171/386.

earned income allowances at the request of ministerial colleagues, which Keynes criticized as '*just unnecessary*' in a budget
'full of good things'. On this Keynes failed to persuade the Chancellor. Keynes, Hopkins and Meade did manage to persuade
Dalton not to rush into producing a new profits tax to replace
EPT, which was abolished from the end of 1946.[24] There were
small reductions in indirect taxation, as there had been in Dalton's first budget.

On death duties Dalton was strongly opposed by his officials.
Since inheritance was a major cause of an unequal income distribution Dalton had long advocated a variant of the scheme put
forward by the Italian economist Eugenio Rignano whereby the
tax on an estate would increase with the number of times it had
changed hands by inheritance.[25] In November 1945 he wanted to
raise the exemption limit on small estates, while increasing the
duties on larger estates; to graduate the legacy and succession
duties (whose rates were currently determined by the relationship of the beneficiary to the deceased); and to introduce his
variant of the Rignano scheme. Except on the exemption limit, he
received support only from Meade, who conceded that the practical difficulties stressed by the other members of the Budget
Committee were 'overwhelming'. Keynes was particularly
critical: in addition to the administrative difficulties he disliked
'this element of "hate" in what could, and should, be a
moderately cheerful and reassuring Budget'. Dalton settled for
steepening the estate duty on large estates while increasing the
exemption limit (which had not been changed for fifty years) to
£2,000 from £100.[26]

[24] Keynes to Chancellor, 1 Apr. 1946, T171/388; Trend, 'Budget', 20 Feb. 1946,
T171/386, and memoranda in T171/388, sect. 7.

[25] Dalton, *Inequality of Incomes*, pt. IV, chs. 9–10; Committee on National Debt
and Taxation, *Report*, Cmd. 2800, 1927, paras. 921–34. Under Dalton's variant of
the Rignano scheme the higher duty that would be attracted when an estate was
passed on a second time would be paid at the time of the first transfer, in return for
which the beneficiary would receive a terminable annuity.

[26] Dalton to Bridges, 'Next Year's Budget', 17 Nov. 1945, T171/386; T171/388,
sect. 9; Meade, *Cabinet Office Diary*, 206, 214, 223, 259; Trend, 'Budget', 20 Feb.
1946, T171/386. Dalton tried again at the beginning of the 1947 budget season.
Faced again with another set of opposing official memoranda on his favourite
ideas, he proposed instead to double the rates of the legacy and succession duties
and to increase the exemptions for small inheritances to close relatives: notes by
Dalton, 11 Sept. 1946 and 5 Jan. 1947, and intervening memoranda on T171/391;
Trend to Bridges, 'Budget', 6 Jan., and Trend to Gregg, 'Budget', 15 Jan. 1947,

Financial reform

Dalton set the nationalization of the Bank of England in train on his first full day in the Treasury, Monday, 30 July 1945. While Sir Herbert Brittain and other Treasury officials started work on the 'Heads of Legislation', Dalton obtained permission on Tuesday from his Cabinet colleagues to introduce two bills in the 1945–6 Parliamentary session: a Bank of England bill and an Investment and Exchange (Controls) bill. (The latter was later split into two bills, saving the more complex exchange control provisions for the third bill, which became the Exchange Control Act, 1947.) On Thursday he saw Lord Catto, who agreed to stay on as the first Governor of the nationalized Bank.[27] On the Tuesday the core members of XYZ (Berry, Durbin, Gaitskell, Jay, Piercy, and Wilmot) also met 'to work on the draft heads of a Bill which Piercy had prepared'. It has been assumed that this draft was for Bank nationalization but it was probably for a National Investment Board.[28] Dalton approved a Treasury draft of the Bank of England Bill to go to the Bank on 14 August. Extensive correspondence then passed between Bank and Treasury before the Bill was published on 10 October 1945.[29]

The major items at issue between the government and the Bank were compensation, the appointment of the Governors and Directors, and the power of the Treasury over the Bank and hence monetary policy. The 'Heads of a Bill on Finance' approved by

T171/389. These changes were included in his third budget, which turned out to be his last opportunity to reform the death duties. His successor as Chancellor, Stafford Cripps, tidied up the system, effectively amalgamating estate duty and the legacy and succession duties by abolishing the latter in 1949.

[27] Pimlott, *Hugh Dalton*, 457; Dalton, *The Fateful Years*, 475, 478–80; Note by Dalton, 4 Aug., Bridges to Padmore, 2 Aug. 1945, T160/1408/F19155/1, PRO. Dalton had visited the Treasury the previous Saturday, 'collected some official papers', and went to spend the rest of the weekend with the Piercys. Nicholas Davenport, in his unreliable memoirs, claimed Dalton visited him the weekend before his first day in office, but on Davenport's own dates that visit was a week later: Davenport, *Memoirs of a City Radical*, 149–50. On Davenport's advice to Dalton see below.

[28] Williams, *Diary of Hugh Gaitskell*, 8. A draft Bank bill prepared by XYZ had been in existence since 1938 (above, p. 71) and there is no copy of a later draft in Dalton's or Piercy's papers, though there is a draft of a bill to set up a National Investment Board: 'Draft bill for National Investment Board', Piercy Papers 8/12. There is also 'A (very hasty) note by W.P.' giving Piercy's 1945 views on financial reform, on the same file.

[29] On the negotiations between Treasury and Bank see also Fforde, *Bank*, 4–16.

the Policy Committee of the Labour Party in 1939 had suggested that from the appointed day the shareholders would be compensated with cash or government securities and the Chancellor would be given the power to appoint the Governor and the Court of Directors and to give instructions to the Governors. By 1945, Piercy (and other members of XYZ) 'like[d] idea taking over going concern with as little visible alteration as possible', retaining the Bank's Charter but adding in the Chancellor's new powers. According to Sir Wilfrid Eady, Joint Second Secretary in the Treasury, Dalton's instructions to his officials at the beginning of August were that the Bank bill should include:

(a) the nomination of the Governor by the Government or possibly the Crown,
(b) the elimination of the voting rights of stockholders,
(c) a reduction in the size of the Court and possibly its reconstruction,
(d) power in the Chancellor to issue such general or particular directions to the Bank as were necessary in the public interest.[30]

Compensation was soon settled and accorded with the party's views. The Treasury's first draft 'Heads of Legislation' proposed the transfer of the existing stock from the private stockholders to the Treasury in exchange for a perpetual annuity equivalent to the existing (since 1923) 12 per cent level of dividends. Dalton had scotched an earlier suggestion from Sir Herbert Brittain that it might be sufficient to remove the stockholders' voting rights (except to elect a minority of the Directors) and to limit permanently their dividends; he preferred the issue of government securities. On seeing the Treasury second draft, the Bank suggested that it would be simpler for the Treasury to issue the stockholders with either £12 annuities for each £100 Bank stock held or £400 3 per cent stock for £100 Bank stock. The latter was adopted, though Dalton initially had some doubts about the implied price in relation to the current market value of Bank stock. The shareholders were bought out with £58m 3% Treasury Stock 1966 or after on 1 March 1946.[31]

[30] 'A (very hasty) note by W.P.', Piercy Papers 8/12; Eady, 'Nationalisation of the Bank of England', 2 Aug. 1945, T160/1408/F19155/1, PRO.
[31] 'Bank of England Bill, Heads of Legislation'. 8 Aug. 1945, Brittain, 'Nationalisation of the Bank of England', 1 Aug., Eady, 'Nationalisation of the Bank of England', 2 Aug., marginal notes by Dalton on both, Bank of England, 'Bank of England Bill—Heads of Legislation, Comments on Treasury Draft of 14/8/45', 28

The Treasury draft provided for the direct appointment by the Prime Minister and the Chancellor of the Exchequer of the Governor and one or perhaps two Deputy Governors, for five-year renewable terms, and for the reduction of the Court of Directors from 24 to 12 persons, all part-time. Eady had suggested two Deputy Governors, one to follow (recent) Bank convention and come up from the ranks of Bank officials, 'as in the case of the Deputy Governor designate, Mr. Cobbold' (who was about to succeed the present Deputy, B. G. Catterns), the other to be an outsider: Dalton suggested one of the two might also be the chairman of the National Investment Board. The Bank preferred to continue with only one Deputy and some full-time Executive Directors, and proposed a Court of sixteen in addition to the Governors, to include not more than four Executive Directors. It also suggested the Governor should be appointed by Royal Warrant for seven-year terms and that the Court be able to nominate Directors with the Treasury's approval rather than the other way round (the Treasury draft having left these options open).[32] The first, second, and third 'Drafts of a Bill', produced after Treasury-Bank meetings on 28 and 31 August with Bridges, Hopkins, Eady and Brittain on the one side and Catto, Catterns and Cobbold on the other, reflected these (and other) differences, though apparently following the Bank's proposals on numbers of Governors and Directors and the Treasury's proposals on their appointment (except for the Royal Warrant) and term of office. When the various points were put to him for decision, Dalton objected to most of the Bank's proposals (except for the Royal Warrant and the number of Directors). Catto subsequently persuaded him to agree to only one Deputy Governor.[33] Dalton was reluctant to

Aug. 1945, and 'Bank of England Bill (Draft of 4th September 1945)', with marginal notes by Dalton, T160/1408/F19155/1, PRO; Sir Norman Chester, *The Nationalisation of British Industry 1945–51* (London, 1975), 237–40.

[32] Eady, 'Nationalisation of the Bank of England', 2 Aug., and Bank of England, 'Bank of England Bill—Heads of Legislation, Comments on Treasury Draft of 14/8/45', 28 Aug. 1945, T160/1408/F19155/1.

[33] 'Note of a meeting held at the Treasury on Tuesday, 28th August, 1945, at 3.45 p.m.', 'Draft of a Bill . . . ', 'Note of a meeting held at the Treasury on Friday, 31st August, 1945, at 10.15 a.m.', Brittain to Bridges, 'Bank of England Bill', 3 Sept., 'Bank of England Bill (Draft of 4th September 1945)', with marginal notes by Dalton, and Catto to Chancellor, 11 Sept. 1945, T160/1408/F19155/1; CP(45)167, Bank of England Bill, Memorandum by the Chancellor of the Exchequer, 10 Sept. 1945, CAB129/2, PRO.

accept only one Deputy largely because he was suspicious of Bank officials who had worked closely with Montagu Norman, Governor 1920–44, one of whom was Cobbold. Cobbold became Deputy Governor on 1 September 1945 and, in spite of Dalton's advice to his successor as Chancellor, Stafford Cripps, not to let Cobbold succeed Catto, Governor on 1 March 1949.[34]

The most contentious issue was, of course, that of Treasury 'directions' to the Bank, which threatened the jealously guarded 'independence' of the central bank from the government and its informal relationships with the City. Brittain noted at the outset:

The wording of this power is a matter of some difficulty. It is undesirable to try to catalogue particular subjects for direction—e.g. bank rate— because we cannot be sure that such a catalogue will cover all eventualities. On the other hand, it would be undesirable for the Treasury to have power to interfere in the day-to-day administration or in the Bank's relations with particular customers.

Dalton responded: 'They [the Treasury] should have the power, but shouldn't use it save in exceptional cases.' The 'Heads of Legislation' shown to the Bank therefore stated: 'Power will be taken for the Treasury to give general or particular directions to the Bank from time to time when the Treasury are satisfied that such directions are necessary in the public interest.' It included a 'possible additional clause':

The Bank of England shall have power, where the Bank considers it necessary in the public interest, and with the approval of the Treasury, to make regulations governing the proportion of assets of different descriptions to be held by banks.[35]

The Bank wanted to make the intention that the government would intervene only in matters of high policy more explicit and the powers over the behaviour of other banks more vague. It proposed that any powers should be given to the Chancellor, not the Treasury, and that the additional clause should allow the

---

[34] Dalton, *High Tide and After*, 47 and 287.
[35] Brittain, 'Nationalisation of the Bank of England', 1 Aug., with marginal note by Dalton, 'Bank of England Bill, Heads of Legislation', 14 Aug. 1945, paras. 4 and 7, T160/1408/F19155/1. Since the UK had no Banking Act (and did not have one until the 1980s) the latter added: 'For the purpose of this Section, "banks" shall mean such institutions as the Treasury may designate as such.'

Bank to make 'recommendations to the Chancellor of the Exchequer in regard to banking practice, and the Chancellor of the
Exchequer ... in consultation with the Governor to make
regulations based on such recommendations'.[36] At the first
Treasury-Bank meeting it was eventually agreed to omit the
words 'general or particular' with respect to directions, leaving
the wording of the other clause for further discussion. At the
second meeting the Bank 'reserved their position' on the directions clause. Catto 'said that he was strongly against any legislation giving powers to regulate the banks, except possibly as
regards the supply of information to the Bank of England' and
would express his views to Dalton. It was nevertheless agreed to
include in the next draft a tentatively worded clause which
allowed the authorities to prescribe reserve ratios for the banks as
well as to require information from them.[37]

The dispute ran for several weeks, complicated by the need to
avoid legal problems in the drafting, both before publication of
the bill and during its passage through Parliament. Catto's
intervention seems to have been crucial. On 3 September,
objecting to the second draft, he proposed two alternative (but
only slightly different) versions of what became clause 4 of the
Bill from the third draft (4 September) on. These both had three
subclauses, providing (1) for Treasury directions to the Bank,
after consultation with the Governor, (2) for the management of
the Bank by the Court of Directors otherwise, and (3) for the
Bank to 'request information from, and make recommendations, to banks in regard to banking policy and practice' and for
the Treasury then to make regulations if necessary. Catto
explained to Bridges:

I should hope directions and regulations will never be needed and that
the Treasury and the Bank will be able, without them, to obtain from the
Bank Community, as in the past, all co-operation necessary to conform
to Government policy. But as I understand that the Chancellor of the
Exchequer and his colleagues consider it essential that the powers

[36] Bank of England, 'Bank of England Bill—Heads of Legislation, Comments on
Treasury Draft of 14/8/45', and 'Bank of England Bill, Heads of Legislation',
T160/1408/F19155/1.
    [37] 'Note of a meeting held at the Treasury on Tuesday, 28th August 1945 ... ',
'Note of a meeting held at the Treasury on Friday, 31st August 1945 ... ', Brittain
to Bridges, 'Bank of England Bill', 3 Sept. 1945, T160/1408/F19155/1.

should be there, it seems to me that the suggested wording conforms to this.[38]

When the third draft was put up to Dalton he was doubtful whether clause 4 covered his intentions, and suspicious of the Bank's motives. As Brittain admitted, it 'would *not* enable the Treasury to force the banks to make loans to the Government'. Catto persuaded Dalton to accept it on the grounds that the Treasury's original clause would have risked scaring bank depositors and that 'the wording proposed ... is as good as can be devised'. It was apparently at this time that the Treasury officials persuaded Dalton that legislation to maintain the system of Treasury deposit receipts was unnecessary, as XYZ had also recognized.[39] In the several drafts after Cabinet discussion of the Bill on 13 September clause 4 read:

(1) The Treasury may from time to time give such directions to the Bank as, after consultation with the Governor of the Bank, they think necessary in the public interest.

(2) Subject to any such directions, the affairs of the Bank shall be managed by the court of directors in accordance with such rules, if any, as may be laid down by the charter of the Bank ...

(3) The Bank may if they think it necessary in the public interest request information from and make recommendations to bankers, and may, if so authorised by the Treasury, issue directions to any banker for the purpose of securing that effect is given to any such request or recommendation.

Humphrey Mynors (then an adviser in the Bank, later a Director and Deputy Governor) later described Catto's role:

He judged correctly the strength of his position if he did not come out in active opposition to the general policy. As a result the Bank was taken

---

[38] Catto to Bridges, 'Draft Bank of England Bill', 3 Sept. 1945, and 'Draft of a Bill ... 3rd Draft, 4 Sept. 1945', T160/1408/F19155/1. Catto's letter continued: 'In a word, the Bank has always worked with the 'velvet glove'. It will continue to do so. But if the necessity arises, the 'iron hand' of the Treasury could then be inside the 'velvet glove'! I should hope and believe, however, that the necessity would rarely, if ever, arise.'

[39] 'Bank of England Bill (Draft of 4th September 1945)' and marginal notes by Dalton, and Catto to Chancellor, 11 Sept. 1945, T160/1408/F19155/1; 'A (very hasty) note by W.P.', Piercy Papers 8/12. Dalton was vulnerable to warnings of scaring bank depositors because there had been something of a scare about deposits in the Post Office Savings Bank during the 1931 general election.

into public ownership with the minimum public controversy and the maximum retention of operational independence.[40]

Dalton moved the second reading of the Bank of England Bill in the House of Commons on 29 October 1945. The small amount of criticism concentrated on clause 4(3) and secured two amendments: that directions could not be specific to particular bank customers and that the banks should be able to make representations to the authorities before directions were issued. In the Lords in January Bill Piercy (now Lord Piercy) defended clause 4(3). With some support from Keynes, he suggested that although it would be 'an easy interpretation' to say that the Treasury could give directions to the Bank:

> the Treasury . . . can never . . . give such a direction to the Bank as will make the Bank think certain steps are necessary in the public interest if in fact the Bank does not think so. That rather subtle point is, I think, one which accounts for the rather peculiar form of the clause. . . . by subsection (3), the right of initiative is left to the Bank.

Catto agreed: 'The initiative is with the Bank of England.' The Lord Chancellor (Jowitt) supported the interpretation.[41]

Dalton and his advisers were pleased with the Bank Bill. When it was first published Berry told Dalton that 'We all think it is a very good Bill and if section IV passes into law unchanged we shall have all we want.' Durbin later complimented Dalton: 'I thought your policy over the nationalisation of the Bank and the control of the banking system—Catto and 4iii et al.—was brilliant.'[42] The Bank of England Act did not, however, give the Treasury the powers XYZ had wanted, as the Treasury ascer-

[40] 'Draft of a Bill . . . 5th Draft, 14 Sept. 1945', T160/1408/F19155/1; printed drafts of 19, 22, and 27 Sept. and 6 Oct. 1945, T160/1408/F19155/2; *Dictionary of National Biography 1951–1960*, 196–8.

[41] *House of Commons Debates*, vol. 415, 29 Oct. 1945, cols. 43–48; Chester, *Nationalisation*, 16 and 67–70; Keynes, 'Bank Bill' (a note literally on the back of an envelope), Piercy Papers 8/64; *House of Lords Debates*, vol. 138, 22 Jan. 1946, cols. 992–3, 1016–18. One minor change to clause 3(4) was made at Committee stage in the Lords. Pethick-Lawrence for the goverment successfully moved an amendment to move the word 'may' in clause 3(4) from before to after 'if they [the Bank] think it necessary in the public interest', in order to make sure the clause conformed to the Lord Chancellor's ruling: *House of Lords Debates*, vol. 139, 31 Jan. 1946, cols. 106–8. On the bill's passage through Parliament see also Fforde, *Bank*, 20–6.

[42] Dalton, *High Tide and After*, ch. 6; Berry to Dalton, 13 Oct. 1945, Dalton Papers 9/1; Durbin to Dalton, 12 Sept. 1946, Dalton Papers 9/2.

tained in 1951 and again in 1957 when it sought the opinion of the Treasury Solicitor. His opinion was clear: Under section 4(1) of the Act the Treasury could give directions to the Bank but section 4(2) implied the directions could only relate to 'the affairs of the Bank of England', while according to section 4(3) the power to seek information from or issue directions to the banks was conferred (as Catto had said) on the Bank not the Treasury.[43] A little later the Radcliffe Committee fudged the issue: although mildly critical of the Bank's interpretation of the 'affairs of the Bank', the committee did 'not think it necessary to form a view' as to whether the Act had changed the existing relationship between the Bank and the Treasury.[44]

Dalton's Investment and Exchange (Controls) Bill was originally intended to make the wartime capital issues and exchange controls permanent. At the end of July Dalton had told his officials that he wanted his financial legislation to cover the nationalization of the Bank, the establishment of a National Investment Board, and government borrowing from the commercial banks as well as capital issues and exchange controls—perhaps the '3-tier bill' that Piercy favoured. The Treasury officials saw 'serious objections' to the second and third proposals which were anyway redundant. The National Investment Board seems to have been dropped by the end of August 1945, and did not appear in any of the drafts of the Bank Bill or the Investment and Exchange Bill.[45]

Under the caretaker government the Treasury had issued instructions to Parliamentary Counsel in June 1945 to prepare a bill for post-war capital issues control. The first drafts of Dalton's investment bill followed those instructions in 'provid[ing] for the control of the borrowing and raising of money, the issue of share, stock and other securities, and the variation of rights connected

[43] Barnes to Eady, 15 June 1951, T233/1401; Anderson to Armstrong, 'Powers of the Treasury against the Bank of England', 5 Sept. 1957, and Lucas, 'Treasury Powers under Section 4 of the Bank of England Act, 1946', 10 Jan. 1958, T233/1664, PRO.

[44] Committee on the Working of the Monetary System, *Report*, paras. 763, 761. *The Economist* had been more forthright: 'the nationalised Bank of 1946 will not differ in any fundamental way from the privately-owned Bank of 1945—or, for that matter, of the past decade' (Feb. 16, 1946, 259).

[45] Brittain to Eady, 1 Aug., and Stainton to Brittain, 28 Aug. 1945, T160/1408/F19155/1; Brittain to Gilbert, 'Legislative Programme—HPC(45)81', 30 Aug. 1945, T233/25, PRO.

with money, shares, stock and securities'.[46] When the Bank of England was asked for its comments in September 1945 it objected that the first clause of the draft went beyond the wartime Defence Regulations in referring to 'borrowing' as well as to 'issues of capital' (a change made partly to avoid legal problems that had arisen during the war). On this occasion the Bank did not win the argument. The Treasury was unsympathetic to the Bank's 'general objection on psychological grounds' and met its other objection that the new capital controls would extend to individual unsecured bank overdrafts by adding a proviso to exclude them. In November Sir Otto Niemeyer reported to the Governors that 'we failed to argue Brittain out of this and he says the Chancellor has supported his view'. Cobbold agreed 'we have shot our bolt and cannot usefully take any further action'.[47] The small change made to meet the Bank did, however, mean in combination with clause 4 of the Bank of England Act that the Labour government would rely on the voluntary wartime control of bank advances.

In October it was decided to split the investment and exchange control legislation into two separate bills, although it was then expected they would be introduced together in Parliament.[48] At the same time Durbin, as Dalton's PPS, criticized the draft Investment and Exchange (Controls) Bill for containing no powers to stimulate investment in a recession. He proposed that it should give the government the authority to provide financial assistance for approved private investment projects in such circumstances. In spite of the Treasury's lack of enthusiasm a second clause allowing for loan guarantees was added. Durbin's proposal allowed for a limit to the amount of assistance provided in any one financial year, which was put at £25 million in the November draft of the Bill. After it was pointed out in the Lord President's

[46] Speed to Compton, 'Post-war capital issues control', 27 June, Shillitto to Brittain, 'Capital issues legislation', 14 Aug., 'Raising of Money (Control), Draft of a Bill . . . 21st August 1945', T233/25.

[47] Niemeyer to Brittain, 'Investment and Exchange (Controls) Bill', 7 Sept., and subsequent correspondence between Brittain and Niemeyer, Brittain to Eady, 'Investment control', 1 Nov. 1945, T233/25, PRO; Niemeyer to Governors, 'Control of Investment Bill', 12 Nov., and note by Cobbold, 14 Nov. 1945, C40/771, BOE.

[48] Note by Cobbold, 15 Oct. 1945, C40/771, BOE; Rowlatt to Solicitor General, 'Investment (Control and Guarantees) Bill, Exchange Control Bill', 25 Oct. 1945, T231/381, PRO.

Committee on 16 November that this figure might look 'niggardly', the limit was raised to £50m.[49]

When the draft Investment (Control and Guarantees) Bill went to the Lord President's Committee it was accompanied by a draft white paper on the planning of investment, announcing that the Capital Issues Committee would be continued and that a 'National Investment Council' would be set up to advise the Chancellor. Dalton told his colleagues that the Council would include the Governor of the Bank, the chairman of the Capital Issues Committee, representatives of industry, the trade unions and the cooperative movement 'and probably an economist and a statistician'; it would 'be charged solely with the duty of advising the Government on the planning of investment in the interests of full employment'. As Meade had recorded after a conversation with Bridges in September, the Treasury had persuaded Dalton that

only the Whitehall machine can really be responsible for planning investment (since it is only one part of the total problem of planning the whole of the national demand for resources and since in any case the state must be responsible for the decisions to be taken); but the Chancellor is bound for political reasons to go a little way towards a National Investment Board.

Asked to assist in drafting the white paper, Meade 'advised Bridges strongly that the Chancellor should make no attempt to pretend that the Consultative Council would perform the functions which others wish to put on an Investment Board but should defend his position by saying that these executive functions should be and will be carried out by HMG itself'. Morrison, briefed by the Economic Section, saw to it that the proposed white paper became merely an explanatory memorandum or, as Meade put it in his diary, 'the Chancellor . . . is not to be permitted to make such an ass of himself'.[50]

At the end of November the Cabinet and its Legislation Com-

[49] 'Chancellor's meeting 3 Oct.', Durbin, 'Note on Clause 1 of Investment and Exchange (Controls) Bill', 3 Oct., Shillitto to Brittain, 'Investment (Control and Guarantees) Bill, Clause 2', 24 Oct., and 'Investment (Control and Guarantees), Draft Bill, 20 October 1945', T233/25; LP(45) 43rd meeting, 16 Nov. 1945, CAB71/19, PRO.

[50] LP(45) 43rd meeting, CAB71/19; Meade, *Cabinet Office Diary*, 135, 148, 170; *Investment (Control and Guarantees) Bill, Memorandum and Draft Order to be made under Clause 1 of the Bill*, Cmd. 6726, Jan. 1946.

mittee approved the bill. Dalton moved the second reading in February, when he noted that some younger Labour MPs, including Christopher Mayhew, thought that it did not go far enough. In his speech he 'deliberately played down' the bill and emphasized that 'The government's ... economic planning [would be done] through a Cabinet Committee not an outside National Investment Council.' In committee stage the title of the bill was altered, on the motion of Mayhew, to the Borrowing (Control and Guarantees) Bill.[51] During its passage through Parliament (it became law on 12 July 1946) Durbin persuaded the Finance Group of Labour MPs to propose to Dalton in April 1946 a further bill on the control of investment. This was to give the Chancellor powers to obtain information on private investment plans, to provide larger amounts of aid, including subsidies, to private investment projects than the Borrowing Bill allowed for, and to ask for government participation in the control of a firm in return for such aid.[52] In September he repeated to Dalton that 'I do not think you have taken sufficient powers to raise national expenditure in face of an American slump'. He feared that such a slump could come in the near future, and (his own) clause 2 of the Borrowing Bill would be 'almost worthless in such a situation'. Although Dalton replied to Durbin that 'Anti-slump precautions ... shall be in the next wave', it was soon 'made clear [to Durbin and the Finance Group of Labour MPs] that there was no question of further legislation for the control of investment' in the immediate future.[53]

The history of the National Investment Council is brief. As Durbin warned Dalton at the outset, it was 'an Advisory Committee and like all advisory Committees will fade into futility

[51] Cabinet 55(45), 22 Nov. 1945, CAB128/2; HPC(45) 31st meeting, 27 Nov. 1945, CAB75/21; Notes on amendments in committee stage on T233/26 and 27; Dalton Diary, vol. 34, 9 Feb. 1946; Dalton, *High Tide and After*, 96. For Mayhew's views on the control of investment see his pamphlet, *Socialist Economic Planning: The Overall Picture* (Fabian Society, Dec. 1946).

[52] Durbin to Benson, Mayhew and Johnson, enclosing 'Draft heads of a further bill on the control of investment', Durbin Papers 3/14, BLPES; 'Copy of a document sent to the Chancellor on 4th April 1946', Piercy Papers 15/91. George Benson and Carol Johnson were the chairman and the secretary of the Finance Group.

[53] Durbin to Dalton, 12 Sept. 1946, Dalton Papers 9/2; Dalton to Durbin, 16 Sept. 1946, Durbin Papers 3/10; 'Letter to the Chancellor of the Exchequer from the Finance Group', 30 Dec. 1946, Piercy Papers 15/91. For Dalton's view of his 'hand-picked' Finance Group see *High Tide and After*, 22–3.

unless it has some *regular* work to do'. He and Piercy and Davenport (who were members of the Council) all tried unsuccessfully
to give it some work by putting up topics for discussion.[54] It first
met on 23 July 1946, with a large number of officials in atten-
dance to represent the government departments concerned with
public investment and, in Brittain's words, 'to keep the Council
on the rails'. It was supposed to meet quarterly and held four
meetings in its first year, but only two thereafter. The first four
meetings were taken up with minor matters relating to the capital
issues control, especially the question of relaxing the wartime ban
on companies' issuing bonus shares.[55] After Dalton's resignation
as Chancellor in November 1947, the Council did not meet, and
Cripps formally wound it up in December 1948, when only
Davenport expressed any disappointment.[56]

Cheaper money

Dalton at the Treasury is most remembered for his *cheaper money
policy*—his attempt to drive down long-term nominal interest
rates rather than to continue with *cheap money* as was generally

[54] Durbin to Chancellor, 'The work of the National Investment Council', 26
Feb., Piercy to Proctor, 'National Investment Council', 2th [sic] July 1946,
enclosing 'National Investment Council, Note by Lord Piercy—23 July 1946',
T228/81; Davenport, 'Economic planning and the investment programme', 20
Jan. 1947, and 'The Stock Exchange inflation and the finance of investment',
T233/164; NIC Paper 16, 'Memorandum by Nicholas Davenport on counter-infl-
ation measures', 22 Sept. 1947, and Piercy to Dalton, 17 Oct. 1947, T233/166; see
also Davenport, *Memoirs of a City Radical*, 154–5. The other members (besides
Piercy and Davenport) were Lord Catto, Lord Kennet (chairman of the Capital
Issues Committee), Sir Albert Gladstone, chairman of the Public Works Loan
Board, Lord Hyndley, chairman of Finance Corporation for Industry Ltd. (the
sister institution to ICFC of which Piercy was chairman), the chairman of the
Stock Exchange Sir Robert Pearson, George Gibson representing the trades
unions and C. E. Prater of the co-operative movement, Sir Clarence Sadd of the
Midland Bank, and Sir Clive Baillieu, president of the Federation of British Industries.
[55] Brittain to Bridges, 13 Sept. 1945, T233/25. The minutes of the first meeting
are on T233/161; the minutes of subsequent meetings (in November 1946,
February, March, August and October 1947) on T233/162–6, PRO. After the 'ex-
haustive' and inconclusive discussions in the NIC, Dalton eventually decided to
allow bonus issues (which he and others disliked because of the opportunities for
profitable speculation at a time of rising security prices) but imposed an additional
stamp duty on them in his April 1947 budget: 'Stamp duty on bonus issues,
historical background', T171/395, PRO.
[56] Davenport to Cripps, 9 Dec. 1948, T233/1021.

expected in light of the white paper on *Employment Policy* and recommended by the National Debt Enquiry. He decided upon it soon after he took office. He took the first step when he announced in his first budget in October the halving of interest rates on the floating debt, returning them to their pre-war levels as recommended by the National Debt Enquiry. He followed it by closing the existing tap offers of bonds at wartime levels of nominal interest rates in December, and, in 1946, offering two new long-term issues yielding 2½ per cent at the time of issue. Both aroused considerable criticism, and it was the reaction to the second, the famous 'Daltons' (2½% Treasury Stock 1975 or after) that effectively ended the cheaper money campaign. This section considers the internal discussions surrounding these issues.[57] In defending his policy Dalton claimed that he had been supported by all his Bank and Treasury advisers, including Keynes and Hopkins, and that only Evan Durbin had warned him that it had 'dangerous inflationary possibilities'.[58] The official Treasury and Bank records bear out his claim.

Writing in 1954 of his experience as Chancellor of the Exchequer Dalton gave his reasons for trying to reduce interest rates in 1945–6:

to save public expenditure on interest, to improve the distribution of income, to encourage investment and to make sure of full employment. The third of these reasons was not, in this period, of much importance ... [since investment was directly controlled]. But I had some further reasons. I wished to help the local authorities to keep down the cost of housing programmes, and thus to keep down rents. . . . And I wished to prepare the way for the series of nationalisation Bills which, during this Parliament, we intended to pass. The higher the national credit, the lower the rate of interest, the less the annual compensation charge corresponding to a given capital value.'[59]

---

[57] I have described these deliberations in 'The origins of cheaper money, 1945–7', *EHR*, 40 (Aug. 1987), 441–7, and 'Cheap money versus cheaper money: a reply to Professor Wood', *EHR*, 42 (Aug. 1989), 401–5. They are discussed from the Bank's point of view in Fforde, *Bank*, 328–30, 333–53. Pimlott, in his otherwise excellent biography, has little to say on cheaper money where he relies almost entirely on Davenport's account (*Hugh Dalton*, 462–5; *Memoirs of a City Radical*, 155–9).

[58] Dalton to the Editor, *The Economist*, 30 Jan. 1951; *High Tide and After*, 124–5, 183.

[59] *Public Finance*, 1954 edn., 235.

The first of these is the classic budgetary reason for low nominal interest rates, which always appeals to Chancellors and their officials. It was one of the two reasons for the post-war continuation of cheap money that Sir Richard Hopkins had given in the report of the National Debt Enquiry, the other being the encouragement of investment, Dalton's third reason. His second, and more 'socialist' reason reflects his long-standing professional concern for income distribution and his view of the burden of the national debt, which also influenced his budgetary aims (above). Cheap money, in the sense of low nominal interest rates on government debt, was a way of minimizing the burden of the national debt; to go further and lower already low nominal interest rates would further reduce rentier incomes and permit more desirable national expenditure. The 'further reasons' reinforced the more general considerations.

Dalton began to think of including lower interest rates in his policy objectives in his first three weeks at the Treasury. He may have discussed the techniques of debt management with Nicholas Davenport at the beginning of his second week.[60] In the Treasury, he asked his officials on 13 August to consider whether local authorities should be allowed to borrow for housing from the central government at a specially low interest rate. They rejected the idea: it would create an undesirable precedent and there were better ways to reduce council house rents. Dalton alluded to these discussions in his first House of Commons speech as Chancellor on 21 August, when, according to *The Economist*, 'the market found [him] rather obscure' on interest rates. He was clearer on 15 September, when he took advantage of the launching of the 'Thanksgiving' national savings sales campaign to mention publicly again that 'he was studying the possibility of cheaper money and lower rates of interest'.[61] (For current market interest rates see Table 3.4.)

[60] Davenport, *Memoirs of a City Radical*, 149. Although Davenport is often inaccurate, there is no reason to doubt the date of their meeting on Sunday, 5 August. Dalton's diary is patchy for his early weeks at the Treasury but Davenport's specific advice on cheaper money (to wait until market expectations were going in the right direction) is recorded in November 1945 (vol. 33, 1 Nov. 1945) and in the Treasury files in January 1946 (Davenport to Dalton, 17 Jan. 1946, T160/1408/F19187).

[61] Brittain to Eady, 15 Aug. 1945, T160/1408/F19187, PRO; Dalton, *High Tide and After*, 51–2; *The Economist*, 18 Aug. 236, 25 Aug. 274, and 22 Sept. 1945, 426.

TABLE 3.4 *Nominal Yields on British Government Securities, Monthly, 1945–7,* %.*p.a.*

End of		Short-dated[1]	Medium-dated[2]	Long-dated[3]	Consols[4]
1945	July	2.41	2.64	2.96	2.83
	Aug.	2.39	2.66	2.95	2.82
	Sept.	2.45	2.63	2.98	2.82
	Oct.	2.55	2.62	2.98	2.70
	Nov.	2.56	2.68	2.99	2.76
	Dec.	2.54	2.70	2.97	2.73
1946	Jan.	2.34	2.55	2.78	2.71
	Feb.	2.24	2.50	2.68	2.70
	Mar.	2.28	2.40	2.69	2.67
	Apr.	1.96	2.17	2.51	2.60
	May	2.13	2.38	2.62	2.50
	June	2.15	2.39	2.60	2.57
	July	2.09	2.36	2.53	2.58
	Aug.	2.04	2.33	2.52	2.59
	Sept.	2.05	2.23	2.48	2.56
	Oct.	1.68	2.05	2.28	2.54
	Nov.	1.78	1.97	2.27	2.53
	Dec.	1.73	1.99	2.29	2.54
1947	Jan.	1.55	1.91	2.22	2.54
	Feb.	1.74	2.04	2.36	2.58
	Mar.	1.90	2.23	2.52	2.64
	Apr.	1.97	2.19	2.48	2.63
	May	1.92	2.16	2.47	2.62
	June	2.08	2.35	2.66	2.68
	July	2.53	2.75	3.00	2.78
	Aug.	2.60	2.69	2.97	2.99
	Sept.	2.69	2.78	2.99	2.99
	Oct.	2.41	2.59	2.79	2.90
	Nov.	2.42	2.76	2.98	2.87
	Dec.	2.54	2.91	3.00	3.01

Notes
[1] Gross redemption yields for 2½% National War Bonds 1952/54.
[2] Gross redemption yields for 2½% Funding Loan 1956/61.
[3] Gross redemption yields for 3% Savings Bonds 1960/70.
[4] Gross flat yields on 2½% Consols.

Sources
Short-dated, medium-dated and long-dated security yields: Bank of England, *Statistical Abstract*, No. 1 (1970), table 30.
Yield on 2½% Consols: Capie and Webber, *A Monetary History of the United Kingdom 1970–1982*, vol. 1, table III(10).

At this time his senior Treasury officials were proposing to follow the recommendations the National Debt Enquiry had made for post-war monetary policy in May 1945: to cut the fixed interest rates on the floating debt, to reduce the rates on short-

and medium-term gilt-edged securities, and to maintain a 3 per cent rate for long-term tap bond issues but provide an early optional redemption date. Dalton wanted to go further:

I am sure that we both can, and should, reduce rates, both short and long. (We discussed this just after I came to the Treasury.) We must not miss the chance of *doing* this as soon as the Savings Campaign finishes.[62]

The Treasury officials initially thought that they would have to wait until the savings campaign ended in November to lower any interest rates. When they discussed their plans with the Bank, however, the Governor argued that they need not, and should not, lower Bank rate. A reduction would be interpreted abroad as inflationary, especially since Bank rate had never been below 2 per cent in the history of the Bank. Furthermore, if Bank rate were left unchanged, the lowering of rates on the floating debt could be presented as 'a technical adjustment' and made immediately after the budget. The Bank proposed the reduction of short-term interest rates should take place in the week of 22–26 October, beginning with a reduction in the clearing banks' call money rates by ½ per cent on 23 October after the budget speech, followed by a reduction in the rate offered by the discount houses at the Friday Treasury bill tender (both on the request of the Governor of the Bank) and then an announcement by the Chancellor that the rate on Treasury deposit receipts was also to go down. Dalton wanted instead to announce the reductions in the budget, so Treasury bill and TDR interest rates were reduced to ½ per cent and ⅝ per cent respectively as from 22 October 1945. In making the request to the bankers on 17 October the Governor explained that the changes had been proposed under the coalition government and were only a return to pre-war levels.[63] When Dalton announced the changes in Parliament his predecessor, Sir John Anderson, pointed out that he would have done the same if he were still Chancellor. In another deliberate attempt to influence expecta-

[62] Brittain to Bridges, 12 Sept., Bridges to Trend, 12 and 28 Sept., and note by Dalton, 14 Sept. 1945, T160/1408/F19187.

[63] Note by Bridges, 18 Sept., Eady to Bridges, 24 Sept., Brittain to Eady, and note by Dalton, 28 Sept., and Cobbold to Brittain, 3 Oct. 1945, T160/1408/F19187, PRO; Cobbold, 'Short-term money rates', 17 Oct. 1945, C42/1, BOE.

tions, Dalton also told the House that he would 'now turn [his] attention . . . to the possibility of securing lower middle-term and long-term interest rates'.[64]

Over the next step in the cheaper money campaign the Bank and the Treasury disagreed. The Bank wanted to continue with the wartime 2½ per cent for medium-term and 3 per cent for long-term government securities while lengthening their maturities. In November it warned the Treasury that with present budget deficits and forthcoming maturities, and the likelihood that recent large subscriptions to the current tap offer of 3% Savings Bonds had been made in anticipation of a fall in long-term rates:

All we are in a position to attack now is the short and medium rates; the long-term rates are more difficult to shift below what investors regard as a practical minimum—if only because they are long-term.

Its reasons against a long-term or irredeemable (that is, with no *final* redemption date) issue at less than 3 per cent included the prediction:

Once a move is made to 2½% for a long-term security, the Market would consider that the worst had happened, would fight shy of the loan and would hopefully await a move in the other direction—we should be regarded as having loosed off the last shot in our locker.

It recommended a conversion offer of 1¾% Exchequer Bonds 1950 for two maturing issues, to be announced on 1 January 1946, closing the existing tap offers of 2½% National War Bonds 1954/56 and 3% Savings Bonds 1965/75 at the end of the year, replacing the latter with a longer, 'irredeemable' bond, 3% Savings Bonds 1985 or after.[65]

In 'three long sessions with the Bank in eight days' the Treasury officials 'pressed the Bank strongly to put forward a scheme on the lines of what we believe to be the Chancellor's views'. They objected to issuing 1¾% Exchequer Bonds 1950, which would have a shorter term to maturity than an earlier issue in 1944, to the length of the 3 per cent bond, and to waiting until January to announce the new issues. Following Keynes's recom-

---

[64] *House of Commons Debates*, vol. 414, 23 Oct. 1945, cols. 1881–2, 2019–20; Dalton Diary, vol. 33, 1 Nov. 1945; see also *The Economist*, 27 Oct. 1945, 601–2.

[65] Bank of England, 'Interest rates', 12 Nov. 1945, T160/1408/F19187. The two issues that could be converted were £207m 2½% Conversion Loan 1944/49 and £444m 2½% National War Bonds 1945/47.

mendations to the National Debt Enquiry, they asked for consideration of a 1½ per cent three-year bond and of a 3 per cent 1955/85.[66] The Bank refused to budge over the short-term issue, arguing that since Exchequer Bonds were still below par their successful issue now would be a step in the direction of cheaper money. It rejected the 3 per cent 1955/85 on the ground that such 'a long option to the Government' would be unpopular with investors: the government would have the option of converting to a lower yield or redeeming the bonds at any time between 10 and 40 years, making the expected yield to maturity very uncertain. The Bank's preferred alternative could not be redeemed or converted for at least 40 years, and therefore had a higher expected yield to investors. The issue of an undated at 3 per cent would also allow the authorities to replace the many maturities coming due in the next decade with dated securities yielding less than 3 per cent. The Bank agreed that the announcements could be made before January. But from the Treasury's point of view a 3 per cent long-term issue was out of the question; Cobbold therefore suggested the two current taps might both be closed without offering a replacement, and the Treasury accepted this compromise. Dalton was critical, but succumbed again to Catto's persuasion. On 27 November he announced the closing of the taps on 15 December and the conversion offer of 1¾% Exchequer Bonds.[67]

In criticizing the compromise proposal, Dalton made clear his intentions to lower interest rates by ½ per cent all along the yield curve in the coming months.

We must improve on this programme. I want to show ½% cuts in interest at various points.

I don't mind the next step being in middle term.

But why not stopping 3% Savings Bonds, put up limit of 3% Defence Bonds to £2,000? Alternatively 2¾% Defence Bonds with no £1,500 limit? We must not discourage the National Savings movement.

[66] Bridges, 'Interest rates', 20 Nov. 1945, T160/1408/F19187, PRO; Peppiatt, 'Interest rates', 14 Nov. 1945, C40/450, BOE. On the earlier issue of Exchequer Bonds see pp. 57–8 above.

[67] Cobbold, 'Interest rates', 14, 15, and 16 Nov. 1945, C40/450, BOE; Brittain, 'Interest rates, Points for meeting with Bank, 15th November', 15 Nov., Brittain to Eady, 'New issues', 17 Nov., Bridges, 'Interest rates', 20 Nov., note by Dalton, 20 Nov., and Trend to Bridges, 'Interest rates', 22 Nov. 1945, T160/1408/F19187. Dalton also announced an increase in the limit on individual holdings of defence bonds, which he had himself suggested in his note.

And what about 'open-market operations'? This used to be a great open-sesame.

A few weeks later he asked why the savings bank funds administered by the National Debt Commissioners could not be used to buy up long-term government securities from the market in order to increase their prices and lower their current yields.[68]

In January Dalton called a meeting of his most senior advisers—Keynes, Hopkins, Bridges, Eady, Catto, and Cobbold—to consider 'the next move in the cheaper money campaign'. He asked them:

(*a*) What more must we do to prepare the way for a long-term issue at 2½?

(*b*) What ought we to do about our succession of 2½% maturities over the next 10 years or so?

(*c*) For what periods could we now issue (i) 1% Bonds, (ii) 1½% Bonds?

(*d*) At what point ought we to reduce the rate on Post Office Savings Bank deposits from 2½% to 2%?

The Bank's advice, which was eventually accepted, was to wait and see what happened to interest rates as the months went by. With current gilt-edged yields (see Table 3.4) a 2½ per cent long-term issue was 'not at present within sight' and a further issue of short-term bonds also 'out of the question' for the time being. A reduction in the savings bank deposit rate, on the other hand, was 'long overdue' but there was no obvious occasion to do this. After a lengthy discussion the meeting agreed to reconsider the position in March.[69]

At the January meeting Keynes's advice was to aim for his National Debt Enquiry proposal of a 3 per cent long-term bond with an early optional redemption date, which he still preferred to a 2½ per cent issue a month later. This was not ambitious enough for Dalton, so Keynes recommended (in February) trying first a 2 per cent ten-year bond and then a 1½ per cent five-year issue.[70] He elaborated on these ideas in a long memorandum

[68] Notes by Dalton, 20 Nov. 1945, T160/1408/F19187, 29 Dec. 1945, T160/1379/F18445/1. On intervention in the gilt-edged market see pp. 135–9 below.

[69] Miss P. C. Shaw to Governor, 14 Jan., Peppiatt to Governors, 'Government borrowing', 15 Jan., Cobbold, 'Government borrowing (Proposed meeting with the Chancellor on 17th January)', 17 Jan., and 'Government borrowing', 18 Jan. 1946, C40/472, BOE. Miss Shaw (later Mrs Trend) was an assistant private secretary to Dalton.

[70] Trend, 'Budget', 20 Feb. 1946, T171/386, PRO.

written on board the liner *Queen Mary* on his way to America for the inaugural meeting of the International Monetary Fund and the World Bank. In it he estimated (incorrectly as it turned out) that the 1946/7 budget deficit would be covered by external financing and 'small savings' so that there was no need to make any new tap issues which would merely lengthen the debt and increase interest payments. He also expected that long-term nominal interest rates would probably fall as fears of higher post-war rates evaporated and holders of medium-term bonds moved into longer issues, which implied it would be difficult to lower the middle of the yield curve. There might be a case for putting a medium-term bond on tap even though there would not be much demand for it initially, because it would be taken up by the market once long rates had fallen. Since Dalton wanted to make some announcement about cheap money in the budget, Keynes suggested reducing some of the administered interest rates that had not been reduced in October, such as those on defence bonds and savings bank deposits, and perhaps also Bank rate. When the time came to issue a long-term bond (at 2½ per cent) the opportunity might be taken to convert 3% Local Loans stock, which had been redeemable at the government's option since 1923, into the new issue; in the meantime the Chancellor should consider reducing the rate on local authority borrowing from the central government. On his return from America, Keynes proposed that Local Loans should be called and a new 2½ per cent twenty-year or more stock offered in conversion. The amount of the new issue should, however, be little more than the £429m Local Loan stock outstanding, because there was no need to fund floating debt and little likely demand for a long-term issue. Its purpose would be to allow Dalton '(a) ... to mark a stage on the progress to cheaper borrowing, and (b) to have a good reason for reducing the borrowing rate to local authorities to 2½ per cent'.[71]

The Bank of England had other ideas. The Treasury having turned down a new 3 per cent issue to replace the last issue of 3% Savings Bonds, the Chief Cashier, Sir Kenneth Peppiatt, now

[71] Keynes, '1946–47 loan programme', 26 Feb., and 'Loan policy', 1 Apr. 1946, C40/472, BOE; see also Fforde, *Bank*, 340–2. Since 1945 all local authorities had been able to borrow from the Public Works Loan Board at interest rates fixed from time to time on the principle that they should reflect the market rates at which the central government could borrow. Keynes overestimated both external financing and small savings in 1946/7: see Table 3.5 below.

proposed a replacement for the 2½% National War Bonds, either another 2½ per cent issue with a twenty-two year term to maturity or a 2¾ per cent issue with an even longer term (issued at a discount so as to permit a slightly longer maturity than issuing at par). Since the Bank's preference was to borrow as long as possible, Keynes's suggested ten-year bond '[did] not make sense from any angle'. Peppiatt and Cobbold agreed with Keynes that rates on defence bonds and savings bank deposits could be reduced, but not Bank rate, and they thought that it was too soon to think of converting Local Loans. The Governor was not in favour of any of the rate reductions proposed by Keynes.[72]

The conference called to discuss Keynes's *Queen Mary* memorandum on 14 March agreed not to consider any new issue before the budget. It also took several important decisions of principle. 'All agreed that the ultimate aim is a 2½% long', and the next new issue would probably be 2½ per cent for as long a term as possible. There would be no reduction in Bank rate or in savings bank deposit rates, but the interest rate on defence bonds could be lowered, and probably announced in the budget. At Dalton's request the National Debt Commissioners were to be allowed to purchase gilt-edged securities again from the market, which they had not done during the war (p. 37).[73] At the next meetings, on 1 and 4 April, when Keynes produced his scheme for calling Local Loans the Bank thought it risky and premature. Furthermore, since the Local Loans were 'irredeemable' they should be replaced with another undated security. Since Dalton objected to the Bank's proposed replacement for 2½% National War Bonds, Catto suggested that he announce in the budget forthcoming repayment of a maturing issue of War Bonds without indicating any replacement. Dalton none the less 'expressed considerable interest in calling the 3% Local Loans now' but the Governor 'offered no prospects of success' and Eady, Hopkins and Bridges supported his alternative proposal. Keynes 'con-

[72] Peppiatt to Governors, 'Government borrowing', 1 Mar., and '1946/47 loan programme', 7 Mar., Cobbold, 'Government borrowing', 11 Mar., and '1946/47 loan programme (Lord Keynes' note of 26.2.46)', 13 Mar., Catto to Chancellor, 14 Mar. 1946, C40/472, BOE.
[73] Cobbold, 'Government borrowing', 15 Mar. 1946, C40/472, BOE; Brittain, 'Chancellor's discussion with the Governor, 14th March 1946', T160/1408/F19187, PRO.

firmed that his first preference would be to say nothing at all in the Budget'.[74] In the budget Dalton reiterated his 'aim . . . to cheapen money and to lower rates of interest to the greatest extent that economic and financial conditions will permit', in announcing a new series of defence bonds with a 2½ per cent return and repayment of the maturing War Bonds on 15 May.[75]

The budget was generally well received. Gilt-edged prices rose and nominal yields on long-term government bonds fell to just over 2½ per cent (see Table 3.4). When Dalton and his senior advisers met on 3 May (without Keynes who had died on 21 April and Catto who was on leave) to decide on a new issue the Deputy Governor recommended a new tap issue of 2½% Savings Bonds 1964/67 at par, to be offered for cash and conversion of the maturing War Bonds. In response to Dalton's 'hope [that] we might now be able to be rather more ambitious', Cobbold argued that 18–21 years at 2½ per cent was 'a bit ahead of the market and we could not expect it to be a great success'. A new short-term bond would not do any better, since there were already plenty of 1¾% Exchequer Bonds still available to be bought from the authorities' large holdings. According to Cobbold, Bridges and Hopkins 'supported these views and the Chancellor agreed. We touched on the question of conversion of Local Loans and the general feeling was that if all went well we might perhaps hope to deal with this by an irredeemable 2½ per cent at the beginning of next year.'[76]

The new issue gave Dalton his excuse to lower the rates at which local authorities could borrow from the central government, which were announced on 31 May. But Dalton was not entirely happy with the results of the issue. The authorities made sure it was a success by buying in maturing War Bonds for conversion into the new stock—over 60 per cent of the £334m converted were official holdings—and supporting the market during the spring and summer by buying other long-term government securities such as the last issue of 3% Savings Bonds.[77] In the first half of May

[74] Cobbold, 'Government borrowing', 1 and 4 Apr., Catto to Chancellor, 3 Apr. 1946, C40/472, BOE; see also Dalton Diary, vol. 34, 12 Apr. 1946.

[75] *House of Commons Debates*, vol. 421, 9 Apr. 1946, cols. 1818–20; Dalton, *High Tide and After*, 181.

[76] Cobbold, 'Government borrowing', 3 May 1946, C40/472, BOE.

[77] Brittain to Eady and Trend, 'National Debt Commissioners' investments', 21 May, Brittain to Pinsent, 24 May 1946, T233/1073, PRO; Pinsent to Brittain, 25 May 1946, C40/438, BOE.

gilts prices were rising; when the new tap opened on 16 May, investors found the terms relatively generous compared with current market yields. There was considerable switching from existing securities whose prices fell heavily. Dalton was extremely annoyed, complaining to Catto that he had received bad advice in his absence and telling him that he 'had totally lost all confidence in Cobbold'. According to Dalton, Catto thought that Cobbold had been too cautious and that he and his advisers should have reconsidered the terms between 3 and 14 May.[78]

The decision in October 1946 to issue a 2½ per cent irredeemable was also a consequence of the decisions taken in the early spring. The final decision on terms was, however, taken at the very last moment. After the 2½% Savings Bond tap was closed, on 16 July, the gilt-edged market recovered, and by September nominal long-term yields were below 2½ per cent (Table 3.4). Catto suggested to Dalton that he could call Local Loans on 16 October, the day of the annual Mansion House dinner for the Chancellor of the Exchequer. Dalton said he would like to offer both a 2½ per cent twenty-year or more bond and a 2 per cent ten-year bond. When he mentioned this to Cobbold,

the Deputy Governor ... [said] he has always been fearful of the moment when it would seem the limit of cheap money had been reached. I said that, in this case, he should back the 2% option, since this would open possibilities of an ever lengthening term for a 2% bond, even though, in fact, we couldn't move very far along this road. Keynes was very keen on a 2% ten year Bond.[79]

The Governor and the Chancellor then went to Washington for the first of the annual IMF/IBRD meetings. In their absence their officials planned a new tap offer of a 2½ per cent irredeemable, callable at the government's option only after forty years. Peppiatt's arguments for such an issue were that the authorities did not hold a sufficiently high proportion of Local Loans outstanding to ensure the success of a conversion, that 'sound finance would, of course, demand that an irredeemable be replaced by another irredeemable', and that to offer a dated long-term bond might be regarded by the market 'as not taking full advantage' of existing market prices and therefore have the same unfortunate

[78] *The Economist*, 25 May 1946, 852, and 8 June 1946, 936; Dalton Diary, 20 May 1946; see also Dalton, *High Tide and After*, 125.
[79] Dalton to Compton, 16 Sept. 1946, T233/149, PRO.

effect as the 2½% Savings Bonds 1964/67. The objections to a short- or medium-term security were the same as they had been earlier in the year. After consulting the Government Broker, the Bank's advice to the Treasury admitted the issue was risky:

(a) . . . It has often been felt that this level [2½ per cent for an irredeemable] would be judged the limit of the cheap money movement, at least for the time being, on long stocks and might therefore cause a general turn in Market sentiment so far as long-term Government securities are concerned.

(b) On the other hand (and this point is emphasised with great strength by those in closest touch with the Market), it would be regarded as unsound to convert an irredeemable into a redeemable stock and such action would be open to heavy (and in their view justifiable) criticism. Moreover it is felt in some quarters that a stock with a very long final date would not be regarded by the market as a stepping stone to a 2½% irredeemable but might be interpreted as a doubt on the part of the Treasury whether they could quite get to that point, and therefore incur the same risks as an irredeemable of marking a final level in the minds of the Market.[80]

The decision was taken on the evening of 14 October. There had already been a setback to gilt-edged prices following a speech on 8 October by the Minister of Fuel and Power (Emanuel Shinwell) which mentioned the possibility of a fuel shortage in the coming winter; the Government Broker had told Cobbold that 'with sentiment as it is today they could not advise us to go ahead with this operation'. At the meeting on 14 October the Governor told Dalton that he was not certain that market demand would be strong enough to make the issue a success, but also not certain conditions would improve, so the Chancellor might prefer to proceed anyway. The Treasury officials present (Bridges, Hopkins, Eric Bamford, a Third Secretary, and Edmund Compton, an undersecretary) were prepared to go ahead if the Bank did not say it was impossible to succeed; Hopkins, the 'most definite and courageous of them all' according to Dalton, argued for taking the plunge: 'He feared that if we held off now . . .

---

[80] Peppiatt, 'Government borrowing programme', 19 Sept., and Cobbold, 'Government borrowing', 20 Sept. 1946, C40/473, BOE; Bank of England, 'Government borrowing—Autumn programme, first thoughts', 27 and 30 Sept. 1946, T233/149, PRO. On the preparation of the Bank's proposal see also Fforde, *Bank*, 349–50. The Government Broker was, from 1786 to 1989, the senior partner of stockbrokers Mullens & Co.

people would start saying that the Treasury had concluded that the 2½% rate could not be achieved and had to be abandoned.' After going over the arguments against a dated stock (on which only Catto had doubts) and a second, shorter stock once again, 'The Chancellor finally decided that Local Loans should be called and a new 2½% Treasury stock 1975 or after issued' from 28 October, the announcement to be made on 16 October. In his announcement Dalton proudly pointed out that it was the first time in the history of the UK national debt that the government had issued a 2½ per cent irredeemable at par and that he had gone further than Chancellor G. J. Goschen whose conversion of 3% Consols in 1888 was to a stock carrying 2¾ per cent for the first fourteen years, then 2½ per cent from 1903.[81]

The Daltons issue is notorious for its 'failure': the stock was heavily supported by the authorities while it was on tap (from 28 October to 11 January 1947), and fell heavily after the tap was closed. Initially it met with a 'mixed reception, the principal point of criticism being the *undated* nature of the stock'. The *Financial Times* compared it with 2½% Consols, the only other undated 2½ per cent stock, whose price had fallen to record lows soon after the First World War, and thought there would be little demand from institutional investors (pension funds, insurance companies, etc.) who were now buying dated stocks. *The Economist* was pessimistic about demand from private investors, who were 'invite[d] to give a complete hostage to the policy of ultra-cheap money for a generation'.[82] On the first day's sales of £50m the *Financial Times* commented that 'earlier predictions of a poor response to the Chancellor's offer may prove to have been too gloomy', but during November sales fell off week by week while criticism of official support of the gilt-edged market was growing more vociferous. The holders of the £429m Local Loans, which were to be repaid on 5 January, had been invited to subscribe their redemption money in Daltons; by 28 November private sector holders of only £46m had done so. It was decided to keep the tap open after 5 January, in the hope of attracting at least enough money into the tap issue to cover the redemption pay-

[81] Cobbold, 'Government borrowing', 9 Oct. 1946, with postscript of 10 Oct., and 'Government borrowing', 15 Oct. 1946, C40/473, BOE; Dalton Diary, vol. 34, 23 Oct. 1946, and *High Tide and After*, 160–4; see also Fforde, *Bank*, 351–2, where the Bank's brief for the Governor to use at the meeting is reproduced.

[82] *Financial Times*, 18 Oct. 1946; *The Economist*, 19 Oct. 1946, 633.

ments to the remaining private sector Local Loans holders. Since
the authorities held £181m Local Loans, Dalton was able to announce on 10 December that nearly three-quarters of the Local
Loans would be converted and that he would not keep the tap
open much longer. After a brief spurt of sales, the Chancellor
agreed on 23 December to the closing of the tap on 11 January.
When the tap closed, a total of £480m Daltons had been sold, but
the authorities held 54 per cent of the total and approximately 60
per cent of the £305m Daltons issued in exchange for Local Loans
stock.[83]

Official support of the gilt-edged market was an integral part
of Dalton's cheaper money policy, as it had been in the wartime
cheap money regime. Wartime practice was for the Issue Department and the NDC to buy up gilt-edged securities nearing maturity, converting them into the new issue if a conversion offer was
made, and to take up a proportion of new tap issues, which the
Issue Department gradually sold to the market. The NDC were
instructed not to buy long-term securities from the market but
only from the tap, and from 1943 were supplied with 3 per cent
terminable annuities whenever the amount of funds to be invested warranted it (above p. 37), enabling the Bank to buy marketable long-term securities from the NDC for the Issue Department
to sell to the market as it bought up shorter stock. At the end of
the war the Bank had envisaged the lifting of the restriction on
NDC investments once the government ceased to be a continuous large-scale borrower, but the cheaper money campaign
delayed the reversion to peacetime practice.

In the autumn of 1945 the issue of the usual £120m 3 per cent
annuity to the savings bank funds was first postponed. When the
Controller of the National Debt Office, H. W. S. Francis, sought
a £240m 3 per cent annuity in November after short-term interest
rates had been lowered, the Treasury was reluctant to issue such
an amount at 3 per cent; at the same time Francis was reluctant to
sell more long-term securities to the Bank without an annuity to
take their place because the lowering of short-term interest rates
had reduced the income of the savings bank funds. The Bank,

[83] *Financial Times*, 11 Dec., 18 and 30 Dec. 1946; Pinsent to Bamford, 28 Oct.
1946, T233/1073; Peppiatt, 'Repayment of 3% Local Loans', 28 Nov., and '2½%
Treasury Stock', 29 Nov. 1946, C40/473, BOE; Compton to Waterfall, 23 Dec.
1946, T233/149; 'Out-turn of the issue of 2½% Treasury Stock 1975 or after', 18 Jan.
1947, T233/150.

wishing to continue to be able to buy marketable long-term stocks from the NDC, recommended issuing the NDC with at least £120m annuities at 3 per cent and permitting them to buy in the market again.[84] When the Treasury proposed to issue £240m 3 per cent annuities, Dalton objected:

No I don't like this. They can continue to hold these funds in liquid form, until we have looked at the whole thing again in the New Year.

He conceded, however, that he would agree to issuing annuities at 2¾ per cent.[85] Cobbold at first thought he would have to accept this but Catto intervened: Dalton agreed to a maximum of £200m 3 per cent annuities, which were issued on 31 December 1945, 'with minimum of publicity'. But he asked: 'Why not use this liquid mass of manœuvre to boost long-term issues, e.g. by steadily buying 3% Savings Bonds and Local Loans? . . . Discuss with Governor in 1946.'[86]

At the begining of the new year the Bank produced a memorandum on intervention in the gilt-edged market. It outlined the practice since the 1930s, and argued that intervention had always been and should continue to be confined to supporting *existing* levels of gilt-edged prices and to facilitating conversions. In the post-war period, 'it would seem likely that our resources will be strained to the utmost . . . in dealing with the large volume of maturing debt', and the authorities would not have the resources to fight market trends. The Treasury officials thought 'the Bank's general policy is reasonable enough'. Since it had just been decided not to take any decision on a new tap issue for a couple of months (above), they proposed 'as an interim measure' a sale from the savings banks funds of £50m long-term stocks in instalments to the Bank in exchange for £50m 1¾% Exchequer

[84] Note by Francis, 9 Oct., Peppiatt, 'Savings banks funds', 12 Nov., and note by Cobbold, 23 Nov. 1945, C40/438, BOE; Francis, 'Savings bank funds', 8 Nov., Brittain to Eady and Trend, 'Investment of savings bank funds', 15 Nov., Bank of England, 'National Debt and Issue Dept. Investment Sales Policy', 30 Nov. 1945, T160/1379/F18445/1, PRO.
[85] Notes by Dalton, 19 and 21 Dec. 1945, T160/1379/F18445/1.
[86] Catto to Cobbold, 28 Dec. 1945, and Note by Cobbold, 3 Jan. 1946, C40/438, BOE; Catto to Dalton, 28 Dec., and Note by Dalton, 29 Dec. 1945, T160/1379/F18445/1, PRO. Catto again raised the spectre of 1931: this time he warned Dalton that a deficiency of income for the savings banks funds would mean either a reduction in the deposit interest rate or a Parliamentary vote to cover the deficiency which 'might . . . frighten Post Office depositors'.

Bonds, whose return would be an improvement on ½ per cent on Treasury bills or Ways and Means Advances.[87]

The decision to allow the NDC to purchase long-term gilt-edged securities from the market was made at the Chancellor's meeting on 14 March when it was decided not to lower the savings bank deposit interest rate (above). Since the savings banks funds' holdings of short-term debt were then very large and included £330m 1¾% Exchequer Bonds, which the Bank wanted to take advantage of current market demand to sell off, 'one last issue' of annuities was made. In deference to Dalton the rate on the £250m issued on 3 May was 2½ per cent rather than 2⅝ per cent preferred by the Bank.[88] The new policy thus came into operation at the same time as the first of the two 'cheaper money' bond issues in May 1946.

When the new tap issue was launched the NDC converted its £154m holdings of the maturing 2½% National War Bonds (a high proportion of which had been bought in the previous six weeks) and took over and converted a further £75m from the Issue Department. Official conversions accounted for over 60 per cent of the total £334m converted. The authorities bought only £12m of the new 2½% Savings Bonds from the tap. Since Dalton preferred that the NDC invest accruing funds in existing long-term securities rather than in the new issue, in order to increase the proportion of the lower interest stocks in private sector portfolios as well as to maintain the income of the funds, the Commissioners invested in the large wartime issues of 3% Savings Bonds. Over the 1946/7 financial year their holdings of 3% Savings Bonds nearly doubled, one-third of the £88m increase taking place during and immediately after the 2½% Savings Bonds issue.[89]

---

[87] Bank of England, 'Government borrowing', 8 Jan., Brittain to Eady and Trend, 'Savings banks funds—investments', 25 Jan. 1946, T233/434, PRO.

[88] Phillips to Brittain, 'Savings banks funds', 12 Apr., Brittain to Eady, 'Savings bank funds' investments', 15 Apr., Brittain to Chancellor, 17 Apr., and notes by Dalton, 21 Apr. 1946, T233/434. There were in fact three later annuity issues, in December 1948, March 1949 and March 1950 (see Ch. 5).

[89] Brittain to Eady and Trend, 'National Debt Commissioners' investments', 21 May, Brittain to Pinsent, 24 May, and Pinsent to Bamford, 1 Aug. 1946, T233/1073, PRO; Pinsent to Brittain, 25 May, and Excell to Chief Cashier, 'C.R.N.D.', 23 Sept. 1946, C40/438, BOE; Compton, 'Stock market transactions by government departments', 25 Nov. 1947, T233/143; Pember and Boyle, *British Government Securities in the Twentieth Century*, 510–11. Jerry Pinsent had replaced H. W. S. Francis as Controller of the National Debt Office in April 1946.

Market support was on a larger scale when it came to the Daltons issue. By this time the monetary consequences of Dalton's policy were beginning to be noticed (see below) and more intervention was needed to hold the line on 2½ per cent. The NDC continued to buy 3% Savings Bonds although they found it difficult to buy large amounts without affecting the price. It was also necessary this time for the authorities to take up large amounts of the stock from the tap—£11m for the Issue Department and £64m for the NDC—in addition to converting their £185m holdings of Local Loans stock. The holdings were difficult to sell off and £275m Daltons were in official hands a year later.[90]

Another way in which Dalton sought to use official intervention in support of cheaper money was to have the NDC underwrite conversions by local authorities of bonds carrying coupons over 3 per cent to lower interest rates. Like other aspects of the cheaper money policy this was a continuation of wartime practice. During the war optional conversions by local authorities and public utility companies had been first prohibited, then permitted only for stocks with coupons above 4 per cent, when the Local Loans Fund was to take up any unconverted local authority stocks for gradual subsequent sale to the market. After reconsidering the ban on conversions of stocks with coupons less than 4 per cent in the spring and autumn of 1945, the Treasury decided to lift it in May 1946—a step of which Dalton strongly approved since one of his arguments for cheaper money was to improve local authority finances. With Dalton's enthusiastic encouragement the 'public stag' underwrote the conversions of £6m local authority stocks to 2¾ per cent issues in the first phase of cheaper money, November 1945–April 1946, and a further £36m

---

[90] Pinsent to Bamford, 28 Oct. 1946, T233/1073, PRO; Peppiatt to Governor, 'Repayment of 3% Local Loans', 28 Nov. 1946, C40/473, BOE; Compton, 'Stock market transactions by government departments', 25 Nov., and 'Investments held by (a) Issue Department (b) N.D.C. funds', 2 Dec. 1947, T233/143. The investment of the savings banks funds in long-term marketable securities instead of non-marketable terminable annuities did not of course solve the problem of maintaining the income of the funds to cover deposit interest and management expenses. The logical solution was to reduce the deposit interest rate, but this was politically awkward. Officials canvassed several alternatives during the autumn and winter of 1946–7 before resorting to a clause in the 1947 Finance Bill to cover the deficiency out of the Consolidated Fund: Compton to Bamford, 14 Sept. 1946, and subsequent memoranda on T233/982 and 983.

to 2½ per cent by the end of 1947, often making a profit on these transactions.[91]

Official intervention in the gilt-edged market in support of 2½ per cent ceased in January 1947. After their heavy underwriting of Daltons the authorities found themselves loaded with very large holdings of the new stock, which the Bank found difficult to sell on a falling market (without further lowering the price). At the same time inflows of deposits into the savings banks were declining, so that the NDC did not have new funds with which to buy long-term securities from the market. The resulting non-intervention was in line with the customary operating procedure but it is unlikely that the Bank would have wished to intervene even if the resources had been available. As it was, the Bank was able to claim later in the year, with almost a straight face, that it had not done more than underwrite new issues under Dalton's cheaper money policy.[92]

The official intervention in the gilt-edged market had begun to receive adverse comment from financial journalists in September 1946. *The Economist* led the chorus, pointing out that the use of departmental funds was not only 'unfunding' the debt (that is, increasing the proportion of short-term debt in the total) but also increasing the money supply. Its evidence was a £260m rise in the London clearing banks' holdings of government securities in the ten months October 1945–July 1946 (compared with a fall of £60m in the similar period of 1944–5) and a rapid rise in clearing bank deposits over those months. In *The Banker* Wilfred King traced the rapid growth of clearing bank deposits in October 1945–August 1946 to the authorities' support of the gilt-edged market.[93] The consequences of the cheaper money policy for government financing, the structure of the national debt, and the money supply are shown here in Tables 3.5–3.8.

Table 3.5 separates the sources of government finance for each quarter of the 1945/6, 1946/7, and 1947/8 financial years into

[91] Sayers, *Financial Policy*, 168–72; Bridges to Trend, 3 May 1946, T160/1402/ F17773, PRO; Note by Dalton, 31 July 1946, T233/303; Pinsent to Trend, and note by Dalton, 24 Oct. 1946, T233/644; Shillitto to Compton, 11 Mar. 1947, and 'Local authority conversions to 2½% stocks (June 1946 to Nov 1947)', T233/299, PRO.

[92] Compton, 'Investments held by (*a*) Issue Department (*b*) N.D.C. funds', 2 Dec. 1947, T233/143; Catto, 'Cheap money policy', 25 Nov. 1947, C42/1, BOE; Fforde, *Bank*, 354–5.

[93] 'Cheap money and "unfunding"', *The Economist*, 7 Sept. 1946, 382–4; 'Gilt-edged and the volume of money', *The Banker*, Oct. 1946, 7–16.

TABLE 3.5 *Central Government Financing, Quarterly, 1945-8, £m*

	(1945)			(1946)				(1947)				(1948)			
	II	III	IV	I	II	III	IV	I	II	III	IV	I	II	III	IV
Above the line surplus/deficit	-697	-698	-721	-90	-275	-212	-126	27	218	-6	22	402	179	74	8
Below the line expenditure[1]	-9	-3	-14	-6	-108	-149	-129	-132	-41	-166	-258	-186	-146	-90	-123
Overall surplus or deficit	-706	-702	-735	-96	-383	-361	-255	-105	177	-172	-236	216	33	-16	-115
Adjustments[2]	-43	7	27	36	10	41	-51	221	-260	-38	-23	80	-77	-9	-37
Changes in TRCs	55	17	46	-153	8	—	12	-139	-6	-6	25	-116	4	45	44
Net overall surplus/deficit	-694	-678	-662	-213	-369	-320	-294	-23	-89	-216	-234	180	-40	20	-108
External financing															
EEA sterling receipts	-3	24	15	13	13	-99	-5	72	-9	11	80	-29	76	36	-21
North American aid + loans, net sterling receipts	-5	-3	47	-24	26	126	85	59	233	358	92	166	16	206	84
Domestic financing															
National insurance funds	17	21	17	23	10	19	17	8	12	23	17	17	15	45	37
Small savings	119	132	204	205	138	45	105	89	31	-19	1	60	-27	-25	-8
Increase/decrease in fiduciary issue	50	50	50	—	—	—	50	—	—	—	-150	—	—	-25	—
Stocks in market[3]	142	168	656	31	194	-91	-41	-123	-26	-111	-87	-261	-34	-29	-17
Market floating debt:															
TDRs	216	47	-486	-77	-169	389	-102	-220	-15	-149	110	-112	177	-18	62
Treasury bills	155	245	174	46	160	-65	189	138	-137	103	21	129	-183	-235	-54

Notes

1 Expenditure expected to bring a cash return in subsequent years, e.g. Post Office capital expenditure, advances to local authorities for capital purposes.

2 Issue Department income *plus* Departmental balances plus sinking funds.

3 Issues of government stocks *less* redemptions of government stocks (including sinking funds) *less* increase in holdings of Issue Department and National Debt Commissioners.

Source

Calculated from 'Exchequer financing and national debt, 1945-51', *Economic Trends* (Dec. 1961), table 1.

external financing, changes in non-marketable debt, and the net effect of operations in marketable debt. In the 1946/7 financial year, in which the cheaper money debt operations were concentrated, external financing, mostly the North American loans, contributed £277m towards a net overall central government deficit of £971m. Small savings contributed £377m. The remainder was covered by a net increase in the floating debt of £320m, which was incurred entirely in the second half of 1946. Net gilt-edged borrowing ceased and turned negative from the end of the first quarter of the financial year. This contrasts strongly with the previous financial year when a deficit twice as large had been met by a similar increase in floating debt, £660m small savings, and £997m net gilt-edged borrowing from the private sector, with no significant contribution from external sources. It also contrasts strongly with the following financial year when external financing amounted to £902m because of reserve losses in the balance-of-payments crisis, inflows of small savings more or less evaporated and the floating debt was reduced by £50m. But the deficit had also shrunk, to £15m overall, so that external financing in effect permitted large-scale repayment of gilt-edged debt.

The resulting shortening of the average maturity of government debt in private sector portfolios is shown in Table 3.6, which provides estimates of private sector holdings of different categories of government debt on 31 March each year 1945–52. In the year to 31 March 1946 the proportion of floating debt in private sector portfolios had dropped from 19 to 15 per cent; in the year to 31 March 1947 it jumped up again to 17 per cent. It fell again the followng year and continued to decline thereafter. As the proportion of floating debt rose in the year of Dalton's cheaper money drive so did the proportion of short-dated gilt-edged debt while that of medium-term gilts fell.

In 1945 monetary growth (both M1 and M3) had declined from wartime double-digit rates (Table 3.7). It accelerated again in 1946, with M1 growing by over 15 per cent and M3 only slightly more slowly. For M1 this rate is the same as the average annual rate of the previous six years, for M3 it is *higher* (see Table 1.4). The monetary base, however, did not revert to its wartime growth and grew by about 6 per cent in 1946. This reflects a post-war decline in demand for currency from wartime levels—currency in circulation grew by about 2.5 per cent in 1946 com-

TABLE 3.6 *Private Sector Holdings of National Debt, by Maturity Class, 31 March 1945–52, £m Nominal (% of Total in Parentheses)*

	Treasury bills[1]	TDRs	Marketable securities[2] With a maximum life of			Small savings[4]	TRCs	Total private sector[5]
			Less than 5 years	5–15 years	Over 15 years[3]			
1945	1,131 (19.2)	1,859	1,297 (8.3)	2,649 (17.0)	5,691 (36.5)	2,273 (14.6)	683 (4.4)	15,583
1946	942 (15.3)	1,559	966 (5.9)	3,071 (18.8)	6,623 (40.4)	2,565 (15.7)	648 (4.0)	16,374
1947	1,504 (17.2)	1,457	1,300 (7.6)	2,610 (15.2)	7,024 (40.8)	2,783 (16.2)	529 (3.1)	17,207
1948	1,407 (15.5)	1,291	1,736 (10.0)	1,869 (10.7)	7,925 (45.5)	2,775 (15.9)	426 (2.4)	17,429
1949	1,313 (14.0)	1,136	2,401 (13.7)	1,188 (6.8)	8,405 (40.0)	2,713 (15.5)	359 (2.1)	17,515
1950	1,841 (13.4)	465	2,100 (12.2)	1,172 (6.8)	8,627 (50.2)	2,669 (15.5)	318 (1.9)	17,192
1951	2,034 (13.2)	284	1,724 (9.8)	2,320 (13.2)	8,226 (46.7)	2,644 (15.0)	386 (2.2)	17,618
1952	1,344 (7.7)	—	2,891 (16.5)	2,049 (11.7)	8,308 (47.3)	2,603 (14.8)	368 (2.1)	17,563

Notes
[1] 'market Treasury bills' *less* holdings of Banking Department of Bank of England and overseas official holders.
[2] Includes government-guaranteed securities.
[3] Includes undated.
[4] National savings certificates and defence bonds.
[5] Some small items have been omitted because there is no breakdown between official and non-official holdings.

Sources
Treasury bills: Calculated from 'Exchequer financing and national debt 1945–51', *Economic Trends* (Dec. 1961), tables 2(*b*) and 4, and Committee on the Working of the Monetary System, *Principal Memoranda of Evidence*, 56.
Marketable securities: 'Exchequer financing and national debt 1945–51', table 3, and Committee on the Working of the Monetary System, *Principal Memoranda of Evidence*, 125.
Small savings and TRCs: Pember and Boyle, *British Government Securities in the Twentieth Century*, 447, 449, 451, 453, 455, and *British Government Securities in the Twentieth Century, Supplement 1950–1976*, 375, 377, 379.

pared with a wartime annual average of 18 per cent—and hides a rapid expansion of bank reserves at an annual rate of 20 per cent in the second half of 1946. Similarly the high growth rates of M1 and M3 reflect rapid expansion of total bank deposits, also on the

TABLE 3.7 *Growth Rates of Monetary Aggregates and Other Variables, Annual, 1945-51, % p.a.*

Year to December	C	R	H	D	M1	M3	P	Money GDP	Real GDP
1945	10.7	11.2	10.8	7.7	8.6	8.2	3.0	−4.3	−6.2
1946	2.5[1]	15.5[1]	5.2	15.2	15.3	14.2	1.9	1.3	−0.6
1947	−4.5	−5.5	−0.9	4.8	1.4	3.7	9.0	7.0	−2.4
1948	−5.2	2.1	−3.1	3.4	2.4	2.2	7.3	10.0	2.6
1949	−0.1	5.2	1.5	0.1	−0.6	0.3	3.0	5.6	3.0
1950	2.6	0.5	2.0	2.6	3.7	2.2	0.6	4.2	3.1
1951	5.3	−0.5	3.5	−1.3	−0.3	−0.3	7.4	11.5	3.6

Notes
C = currency in circulation outside banks
R = reserves of UK commercial banks
H = C + R
D = net deposits of UK commercial banks
M1 = currency in circulation + demand deposits of UK commercial banks
M3 = C + D
P = GDP deflator
[1] November to November, because reported bank reserves dropped when the London clearing banks gave up 'window-dressing' their published reserves in December 1946.

Sources
C and R: Calculated from data on currency in circulation in *Monthly Digest of Statistics*, 1946–52, and Capie and Webber, *A Monetary History of the United Kingdom 1870–1982*, vol. I, table II(2), cols. V and VI.
D, M1 and M3: ibid., tables I(2) and I(3).
Money GDP, real GDP, GDP deflator: Feinstein, *National Income, Expenditure and Output of the United Kingdom 1855–1965*, tables 3, 5, and 61.

order of 15 per cent for the year, not of currency in circulation. Taking into account the rate of increase in prices (the GDP deflator) *real* money balances, whether measured by M1 or M3, *grew by no less than 12 per cent*, a rate achieved in wartime only in 1941, and then only for M1 (see Table 1.4).

Table 3.8, which gives the 'proximate determinants' of the behaviour of M3 on a monthly basis for 1945–7, also indicates the peculiarities of 1946 (and 1947). The post-war decline in the demand for currency shows up as a rise in the deposit-currency ratio in 1946, although this did not continue in the first half of 1947. In the behaviour of the deposit-reserve ratio, which had been stable around an average of 11.4 in 1944 and 1945 (see Table 1.5), there are two striking features in 1946. The first is the large downward blips in July and October–November, indicating

TABLE 3.8 *The Money Stock (M3) and its Proximate Determinants, Monthly, 1945–7*

	M3, £m	H, £m	D/C	D/R
1945				
July	6,853.4	1,652.6	4.94	11.15
Aug.	6,953.7	1,670.6	4.90	11.41
Sept	7,025.1	1,697.8	4.77	11.79
Oct.	6,951.5	1,685.7	4.87	11.20
Nov.	6,892.1	1,683.9	4.70	11.64
Dec.	6,955.3	1,728.1	4.65	11.20
1946				
Jan.	6,880.7	1,740.4	4.44	11.47
Feb.	6,772.9	1,685.5	4.59	11.41
Mar.	6,847.5	1,692.7	4.62	11.53
Apr.	6,981.0	1,701.4	4.72	11.64
May	7,125.3	1,711.6	4.87	11.56
June	7,214.7	1,751.3	4.73	11.76
July	7,255.5	1,765.9	4.96	10.73
Aug.	7,400.6	1,774.7	4.84	11.81
Sept.	7,488.5	1,766.2	4.99	11.78
Oct.	7,566.7	1,778.5	5.13	11.35
Nov.	7,663.6	1,788.5	5.19	11.40
Dec.	7,945.7	1,812.2	4.83	14.06
1947				
Jan.	7,918.3	1,830.2	4.86	13.33
Feb.	7,864.1	1,800.7	4.79	14.26
Mar.	7,046.6	1,826.2	4.78	13.90
Apr.	7,947.1	1,830.5	4.79	13.65
May	8,047.4	1,826.2	4.87	14.00
June	8,026.9	1,830.4	4.83	13.98
July	8,018.4	1,850.3	4.80	13.55
Aug.	8,018.0	1,837.0	4.83	13.74
Sept.	8,083.3	1,818.0	4.95	13.99
Oct.	8,139.3	1,804.0	5.05	14.13
Nov.	8,302.8	1,792.3	5.28	14.23
Dec.	8,238.4	1,801.4	5.30	13.47

Notes

$$M3 = H \cdot \frac{D/R\,(1 + D/C)}{D/R + D/C}$$

where M3 = currency in circulation plus net deposits of UK commercial banks, C = currency in circulation outside banks, R = reserves of UK commercial banks, D = net deposits of UK commercial banks, and H = C + R

Sources
As for Table 3.7.

reserves rising temporarily faster than deposits. The second is the permanent rise to a new average level of 14.0 at the end of the year, because of the abolition of the clearing banks' practice of 'window-dressing' their published reserves by bunching their maturities of Treasury bills at halfyear ends.[94] The table reinforces the impression from Table 3.7 that the cheaper money drive in 1946 produced a sizeable acceleration of monetary growth. As the authorities bought up gilt-edged stocks from banks, other institutional investors, and individual private sector holders, so the banks' reserves and deposits increased rapidly. The banks could take up the increasing floating debt without cutting back on their advances, and the national debt was being 'unfunded' at the same time as the money supply was rapidly increasing.

Reactions and reasons

This chapter has described the financial policy pursued by Dalton in his first eighteen months at the Treasury, concentrating on the legislative steps taken to reform the financial system in line with Labour party policy and on his drive for cheaper money which was a more personal campaign. Here I mention the reactions of Dalton's former party advisers to his efforts in 1945–6 to pursue a 'socialist' monetary policy, before providing some conclusions on 'why Dalton did it'—that is, why he chose to try to push down nominal interest rates in an inflationary situation and why his official advisers in the Treasury and the Bank of England were willing to assist him in the attempt.

Dalton was understandably pleased to have brought the Bank of England into public ownership and control with practically no fuss. He and his former advisers were not concerned that the legislation did not give the government direct control over the commercial banks—not so much because they did not realize the Treasury's powers were so limited (above pp. 116–17) but because they did not in 1945 *want* to make any radical change in the relationship between the Bank and the Treasury.[95] As XYZ had pointed out during the war, wartime financial arrangements provided the possibility of increasing control over the financial system without legislation other than to formalize the existing

[94] The classic description of 'window-dressing' is in the report of the Macmillan Committee which recommended its abolition: Committee on Finance and Industry, *Report*, Cmd. 3879, 1931, paras. 368–70; see also R. S. Sayers, *Modern Banking* (1st edn., 1938), 36–40.

[95] Dalton, *High Tide and After*, ch. 6; Pimlott, *Hugh Dalton*, 457–61; above pp. 145–6.

relations between the Bank of England and the Treasury by nationalizing the Bank. Thus Dalton took no powers to compel the banks to lend to the government but relied on the continuation of Treasury deposit receipts. It was also easy for the Bank and Treasury officials to persuade Dalton not to establish a National Investment Board, since the Treasury and the Economic Section of the Cabinet Offices were already taking steps to implement the public investment recommendations of the white paper on *Employment Policy* (above). But here his former advisers were more critical.

In their criticisms of Dalton's financial policy, his former advisers pointed to both the lack of financial reform and the inflationary risks of the cheaper money policy. The major criticism, voiced by Durbin, Davenport, Piercy, and Mayhew, was that the failure to create a National Investment Board meant a failure to control private investment, especially in a slump (above). They were generally less critical of cheaper money, mainly because in 1946 they still feared deflation and unemployment more than inflation. In May 1946 Durbin circulated to his fellow members of XYZ a paper about the possibility of a US slump before the next general election. At the next meeting XYZ first had

a short discussion . . . on two points . . .
(*a*) Does a boom in stocks and shares matter?
(*b*) Where does the money come from to sustain gilt-edged prices particularly?

On (*a*) they thought a stock exchange boom did not matter much in itself; on (*b*) they rejected the suggestion made by one of their number (Stockdale) that the demand for gilt-edged securities was coming only from the banks, 'E.D. den[ying] that such inflationary circumstances had existed'. Although Durbin also denied that 'there were any signs today of an inflation', Jay at least disagreed, 'instanc[ing] the rise in prices of cars and . . . clothing'.[96]

In June XYZ discussed the Anglo-American loan agreement and

[96] 'XYZ meeting—22 May 1946', Piercy Papers 15/117, BLPES; Durbin's paper marked 'Circulated to XYZ 10.5.46' is on the same file. The members at this time were Durbin, Gaitskell, Jay, Mayhew, Piercy, Lawrie, Edmund Stockdale of Reed and Brigstock, a City firm, and A. Radomysler, a lecturer in economics at LSE. Berry, who had worked for the Allied Control Commission in Germany before joining Union Discount, had returned to Germany as Regional Commissioner at Hamburg: George and Pamela Cleaver, *The Union Discount, A Centenary Album* (London, 1985), 59; Dalton, *High Tide and After*, 97 n.

the proposed International Trade Organization, concluding that the former was 'O.K.' and the latter 'worth a trial'. The major concern was still, especially for Durbin, the prospect of an American slump, when these international agreements were '[bound to] break down'. In July Durbin still 'maintained from the ... figures that there was little evidence' of inflation. By October he and other members of XYZ were less sanguine, observing an acceleration in inflation in data on prices, the available monetary aggregates, and wage rates. They accepted that the rapid rise in bank deposits was a direct result of the cheaper money policy, but they did not all think it was 'dangerous'.[97] It is presumably at this time that Durbin warned Dalton of the inflationary risks of his policy. By the time of the 1947 balance-of-payments crisis, however, Durbin advocated only a '*mild deflationary policy* to relieve pressure on the controls', because the available data were by then suggesting a slowdown in monetary growth and in consumers' expenditure.[98]

After the alarms and diversions of 1947 (see Chapter 4) XYZ returned to review the issue of financial reform in 1948, initially under four headings: foreign exchange control, international financial machinery, control and direction of the long-term capital market, and control and direction of the short-term capital market. Apart from the operation of UK exchange control and the current roles of the IMF and the World Bank, they considered what the nationalized Bank of England was doing to control the capital market, whether the commercial banks should be subject to more control, 'what, if anything, are the National Investment Board [*sic*] and the Capital Issues Committee doing', and whether there were needed changes in the stock exchange or the discount market. To these questions drawn up by Durbin the answers of the individual members (now including another Oxford economist, later Labour MP, Tony Crosland) were by and large negative.[99] The Bank of England Act was still thought to

[97] 'XYZ meeting, 23rd October, 1946', Piercy Papers 15/64.
[98] 'Dollar crisis' and 'Summary of E. Durbin's programme', Piercy Papers 8/63.
[99] 'Survey of financial machinery', Piercy Papers 15/117. The replies are in the same file: 'XYZ, Suggested reforms in financial machinery, July 1948', 'The London and Provincial Stock Exchanges and their services', 'Control and direction of the short-term capital market', 'International financial machinery', 'Control and direction of the long-term capital market', and 'Suggested reforms in financial machinery, October 1948'. Although only one ('International financial machinery' by Crosland) is signed, several attribute views to individual members,

give the authorities adequate control over the commercial banks, so that 'there is no case for [their] nationalisation', although there was a case for an inquiry into the high costs of their operations. There was little political point in proposing reforms of the Stock Exchange or discount market, in spite of the prevalence of speculation, for there was not 'much material there for a popular cry'. There was little criticism of external arrangements, except that the remaining gaps in the exchange controls should be closed. Where there was dissatisfaction was over the control of investment: XYZ suggested that the National Investment Council should be merged with the official Investment Planning Committee and the activities of the Capital Issues Committee co-ordinated with the overall planning of investment. This would be particularly important when the inflationary transitional period was over: 'Once present restrictive controls . . . are abandoned . . . this machinery . . . will be needed as a guide and supplement to monetary and fiscal policy.'[100]

By the time XYZ put together their answers to Durbin's questionnaire, Durbin had drowned off the Cornish coast in September. XYZ did not consider current monetary policy again until 1951 (see Chapter 6).

Before returning to Dalton's reasons for his monetary policy, there is one other of his former advisers whose reaction to the policy should be mentioned. Nicholas Davenport had left—or been eased out of—XYZ by the mid-1930s but he had continued to provide Dalton with advice, especially in 1945-7 when Dalton was Chancellor and specifically on how to bring about lower long-term interest rates. He later claimed that Dalton was ignorant of the working of monetary policy and of operations in the gilt-edged market.[101] But in the spring of 1946 Dalton was quite clear on the nature of official intervention in the market—which implies that *if* he *had* been ignorant earlier he had learned much from Davenport's coaching. In January 1947 Davenport did warn

and the last summarizes the outcome of the discussions. Tony Crosland, Fellow and Lecturer in Economics at Trinity College, Oxford, had been invited to join XYZ at Dalton's instigation in January 1948: Dalton to Crosland, 20 Jan. and 5 Feb. 1948, Crosland Papers 9/1, BLPES.

[100] 'Suggested reforms in financial machinery, October 1948', 'Control and direction of the long-term capital market' and 'XYZ, Suggested reforms in financial machinery, July 1948', Piercy Papers 15/117.

[101] Above, nn. 27 and 60; *Memoirs of a City Radical*, 149, 155-7.

Dalton that the stock exchange boom was 'dangerous' and potentially inflationary because of the capital gains being made by speculative investors. But his recommendation was for the authorities to direct insurance companies to invest a certain proportion of their assets in government securities in order to maintain nominal long-term yields at 2½ per cent. He repeated this recommendation during and after the convertibility crisis, when he also argued against raising interest rates.[102]

Dalton's longer-run aim in wanting lower nominal interest rates after the war is quite clear: it was—to use, as Dalton did, Keynes's phrase—the 'euthanasia of the rentier'. As his biographer has remarked, he 'approached all economic questions . . . primarily from the point of view of distribution'; cheaper money would keep down the burden of the debt and help to reduce income inequality.[103] What needs to be considered is why he, and his official advisers, thought it was a *feasible* as well as a desirable policy in the immediate post-war inflationary situation. The first part of the answer is the influence of the Keynesian liquidity-preference theory of interest rates. When Joan Robinson had used Keynesian interest-theoretical arguments to advocate a permanent low interest-rate policy in Dalton's party committee in 1943, Dalton had noted her arguments with approval. Keynes used the same arguments two years later in the National Debt Enquiry to persuade senior Treasury officials of the practical possibility of maintaining wartime cheap money, and in 1946 he was to provide Dalton with specific recommendations on tactics for the cheaper money campaign, which also assumed the authorities could set nominal interest rates where they liked as long as they were prepared to allow the composition of the debt to reflect assetholders' preferences and expectations. Hence Dalton's cheaper money policy reflected more the Keynesian advice of Joan Robinson and of Keynes himself than the more cautious recommendations of other economists in the Labour Party in the 1940s.

[102] 'The Stock Exchange inflation and the finance of investment', T233/164; Davenport to Dalton, 8 July 1947, Piercy Papers 10/64; NIC Paper 16, 'Memorandum by Nicholas Davenport on counter-inflation Measures', 22 Sept. 1947, T233/166. On insurance company investments see also pp. 195–8 below.
[103] Dalton to Crosland, 'Keynes', 6 Feb. 1951, Crosland Papers 10/2, BLPES; Dalton, 'Note on Rate of Interest, etc.', May 1951, Dalton Papers 9/19; Pimlott, *Hugh Dalton*, 142.

The second part of the answer is the argument, again put forward by both Robinson and Keynes during the war, that since controls would be needed to restrain inflation after the war, monetary policy could be directed to targets other than combating post-war inflation. This goes some way to explain why Dalton did not fear inflation as a result of his cheaper money policy, but not all the way, for one of his objectives in 1945–7 was to prevent inflation in the post-war transitional period. He made this clear in his October 1945 and April 1946 budget speeches and saw himself as limiting income tax concessions and expenditure increases in order not to increase inflationary pressure at that time. But for anything except the short term he was more worried about unemployment than about inflation, and therefore *desired* some persistent pressure on the controls. He stated this 'doctrine' most clearly in January 1950:

Don't rely mainly on *financial* controls to prevent inflation. Always keep demand just above supply in order to hold full employment, & rely on *physical* controls—especially on total imports, capital export, building, location & essential materials—even when no longer 'in short supply'—to hold inflation. Really, therefore, though this is not the way anyone puts it—'always have a bit of inflationary pressure, but use physical controls to prevent it breaking through.[104]

In the spring and summer of 1946, when Dalton was pushing cheaper money, inflation seemed to be abating or at least not increasing, so that he believed risks could be taken with both monetary and fiscal policy. He opposed his officials' attempts then and in 1947 to reduce or at least limit the cost-of-living subsidies both because he knew that many in the Labour party would object to their removal and because he thought their maintenance helped to reduce pressure for wage increases.[105] In assuming that

[104] Dalton Diary, vol. 38, 24 Jan. 1950. Dalton was commenting on a paper by Gaitskell and Jay on 'Controls and economic policy' (below Ch. 6). At least for the transitional period Keynes may have shared this attitude: Cairncross, *Years of Recovery*, 413.

[105] His clearest statement on subsidies is his note, 'Cuts in expenditure', (Oct. 1947), T171/392; see also Dalton Diary, vol. 35, 19 and 23 Oct. 1947. Douglas Jay, by then his PPS, shared his views (see his 'Budget and food subsidies', 10 Oct. 1947, T171/392). The Finance Group of Labour MPs made their strong opposition to reductions in food subsidies clear to both Dalton and Cripps: Benson to Chancellor, 4 Nov. 1947, T171/392; Carol Johnson, 'Finance Group, Note of discussion held on 11th February [1948] on suggestions on the Budget for the consideration of the Chancellor', T171/394.

if inflation did increase in 1946 it could be kept at bay by maintaining cost-of-living subsidies and going slow with post-war tax reductions, he was almost certainly overestimating the power of controls to prevent open inflation. But from his vantage point in 1946, if the cheaper money policy were to produce inflationary pressure in *later* years, that would be a *benefit* not a defect of the policy, for there would then be less pressure from other sources and a threat of unemployment.

Finally, why were Dalton's official advisers so acquiescent? In answering this question one must distinguish, as usual, between the Treasury and the Bank.

The Treasury's reasons were in the first instance those given by Hopkins in the National Debt Enquiry report: a desire to keep down the cost of the debt for the usual budgetary reasons and the hope that cheap money would help to maintain a high level of employment in line with the commitment of the *Employment Policy* white paper. The officials shared Dalton's fears about post-transitional period unemployment (see Chapter 1). Dalton's cheaper money was only a variant of cheap money and would attain the same objectives. Keynes had different reasons from the permanent Treasury men for the advice he gave Dalton in the spring of 1946, for he did not share the general expectation of a short transitional period nor the authorities' traditional preference for long-term borrowing. Since he made clear his preference for maintaining 3 per cent as the nominal yield on long-term government debt, he appears to have simply accepted the Chancellor's determination 'to do better than 3 per cent' and advised him accordingly.

The Bank of England's role in aiding and abetting Dalton in his two bond issues was more Machiavellian. It did not agree with Dalton's or Keynes's ideas on post-war monetary policy and debt management (Chapter 1). It thought the Treasury over-optimistic in aiming to maintain wartime levels of interest rates—let alone 2½ per cent—through the transitional period. It none the less went along with the attempt to issue very long-term bonds with low coupon interest rates, because any success in this respect would assist in managing the greatly increased government debt resulting from the war. Hence the willingness, even if without enthusiasm, to take the explicitly acknowledged 'gamble' of putting Daltons on tap in the autumn of 1946, as long as they were 'irredeemable'.

One last point. After his fall from office Dalton made it clear on several occasions that his drive for cheaper money had been supported by his Bank and Treasury advisers, including Keynes. (As this chapter shows he was quite justified in making this claim.) Since Keynes died before Dalton took the last step of trying to issue irredeemables at 2½ per cent, it is often asked whether Keynes would have continued to support the cheaper money policy in the autumn of 1946. The answer is surely that he would not. Without the Bank's (or the Treasury's) obsession with funding the debt and without Dalton's enthusiasm for 2½ per cent, he would have had no reason to advise Dalton to take the gamble of issuing Daltons.

4

The End of Cheaper Money

'1947 was a pig of a year.'[1]

1947 was a year of crises. First there was the 'winter crisis' (to borrow Alex Robertson's phrase)—exceptionally severe weather and a chronic shortage of fuel which officially reached crisis proportions from 10 February to 3 March.[2] Hard on its heels came the 'summer crisis'—over the deteriorating balance of payments and then the convertibility of sterling under the terms of the Anglo-American Financial Agreement. It was not until after convertibility, introduced on 15 July, had been suspended on 20 August that Dalton would think of resuming his cheaper money campaign in order to finance the nationalization of the railways at 2½ per cent. It was too late: gilt-edged prices had been sliding for most of the year and nominal yields on long-term government bonds were back around 3 per cent. Dalton nevertheless continued to affirm his commitment to cheaper money until he resigned as Chancellor of the Exchequer on 13 November. The day before, on the way into the House of Commons to present a supplementary budget, he had inadvertently leaked some of its contents to a journalist acquaintance.[3] His successor, Sir Stafford Cripps, reluctantly agreed in December that the railway nationalization compensation stocks would be issued with a 3 per cent coupon at par. The recognition by Labour ministers of inflation as a serious problem that could not be assumed to be about to disappear with the onset of a post-war slump, had led to a major reorientation of budgetary policy in Dalton's budgets of April and November, but not in monetary policy. Meanwhile the criticisms of Dalton's monetary policy had been mounting, and

---

[1] Dalton, *High Tide and After*, 291.
[2] Alex J. Robertson, *The Bleak Midwinter 1947*, vii.
[3] On the resignation see Pimlott, *Hugh Dalton*, ch. 29.

outside and official concern with inflation increasing, while the monetary expansion was slowing down.

This chapter first outlines the balance-of-payments problem in 1947 and Dalton's two 1947 budgets, before describing the authorities' gradual abandonment of the cheaper money policy in 1947. The remainder of the chapter is concerned with the longer lasting impact of the policy and the nature of the problems it posed for the Labour governments for the rest of their period of office. (How they perceived those problems and tried to tackle them is the subject of the following two chapters.) The discussion includes consideration of the alternative hypotheses about the impact of cheaper money and its relation to the crises of 1947. It concludes by asking whether the failure of Dalton's experiment was inevitable.

Since the monetary policy decisions of 1947 were intimately connected with the finance of the nationalization programme, that subject is also discussed here, mostly in an appendix.

The balance of payments and the budget

In 1946 the state of the UK balance of payments and the domestic economy had been very encouraging. Strong export growth and domestic capital investment held out the hope of a smooth, fully employed transition to peace. Consumers' expenditure and imports of goods and services were also expanding strongly but not so strongly as to prevent a reduction in the current account deficit. In 1947, however, a 45 per cent increase in merchandise imports swamped a 23 per cent rise in merchandise exports. The trade deficit rose from £103m to £361m and the current account deficit from £230m to £381m (see Table 3.1). The current account of the rest of the sterling area was also deteriorating rapidly, and there were large capital outflows from the UK, reinforcing the effect on the reserves. In spite of the utilization of the North American loans, UK official international reserves, which had increased by £54m in 1946, fell by £152m to £512m by the end of 1947 (Table 4.1).

Consumers' expenditure on goods and services at current prices rose less in 1947 than in 1946, by 10.4 per cent compared with 13.8 per cent. Gross domestic fixed capital formation in-

TABLE 4.1 *UK Official International Reserves, End Quarters, 1945–51*

		£m[1]
End of 1945	I	603
	II	624
	III	603
	IV	610
1946	I	587
	II	567
	III	661
	IV	664
1947	I	586
	II	593
	III	587
	IV	512
1948	I	552
	II	473
	III	437
	IV	457
1949	I	471
	II	406
	III	349/509
	IV	603
1950	I	709
	II	865
	III	984
	IV	1178
1951	I	1342
	II	1381
	III	1167
	IV	834

Note
[1] Sterling equivalent of gold and convertible foreign currencies held by EEA, calculated on basis of US$4.03 = £1 up to September 1949 and US$2.80 = £1 thereafter.

Source
Bank of England, *Statistical Abstract*, No. 1 (1970), table 27.

creased by 29.6 per cent compared with 164.3 per cent in 1946 (Table 4.2). But the reduction in government current expenditure in 1947 was less than half the fall the previous year. There was also an increase of stocks of £269m compared with a decrease of £126m in 1946. Total domestic expenditure at current prices rose by 8.5 per cent in 1947 whereas it had fallen by 3.5 per cent in 1946. With this increase in absorption it is not surprising that the current account deteriorated or that inflation accelerated (see Table 4.3). Although the increase in the rate of increase of the

TABLE 4.2 *Gross Domestic Product, by Category of Expenditure, 1945–8, at Market Prices, £m*

	1945	1946	1947	1948
Consumers' expenditure	6,391	7,273	8,028	8,609
Government current expenditure on goods and services	4,190	2,282	1,735	1,756
Gross domestic fixed capital formation	350	925	1,199	1,422
Value of change in stocks	−200	−126	+269	+175
Exports of goods and services	800	1,430	1,652	2,196
Less Imports of goods and services	1,700	1,825	2,228	2,434
Gross domestic product at market prices	9,831	9,959	10,655	11,724

Source
Feinstein, *National Income, Expenditure and Output of the United Kingdom 1855–1965*, tables 2 and 3.

TABLE 4.3 *Prices and Wages, 1945–51, 1913 = 100*

	GDP deflator	Retail prices	Average weekly wage rates
1945	263.6	226	368
1946	268.6	236	383
1947	292.9	249	412
1948	314.3	268	449
1949	323.6	275	468
1950	325.7	293	490
1951	349.8	311	538

Source
Feinstein, *National Income, Expenditure and Output of the United Kingdom 1855–1965*, tables 61 and 65.

retail price index was small (4.4 per cent to 5.5 per cent), the GDP deflator rose by just over 9 per cent in 1947 compared with less than 2 per cent in 1946. In addition to rising import prices—the import price deflator calculated by Feinstein rose by 21 per cent in 1947 compared with 7 per cent in 1946—there were large increases in capital goods prices and export prices. The price deflator for capital goods increased by 4.6 per cent in 1946, 11.2 per cent in 1947, that for exports 6 per cent in 1946, 15.5 per cent in 1947.[4]

The deterioration in the terms of trade helped to increase the trade deficit in 1947. The winter crisis also contributed. In the first quarter of the year industrial output and exports were reduced by

[4] Feinstein, *National Income*, table 61; see also Cairncross, *Years of Recovery*, ch. 2, esp. 39–40.

a shortage of fuel and power and by transport difficulties—
which exacerbated the fuel shortage—in the blizzards and
freezing conditions of late January, February, and early March.
Coal had been in increasingly short supply throughout the war,
but in spite of clear warnings to ministers by Jay and Meade
among others in 1946, and increasing awareness of the problem
outside Whitehall, it did not hit the government as a crisis until
early 1947. On 7 February the Minister of Fuel and Power announced the complete suspension of the supply of electricity to
industry in the South-east, the Midlands, and the North-west,
and drastic restrictions on household and other consumers. Unemployment shot up over 2 million. In April official estimates
first put the loss of exports at £100m, and immediately revised it
to £200m, although the latter figure now appears to be an over-
estimate.[5]

No sooner had the fuel crisis officially ended than the Cabinet
was confronted with the balance-of-payments crisis. In March
the Chancellor warned his colleagues that the reserves, and the
North American credits, were now running down at an increasing rate.[6] Dalton had been preoccupied with the balance of payments since January, fighting in Cabinet to reduce first overseas
military expenditure and then, with less success, planned
imports for 1947/8. In the absence of the Lord President, Herbert
Morrison, through illness he was also chairing some of the
ministerial committees on economic matters in January–April, as
well as preparing his third budget presented on 15 April. After
the budget the inconclusive ministerial discussions went on: as
Dalton put it, 'between my third Budget on April 15th and convertibility on July 15th, we debated much but decided little'.[7]

The convertibility crisis did not creep up on the Labour government unawares, even though most ministers had been disin-
clined to heed Dalton's warnings. In February Dalton had raised
the possibility of asking the Americans to allow postponement of

[5] Robertson, *The Bleak Midwinter*, esp. chs. 1 and 7; Cairncross, *Years of Recovery*, ch. 13.

[6] CP(47)100, 'Exhaustion of the dollar credit: Memorandum by the Chancellor of the Exchequer', 21 Mar. 1947, CAB129/117, repr. in Sir Richard Clarke, *Anglo-American Economic Collaboration in War and Peace 1942–1949*, ed. Sir Alec Cairncross (Oxford, 1982), 156–7; Cabinets 30(47) and 33(47), 20 and 27 Mar. 1947, CAB128/9, PRO; Dalton, *High Tide and After*, 220–2.

[7] Ibid. 193–9, 220–2, 254–9; Pimlott, *Hugh Dalton*, 480–2; see also Cairncross, *Years of Recovery*, 131–3. On the budget see below.

convertibility but his officials and the Bank had advised against in spite of their doubts as to whether convertibility could be sustained. In the Treasury at least it was hoped that since a large amount of convertibility had already been allowed in advance of 15 July, that date would not intensify the existing reserve losses.[8] Since the US ratification of the Anglo-American financial agreement in July 1946, the UK monetary authorities had been negotiating supplementary payments agreements with several countries providing them with 'transferable accounts' from which sterling could be transferred into other countries' transferable accounts or into already convertible 'American accounts'. Of the six countries which had supplementary agreements with Britain before July 1947, at least one, Belgium, had taken advantage of this early convertibility. It was also not clear whether such transactions were a major factor in the reserve loss. The balance-of-payments position of Britain and the rest of the sterling area *vis-à-vis* the dollar area was quite worrying enough.[9] (On the sterling area balance of payments see below.)

As Professor Pressnell has pointed out, the awareness of a growing world dollar shortage and the perception that Britain's balance-of-payments problem was part of this wider development, led Treasury officials to consider seeking some relaxation of the non-discrimination obligations of the loan agreement, perhaps during the round of negotiations over an International Trade Organization currently taking place in Geneva, rather than suspending convertibility.[10] Convertibility of sterling into dollars for current transactions was worth keeping because many of the

---

[8] Ellis-Rees, 'The convertibility crisis of 1947', T276/3, PRO, part II, paras. 1–10; Fforde, *Bank*, 161–6; see also Cairncross, *Years of Recovery*, 126–30, and Dalton, *High Tide and After*, 257–8. This mixture of optimism and apprehension was also to be found outside the Treasury: see, for instance, *The Economist*, 'After July 15th', 19 July, 1947, 117–18.

[9] Above, p. 101; Ellis-Rees, 'The convertibility crisis', part II, paras. 12–47; Fforde, *Bank*, 132–40; Cairncross, *Years of Recovery*, 130–5. The six countries were Argentina, Portugal, Belgium and Luxembourg, the Netherlands, Italy, and Brazil, with net sterling liabilities prior to the agreements totalling £313m; in July a further eight countries, with sterling liabilities of £132m, concluded agreements (Clarke, *Anglo-American Economic Collaboration*, 185). For the (interesting) story of one of these agreements see Marcelo de Paiva Abreu, 'Brazil as a creditor: sterling balances, 1940–1952', *EHR*, 43 (Aug. 1990), 457–68; one point that emerges is that the Anglo-Brazilian 'agreement' of May 1947 was an informal exchange of letters.

[10] Pressnell, 'The 1947 Crisis', paper presented to the Post-war Policy Seminar, Oxford, Jan. 1989, and Pressnell to Howson, 27 Mar. 1989.

sources of UK imports desired payment in dollars or convertible currencies and sterling would be more widely held if it were convertible. Hence:

rather than operate in the field of convertibility, we should be better advised to concede our formal version of transferability (with safeguards) and to bring any bargaining pressures to bear in the form of trade discrimination.[11]

Non-discrimination, on the other hand, rendered even savage cuts in the import programme less effective than they otherwise would be in reducing pressure on Britain's reserves. The Cabinet therefore agreed the President of the Board of Trade (Cripps) should 'make every effort to secure the agreement of the United States Government to a relaxation of the non-discrimination provisions' of the loan agreement.[12]

By the time, however, that Treasury officials began to talk to their American counterparts, the possibility of a European Recovery Programme raised by US Secretary of State George Marshall in a speech at Harvard University on 5 June meant that Britain had to wait to see whether and to what extent this would take the form of American aid. Ernest Bevin, the Foreign Secretary, had seized upon Marshall's point that American aid to Europe would be conditional on European initiative to produce a joint programme and entered into discussions with the French and Soviet foreign ministers in Paris as well as with Will Clayton from the US State Department in June. The British and French foreign ministers agreed to invite other European nations to a conference in Paris in July in order to set up an organization to produce a joint European plan for submission to the Americans by 1 September. An *ad hoc* Committee on European Economic Cooperation (CEEC), the forerunner of the Organization for European Economic Cooperation (OEEC) established the following spring, was at work in Paris throughout the summer. After the CEEC's first attempts at a report had been revised to meet

[11] R. W. B. Clarke and A. T. K. Grant, 'The dollar crisis', 30 May 1947, para. 7, T236/782, PRO; see also Clarke, 'Alternative courses of action', 21 July 1947, T229/136 (of which the final version, dated 23 July, is reproduced in *Anglo-American Economic Collaboration*, 175–80).
[12] Cabinets 52(47) and 56(47), 5 and 24 June 1947, CAB128/10. On the effects of non-discrimination, which had been required since 31 December 1946, see also Clarke, 'The world dollar crisis', 14 June 1947, T236/782, paras. 1–10.

American requirements, several more months were to elapse before Congress passed the Economic Cooperation Act in the spring of 1948.[13]

The date for general convertibility under the loan agreement arrived and the dollar drain accelerated. At the end of July Dalton reported the monthly reserve losses since the beginning of the year:

		$m
January		137
February		224
March		323
April		307
May		334
June		308
July	possibly	500

This contrasted with a loss of $70m in 1946 III and $123m in 1946 IV. Seventy-three per cent of the American loan had been spent (plus 59 per cent of the Canadian); at the current rate of drawings it would be exhausted by October. Dalton sought more import cuts, but received little support; the Cabinet could not make up its mind on what to to do to halt the drain.[14] Pressnell suggests that

What pushed suspension of convertibility to the forefront in August was impending crisis at Geneva. Either the trade negotiations would break down, bringing Anglo-American tension, or, leading to the same result, Britain would approve in mid-August, on signing the GATT [General Agreement on Tariffs and Trade], constraints on discrimination which she intended, nevertheless, to break forthwith. Cripps [President of the Board of Trade] made clear that the double-dealing implied in that second possibility was unthinkable.

So it had to be suspension of convertibility,

which the Cabinet agreed to on Sunday, 17 August. It was announced after frantic Treasury discussions in Washington to

---

[13] See Bullock, *Bevin*, chs. 10 and ll, sects. 6 and 7, Milward, *Reconstruction of Western Europe*, ch. 2, and Hogan, *Marshall Plan*, ch. 1, 2, and 3, sect. 2.

[14] Cairncross, *Years of Recovery*, 135–7; GEN179/6th meeting, 29 July, and GEN179/17, 'The Dollar Position, Note by the Chancellor of the Exchequer', 29 July 1947, CAB130/19; Dalton Diary, vol. 35, 29 and 30 July 1947, repr. (with one omission relating to monetary policy) in Pimlott (ed.), *Political Diary of Hugh Dalton*, 400–5.

avoid legal default on the loan agreement, shortly after 9 p.m. on Wednesday, 20 August.[15]

The renewed inconvertibility of the pound meant that the privilege of free transferability of sterling in 'transferable accounts' to American accounts or to other countries not in the sterling or transferable account areas was withdrawn. New monetary agreements were negotiated in place of the supplementary monetary agreements. Restrictions on the use of the sterling area dollar pool were tightened instead of given up as required by the loan agreement. But sterling in a transferable account could still be paid to the accounts of other transferable account countries (though the number of these was reduced) and sterling in American accounts remained freely convertible into dollars and transferable to (though not from) transferable account countries. This limited convertibility was not strictly confined to current transactions, since the Bank of England left it to the overseas sterling area countries' exchange controls to determine whether particular payments should be permitted outside the sterling area. The payments agreements negotiated by the Bank with nonsterling area countries also did not clearly distinguish between current and capital account transfers.[16]

After the suspension Dalton finally obtained Cabinet agreement for his desired cuts in imports, especially from North America. The Cabinet also agreed to cut the investment programme in October. Dalton was strongly supported by Cripps, who was now Minister of Economic Affairs.[17] Attlee's appointment of Cripps to this new position was the unexpected outcome of a bout of political intrigue launched by Cripps and encouraged

[15] Pressnell, 'The 1947 Crisis', 12–13; Cairncross, *Years of Recovery*, 137–40; Cabinets 71, 72, and 73(47), 19, 20, and 21 Aug. 1947, CAB128/10; Pimlott (ed.), *Political Diary of Hugh Dalton*, 409–11; Fforde, *Bank*, 156–8. Pressnell's conjecture is borne out by, among other evidence, the line the government initially intended to take in Washington, namely: 'We wanted to maintain convertibility, and it was in our own and the United States interest that we should do so. But if this was to be done it was essential that there be a limit on the demands for dollars which other countries put upon the United Kingdom. . . . This would necessarily also involve elasticity in the interpretation of our non-discrimination obligations on e.g. the lines under discussion in Geneva.' (GEN179/21, 'Washington Talks', 8 Aug. 1947, para. 2(ii), CAB130/19)

[16] Cobbold to Eady, 16 Oct. 1947, T236/1667, repr. in Clarke, *Anglo-American Economic Collaboration*, 181–7; Cairncross, *Years of Recovery*, 127–8.

[17] GEN197/1, 'The 1948 Dollar Programme', 11 Oct. 1947, CAB130/27; Cabinet 81(47), 20 Oct. 1947, CAB128/10; Cairncross, *Years of Recovery*, 140–2.

by Dalton with the intention of replacing Attlee as Prime Minister. Cripps took over the responsibilities of the Lord President for economic planning, which he had previously assumed while Morrison was ill earlier in the year; he had the assistance of a Central Economic Planning Staff (CEPS), with Sir Edwin Plowden as Chief Planning Officer, which had been established in the spring.[18] He took his new role and the CEPS to the Treasury when he succeeded Dalton immediately after the latter's fourth budget in November. That post-crisis budget strengthened the deflationary measures Dalton had taken in his April budget in response to the worsening balance of payments.

As usual official preparations for the 1947 budget had begun the previous summer. On this occasion the Budget Committee had asked the Economic Section for a 'full dress paper on the control of inflation'. The Section paper, which was very much Meade's, began by estimating the magnitude of inflationary pressure in the markets for consumption and investment goods, allowing for accumulated wartime savings, pent-up demands for goods, and the current shortfall of supplies of consumer goods below normal peacetime demands. It argued for greater reliance on financial rather than physical controls for controlling inflation, keeping up those taxes which tended particularly to reduce consumption, while allowing some relaxation of import restrictions in order to increase the supply of consumer goods. The cost-of-living subsidies should be phased out; they were increasingly expensive and a rise in retail prices would help to reduce the inflationary gap in consumption. The impact could be softened by introducing a new and more realistic cost-of-living index (which was already under consideration in the Ministry of Labour). Finally, given the white paper on *Employment Policy*,

It is presumably the accepted doctrine that the maintenance of total demand will require Budget deficits in certain years, but that every attempt will be made to offset this as far as possible by Budget

---

[18] On the political developments see Dalton, *High Tide and After*, ch. 29, Morgan, *Labour in Power*, 350–6, and Pimlott, *Hugh Dalton*, 500–19; on the establishment and role of CEPS see Edwin Plowden, *An Industrialist in the Treasury, The Post-War Years* (London, 1987), esp. chs. 2 and 3. Cripps announced the CEPS in March in the House of Commons debate on the *Economic Survey for 1947* (which Cripps had helped to draft): *House of Commons Debates*, vol. 434, 10 Mar. 1947, cols. 69–71.

surpluses in good years. If this principle is adopted, there can be no doubt that next year is a year when, if ever, there should be a Budget surplus,

because of the severe inflationary pressure.[19]

The other members of the Budget Committee were in 'general agreement' with Meade's suggestions, though they thought the cost-of-living subsidies should 'gradually and quietly be tapered off with as little noise as possible'. The Chancellor, at first apparently 'clearly very attracted by the general lines' of the paper, was opposed to cutting the subsidies because it would be politically unpopular and could increase pressure for wage increases.[20] In his budget speech he committed the government to maintaining the existing policy at least until the introduction of the new cost-of-living index, when 'we shall have to devise . . . a modified policy, which will no longer aim at an absolute stability . . . but will still continue, at a lower cost, to exercise a stabilising influence upon the index'.[21] Later in the year, after the convertibility crisis, he reluctantly agreed to a ceiling on the cost of food subsidies.

In his April 1947 budget Dalton was concerned again with inflation, which he had thought to be abating a year earlier. He told the Commons: 'deflation is no longer the immediate danger today. The immediate danger is of an inflation going beyond bounds, and breaking through the various controls we have set up.' With a high level of employment and with prices rising 'faster than we like', 'I submit . . . that there can be no doubt that . . . this is a good year for a good surplus.' The warnings from his officials and the Economic Section, which Meade had repeated more forcefully after the preparation of the draft Economic Survey for 1947, had not been without effect. In August 1946 Dalton had been wanting a balanced budget for 1947/8; at the end

[19] Meade, *Cabinet Office Diary*, 272, 281; Meade, 'Control of inflation', (June 1946), T171/389, PRO, reprinted in his *Collected Papers*, vol. 1, ch. 17. The existing cost-of-living index, based on the consumption patterns of working-class households in 1904, gave undue weight to items such as bread and sugar. An advisory committee reported in March 1947 in favour of a new index, which was introduced in the summer.

[20] Meade, *Cabinet Office Diary*, 292–3; Note by Trend, n.d. but July 1946, T171/389. Cairncross and Watts (*Economic Section*, 240–2) discuss Meade's memorandum at some length but surprisingly claim that there is 'no indication' of how the paper was received by the Budget Committee.

[21] *House of Commons Debates*, vol. 436, 15 Apr. 1947, col. 46.

of the year he decided he wanted a small surplus, to be achieved mainly by reductions in expenditure. A few income tax concessions were to be covered by tax increases elsewhere.[22] The size of the desired surplus increased in the first quarter of 1947, as a result of the fuel crisis, the increasing current account deficit, and rising world prices, and the estimated surplus for 1947/8 given in the budget speech was £270m. The realized surplus was increased to £636m. by the November budget (see Table 3.3).

Dalton's own ideas on the tax changes he wanted in his budget included increases in profits taxation, in stamp duties on financial transactions, and in death duties. Meade suggested profits taxation should differentiate between distributed and undistributed profits, so as to be able to tax the former more heavily in times of inflationary pressure and vice versa in deflationary years. The budget increased the tax on distributed profits to 12½ per cent while leaving the rate on retained profits at 5 per cent.[23] When Dalton decided over Christmas 1946 on a budget surplus, he also told his private secretary, Burke Trend, that 'the Budget should be, in the main, a direct taxation Budget and should not deal very much with indirect taxation'. In the budget there was no change in the standard rate of income tax, an increase in the earned income allowance to its 1940 level, and an increase in children's allowance to the pre-war level. There were a few reductions in purchase tax, which need not be detailed here. As a result of the fuel crisis Dalton also reimposed

---

[22] *House of Commons Debates*, vol. 436, col. 54; Meade, 'The Economic Survey for 1947 and the Budget for 1947/48', undated but late Nov. 1946, T171/389; Meade, *Cabinet Office Diary*, 311; Trend to Bridges, 6 Jan. 1947, T171/389. In his memorandum Meade estimated the excess of consumption demand over resources available for consumption in 1947 at some £560m; Cairncross and Watts give the date of this paper as January 1947 (*Economic Section*, 239 n. and 242) but it was on the agenda for the meeting of the Budget Committee on 4 December 1946 (Bridges, 'Budget Committee', 4 Dec. 1946, T171/391). Meade put in another memorandum on similar lines after the publication of the *Economic Survey for 1947*, which, as Cairncross and Watts note (p. 239), was too late to affect decisions already made: Meade, 'The Economic Crisis and the Budget for 1947/48', Gilbert to Bridges and Bridges to Trend, 14 Mar., and note by Dalton, 16 Mar. 1947, T171/389.

[23] Meade, *Cabinet Office Diary*, 312; Bridges, 'Budget Committee', 15 Nov. and 4 Dec. 1946, and subsequent memoranda on T171/391, section 1; Trend to Bridges, 'Budget', 31 Oct. 1946, and subsequent memoranda on T171/391, section 2; Note by Dalton, 11 Sept. 1946, and subsequent memoranda on T171/391, sect. 3. Dalton doubled a number of the stamp duties in the budget. On death duties see p. 109 above.

purchase tax on domestic cooking and heating appliances which he had exempted eighteen months previously in his first budget.[24]

Two last items in the April 1947 budget merit a mention. As in 1946 Dalton felt obliged for political reasons to repay some post-war credits but was restrained from doing any more than offering to repay those of old-age pensioners for the last two years of the war. He also dramatically doubled the customs duties on tobacco, not for the sake of the Exchequer or the health of the nation but for the balance of payments, by reducing the amount of dollars spent on importing American tobacco. The 'final picture' which he wished to leave at the end of his three-hour long speech was that:

Our internal financial position is much better, and our external trading deficit is a good deal worse than it would have been reasonable to anticipate two years ago. In this Budget, I have proposed measures which, I hope, will strengthen both the internal and the external position. If these measures prove not sufficient, stronger and more drastic measures will have to follow, and His Majesty's Government will take the responsibility for proposing these in due course.[25]

The 'stronger and more drastic measures' were taken in the supplementary budget Dalton presented on 12 November. Dalton later thought he should have gone for a larger surplus in April, 'particularly as some of my tax increases—on legacies, successions and stamps—were taxes on capital, good for distribution but not for closing the inflationary gap'.[26] During the convertibility crisis he began to contemplate an autumn budget which would close the gap by cutting expenditure and by raising taxes, other than income tax, in simple ways.

Its sole purpose, if it were decided to have one, would be to lessen the inflationary pressure by 'mopping up' some purchasing power and at the same time to illustrate the Government's intention that there must be 'equality of sacrifice' as between different sections of the community.

His ideas for tax increases were increasing the tax on distributed profits and purchase tax by doubling the rates. He also wondered whether to raise tobacco duty again.[27] The Economic Section esti-

[24] Trend to Bridges, 'Budget', 6 Jan. 1947, and subsequent memoranda on T171/389, sect. 5; *House of Commons Debates*, vol. 436, cols. 71–5, 85–7.

[25] *House of Commons Debates*, vol. 436, cols. 76–7, 87–90.

[26] *Public Finance*, 1954 edn., 243.

[27] Dalton to Bridges, 11 Aug., and Trend to Bridges, 8 Sept. 1947, T171/392, PRO.

mated the inflationary gap very approximately at £400m for calendar 1948. Although Dalton found the Section paper 'very inconclusive and admittedly sketchy', he agreed with its 'wise last sentence' which pointed out that 'the disadvantages attendant on assuming too large a gap are much less than those, so much in evidence now, of planning for one which turns out to be too small'. The estimate of the gap was raised to £600–650m a couple of weeks later, when the senior Treasury officials unsuccessfully urged a 50 per cent cut in the cost-of-living subsidies. By late October they were trying only for a commitment to a £300m ceiling on the cost of the subsidies; in finally agreeing to a ceiling Dalton insisted that it be the £392m estimated for 1947/8 at the beginning of the financial year.[28]

On the other measures in the budget, which Dalton discussed with the other 'Big Five' ministers (Attlee, Morrison, Bevin, and Cripps), it was agreed to double the rates of profits tax on both distributed and undistributed profits, and to raise purchase tax rates across the board. The duties on tobacco and on wine and spirits were also to be increased, but *not* that on beer. The increase in tobacco duty was abandoned, however, because the previous increase was not having much effect in saving dollars, and the beer duty raised instead by the equivalent of 1*d*. a pint. There was also to be a betting duty on some forms of betting which it was easy to tax. The tax changes were estimated to bring in an extra £48m in the rest of 1947/8 and £208m in a full financial year.[29]

The abandonment of cheaper money

In his April 1947 budget speech Dalton took the opportunity to defend his cheaper money policy, which had been under threat since the beginning of the year.[30] The 'peak' of cheaper money had been reached on 26 November 1946, when 2½% Consols stood at par, during the tap issue of 2½% Treasury Stock 1975 or

[28] 'The Inflationary Pressure', 1 Sept., Note by Dalton, 6 Sept., Bridges, 'Autumn Budget', 23 Sept. and 22 Oct. 1947, T171/392; *House of Commons Debates*, vol. 444, 12 Nov. 1947, 395-7. The long run of official memoranda on the question of the subsidies is in T171/392, sect. 2.

[29] Trend to Bridges, 'Budget', 20 Oct. 1947, and 'Supplementary Budget, 1947', T171/392: *House of Commons Debates*, vol. 444, 12 Nov. 1947, col, 407.

[30] *House of Commons Debates*, vol. 436, 60-6. He later admitted: 'my defence was long and at times rhetorical and even a bit shrill' (*High Tide and After*, 230).

after. After the issue closed on 11 January the authorities stopped intervening in the gilts market in support of cheaper money (Chapter 3). Without support the newly issued Daltons held their price for only a matter of days, falling below par by 15 January. As the 'winter crisis' gathered momentum, stock exchange prices including government bonds inevitably fell, the 'irredeemables' most of all. By mid-March Daltons were down to 95 (yielding 2.63 per cent) in spite of Dalton's statement in the Commons debate on the economy that he still regarded 2½ per cent as 'the appropriate long-term rate, in present conditions, for British Government borrowing'. 'Plainly', wrote one financial commentator, 'the Chancellor's bull tactics in the market have lost a good deal of their old magic.'[31]

There was some recovery in gilt-edged prices, including the irredeemables, after the budget.[32] It did not last beyond the middle of May (when Daltons were just over 97). By the middle of June gilt-edged prices were lower than they had been in May 1946 before the first of Dalton's two 'cheaper money' long-term bond issues. *The Economist* did not fail to point out the inconsistency between Dalton's stated intention to persevere with cheaper money and the facts of the gilt-edged market, including the lack of support from the NDC during and since the fuel crisis.[33] In the first two weeks of convertibility gilts prices fell precipitously, with Daltons reaching a yield of 3 per cent on 31 July, and continued to fall in the remaining three weeks of convertibility in spite of some intervention by the Bank (see below).

During the summer crisis the possibility of a deliberate change in monetary policy was discussed, briefly and very quietly, by Bank of England and Treasury officials, as something which (along with devaluation or depreciation of the pound) might have to happen if Britain did not receive Marshall Aid. Even then

---

[31] *House of Commons Debates*, vol. 434, 10 Mar. 1947, col. 1076; *The Economist*, 2 March 1947, 428.

[32] *The Economist* grudgingly admitted the budget was 'acceptable'; with respect to monetary policy, however, 'He said nothing to defend himself against the charge of having pursued his policy at the cost of a large-scale creation of liquid credit, contrary to the debt-funding tactics that are appropriate to a dis-inflationary policy.' (ibid. 19 April 1947, 569–70).

[33] 'Cheap money now', 5 July 1947, 25–6: see also 21 June 1947, 993.

Hopkins thought that 'significant changes in interest rates were ruled out by the size of the National Debt' and that the authorities would have to rely on a budget surplus and capital controls to fight inflation. Cobbold, on the other hand, thought that in that situation 'the whole question of Government credit, issue of nationalisation stocks, etc. [would] need re-examination'.[34] More serious discussion of monetary policy, involving the Chancellor, took place in the autumn when Dalton was preparing his supplementary budget.

The government had not had to make any new bond issues to the market after Daltons in 1947. There was a new issue of savings certificates in April (with a yield of a little over 2½ per cent if held to maturity), but there were no maturing government stocks and the budget was moving into surplus from the first quarter of 1947. Although the above-the-line surplus realized in the first half of 1947 becomes a net overall deficit when various adjustments (for below-the-line expenditure etc.) are made, this deficit was small in 1947 I and II (£23m and £89m). It was also more than covered by external financing in those quarters and in 1947 III (see Table 3.5), so that the domestic borrowing requirement was negative in 1947 I (the last, tax-gathering quarter of the 1946/7 financial year) and remained negative for the next six months. In spite of a much reduced inflow of small savings, a reduction in the amount of the gilt-edged debt held by the private sector could be accompanied by a reduction in the floating debt in 1947 I–III, and only a small increase in the latter in 1947 IV. Further, because of the lack of official intervention, the reduction in market holdings of gilt-edged debt in the first half of 1947 was not matched by an increase in official holdings of such debt (see below). 1948, however, was to be 'a year of unexampled activity in the gilt-edged market' in spite of the budget surplus. The railways were to be nationalized on 1 January, and on that day the government would have to issue £1,000m government-guaranteed stock in compensation. Further nationalization compensation issues amounting to some £600m would probably have to be made later in the year. The authorities would also have to convert £300m 3% Conversion Loan 1948/53 on its earliest redemption date, plus some £150m

---

[34] Mynors, 'Meeting at the Treasury 2nd July 1947', 3 July, and Cobbold to Governor, 23 July 1947, G1/101, BOE; see also Fforde, *Bank*, 150–1.

government-guaranteed stocks, unless they wished to admit long-term interest rates had returned to 3 per cent.[35]

Decisions on the form of the compensation to be paid for transport nationalization in the winter of 1946–7 had determined the nature of the debt management problem the authorities faced at the end of 1947. The crucial decisions were that compensation would be based on the market value of the railway companies' shares, for which an equivalent amount of government-guaranteed stock would be issued, and that there would be a single large issue of transport stock, to be made on one date. Despite criticism the same principles of compensation were followed in the electricity, gas, and iron and steel nationalizations in 1948, 1949, and 1951 (see Appendix). The major criticism of the transport scheme was that the former shareholders would suffer a considerable drop in income given the low level of gilt-edged interest rates under cheaper money. In order to ensure that the transport stock would carry a 2½ per cent coupon, Dalton himself proposed that the railway shares could be valued for compensation purposes as the average of either their mid-monthly Stock Exchange quotations for February–July 1945 or their daily quotations for 1–8 November 1946. This did not prevent criticism of the scheme, or enable the stock to be issued at 2½ per cent, but it increased the cost of nationalization. Dalton also committed the authorities to some extent on the maturity of the transport stock, by promising in Parliamentary debate on the Transport Bill that it would be a dated stock redeemable 'within the century'.[36]

When Dalton was contemplating an autumn budget, he asked his officials for advice on 'what steps we should be taking between now [September] and next January to get the market adapted' for the issue of the transport stock. He was 'determined that this shall be done by a 2½ per cent issue at par—though he does not mind how short dated the stock has to be, even down to 10 years, to achieve this object'. In his speech at the annual

---

[35] Compton, 'The 1948 gilt-edged market', 17 Sept. 1947, T233/143, PRO. In the event two of the nationalization issues were delayed (see Appendix), and the maturing stocks went unconverted (below).

[36] Chester, *Nationalisation*, ch. III, esp. 261–74; *The Economist*, 'Nationalisation on the Cheap', 23 Nov. 1946, 836–8, and 'Transport Questions Unanswered', 21 Dec. 1946, 1007–8; see also 'The Doctor's Dilemma', *The Economist*, 18 Oct. 1947, 649–50. On the criticism see also J. E. Allen, 'Railway Compensation Examined', *EJ* 58 (Mar. 1948), 125–8.

Mansion House dinner in October he implied that he still aiming for 2½ per cent for the transport issue.[37] The official Treasury advice was straightforward:

We can do one or more of three things: (*a*) prepare the market between now and January 1st by official buying of gilt-edged, (*b*) adjust the issue terms of Transport Stock on January 1st, so as to secure the highest possible issue price, and (*c*) support the market after the January 1st issue so as to maintain Government credit and keep the way clear for the 3% Conversion, Electricity and other operations that have to take place later in the year. . . . (*a*) and (*b*) should be avoided, and . . . the general plan of campaign should be to concentrate on (*c*), but judiciously and not . . . to the point of aggravating the inflationary pressure.

On (*a*) Edmund Compton (undersecretary) pointed out that the current income of the National Debt Commissioners' funds was low and that the Issue Department was already holding large amounts of 3% Conversion Loan, Daltons, and 1¾% Exchequer Bonds. The Issue Department could intervene on a large scale by using its floating debt holdings but market Treasury bills or TDRs would increase. Then 'bank deposits will go up, and everyone is on the look out for this as a statistical red light and warning that an inflationary situation is developing'. The potential inflation would become actual if the holders of the increased bank deposits bought goods instead of reinvesting in gilt-edged securities. Therefore the resources should be saved for market support *after* 1 January, if necessary on a considerable scale, but 'the limit to such action should be, not the cash in the Issue Department but the movement of bank deposits resulting from such action'. As for (*b*), 'with the present market, we could not justify 2½% at par for any stock unless it had a final maturity of 4.5 years'. Such a short stock would not be held by private investors, who would want to sell it immediately, and the Transport Commission would be saddled with short-term borrowing.[38]

Dalton had specially asked for Sir Richard Hopkins's views. Hopkins entirely agreed with Compton that 'it would be quite disastrous from the point of view of confidence, as well as very bad finance, to issue a short Nationalisation Stock'. He took a different stand on intervention, for he thought that to issue

[37] Trend, 'Budget', 8 Sept. 1947, T171/392, PRO; 'The Doctor's Dilemma', *The Economist*, 18 Oct. 1947, 649–50.
[38] Compton, 'The 1948 gilt-edged market', 17 Sept. 1947, T233/143, PRO.

nationalization stocks at 3 per cent 'would be a confession of failure of a striking part of Government policy'. Hence the authorities needed 'a forthright [surplus] Budget, followed by resolute action' in the form of large-scale intervention to bring 2½ per cent Savings Bonds back to par in order to permit a 20–25 year 2½ per cent transport stock, issued at a discount if necessary. He warned that the policy was risky, especially 'if pursued with a faint heart'. Sir Wilfrid Eady, on the other hand, was pessimistic, believing that intervention would fail unless the market had started moving upwards of its own accord: 'All very orthodox and timid, no doubt, but the conclusion is to wait and see.'[39]

Dalton later recorded that he 'had been too tired that summer and autumn to fight the Bank in favour of intervention [and] had, in fact given up that ghost, for the time being at any rate'. (As his biographer reports, he was exhausted almost to the point of collapse.) But he was not easily defeated: if the usual method of support was not practicable, why not assist the market by either switching the £35m 1¾% Exchequer Bonds 1950 held by the National Land Fund into longer-term securities or issuing a 2½ per cent medium or long-term security acceptable (at par) in payment for death duties, perhaps in conversion of 3% Conversion 1948/53? His unenthusiastic officials discussed both suggestions with the Bank who advised that neither could have much beneficent effect on the gilt-edged market and might make things worse.[40] In discussions with the Governors in November Dalton raised the idea of a 'death duty stock' again, when he suggested he could announce in his forthcoming budget the repayment of 3% Conversion Loan on 1 March 1948 and a new tap issue. Catto replied that 'to open a 2½% "Death Duty" tap at this moment would be interpreted as a sign of weakness rather than of strength'. He suggested instead an offer of conversion into an outstanding stock, 2½% Funding Loan 1956/61. Dalton first agreed and then

[39] Hopkins to Bridges, 'The gilt-edged market', Note by Hopkins, 25 Sept., Eady to Bridges, 30 Sept. 1947, T233/143. Hopkins appended the passage from the *General Theory* that he had quoted in the report of the National Debt Enquiry (quoted in ch. 1 above).

[40] Dalton Diary, vol. 38, 20 Oct. 1950, BLPES; Pimlott, *Hugh Dalton*, 508–9, 516, 518–19; Trend to Bridges, 'Cheap money', 21 Oct., Bamford to Eady and Bridges, 'Cheap money', 22 Oct., Bridges to Trend, 'Transport stock and cheap money', 29 Oct. 1947, T233/143, PRO; Peppiatt to Cobbold and Niemeyer, 'Gilt-edged market', 22 Oct., and Cobbold, 'Extract from Note of a meeting at 11 Downing Street', 4 Nov. 1947, C40/407, BOE.

changed his mind, saying in his budget speech only that he would shortly make an announcement about the 3% Conversion Loan. After the budget the market deteriorated and the Bank advised the Treasury not to attempt a conversion. The loan was repaid on 1 March 1948.[41]

After Dalton resigned on 13 November, he offered his successor advice on the terms of the transport stock. It was, of course, to 'stand and fight, on the 2½ per cent line'—either by issuing a long-term stock at a discount or by offering a mixture of short- and long-term stock to the railway shareholders.[42] When Cripps was briefed on the issue, the Governor 'stated emphatically that, as he had warned Mr Dalton on several occasions, a long 2½% stock was not at present in the picture'. Since 'it was felt that there was strong political objection to making a 3% issue ... because it would seem a complete reversal of the Government's policy about interest rates', it was 'concluded that the objective to hope and aim for was a 2¾% stock with the latest possible date'.[43]

On 3 December the Bank reported the view of the Government Broker that a 2¾ per cent stock at par could not be issued for more than thirteen years. Market intervention before 1 January was 'out of the question. They cannot intervene on a falling market'. The Bank also successfully argued against issuing at a discount, because it would be 'a great sign of weakness' and administratively inconvenient. Cripps continued to resist 3 per cent for transport stock, deferring his provisional decision on the terms until 19 December, when he ruefully 'noted that as the result of decisions already taken ... the scope of the decisions remaining was very much narrowed', relating only to the details of the maturity of a 3 per cent long-term stock. 3% British Transport Guaranteed Stock 1978/88 (which the market nicknamed 'Long Transport') was issued on 1 January 1948 in the biggest operation

[41] Trend, 'Cheap money', 4 Nov. 1947, T233/143; Peppiatt to Governors, '3% Conversion Stock 1948/53', 7 Nov., Note by Peppiatt, 11 Nov., and Cobbold to Governor, 21, 25, and 27 Nov. 1947, C40/476; *House of Commons Debates*, vol. 444, 12 Nov. 1947, cols. 392–3.

[42] This suggestion came from Nicholas Davenport: see his 'Notes on the gilt-edged market', 28 Nov. 1947, Dalton Papers 9/3, BLPES. Dalton also made suggestions to Cripps for the 1948 budget and on the next Governor of the Bank: *High Tide and After*, 287–91.

[43] Cobbold to Governor, 25 Nov. 1947, C40/476, BOE; see also Bamford to Eady, 1 Dec. 1947, T233/143.

in the gilt-edged market since the conversion of 5% War Loan in 1932.[44]

A logical consequence of the admission that the rate for long-term government borrowing was now back to 3 per cent was to raise the rate at which local authorities could borrow from the central government. Dalton had reduced the rate for long-term loans to 2½ per cent in May 1946. This had been out of the line with the market since the summer of 1947, but at that time 'hope had not been abandoned of improving Government credit up to or near 2½%'. (At the same time the Treasury had closed the market to local authority bond issues until after the transport operation.) When agreeing to 3 per cent for the transport stock on 19 December Cripps agreed to the raising of the local authority long-term (over 15 years) borrowing rate to 3 per cent, which was announced a few days after the announcement of the terms of Long Transport.[45]

After their absence from the gilt-edged market in the first half of 1947, the authorities had resumed intervention in the second half of the year. In accordance with their usual practice when faced with forthcoming maturities they began buying up 3% Conversion Loan in the third quarter of 1947. The Issue Department accumulated over £100m by the end of the year, while NDC holdings rose from £10m in March to £25m by the end of October. The Issue Department had also bought some 2½% Savings Bonds and 2½% National War Bonds with 1949 and early 1950s maturities in late July and early August 1947 during the convertibility crisis.[46] In January 1948, following the issue of the transport stock, the authorities bought a range of securities, including 3% Conversion Loan,

---

[44] Bamford, 'Note of a discussion with the Bank on Cheap Money and Transport Stock on Wednesday, 3rd December', 5 Dec. 1947, T233/143; 'Transport Stock, Discussion on 3rd December', and 'Transport Stock, Note of a discussion in the Chancellor of the Exchequer's room No. 11 Downing Street on 19th December, 1947', T233/337, PRO. On the Bank's attitude to intervention in 1947 see also Fforde, *Bank*, 355–7.

[45] Compton, 'Government credit and terms of Exchequer borrowing', 15 Dec. 1947, T233/142; 'Transport Stock: Note of a discussion ... on 19th December 1947', T233/337, PRO; Cobbold to Governor, 24 and 29 Dec., and Bamford to Cobbold, 'Transport Stock', 29 Dec. 1947, C40/807, BOE; *The Economist*, 10 Jan. 1948, 66–7.

[46] Compton, 'Investments held by (a) Issue Department (b) N.D.C. Funds', 2 Dec. 1947, T233/143; Pember & Boyle, *British Government Securities in the Twentieth Century*, 511; Dalton Diary, vol. 35, 29 July 1947; see also Brian Tew, 'A First Look at Exchequer Financing under the Labour Governments', 24 Oct. 1960, 8.

with the triple objectives of (i) supporting Transport Stock; (ii) adding to our collection of 3% Conversion Loan against redemption on 1st March; and (iii) feeding the market with the National War Bonds and the Exchequer Bonds that the market needs as shorts.

The market had regarded the terms of Long Transport as somewhat ungenerous and the new stock had opened at a discount on 2 January. On that first day of trading its price rose from 97 to 98 where it remained for most of the rest of the month, reflecting, as Compton described it, 'steady but by no means spectacular market support by the authorities' in the form of NDC purchases of £22m Transport Stock.[47]

In February the Issue Department began at last to sell off its £95m holdings of Daltons, which it continued to do for the rest of the year, thus reverting to the conventional practice of selling off securities as demand arose while buying up those nearing maturity. In February the authorities also considered resuming the issue of terminable annuities to the NDC to absorb large inflows of savings bank deposits. As Pinsent, Controller of the National Debt Office, later described it, 'we were hardly able to invest our money as fast as it came in, in spite of the fact that we were actively supporting the new Transport issue'. In March, however, the Government Broker, Sir Edward Cripps, asked for assistance in supporting the market in advance of the electricity nationalization issue on 1 April. To quote Pinsent again,

On March 16th . . . [he] appealed for help, and I arranged by telephone with you [Compton], the Bank, and the Ministry of National Insurance, to switch all Unemployment Fund purchases from Treasury '75s to Transport Stock, and to put £5m at . . . [his] disposal from Savings Banks Funds for the purchase of 3% Savings Bonds '65-75. Not for the first time we found ourselves much in the position of the Red Queen. Cripps had in turn to support 3% Savings Bonds '60-70, and the pace went faster and faster until we had actually put £m41 into the two series of Savings Bonds and into Transport Stock, up to and including yesterday [1 April]. Today we have had to call a halt'

because the savings banks funds' resources were exhausted. There was therefore no need for the annuity to which the Chan-

[47] Compton to Bamford, 29 Jan. 1948, T233/1073; 'British Transport Stock', *The Economist*, 3 Jan. 1948, 25–6; London and Cambridge Economic Service, *Bulletin*, 18 Feb. 1948, 17–18; 'Operation Transport, 4. First Month', in Pember and Boyle, *British Government Securities in the Twentieth Century (First Supplement, March 1948)*.

cellor had agreed in principle in February.[48] In addition to such flurries of support for nationalization issues the NDC also supported local authority issues, which were resumed with the assistance of the 'public stag' in May 1948. The Bank of England would have preferred a return to market underwriting, but underwriting by the NDC was cheaper for the local authorities.[49]

As a result of the authorities' intervention in late 1947 and early 1948 official holdings of marketable government and government-guaranteed securities increased by £187m in the second half of 1947, most of the increase being 3% Conversion Loan, fell by £54m in 1948 I when Conversion Loan was redeemed and rose by £31m in 1948 II. Over the 1947/8 financial year such holdings rose by £155m compared with £104m in 1946/7. Intervention in 1947/8 was thus sizeable in total even if it did not in any quarter reach the heights of 1946/7.[50] Since it did not involve such large purchases of *long-term* securities as in 1946/7 it did not significantly alter the maturity composition of private sector holdings of government debt (see Table 3.6). The monetary consequences of intervention were also lessened by the reduction of market floating debt of £50m compared with the £320m rise in 1946/7. The adjusted deficit of 1947/8 was much more than covered by external financing (a total of £902m compared with a net overall deficit of £359m); the resulting negative domestic borrowing requirement permitted a reduction of both gilt-edged and floating debt in the hands of the public even while inflows of small savings were beginning to be replaced by outflows (Table 3.5).

The behaviour of the monetary aggregates was very different in 1947 from what it had been in 1946 (see Tables 3.7 and 3.8). The monetary base essentially did not grow at all over 1947 (compared with 6 per cent in 1946). With the deposit-currency ratio con-

[48] Pinsent to Compton, 2 Apr., and Compton to Bamford, 'Investment of N.D.C. cash in annuities', 18 Feb. 1948, T233/1073; Peppiatt to Governors, 18 Mar. 1948, C40/438; and Compton, 'Investment of savings bank funds in an Exchequer annuity', 24 Mar. 1948, T233/435. The next annuity issue was made in December: see ch. 5.

[49] Bamford, 'Local authority conversions', 26 Apr., and 'Local authority conversions: N.D.C. underwriting', 3 May, and Notes by Cripps, 27 Apr. and 3 May 1948, T233/665.

[50] 'Exchequer financing and national debt, 1945–51', *Economic Trends*, Dec. 1961, table 1; Tew, 'A second look at Exchequer financing under the Labour governments', 24 Nov. 1960, table 1.

tinuing to rise from its wartime low levels and the deposit-reserve ratio steady about 14.0, bank deposits grew by 4.8 per cent (15.2 per cent in 1946), M1 by 1.4 per cent (15.3 per cent), and M3 by 4.9 per cent (14.2 per cent). *Real* money balances *fell* by 6.6 per cent for M1 and 4.76 per cent for M3. Although the monetary base resumed its growth in 1948, the rates of monetary growth in 1947 were to be typical of the next four years.

The impact of cheaper money

Almost all the literature on Dalton's monetary policy implies that the impact of his 'cheaper money' experiment was limited: widespread direct controls prevented its having much effect and the policy was short-lived and did not survive the winter and summer crises of 1947. It is true the policy was short-lived; indeed, as the last section shows, it had effectively been abandoned *before* the winter crisis. The purpose of this section is to suggest that its effects were not limited or short-lived but serious and persistent, essentially because it exacerbated the 'monetary overhang' from the war.

The simplest measure of the monetary overhang is provided by the ratios of the money stock (M1 or M3) to national income. Table 4.4 gives annual figures for three decades. These show clearly both the wartime and Daltonian increase in this measure of private sector liquidity to historically very high levels, which peaked at 57 per cent (M1) and 79 per cent (M3) in 1946, and the gradual return to pre-war levels in the remaining years of the Attlee goverments.

Most of the well-known judgements on Dalton's monetary policy were made at a time when economists generally did not rate the power of monetary policy highly. H. D. Henderson and R. F. Harrod, for instance, in their contemporary attacks on the inflationary policies of the Labour government, thought the contribution of cheaper money to the inflation had been 'a very minor factor . . . so unimportant relatively to other factors as to be scarcely worth considering' (Henderson) and 'not . . . having any immediate bearing, if any bearing at all, on the problem of inflation' (Harrod). Henderson did 'not believe that a single industrialist or trader would be deterred . . . from a single act of real

TABLE 4.4 *Money to Income Ratios, Annual, 1930–59*

	M1/Y	M3/Y
1930	0.30	0.54
1931	0.30	0.56
1932	0.33	0.63
1933	0.34	0.63
1934	0.34	0.61
1935	0.35	0.61
1936	0.37	0.63
1937	0.35	0.60
1938	0.33	0.54
1939	0.34	0.55
1940	0.33	0.49
1941	0.35	0.51
1942	0.37	0.52
1943	0.39	0.55
1944	0.44	0.62
1945	0.50	0.70
1946	0.57	0.79
1947	0.53	0.76
1948	0.49	0.70
1949	0.47	0.67
1950	0.46	0.65
1951	0.41	0.58
1952	0.38	0.55
1953	0.36	0.54
1954	0.36	0.53
1955	0.33	0.48
1956	0.31	0.45
1957	0.29	0.44
1958	0.28	0.43
1959	0.28	0.43

Sources
M1 and M3: Capie and Webber, *A Monetary History of the United Kingdom,
Volume I: Data, Sources, Methods*, tables I(2) and I(3).
Y (GNP at market prices): Feinstein, *National Income, Expenditure and Output of
the United Kingdom 1855–1965*, table 3.

investment' or that savings would be significantly increased by
higher interest rates, even though aggregate investment was
excessive in relation to current savings. Harrod assumed the
mantle of Keynes to claim that 'in circumstances such as the
present the undoctored functioning of the capital market would
not secure us a high enough rate of interest to prevent inflationary pressure', so that we might as well enjoy the budgetary

benefits of low interest rates.[51] There were exceptions, notably Meade who did not share the contemporary belief in low interest-elasticity of investment (see Chapter 1). In mid–1946 he noted:

Every industry is going round making plans for investment on the assumption that 3 per cent or even 2½ per cent represents the true 'opportunity cost' for capital. Then a little man in a bowler hat with an application form for a building licence to be filled in in triplicate runs round to start the process of scaling all the demands down—not in the economic way of asking everyone to do their calculations on a 10 per cent basis but on some mystical principle of social priorities.

After he left government service he argued cogently for higher interest rates in 1948 to 'ration' investment projects.[52] Lionel Robbins, back at LSE since January 1946, was also not inclined to acquit Dalton of the charge of exacerbating inflation by his cheaper money policy, which he thought had 'produced an appreciation of values tending greatly to encourage spending, not only of income but also out of capital'—although at the beginning of 1947 he thought that 'exaggerated stress has been laid upon the danger of inflation arising from an excessive volume of spending' and was more worried about cost inflation. His colleague Frank Paish was unusual in 1947 in straight-forwardly blaming Dalton's monetary expansion for increasing consumer demand.[53]

Other critics who allowed for the possibility of real balance effects on consumption thought they would be small. Thus C. M. Kennedy, in his famous assessment of post-war monetary policy up to 1950, though he emphasized the windfall capital gains made by security holders under the cheaper money policy, concluded:

[51] H. D. Henderson, 'Cheap money and the budget', *EJ*, 57 (Sept. 1947), 265–6; R.F. Harrod, *Are these Hardships Necessary?* (London, 1947), 124–6. Not surprisingly Dalton later quoted both comments with satisfaction: *Public Finance*, 4th edn, 239 n.

[52] Meade, *Cabinet Office Diary*, 274; *Planning and the Price Mechanism: the Liberal–Socialist Solution* (London, 1948), 26–33.

[53] Robbins, 'Inquest on the crisis', *Lloyds Bank Review* no. 6 (Oct. 1947), 12–13, and 'Economic prospects', ibid., no. 3 (Jan. 1947), 26–7; F. W. Paish, 'Cheap Money Policy', *Economica* 14 (Aug. 1947), 175. Leslie Pressnell remembers Paish giving his article as a lecture: 'marvellous stuff, and exhausting, in a crowded lecture room' (information from Professor Pressnell).

It is . . . only too easy in retrospect to over-estimate it [the impact of cheaper money], and to attribute the inflationary stresses . . . in too large a measure to the controversial monetary policy. . . . [W]hether or not these [inflationary] pressures were aggravated to any appreciable extent by Cheaper Money remains in the writer's view a matter of doubt.[54]

J. C. R. Dow in his evidence to the Radcliffe Committee, dismissing the importance of the real balance effect, claimed that 'It seems more illuminating to describe the abnormal [post-war] demand [for consumer goods] as an effect of the *real* depletions imposed on consumers during the war, than as an effect of their high liquid asset holdings.' Although 'the cheap money policy of . . . 1945–1947 must undoubtedly have increased the pressure of demand . . . it is . . . doubtful whether the mistake was in any way serious. Cheap money may have encouraged investment. But investment expenditure was well controlled . . .'.[55] In 1964 he still thought 'it must remain doubtful whether cheap money was seriously harmful. Investment demand—high in any case, and subject moreover to direct controls—cannot have been greatly stimulated by a half per cent interest-rate incentive. Nor was home demand a main cause of the two particular crises of 1947.'[56]

If monetary policy is thought to operate only through a single narrow channel of interest-rate changes on relatively interest-inelastic investment, then the impact of a policy like Dalton's in an already inflationary situation with planned and controlled physical investment will necessarily seem limited. Once one allows for real balance and other wealth effects on consumption, the scope for cheaper money to influence expenditure is much wider. Before looking at the evidence for such effects in 1946–7 it is useful to outline the theoretically possible ways in which monetary expansion can affect other economic variables.

[54] C. M. Kennedy, 'Monetary policy', in G. D. N. Worswick and P. H. Ady (eds.), *The British Economy 1945–1950* (Oxford, 1952), 195.

[55] Dow, 'The Economic Effect of Monetary Policy 1945–57', Parts 2 and 3 (quotations from the 'Note on "Liquidity" or "Cash Balance" Effects' which follows para. 124, and from para. 129), in Committee on the Working of the Monetary System, *Principal Memoranda of Evidence*, vol. 3 (London, 1960), 76–105. He explicitly contrasted his own view, which was based on the available econometric evidence, with that of Don Patinkin in *Money, Interest and Prices* (New York, 1956), 22.

[56] *Management of the British Economy 1945–60*, 21–2.

Following (and quoting) Friedman and Schwartz,

the effects of a[n unanticipated] shift from one rate of monetary growth to another can be ... classified under three headings: (1) the impact effect which includes the Keynesian liquidity effect and a first-round loanable funds effect; (2) an intermediate-run effect on real income and the price level; and (3) a long-run price anticipation effect . . .[57]

The 'liquidity effect' refers to the reduction of nominal interest rates on financial assets that will accompany faster monetary growth; the 'loanable funds effect' to the fact that in a modern capitalist economy where the increased monetary growth comes through the banking system, the impact effects of monetary expansion will also mean an increased willingness to lend on the part of the commercial banks. These two short-run effects will, of course, operate simultaneously in practice.

In the 'intermediate run' lower nominal interest rates and increased real money balances will both tend to increase expenditure, for several reasons. These include the increased opportunity cost of holding money and financial assets in place of physical assets, which should induce a reallocation of portfolios by both households and firms to include a higher proportion of real assets, as well as the increased ease of borrowing to finance (consumption or investment) expenditures. On the older Keynesian view the main 'channel of monetary policy' was seen as the effect of the first-round reduction on investment spending; on the broader 'portfolio' view the readjustment of portfolios in face of increased money balances would induce expenditure on a wider range of real assets, consumption goods and services as well as capital investment. On both views the increased expenditures will raise nominal income, usually both real output and prices. In a growing economy one will therefore observe a faster growth of real output and an increase in the rate of inflation (though in an open economy the behaviour of the latter will also partly depend on inflation in other countries, to an extent depending on the exchange rate regime). Since the demand for money depends on income as well as interest rates, faster nominal income growth will tend to bring nominal interest rates back

[57] Milton Friedman and Anna J. Schwartz, *Monetary Trends in the United States and the United Kingdom, Their Relation to Income, Prices and Interest Rates, 1867–1975* (Chicago, 1982), 480.

to their initial level—unless there is a further acceleration of monetary growth.

In the longer run, as all 'monetarist' economists since Fisher have emphasized, a higher rate of inflation would come to be generally anticipated by lenders and borrowers, lowering *real*, inflation-adjusted interest rates, Since lenders would want to receive and borrowers would be prepared to pay higher interest rates, nominal interest rates would tend to move *above* their original levels.

How much of this theoretical sequence can be discerned in actual behaviour in Britain in 1946-7? The behaviour of nominal interest rates and the money supply has been documented already (above p. 124 and pp. 141-5). The Dalton episode can certainly be seen as an example of an unanticipated shift (increase) in the rate of monetary expansion, which permitted the initial lowering of nominal interest rates that Dalton desired. As will be shown below, these low nominal rates became harder to sustain as, on the one hand, people adjusted their spending to take advantage of cheaper money's 'benefits' and on the other their expectations of future monetary and price behaviour changed. Changed expectations were the proximate cause of the breakdown of the policy since the authorities were not prepared in 1947 further to increase the rate of monetary expansion in order to maintain 2½ per cent in face of changed expectations. The return to a slower rate of monetary growth in 1947 should probably, therefore, *not* be regarded as unanticipated.

As nominal interest rates fell and monetary growth rose in 1946, the non-bank private sector found itself with higher real balances (which rose by 12 per cent in that year alone, according to the estimates in Table 3.7). Holders of financial assets other than money found their wealth increased by the large rise in the market values of their stocks and shares, the latter increased by investors switching into them as gilt-edged yields fell. According to one City estimate the appreciation of a representative group of equity shares was 'no less than 20%'. These capital gains were, unlike interest income, tax-free, which would have provided additional inducement to realize them and spend the proceeds on real assets.[58] These consequences of Dalton's policy occurred

[58] Davenport, 'The Stock Exchange inflation and the finance of investment', (Jan. 1947), T233/164, PRO.

TABLE 4.5 *Consumers' Expenditure, at Current and Constant Prices 1945-8, % Change from Previous Year*

	1945	1946	1947	1948
Current prices				
Food, drink, tobacco	5.2	8.0	12.6	9.3
Housing, fuel, light	7.4	11.1	8.7	5.6
Clothing	4.7	19.3	15.4	22.6
Durable and other household goods	18.6	48.0	19.1	9.2
Travel and communication	20.1	23.0	6.9	-1.9
Services	11.3	19.2	5.6	1.7
Total	9.3	13.8	10.4	7.2
Constant prices (1938 = 100)				
Food, drink, tobacco	4.1	13.6	3.8	0.4
Housing, fuel, light	2.2	9.4	4.4	2.3
Clothing	1.8	19.0	12.8	10.8
Durable and other household goods	13.3	40.7	10.5	3.3
Travel and communication	17.9	19.1	-1.1	-2.5
Services	6.2	-3.3	-0.9	-1.0
Total	6.3	10.3	3.1	0.9

Source
Calculated from Feinstein, *National Income, Expenditure and Output of the United Kingdom 1855–1965,* tables 24 and 25.

when the non-bank private sector was already highly liquid as a result of wartime cutbacks on consumption and accumulated savings largely in the form of bank deposits, 'small savings' and readily marketable government debt.

Much of the increase in consumers' expenditure in 1946 must be attributed to a post-war rise in dissaving which would have taken place anyway as soon as consumer goods became more readily available. But the size of the increases in 1946 over 1945 is striking (Table 4.5). The largest increases were in durable and other household goods, nearly 50 per cent in nominal terms and over 40 per cent in real terms, followed by clothing and travel each around 20 per cent at current and constant prices. In 1947, when the overall growth of consumers' expenditure slowed, the same categories rose more rapidly than the others, but the differences between the rates of growth were considerably smaller. At the beginning of 1947 the *Economic Survey* (Cmd. 7048, paras. 53–6) commented on the importance of the 'heavy purchasing power' in the level and pattern of consumption in 1946: 'if an attempt were made to use all this purchasing power, the [available] goods would vanish even more rapidly from the shops.' It noted the 'very apparent' effect on the consumption of services, where expenditure on passenger travel and entertainments was over 50 per cent above pre-war. This evidence cannot be taken far (for it is equally consistent with both 'real' and 'monetary' explanations of 1947 consumption behaviour) but taken in conjunction with contemporary comments that by the end of 1946 the realization of stock exchange gains were boosting consumption of 'luxury' goods, it suggests that the wealth effects of monetary expansion were *already* threatening to exacerbate the problems of post-war adjustment in an inflationary way. (Allowing for lags one would expect most of the effect of monetary expansion in 1946 to appear in 1947.)

Before looking at the signs of increased inflationary pressure in 1947, there is the contribution of investment expenditure to be considered. Here the contemporary scepticism that monetary policy had little to do with the behaviour of investment might perhaps be justified, since investment, public and private, was planned and controlled. But there is Meade's observation already quoted, and the fact that the investment controls had to be severely tightened in 1947 after it had become 'increasingly obvious in the course of 1946 that fixed investment was roaring away faster than any other element in GDP'.[59] As with consumers' expenditure, this suggests that the low interest rate policy was adding to existing pressures—in this case already serious due to an overambitious investment programme. Table 4.6 indicates just how ambitious this programme was, since it shows an enormous increase in investment in buildings and works compared to pre-war as well as wartime levels.

There is considerable evidence of an intensification of inflationary pressure in 1947. The behaviour of the available price and wage series has been noted above (Table 4.3). In spite of the continuation of wartime price controls and cost-of-living subsidies, which imply that reported prices underestimate the extent of inflation, there was a large increase in the rate of inflation in 1947 which cannot be blamed entirely on higher import prices. Repressed inflation shows up in the increased cost of the cost-of-living subsidies—running at about £250m a year in August 1945, they rose to £367m for the financial year 1946/7 and £425m for

---

[59] Cairncross, *Years of Recovery*, 448–52; see also Dow, *Management of the British Economy*, 151.

TABLE 4.6 *Gross Domestic Fixed Capital Formation, at Current and Constant Prices, by Type of Asset, 1938, 1945–8, £m*

	1938	1945	1946	1947	1948
Current prices					
Ships and vehicles	79	90	170	230	249
Plant and machinery	184	120	200	360	500
Buildings and works	329	140	550	610	673
Total	592	350	925	1,199	1,422
Constant prices (1938 = 100)					
Ships and vehicles	80	50	90	110	110
Plant and machinery	183	70	130	180	220
Buildings and works	329	70	260	270	270
Total	592	190	480	560	600

Source

Feinstein, *National Income, Expenditure and Output of the United Kingdom 1855–1965*, tables 39 and 40.

1947/8[60]—but here rising world food prices were largely to blame. It also shows up in the rapid running down of stocks in 1947, which as Hicks for one (Robbins was another) pointed out at the time, was 'just the sort ... of thing ... one would expect to happen as a result of inflationary pressure in a controlled economy'.[61]

The inflationary pressure spilled over on to the balance of payments. Before looking at the external sector it should be admitted that it is difficult to disentangle the monetary factors contributing to the build-up of inflationary pressure in 1947 from other factors such as the excessive investment plans and pent-up consumer demand. I do not want to claim, however, more than that Dalton's monetary expansion—on top of the existing 'monetary overhang' from wartime finance—would have increased domestic absorption in 1947 and subsequent years. While wartime direct controls were extensive, and had not yet been relaxed, they were never totally comprehensive, and allowed scope for increased aggregate demand to be concentrated on the uncontrolled or loosely controlled goods, especially as more consumer

---

[60] *House of Commons Debates*, vol. 421, 9 Apr. 1946, col. 1810, and vol. 436, 15 Apr. 1947, col. 44.

[61] J. R. Hicks, 'The empty economy', *Lloyds Bank Review*, no. 5 (July 1947), 2; Robbins, *The Economic Problem in Peace and War* (London, 1947), 60.

goods became available.[62] As already mentioned domestic expenditure at current prices rose by 8.5 per cent in 1947 compared with 3.5 per cent in 1946, and the rapid export growth of 1946 slowed to 23 per cent. At the time there were many complaints that manufacturers were devoting too much of their efforts to supplying the domestic market rather than exporting.[63] Imports rose by 45 per cent—but here of course rising import prices *were* important, especially since imports were controlled. Hence one should attribute a large part of the deterioration of the UK balance of payments to excessive domestic absorption, and hence inflationary domestic macroeconomic policy, even though the size of the reserve drain, especially under convertibility, was increased by other factors.

Those other factors included deterioration in the current account of the rest of the sterling area and capital outflows from the UK. Under the wartime and early post-war exchange control regime it was not Britain's balance of payments that determined her reserve position but the state of the balance of payments of the whole sterling area *vis-à-vis* the rest of the world. In wartime, with capital flows out of the sterling area strictly controlled, the combined current account of the sterling area with the dollar area was the determining factor and that depended on the sterling area's exports to the rest of the world and on the area's imports from outside the sterling area which were subject to import controls of varying degrees of strictness. In peacetime, as payments agreements between Britain and nonsterling area countries became less bilateral and sterling approached dollar convertibility (in principle only for current transactions), capital flows became an influence again, since sterling balances were increasingly less confined within the sterling area and the UK authorities had no surveillance over whether the balances transferred were for current or capital transactions. As with current payments it was capital flows in or out of the whole sterling area that mattered.

Table 4.7 shows the very large swings in the current account of the sterling area in 1947. The total sterling area deficit doubled,

---

[62] Dow, *Management of the British Economy*, ch. 6; Cairncross, *Years of Recovery*, 344–51.

[63] For example, in the *Economic Survey for 1947*, paras. 73–4, 80–1, 127, and Robbins, 'Inquest on the crisis', 10–15.

TABLE 4.7 *Sterling Area Balance of Payments, Current Account, 1946–51, £m*

	1946	1947	1948	1949	1950	1951
UK	−344	−545	−26	+6	+258	−465
RSA	−101	−425	−254	−369	+124	−163
Total	−445	−970	−280	−363	+382	−628

Source
Bank for International Settlements, *The Sterling Area* (Basle, 1953), 35.

with the overseas sterling area contributing 62 per cent of the deterioration. Table 4.8 shows the UK balance of payments with the dollar area. In 1947 the current account deficit with the dollar area amounted to £506m, and the rest of the sterling area deficit with the dollar area added £299m to the payments to be made to the dollar area. As Cairncross has pointed out,

Most of the dollar drain in 1947 can be accounted for by a [sterling area] current account deficit with the dollar area. ... The net deficit of the United Kingdom alone amounted to £510 million to which must be added the rest of the sterling area's deficit of £222 million, making a total equal to nearly three-quarters of the gold and dollar drain of £1,024 million.

TABLE 4.8 *UK Balance of Payments with Dollar Area, Annual 1946–9, £m*

	1946	1947	1948	1949
Exports of goods[1]	100	130	196	194
Imports of goods[1]	390	567	406	442
Trade balance	−290	−437	−210	−248
Net invisibles	−9	−69	−31	−43
Current balance excluding grants	−299	−506	−241	−291
Marshall Aid	—	—	+144	+244
Current balance	−299	−506	−97	−47
Intergovernmental loans (net)[2]	+247	+776	+82	+75
Long-term capital flows (net)	+61	+18	−24	+35
Overseas sterling holdings	−1	−15	+1	+12
Gold and dollar reserves	−54	+152	+55	+3
RSA sales of gold in UK (net)	+82	+77	+55	+68
Other transfers	−36	−502	−72	−146

Notes
[1] fob.
[2] Includes UK subscriptions to IMF and IBRD.

Source
United Kingdom Balance of Payments, 1946–57 (HMSO, 1959), table 4.

The rest of the reserve loss can be accounted for by capital out-flows from the sterling area as a whole.[64] Total outflows of capital from the UK in 1947 amounted to £500–600m, partly but not mainly the running down of sterling balances for there were sizeable capital transfers to the rest of the sterling area, especially to South Africa (£300–400m), and transfers to the non-dollar and non-sterling areas (£200m), some part of which may have been capital transfers. (South Africa was a particular problem, for it was receiving capital flows from other parts of the sterling area, especially India on the verge of independence, and its receipts of sterling enabled it to supply less gold to the London market in payment for its imports.[65]) Furthermore, the capital movements appear to have been augmented by speculative outflows in the summer, especially in 1947 III.[66]

Thus by 1947 the British economy was no longer insulated in the way Dalton had liked to assume in 1946. It was instead a fairly open economy with a fixed exchange rate suffering the conse-quences of unduly expansionary domestic financial policies. If one puts the argument into the framework of the 'monetary theory of the balance of payments'—ignoring the complications to be allowed for shortly—one would say that 1946 witnessed a fall in 'hoarding' (that is, accumulation of money balances) due to the desire to use accumulated savings to finance consumption expenditure, especially on durable goods, and at the same time a rapid increase in the money supply due to domestic credit expan-sion under Dalton's interest rate policy. The resulting excess supply of money (caused by both a fall in money demand and an increase in money supply) led to a major worsening of an existing

[64] *Years of Recovery*, 145–62. The figures cited by Cairncross (p. 145) differ slightly from those in Table 4.8 because they are derived from an earlier set of official balance-of-payments estimates. Unfortunately, as Cairncross em-phasizes, there is no single set of estimates to be relied upon because only some of the components of the earlier estimates have been subsequently revised. As Cairncross also emphasizes, the even greater uncertainty of the contemporary estimates bedevilled officials' efforts to analyse the causes of the drain in 1947, but the different factors involved were soon recognized, even if not accurately quantified: for one of the best analyses see EC(S)(47)30, 'Some aspects of the balance of payments crisis, Note by Mr J. M. Fleming', 8 Sept. 1947, T230/447, PRO. (Marcus Fleming was Deputy Director of the Economic Section.)
[65] See unsigned memoranda to Bridges and Trend, 3 June, and 'Our dollars', 12 June 1947, T236/782, PRO. In October 1947 South Africa was excluded from the dollar pooling arrangements although remaining in the sterling area.
[66] Cairncross, *Years of Recovery*, 160–1; Pressnell, 'The 1947 crisis', 10.

balance-of-payments deficit. Since 'hoarding' and 'dishoarding' are by definition the difference between money income and absorption, this description is consistent with the absorption approach to the balance of payments, which was coming into use among economists—especially in the government's Economic Section—in 1947; it only differs in stressing the monetary causes and consequences of excessive absorption.

The 'monetary theory' interpretation of the problems of 1947 would go on to predict that the reserve losses resulting from the balance-of-payments deficit would reduce the money supply (or at least its rate of growth) until the excess money and the payments deficit were eliminated. However, the links between the reserves and the money supply in the 1940s do not fulfil the requirements of the monetary theory, even when sterling was freely convertible. The reserve losses of 1947 did not reflect only UK dishoarding but resulted from the whole sterling area balance-of-payments deficit, and reserve losses were not automatically translated into changes in the UK money supply, because of the sterilization of reserve flows provided by the Exchange Equalization Account. Table 4.9 shows that the reserves and the monetary base moved in opposite directions from quarter to quarter almost as often as they moved in the same direction in 1947–51. None the less the 'monetary theory' interpretation is useful in drawing attention to the idea that the 'dishoarding' produced by previous monetary expansion, and hence a high level of absorption, would persist unless and until the surplus money balances had been removed.

In the second half of 1947 and early 1948 there were significant decreases in the monetary base. As already mentioned the rates of growth of M1 and M3 were much lower in 1947 than in 1946 and with prices rising rapidly real balances fell considerably. As monetary growth continued at a modest rate in and after 1948, real balances continued to fall, though more slowly. Prices were rising more slowly in 1948–50. The Daltonian increase in real balances seems to have been worked off by 1949 but the monetary overhang from the war (measured by money-to-income ratios) persisted until the early 1950s (see Table 4.4). This very high degree of private sector liquidity could have been worked off earlier if it had not been for Dalton's cheaper money policy which increased the size of the overhang and delayed the adjustment.

TABLE 4.9 *Quarterly Changes in UK Official International Reserves and in the Monetary Base, 1945 II–1951 III, £m*

		Reserves	Monetary base
1945	III	−21	+84
	IV	+7	+30
1946	I	−23	−35
	II	−20	+58
	III	+94	+15
	IV	+3	+53
1947	I	−78	+8
	II	+7	+4
	III	−6	−15
	IV	−75	−17
1948	I	+40	−109
	II	−59	+21
	III	−36	−5
	IV	+20	+38
1949	I	+14	−43
	II	−65	+35
	III	−76	−12
	IV	+94	+46
1950	I	+106	−65
	II	+156	+89
	III	+119	−61
	IV	+194	+68
1951	I	+164	−42
	II	+39	+37
	III	−214	0

Sources
Changes in reserves calculated from Bank of England, *Statistical Abstract*, No. 1, 1970, table 27; changes in monetary base calculated from Tables 3.8 and 5.10.

This last point hints at a possible further implication, namely a monetary explanation of the devaluation of the pound sterling in 1949. The continued monetary overhang from the war would have maintained domestic absorption at a higher level than it would otherwise have been and insofar as a continued high level of domestic absorption contributed to the need for a devaluation in 1949 it would have exacerbated it. There were, however, more fundamental factors making for a post-war devaluation of sterling, such as the permanent deterioration in the current account of Britain's balance of payments brought about by the war and the related changes in the world economy which made all European currencies overvalued in relation to the US dollar in the early post-war years (see the next chapter). It is possible, though, that Britain did not reap the full benefits of the devaluation after the event because domestic demand continued to be insufficiently restrained by monetary and fiscal policy.

One other effect of excessive monetary expansion I have so far played down, namely the impact on prices. This is partly because of price controls and the other measures the wartime and immediate post-war governments took to repress inflation. It also reflects the fact that in an open economy with a fixed exchange rate domestic prices will be heavily influenced by world prices. Unless one adopts the simplest version of the 'monetary theory' of the balance of payments, however, one does not have to assume UK post-war inflation simply reflected the behaviour of prices in the rest of the world, especially in the large US economy. During the war UK prices had risen faster than US prices. In 1946 US prices jumped when price control was abandoned, so that by 1947 US prices had risen more than UK prices since 1939 (see Table 5.12 in the next chapter). Over the next two to four years (depending on which price indices are used) UK prices 'caught up' with US prices again, since US prices fell slightly in the mild 1948-9 US recession while UK prices went on rising, even though slowly, both before and after the devaluation of sterling in September 1949. Although the comparison over the whole twelve-year period confirms that price levels of open economies in a fixed exchange rate world cannot diverge much from each other in the longer run, the short-run differences are revealing. The slower inflation in Britain than in America in 1946-7 suggests that controls had helped to keep inflation at bay in face of the pressures coming both from domestic demand and from rising import prices.

The failure of cheaper money

Before considering further the consequences of Dalton's cheaper money policy and the reasons for its failure, it is only fair to note some successes of the policy, from Dalton's point of view at least. The first was the reduction of the cost of debt service for both central government and local authorities. Dalton's lowering of the fixed nominal interest rates on the floating debt lasted for six years and saved the Exchequer some £30m a year. According to

Treasury estimates provided to Dalton in 1949, his cheaper money policy had saved another £6.5m a year on gilt-edged debt and £1.4m on small savings (with the issue of 2½ per cent instead of 3 per cent defence bonds). Local authorities had been saved £2.6m a year by borrowing from the central government at lower nominal rates of interest and by converting their market issues with coupon rates of 3 to 5 per cent to new issues carrying 2¾ or 2½ per cent.[67] As Kennedy pointed out, the savings on long-term gilt-edged debt were partly offset by the increased cost of the nationalization programme (see below) but the reduction in short-term interest rates 'continued to give benefit to the Exchequer in the servicing of the floating debt right up to the fall of the Labour Government in October 1951'.[68] Table 4.10, which gives the proportion of total current expenditure devoted to debt interest by central government and local authorities in 1945–59, illustrates the greater benefit of cheaper money to the latter. For the local authorities this proportion averaged 10.7 per cent a year in 1946–51 compared with 17.7 per cent in the 1930s and 12.9 per cent in the rest of the 1950s. For the central government the proportion, while much lower than the 25.7 per cent of the later 1930s (that is, after the conversion of 5% War Loan in 1932), declined fairly steadily from 16.5 per cent in 1947 to 12.6 per cent by the end of the 1950s.

Dalton's second aim in pursuing cheaper money (see Chapter 3) had been 'to improve the distribution of income'. A related aim was to reduce the cost of the nationalization programme: as he remarked when criticism of the transport nationalization scheme was at its height, 'gradually our opponents are, perhaps, beginning to see some connection between the cheap money drive and the terms of nationalisation. "The euthanasia of the rentier" is proceeding apace.'[69] On both counts his cheaper money policy was a failure, which he later recognized. The rise in security prices as nominal interest rates were pushed down to 2½ per cent

[67] Dalton, *Public Finance* 1954 edn., 237–8. The figures derive from Shillitto to Compton, 11 Mar. 1947, T233/299, which provides the estimates for local authorities' savings Dalton gave in his April 1947 budget speech (*House of Commons Debates*, vol. 436, 15 Apr. 1947, col. 63), and Jay to Dalton, 25 Nov. 1949, T233/299 and Dalton Papers 9/7, which updates the earlier estimates. In his papers Dalton has attributed the table of 'Cheap money savings' which he reproduced in his book to Joan Robinson, but the figures are identical with the Treasury's.

[68] 'Monetary policy', in Worswick and Ady, *British Economy 1945–1950*, 203–5.

[69] Dalton Diary, vol. 34, 29 Nov. 1946, BLPES.

TABLE 4.10 *Interest Payments on UK Central Government and Local Authority Debt, Annual, 1945–59*

	Central government		Local authorities	
	£m	% of total current expenditure	£m	% of total current expenditure
1945	450	8.7	63	11.9
1946	486	13.3	61	10.6
1947	519	16.5	61	9.5
1948	509	15.5	66	10.1
1949	507	14.5	72	10.8
1950	507	14.3	81	11.5
1951	550	13.9	89	11.4
1952	609	13.5	104	12.1
1953	639	13.6	123	13.2
1954	637	13.2	142	14.1
1955	708	14.3	161	14.6
1956	723	13.7	193	15.4
1957	705	12.9	221	16.0
1958	780	13.4	241	16.2
1959	774	12.6	262	16.4

Source
Feinstein, *National Income, Expenditure and Output of the United Kingdom 1855–1965*, tables 13 and 14.

brought large windfall capital gains to their holders and it increased the share values used to calculate the amount of compensation paid to the owners of the railways. The railway shareholders gained considerably from the return of interest rates to 3 per cent during 1947, for they received transport stock with a 3 per cent coupon in amounts based on valuation of their railway shares at 2½ per cent. They thus received more compensation than they would have done if nominal long-term interest rates had remained at 3 per cent through 1946—although this effect was also due to the decision to allow November 1946 valuations instead of 1945 ones (above p. 169). As for rentiers more generally, Dalton was persuaded by Tony Crosland in 1951 that his cheaper money policy might have benefited them insofar as windfall capital gains on stock exchange securities had enabled their owners, the wealthier members of the community, to live on their capital.[70]

As for his aim of 'mak[ing] sure of full employment' Dalton

[70] Dalton Diary, vol. 39, 21 Mar. and 26 June 1951, BLPES. Dalton took quite a lot of persuading: see ch. 6 below.

understandably did not see his monetary (or fiscal) policy as a failure. He would none the less have been disturbed to think that his cheaper money policy had been seriously inflationary (even when he had admitted it might have increased consumption expenditure), since he did not wish the transition to socialism to be jeopardized by inflation. He was naturally glad to accept the common contemporary judgement of 'most serious economists' that the policy had not been *actually* inflationary ... in any important degree.'[71]

Finally, I come to the important question of whether the failure of cheaper money was inevitable. This question can be subdivided into whether the policy was bound to break down sooner or later because of its inflationary consequences, and the narrower question of whether it could have survived the vicissitudes of 1947 and allowed the nationalization of the railways at 2½ per cent. Dalton later speculated that 'if I (and my successor) had held on through 1947 ... [and issued Long Transport at 2½ per cent at par], and if we had used to the full all the means at our disposal to hold the long-term rate at 2½ per cent, we *might* have succeeded in "conditioning the market" to this rate'—but he admitted this could well have had excessively inflationary consequences. He also claimed that he 'could certainly have held the long-term rate' at 2½ per cent if only he had the power to compel the insurance companies and other large institutional investors to hold a minimum proportion of their assets in gilt-edged securities.[72] To investigate these claims it is necessary to consider more closely than I have done so far the timing of the break in interest rates and its proximate causes.

The turning point came during the issue of Daltons in the winter of 1946–7. At the time the authorities took their risky decision to issue the stock there were analyses in the financial press of the monetary consequences of cheaper money as well as increasing concern over the possibility of a winter fuel shortage. For instance, Wilfred King in *The Banker* was pointing out that the private sector was probably becoming less willing to hold securities as a result of post-war dissaving and because Dalton's policy was making securities less attractive as an alternative to holding money. This 'increasing "liquidity preference" of the public' was

---

[71] *Public Finance*, 1954 edn., 238–9.   [72] Ibid. 239–40, italics in original.

increasing the amount of official intervention needed to maintain gilt-edged prices. He warned investors:

If the 'departments' really are being obliged to take up abnormally large quantities of securities from the public, and if it is fully perceived that these operations are the cause of an increase in the volume of money which the Government obviously does not like, a brake might be put upon the cheaper money progression.[73]

In mid-November the *Financial Times* was asking 'Has the Rise in Gilt-Edged Gone Too Far?'; a further reason for expecting a rise in interest rates occurred when the transport nationalization compensation scheme was announced, and criticized, since it implied that the expropriated railway owners might rush to sell off their transport stock when it was issued.[74]

In these unpropitious circumstances it is hardly surprising that Daltons were not eagerly bought by private sector investors. The post-tax return to individual investors on long-term government securities was already negligible with high rates of income tax and low nominal yields; an anticipated capital loss due to even a small rise in interest rates would produce a large negative expected return. Hence any change in market expectations of future interest rates would produce large shifts in assetholders' desired portfolios and large falls in gilt-edged prices in the absence of large-scale official intervention. In a thin market even a few doubts about the continuance of Dalton's cheaper money drive could prompt a rise in yields and serve to reinforce fears of higher interest rates.

A sign of a change in market expectations in late 1946 is visible in the behaviour of the relative yields on short- and long-term marketable government securities. In the first nine months of 1945 the yield curve rose quite steeply from around 2 per cent for bonds with five years to maturity up to near 3 per cent for irredeemables (2½% Consols). Over the next twelve months it flattened: in September 1946 yields ran from 2 per cent for five years to maturity to 2½ per cent for irredeemables. By the end of the year the yield gap had widened again: market yields on the shorter

[73] 'Gilt-edged and the volume of money', *The Banker*, (Oct. 1946), 8–11.
[74] *Financial Times*, 16 and 18 Nov. 1946; *The Economist*, 23 Nov. 1946, 839; W. Manning Dacey, 'The cheap money technique', *Lloyds Bank Review*, no. 3 (Jan. 1947), 49. On the *FT*'s sustained and often vitriolic criticism of Dalton see also David Kynaston, *The Financial Times, A Centenary History* (London, 1988), 172–80.

bonds had fallen, suggesting a switch in demand to the shorter issues (while the nominal yield on the longer issues was being held up by official support). Over 1947 the yield curve was to steepen further without intervention to hold the long rate below 3 per cent.

Once assetholders' expectations had changed from expecting falling interest rates to anticipating higher rates, then (unless something fortuitously happened to change expectations again) there was no way that the authorities could keep 2½ per cent without continually increasing expansion of the money supply. As we have seen, the Bank of England stopped intervening in the gilt-edged market in January 1947, so it was never put to the test what scale of intervention would have been necessary to keep 2½ per cent nominal yields on irredeemables. If the authorities had tried to do so they would have found themselves confronted with what the Controller of the National Debt Office would have called the 'Red Queen' problem (above p. 174)—having to buy up more and more long-term debt in order to keep gilts prices at the same level. This is of course one aspect of the medium to longer run consequences of monetary expansion to be expected on theoretical grounds (see pp. 180–1 above), that sustained monetary expansion, although it will first lower nominal interest rates, will subsequently tend to push them back to and even beyond their original levels.

This line of argument thus implies the failure of Dalton's cheaper money policy was inevitable sooner or later. It came sooner rather than later because of the Bank's withdrawal from the gilt-edged market for the first half of 1947. The cheaper money policy was not a casualty of the winter or summer crises of 1947 because it was already effectively over by the time they materialized. (Although one might want to argue that the prospect of the first crisis contributed to the change in market expectations there were several other reasons for investors to have doubts in the autumn of 1946 whether cheaper money could be sustained through the coming winter.)

What about Dalton's claim that he could have stopped the rot in the gilt-edged market by requiring large institutional investors such as insurance companies to hold certain proportions of gilt-edged debt in their asset portfolios? This proposal derived from Davenport who put up for discussion in the National Investment

Council in July 1947 that the insurance companies should be required to invest their new income in government securities as they had done during the war. The Treasury pointed out that the voluntary agreement which had ended in July 1946 had only been to invest in new tap issues, that the government did not have any statutory power to do more, and that the insurance companies were bound to hold a high proportion of gilt-edged securities anyway. At the October Council meeting it was agreed, at Dalton's request, that the Treasury 'should consider the desirability of reopening discussions with the British Insurance Association on its gilt-edged investment policy, if a statistical analysis of the situation at the end of the year [1947] showed that such action seemed to be required'; since Dalton resigned soon afterwards, nothing came of this.[75]

Davenport claimed that the insurance companies had been heavy sellers of government stocks in 1947, especially of Daltons early in the year, and that in a thin market dominated by institutional investors this had been a major factor contributing to the downfall of cheaper money. Table 4.11 gives the proportions of insurance company portfolios held in various types of assets in 1938–52. It shows that the companies increased their holdings of government and government-guaranteed securities considerably during the war, from 20 per cent of their total assets in the late 1930s to over 40 per cent by 1945, and ran them down afterwards. The assets taken up instead were not so much mortgages and loans, which had accounted for 20 per cent of the companies' pre-war portfolios, but rather equities and property—which was the beginning of a long sustained trend in an inflationary environment.[76] Although they still held 30 per cent of their assets in government securities in 1952 (and did not get down to the pre-war 20 per cent until the end of the 1950s), there was also a marked and temporary fall in their holdings in 1947. In absolute

[75] Davenport to Dalton, 8 July 1947, Piercy Papers 10/64, BLPES; 'National Investment Council, Fifth meeting . . . 8th August, 1947', T233/165, PRO; Radice, 'Insurance companies and gilt edged investment', 15 Oct., and 'National Investment Council, 7th meeting—20th October, 1947, Record of Discussion', T233/166; Davenport, 'Notes on the gilt-edged market', 28 Nov. 1947, Dalton Papers 9/3, BLPES.

[76] Barry Supple, *The Royal Exchange Assurance, A History of British Insurance 1720–1970* (Cambridge, 1970), 518–19, 527–8; Committee on the Working of the Monetary System, *Report*, paras. 244–8; see also Leo T. Little, 'Insurance companies and industrial capital', *The Banker*, (Aug. 1950), 80–7.

TABLE 4.11 *Insurance Company Portfolios, by Type of Asset, Annual, 1938–52, % of Total*

	Mortgages	Loans	BGS[1]	Other Securities	Equities	Property	Cash and other assets
1938	11.0	9.8	21.2	11.6	34.6	5.6	6.2
1939	10.9	10.8	19.8	11.2	34.6	5.8	6.9
1940	9.9	12.4	25.7	10.9	36.1	5.5	0
1941	9.2	11.9	29.4	10.2	32.2	5.3	1.9
1942	8.4	10.4	33.1	9.6	30.5	5.0	3.0
1943	7.7	9.2	35.4	9.4	29.1	4.9	4.3
1944	7.0	7.7	38.7	9.0	27.7	4.8	5.1
1945	6.3	6.3	41.4	8.8	26.4	4.7	6.1
1946	5.9	5.9	39.9	8.5	27.8	4.7	7.4
1947	6.0	5.6	35.9	8.7	30.1	5.0	8.8
1948	6.5	4.5	39.0	8.8	26.8	5.2	9.2
1949	6.8	4.1	37.1	9.6	27.1	5.5	9.6
1950	7.7	3.8	33.1	9.8	28.5	5.8	11.3
1951	8.7	3.7	31.7	9.6	29.3	6.4	10.6
1952	9.5	3.7	30.0	9.7	29.7	6.7	10.6

Notes
[1] British government and government-guaranteed securities.
[2] Commercial and municipal securities, foreign government and municipal securities.

Source
Calculated from David K. Sheppard, *The Growth and Role of UK Financial Institutions 1880–1962* (1971), table (A) 2.5.

terms they reduced their £1,007m 1946 holdings to £977m in 1947 and increased them again to £1,131m in 1948. This suggests that there was indeed, as one authority on insurance company investment has described it, 'a reaction against British Government Securities' as a result of Dalton's cheaper money policy.[77]

If the reduction in the insurance companies' holdings of government securities had been concentrated in the longer dated stocks it would go far to explain the fall in their prices in early 1947. This does not mean that the downturn would not have occurred in the absence of such a switch. If the companies had still been investing in new tap issues as they had during the war then the Daltons issue would have been less unpopular, but there were plenty of other reasons why private and institutional investors would be bearish about the future of cheaper money and

[77] David K. Sheppard, *The Growth and Role of UK Financial Institutions 1880–1962* (London, 1971), Table (A) 2.5; G. Clayton, 'The role of the British life assurance companies in the capital market', *EJ* 61 (Mar. 1951), 92.

hence why their fears were likely to be realized in the gilts market in the early months of 1947. If the insurance companies had been obliged to invest their new income in government securities or to hold a certain minimum proportion, say 40 per cent, of their assets in gilt-edged securities, this would have increased their demand for gilts in 1947 by around £110m.[78] But such a requirement would not have prevented their switching between different maturities of government securities. Although insurance companies, especially life insurance companies, generally have a preference for longer-dated securities, 'they may ... "take a view" on the course of gilt-edged prices, and go shorter if they think that yields are likely to rise'.[79] Switching out of the longest stocks by institutional investors was noted by several commentators in the winter of 1946–7.

It is, therefore, difficult to believe that if insurance companies had been subject to restrictions on the composition of their asset portfolios and had had to maintain their holdings of government securities at wartime levels, this would have done more than *delay* the end of cheaper money. Some commentators have suggested that if Dalton could have convinced investors in the early months of 1947 that nominal interest rates would remain at their current low levels the high level of liquidity preference would have abated and the demand for long-term government bonds revived.[80] With the alarms and diversions of 1947 gilt-edged prices would have needed at least intermittent but at times probably heavy official support to weather the crises. Unless this support was short-lived its monetary consequences would increase the amount of intervention needed and the authorities would eventually have been forced to draw back.

This conclusion rests on the assumption that the government would have become concerned about the inflationary consequences of monetizing government debt. In other words, the cheaper money policy was bound to be abandoned once the government's macroeconomic policy stance was directed toward

---

[78] Calculated from data in Clayton, 'The role of the British life assurance companies in the capital market', table I, and Sheppard, *Growth and Role of UK Financial Institutions*, table (A) 2.5.

[79] Committee on the Working of the Monetary System, *Report*, para. 245.

[80] Dacey, 'The cheap money technique', *Lloyds Bank Review* no. 3 (Jan. 1947), 63; Joan Robinson, 'The rate of interest', *Econometrica*, 19 (Apr. 1951), 110; Kennedy, 'Monetary policy', 201.

fighting inflation, as it came to be in 1947, even if monetary policy itself was not given a significant role in the anti-inflationary policy.

APPENDIX

The Finance of Nationalization

Since the 1930s the Labour Party had accepted that full compensation should be paid to the expropriated owners of industries nationalized by a Labour government. In 1945 these industries were to be, according to the election manifesto, the fuel and power industries, inland transport, and the iron and steel industry, as well as the Bank of England. The 1945–51 Labour governments had, therefore, to decide on the method of calculating the amount of compensation and on the form of its payment for each of the industries in their nationalization programme.

In September 1945 Herbert Morrison opened the discussion with a list of eight questions to his fellow 'socialising ministers'—Cripps and Dalton and the Ministers of Supply, Fuel and Power, and Transport (Wilmot, Shinwell, and Barnes)—on compensation and other issues such as pricing policy. Following both Morrison (in his *Socialisation and Transport* (1933)) and the TUC (in its *Interim Report on Post-war Reconstruction*), the ministers favoured 'net maintainable revenue'—that is, the prospective earning power of an undertaking—capitalized at an appropriate number of years purchase as the basis of compensation, and payment in government or government-guaranteed stock.[81] In due course an official committee on the socialization of industries reported early in 1946. On the calculation of compensation it argued for capitalized 'net maintainable revenue', which was 'theoretically the most satisfactory basis', rather than the market valuation of shares: securities quoted on the Stock Exchange represented only part of the capital in most industries, market valuations 'tended to reflect unduly the dividend policy of the directors', and there would be problems with holding companies only part of whose assets were to be nationalized. However, since 'net maintainable revenue' would have to be estimated by an arbitration tribunal, some

[81] The questions are enclosed with Morrison to Cripps, Dalton, Wilmot, Shinwell, and Barnes, 3 Sept. 1945, CAB124/915 and T230/106; the replies are on T234/1, PRO. The idea of the questions had come from Meade (*Cabinet Office Diary*, 123, 130). As Minister of Transport in the second Labour government Morrison had introduced the bill to nationalize London's transport system; for his views and those of the TUC see Chester, *Nationalisation*, 217–20, 225–8.

'short cut' would have to be found for the hundreds of separate under-takings comprising the gas and electricity industries. As for the form of compensation it should usually be a government-guaranteed stock issued on behalf of the particular industry. An exception was the coal industry, where a straight government stock would be more appro-priate, because there were 'strong psychological arguments, arising out of the industry's past history, against leaving any suggestion that the employees are working for a body of stock-holders rather than the State'.[82]

Although the government kept to the principle of net maintainable revenue in the nationalization of the Bank of England, the coal industry, and Cable and Wireless Ltd. (a company which operated a telecom-munications service between Britain and the Commonwealth), it resor-ted to the administratively simpler expedient of market valuation for the other industries.[83] Except for the coal industry, Cable and Wireless, and the Bank of England, and for civil aviation, where no stock was issued, it issued government-guaranteed stock. (Most of Britain's aviation indus-try was already in the public sector, and the few private companies were purchased by private negotiations.) In each case the terms of issue of the compensation stocks raised a problem of debt management for the mon-etary authorities, whose decisions on the issues are outlined here. The industries nationalized, with the dates of their takeover, and the stocks issued in compensation are listed in Table 4.12.

I begin with three small nationalization issues which did not pose serious problems for the authorities. The first nationalization compensa-tion stock issued was £58m 3% Treasury Stock 1966 or after to the Bank of England shareholders on 1 March 1946. Since the dividend on Bank Stock had not been changed for twenty-three years it was easy to decide the 'net maintainable revenue' for an indefinite future, and since Dal-ton's drive to lower long-term interest rates was not then under way a 3 per cent issue at par was appropriate. The second compensation issue was made solely to the National Debt Commissioners during the tap offer of Daltons. When the National Coal Board took over the ownership of mining royalties, which had been nationalized under the Coal Act of 1938, on 1 January 1947 the NDC received £78m 2½% Treasury Stock 1986/2016 in exchange for their holding of £69m 3% Coal Commission Stock 1986/2016. The Bank had suggested that they could be issued with Daltons, but Dalton stipulated that nationalization issues have a final

---

[82] SI(O)(46)12, Official Committee on the Socialisation of Industries, First Re-port, 21 Feb. 1946, paras. 9–24, and SI(M)(46)18, Official Committee on the Socialisation of Industries, Second Report, 10 May 1946, paras. 22–5, T234/1; see also Chester, *Nationalisation*, 221–4, 235–6.

[83] See ibid., ch. 3, for details of the decisions on the method of determining the amount of compensation paid in each industry.

TABLE 4.12 *The Nationalization Programme, 1945–51*

Industry	Vesting date	Compensation stock	Amount issued £m	Date of issue	Price of issue
Bank of England	1 Mar. 1946	3% Treasury Stock 1966 or after	58	1 Mar. 1946	Par
Civil aviation	1 Aug. 1946	None issued	—		
Cable & Wireless	1 Mar. 1947	3% Savings Bonds 1960/70	16	1 Mar. 1949	102
		3% Savings Bonds 1965/75	16	1 Mar.	102
Coal	1 Mar. 1947	2½% Treasury Stock 1988/2016[1]	79	1 Jan. 1947	100½
		3½% Treasury Stock 1977/80	262	15 June and 15 Dec. 1950–6	[2]
Transport	1 Jan. 1948	3% British Transport Guaranteed Stock 1978/88	1054	1 Jan. 1948	Par
		3% British Transport Guaranteed Stock 1967/72	13	1 Jan. 1948	Par
		3% British Transport Guaranteed Stock 1968/73	139	1 Apr. 1948 and subsequently	[3]
Electricity	1 Apr. 1948	3% British Electricity Guaranteed Stock 1968/73	344	1 Apr. 1948	Par
Gas	1 Apr. 1949	3% British Gas Guaranteed Stock 1990/95	189	1 May 1949 and subsequently	Par
Iron and steel	15 Feb. 1951	3½% British Iron and Steel Guaranteed Stock 1979/81	246	15 Feb. 1951	Par

Notes
[1] To National Debt Commissioners.
[2] First issue at par, later issues at varying prices.
[3] Initial issue (for railway wagons) at par, later issues (for road passenger transport and road haulage undertakings) at varying prices.

Sources
Sir Norman Chester, *The Nationalisation of British Industry 1945–51*, chs. 1 and 3; Pember and Boyle, *British Government Securities in the Twentieth Century, Supplement 1950–1976*, 186, 192–3, 228, 232, 244, 254, 358.

redemption date. The Controller of the National Debt Office had grumbled at getting a stock for the savings banks funds with a 2½ per cent coupon in place of one carrying 3 per cent; hence the old stock was valued at 113½ in order that the new stock would provide the same income to 1986 as the old stock. The new stock was issued at a small premium following the wartime principle of making each new issue on slightly worse terms than its predecessor (Daltons in this case).[84] One small issue for nationalization was not thought to warrant a special stock. When Cable and Wireless was acquired in March 1949, £16m each of two of the larger wartime issues of 3% Savings Bonds were issued at current market prices, after the Bank had assured the Treasury that this would not depress the market prices of the bonds.[85]

The most difficult debt management decision in connection with nationalization arose with the £1,000m government-guaranteed transport stock on 1 January 1948. This was the largest single compensation issue, which would have constituted a major problem in itself; the difficulty of setting the terms of issue was compounded by the fact that the decision was also a decision on the fate of the cheaper money policy (see Chapter 4 above). However, as indicated in Chapter 4, the scope of the final decision in December 1947 was narrowed by decisions made up to a year earlier.

After the criticism of market valuation of the private railway companies' shares as the basis for the amount of compensation to be paid, which was announced in November 1946, Treasury officials had considered the possibility of alleviating the 'hardship' to the shareholders that would be caused by the low nominal yields on gilt-edged stocks under the cheaper money policy, because they did not want to see large-scale switches out of the new stock which would lower gilt-edged prices. One possibility was to offer a second, alternative stock for holders concerned mainly with income, for 'if we can reconcile a fair proportion of such holders to stay in gilt-edged, it will greatly improve our chances of successfully managing not only the nationalisation programme, but also the cheap money programme'. They rejected as an option a security issued at a premium with a high coupon interest rate and an early redemption date: it would place an increased interest burden on the Transport Commission and an early redemption date was 'unsound finance'. They discussed with the Bank another alternative security, namely a Goschen-type issue with an

[84] Francis to Compton, 19 Nov. 1945, C40/786, BOE; Pinsent to Compton, 'Coal stock', 3 Sept., Yeomans to Compton, 'Coal nationalisation', 10 Dec., Compton to Pinsent, 'Coal Commission stock', 12 Dec., Compton to Bamford and Brittain, 14 Dec., and Compton to Dalton, 'Issue of Government Stock on 1st January, 1947, in exchange for Coal Commission Stock', 20 Dec. 1946, T233/49, PRO; for the valuation of the old stock and the calculation of the premium on the new see also C40/474, BOE.

[85] Eady to Compton, 'Cable and Wireless', 7 Jan. 1949, and subsequent correspondence on T233/343, PRO.

interest rate declining from an initial 2¾ or 3 per cent for, say, eighteen years to a final 1 per cent after forty years. The Bank advised against giving the shareholders any option, which might prove more popular than a 2½ per cent long-term offered at par and would anyway be administratively very difficult. The Bank doubted whether a Goschen issue would be successful with the interest rates suggested by the Treasury.[86] Thereafter the intention was to issue only one transport stock.

In the autumn of 1947 the possibility of options was raised again since Dalton and Jay had received similar suggestions from Davenport and others, but not seriously reconsidered because of the administrative difficulties emphasized by the Bank. Davenport's suggestion at that time was to offer the choice between a short-term (four or five years to maturity) with a 2 per cent coupon and a long-term (twenty years or more) with a 3 per cent coupon. Another stockbroker proposed three options, the third being a stock acceptable at par in payment for death duties.[87]

In February 1947 the Treasury also agreed to the Bank's and the railway companies' proposal that the amount of compensation stock should be fixed once-for-all on the vesting date, 1 January 1948, a decision made mainly for the considerable administrative convenience but one which the authorities later regretted.[88] Exceptions to the principle of a single large issue for transport nationalization were none the less made. One was for the holders of the £13m London Passenger Transport Board 3% Guaranteed Stock 1967/72, the only government-guaranteed stock in the securities taken over in the transport nationalization. The Treasury ascertained in November 1946 that it would be legal to issue a lower interest rate stock in exchange, despite the doubts raised by the Ministry of Transport and the Bank of England. When the Minister of Fuel and Power pointed out in February 1947 that the problem would recur with the electricity nationalization the Treasury backed down and agreed to issue a separate stock with the same terms as the LPTB stock.[89] The other

[86] Compton to Bamford, 'Transport bill: Hardship to railway stockholders', 7 Jan., Bamford to Holland-Martin, 10 Jan., and Holland-Martin to Bamford, 'Railway compensation stock', 15 Jan. 1947, T233/229, PRO.

[87] Davenport to Jay, 16 Oct., Eady to Bridges, 22 Oct., Bridges to Trend, 22 Oct., and 'Transport stock and cheap money', 29 Oct. 1947, T233/143, PRO; Cobbold, 'Transport compensation—options', 21 Oct. 1947, C40/807, BOE. On 'death duty stock' see p. 171 above.

[88] Compton, 'Transport Bill: arrangements for issue, etc. of compensation stock', 19 Feb., and Bamford to Trend, 'Transport Bill: arrangements for the issue of compensation stock', 24 Feb. 1947, T233/229; see also below.

[89] Eady to Miss Shaw, 'L.P.T.B. 3% Guaranteed Stock', 18 Nov. 1946, Shinwell to Dalton, 'Electricity Bill, Government guaranteed stocks', 8 Feb., Trend to Bamford, 15 Feb., Bamford, 'Treatment of government-guaranteed stocks under the nationalisation programme', 4 Mar., and Trend to Chancellor, 5 Mar. 1947, T233/232.

exception, British Transport 3% Guaranteed Stock 1968/73, was issued to the owners of railway wagons not owned by the railway companies on the same day (1 April 1948) and the same terms as the electricity nationalization stock and (later) for road haulage undertakings (below).

When Cripps succeeded Dalton as Chancellor he accepted the official advice that there should be no options offered to railway shareholders. On 21 November he also accepted that the best terms the authorities could hope for on the transport stock were 2¾ per cent at par for twenty-five years. He was then 'strongly against a 3% issue' and did not agree to 3 per cent until a month later after the Bank had persuaded the Treasury that the stock should not be issued at a discount.[90] The maturity dates thirty to forty years hence were chosen by reference to the current market values of the wartime 3% Savings Bonds on 1 January 1948.[91]

In the electricity nationalization bill, published on 12 January 1947, the basis of compensation to the private shareholders was again the market value of their shares. The compensation stock was to be issued, and its terms fixed, on the vesting date, 1 April 1948.[92] In early March, when the authorities began seriously to consider the terms, the Bank pressed for issuing at par for administrative convenience as with the transport stock. Cripps resisted, for the market had weakened since the issue of Long Transport and a 3 per issue at par would now require a maturity of seventeen to twenty-seven years compared with the thirty to forty years of Long Transport. 'It is very important', he told his officials, 'that Electricity Stock should *not* (repeat not) be issued on terms more adverse than the Transport Stock so far as our credit policy is concerned.' As the Chancellor's private secretary put it, he was 'anxious that we should not be caught napping on the relevant date and be compelled, if we wished to issue the Stock at par, to concede an interest rate of 3½%'. Cripps postponed the decision on the price of issue until 19 March, 'after the Deputy [Governor] had admitted that the printing timetable did not require an earlier decision'.[93] By 19 March the Bank had, as the Treasury officials anticipated, intervened to raise gilt-edged prices and was prepared to push them a little higher (though not so far as to bring Long Transport to par). Cripps then agreed to issuing the electricity stock at

[90] Cobbold to Governor, 25 Nov. 1947, C40/476, BOE; Bamford to Eady, 1 Dec. 1947, T233/143; above pp. 172–3.

[91] Bamford to Eady, 'Transport stock: terms of issue', 11 Dec., Compton, 'Transport stock terms', 19 Dec., and Bamford, 'Transport stock, Note of a discussion in the Chancellor of the Exchequer's room No. 11 Downing Street on 19th December, 1947', T233/337.

[92] Chester, *Nationalisation*, 280–92.

[93] Cobbold to Bamford, 5 Mar., Compton to Bamford, 'Electricity compensation, Points for Chancellor's meeting on 9th March', 9 Mar., Compton to Bamford, 8 Mar., Note by Cripps, 8 Mar., Note by Trend, 9 Mar., and Radice to Compton, 17 Mar. 1948, T233/269, PRO.

par. He also agreed to issuing a second transport stock for privately owned railway wagons on the same terms as the electricity stock in preference to issuing to a tranche of Long Transport at a discount. On 31 March the Bank recommended maturity dates of 1 April 1968 to 1 April 1973 for the two stocks, which the Chancellor approved the next day.[94]

Discussion of the compensation stock for gas nationalization also commenced early in 1948, when criticism of the 'cheeseparing' terms of Long Transport in the financial press and in Parliament prompted the Bank to propose that the terms of issue should be fixed 'at or about' the vesting date rather than on a single date announced months in advance. Although the Treasury was initially reluctant to break with precedent the Chancellor agreed to amend the bill then being debated in the House of Commons. Later in the year the authorities settled on 1 May 1949 as the relevant date (as further away from and therefore less likely to be affected by reaction to the budget than the vesting date of 1 April).[95] At the beginning of April 1949 the Treasury agreed to deciding the terms at close of business on Friday, 29 April, rather than waiting until Monday, 2 May, and to the Bank's usual request to issue at par, because with the gilt-edged market 'very firm' there was no difficulty in issuing a 3 per cent stock. On 28 April the Chancellor 'agreed 3% 1990–1995 or 1989–1994, with Pref[erence] for former at discretion of Governor', these dates having been recommended by comparison with 3% Savings Bonds 1965/75 and the other nationalization stocks.[96]

On 2 May only £60m British Gas 3% Guaranteed Stock 1990/95 was issued. The remainder was issued over the following year as the valuations of securities not quoted on the Stock Exchange were completed. Since the strength of the gilt-edged market in the spring of 1949 did not last, only £77m was issued when it stood at or above par, and the market values of the £34m issued between 28 June and 22 August during the sterling crisis were in the range of 89½–95½. By September 1949 the cries of protest from shareholders and in the press over the payment of compensation in a stock now worth much less than

[94] Note by Trend, 19 Mar., and Bridges to Chancellor, 'Electricity Stock', 31 Mar. 1948, T233/270; see also Compton to Radice, 12 Mar., Compton to Bamford, 'Compensation for privately-owned railway wagons', 12 Mar., and Compton to Wilson, 19 Mar. 1948, T233/339. On the Bank's market intervention in March see p. 174 above.

[95] Chester, *Nationalisation*, 302–4; Compton to Bamford, 'Gas compensation', 12 Jan., Compton, 'Legislation Committee Tuesday 20th January, Gas compensation stock', 19 Jan., and Compton to Holland-Martin, 20 Jan. 1948, T233/601; Cobbold to Eady, 21 Aug., and Compton to Eady, 24 Sept. 1948, T233/602.

[96] Compton to Wass, 'Gas compensation', 26 Mar., and Eady to Trend, 'Gas compensation stock', 5 Apr. 1949, T233/602; Eady to Bridges, 'Gas compensation stock', 22 Apr., and Note by Cripps, 28 Apr. 1949, T233/603.

its nominal value led the Ministry of Fuel and Power to seek to provide some redress.[97] The question went up to the Cabinet Economic Policy Committee in November, but Cripps successfully resisted on the grounds of an undesirable precedent and the 'almost insuperable' administrative difficulties. It fell to Gaitskell as Minister of Fuel and Power to defend the decision in the House of Commons in December.[98]

When briefing Gaitskell for the debate, the Treasury mentioned one argument that he should not use in public, namely that the Bank had advised once-for-all fixing of the terms of the gas nationalization stock because 'if on each conversion date the Treasury had to take a fresh look at the market values of Government securities and revalue compensation stock at that date, this would be bad for Government credit and embarrassing for Government borrowing operations'.[99] Such 'serial valuation' had, however, been adopted in the case of the coal industry, the first major industry to be nationalized by the Labour government. Here the government had adopted 'net maintainable revenue' as the basis of compensation, which was to be paid, in government stock, to hundreds of coal companies rather than to shareholders. The process of valuation turned out to be extremely protracted, so that the first issue of 'coal stock' was not made until June 1950, after an amending bill to the Coal Industry Nationalization Act had been passed to permit the delay. On the advice of the Bank the Treasury proposed to include a change to once-for-all valuation in the coal industry amending bill, but the Ministry of Fuel and Power refused.[100] After the problems with the gas stock, however, the Bank changed its mind and recommended 'date of issue' valuation at six-monthly intervals for coal compensation. It also recommended it for iron and steel, whose nationalization bill was then going through Parliament; the Treasury agreed in principle but rejected it because it would involve amending the iron and steel bill and hence

[97] 'British Gas 3% Guaranteed Stock 1990–95', 29 Nov. 1950, T233/608; Radice to Wass, 1 Sept., Compton to Radice, 2 Sept., Rhodes to Radice, 6 Sept., and Gaitskell to Cripps, 4 Oct. 1949, T233/605.

[98] Eady to Armstrong, 22 Oct., Note by Cripps, 22 Oct., Cripps to Gaitskell, 3 Nov. 1949, T233/605; Ayres to Trend, 12 Nov., Radice to Trend, 14 Nov., Trend to Chancellor, 'Economic Policy Committee, Gas Act—Compensation, Memorandum by the Chancellor of the Exchequer and the Minister of Fuel and Power', 15 Nov. 1949, T233/390; *House of Commons Debates*, vol. 470, 12 Dec. 1949, cols. 2417–28; see also Chester, *Nationalisation*, 306–7.

[99] 'Brief for debate on the Opposition Motion relating to Gas Compensation', T233/607.

[100] Compton to Eady, 'Coal compensation', 4 Nov., and Compton to Eady, 10 Nov. 1948, T233/495, PRO; see also Yeomans to Compton, 17 Sept., Compton to Niemeyer, 'Coal compensation', 27 Oct., and Compton to Niemeyer, 13 Nov. 1948, C40/476, BOE.

increase the current agitation for a change in the Gas Act.[101]

The first of the coal compensation issues was made on 15 June 1950. At the beginning of the year the authorities had provisionally agreed to issue it in March, but after Attlee's announcement on 10 January of a general election six weeks later, Cripps 'could not agree to an issue in early March . . . the question of date would have to be decided after the Election'. In May he agreed to 15 June.[102] The officials then had to settle the title and terms of the stock. Since long-term gilt-edged yields had been above or slightly over 3½ per cent for much of the previous twelve months, the Bank thought 3½ per cent 'could be regarded as appropriate'. The maturity dates were chosen on the day of issue as 1977/80 since a recent issue of government-guaranteed stock for the Electricity Board with a 3½ per cent coupon and twenty-six to twenty-nine years to maturity stood at a small premium.[103] Serial valuation meant that while the first issue was at par, the second on 15 December 1950 was at a premium, to yield the current long-term gilt-edged rate of 3.34 per cent, and subsequent issues were at varying discounts, giving higher yields. When the last issue was made on 15 December 1956 (at 75⅛) a total of £262m had been issued.[104]

The Labour government dithered over the nationalization of the iron and steel industry, on which their views were divided. Unlike the other nationalized industries it had not been in *Labour's Immediate Programme* in 1937. It was added to the party's 'shopping list' in the 1945 election manifesto, after it had been included in the TUC's *Interim Report on Post-war Reconstruction* and after the 1944 party conference, when left-wing critics of Dalton's policy document, *Full Employment and Financial Policy*, had successfully moved a resolution that the party should commit itself to 'the transfer to public ownership of the land, large-scale building, heavy industry, and all forms of banking, transport and fuel and power'.[105] The new government waited until the British Iron and Steel Federation had submitted its own proposals for the reorganization of the industry before deciding in April 1946 on nationalization in principle and at the same time agreed to defer the legislation until the 1947-8 session of Parliament. In 1947 the Cabinet wasted considerable time and energy in arguing backwards and forwards for several months over whether to delay the legisla-

[101] Bernard to Eady, 19 Aug., Radice to Eady, 26 Aug., and Eady to Deputy Governor [Bernard], 29 Aug. 1949, T233/896; see also Beale to Peppiatt and Governors, 'Compensation for nationalised industries (Governor's note dated 21.10.49)', 25 Oct. 1949, C40/786, BOE.

[102] Radice to Tozer, 20 May 1950, C40/786.

[103] Bailey to Parsons, 'First issue of coal compensation', 23 May, Bailey to Radice, 26 May, and Peppiatt, 'Issue of Treasury stock for coal compensation', 15 June 1950, C40/786, BOE.

[104] Pember and Boyle, *British Government Securities in the Twentieth Century, Supplement 1950–1976,* 228.

[105] Chester, *Nationalisation,* 4–8.

tion until 1948-9 and over whether to accept an alternative scheme of reorganization not involving full nationalization put up by Morrison and Wilmot (then Minister of Supply). Eventually it settled on postponement (and Wilmot lost his job).[106]

As already indicated the compensation provisions of the Iron and Steel Act followed those for transport, electricity and gas, although the possibility of 'serial valuation' as used in coal was considered in August 1949 and again after the Act was passed.[107] The authorities therefore in October 1950 set the vesting date with great care as 15 February 1951. They also agreed to fix the terms of the compensation stock on that date, anticipating that it would be 3½ per cent long-term at par. They set the maturity dates by reference to the current yield of the 3½ per cent electricity stock; in order to permit them to go as long as possible the Government Broker intervened in the few days immediately before the issue to keep up the prices of the other nationalized industry stocks. He also supported the steel stock, 3½% British Iron and Steel Guaranteed Stock 1979/81, when dealings opened.[108]

On 31 March 1946, when only the Bank of England had been nationalized, total gilt-edged debt (including government-guaranteed issues) stood at £13,168m, of which £1,587m was held by the NDC. Five years later, two weeks after the Labour governments' last nationalization, the total gilt-edged debt was £15,280m (including £2,457m held by the NDC), of which nationalization compensation issues accounted for £2,107m (including £319m held by the NDC), 13.8 per cent of total gilt-edged issues and 7 per cent of the whole UK national debt. The nationalization compensation issues had, however, amounted to almost the whole of the £2,112m increase in gilt-edged outstanding over the previous five years.

[106] Ibid. 35-8; Dalton, *High Tide and After*, ch. 30; Morgan, *Labour in Power*, 110-21.

[107] Above; Radice to Johns, 16 Dec., Johns to Radice, 22 Dec. 1949, Radice, 'Valuation of iron and steel compensation stock', 7 Jan. 1950, and Drake to Trend, 30 Sept. 1950, T233/896.

[108] Trend to Eady, 'Iron and Steel Act—vesting date', 2 Oct. 1950, and subsequent correspondence on T233/425; Parsons to Trend, 'British Iron and Steel Stock', 23 Nov., and Eady to Trend, 'Steel Stock', 29 Dec. 1950, T233/897, PRO; Beale to Peppiatt and Deputy Governor, 'Iron and steel compensation stock', 1 Feb., Bernard, 'Deputy Governor's Note', 14 and 15 Feb., and Notes by Mullens, 12, 14, 15, and 16 February 1951, C40/823, BOE. The last of the industries to be nationalized by the Attlee governments, the iron and steel industry was the first to be 'privatized', though not for long. The Conservative party pledged to denationalize the industry and the Conservative government elected in October 1951 gradually sold off the component companies beginning in October 1953. Four years after the last sale in 1963 the second Wilson Labour government nationalized the industry again. On the denationalization see Kathleen Burk, *The First Privatisation* (London, 1988) and Fforde, *Bank*, 733-43.

5

Monetary Policy and Devaluation 1948–50

This period might be described as the St Lucy's day of monetary policy: for a year or two in the middle of the period there is scarcely a sentence in any official statement which mentions credit or interest rates. It is probably correct to say that the aim was a 'neutral' money policy, which would not work against the general aim of disinflation ...[1]

AT the beginning of 1948 the economic problems facing the Labour government looked rather different from what they had appeared to be twelve months earlier. The interrelated difficulties of inflation, the balance of payments and the 'dollar drain' were now recognized as more immediate problems than the prospect of an imminent slump and unemployment. 1947 had not only brought recognition of these problems but also some progress in tackling them. Although the loss of gold and dollar reserves was 'still running at a dangerous rate in the early weeks of 1948', the overall UK balance of payments was improving. Exports had almost reached their target level for 1947 in spite of the winter crisis and imports, especially from dollar sources, had been drastically cut after the summer crisis.[2] Although the scope and scale of Marshall Aid from the USA to Britain were still uncertain until the ERP legislation had passed Congress and the UK had signed its Marshall Aid agreement with the US administration (in June 1948), there was cautious optimism that it would ease the burden of balance-of-payments adjustment. Domestic fiscal policy was, after Dalton's two budgets in 1947, geared to preventing inflation at home. With respect to monetary policy, however, the new Chancellor of the Exchequer, Stafford Cripps, had only gone so far as to acquiesce reluctantly in the

---

[1] Dow, *Management of the British Economy*, 227–8.
[2] *Economic Survey for 1948*, Cmd. 7344, Mar. 1948, paras. 2, 9–11.

reversion to a cheap, rather than a cheaper, money policy. The problem of the appropriate monetary policy for an inflationary environment in which the 'monetary overhang' from wartime and Daltonian finance persisted remained. It was to preoccupy the UK monetary authorities for the rest of the post-war Labour government's' period of office.

The balance-of-payments problem was also to continue through Cripps's time at the Treasury and that of Hugh Gaitskell, who became Minister of State for Economic Affairs in February 1950 and Chancellor of the Exchequer when Cripps resigned because of ill-health in October 1950. In spite of considerable success in bringing about overall current balance in the UK balance of payments, and in 'disinflation' by means of surplus budgeting and a voluntary 'incomes policy', the government decided to devalue the pound from US$4.03 to $2.80 in September 1949. A further balance-of-payments crisis broke out in 1951 after the Korean war and British rearmament in 1950–1. The crisis was at its height when the Labour party was defeated in the general election of October 1951.

Under the two Chancellors Bank rate stayed at 2 per cent and the fixed interest rates on Treasury bills and Treasury deposit receipts remained at the ½ per cent and ⅝ per cent to which Dalton had lowered them in October 1945, while nominal yields on long-term government bonds gradually rose to nearly 4 per cent by October 1951. The upward drift of interest rates accompanied slow growth of the money supply, observed at the time in the deposits of the London clearing banks published each month. The only visible deliberate monetary policy steps were several 'requests'—in December 1947, April and October 1949, and April 1951—to these banks to moderate their lending in particular directions.

It is now known from official records, what was previously only suspected, that the official silence on monetary policy hid a prolonged dispute between ministers, Treasury officials and the Bank of England on the use of monetary weapons, a dispute which was especially lively at the time of the devaluation and when Gaitskell was Chancellor.[3] The major participants on the govern-

[3] For previous accounts of the dispute see my 'The problem of monetary control in Britain, 1948–51', *JEEH* 20 (Spring 1991), 59–92; Cairncross, 'Prelude to Radcliffe', *Rivista di Storia Economica* 4 (1987), 2–10; Cairncross and Watts, *The Economic Section 1939–1961*, 213–15; and Fforde, *Bank*, 359–96.

ment side included Douglas Jay, who became Dalton's PPS in October 1947, Economic Secretary to the Treasury from December 1947 to February 1950 and Financial Secretary from February 1950 to October 1951; Hugh Gaitskell from February 1950, first as Minister of State for Economic Affairs and then as Chancellor; and Robert Hall, who succeeded James Meade as Director of the Economic Section in the summer of 1947. The dispute can be divided into three phases: the first round of Treasury-Bank discussions in 1948 initiated by Douglas Jay; the efforts of the Governor of the Bank of England, Dalton's *bête noire* C. F. Cobbold, to change the stance of domestic monetary policy in 1949, both before and after devaluation; and the Governor's renewed campaign in 1951, which finally succeeded in November after the fall of the Labour government with a Conservative Chancellor of the Exchequer, R. A. Butler. After outlining the background to the monetary policy discussions—the behaviour of the balance of payments and of the domestic economy and the 'disinflationary' budgetary policy pursued under Cripps—this chapter describes the first two rounds of the dispute, especially from the point of view of the Treasury ministers and their officials. Since the major participants in the monetary debate also played important roles in the decision to devalue the pound, some attention is also given to the arguments for and against devaluation used in Whitehall and to a lesser extent in the Bank of England in 1948–9.[4] The next chapter discusses the continuation of the monetary dispute in 1950–1 and its final resolution in the winter of 1951–2 along with the economic developments during Gaitskell's period at the Treasury, while the concluding section of this chapter discusses the relations between the authorities' 'inactive' monetary policy and the behaviour of monetary variables in 1948–51.

The background

Tables 5.1 and 5.2 show the vicissitudes of the UK balance of payments in 1948–51. On current account the deterioration of 1947 was followed by an improvement sufficient to produce a

---

[4] For a full account of the devaluation episode see Cairncross, *Years of Recovery*, ch. 7, and for the Bank's role Fforde, *Bank*, ch. 4(e).

TABLE 5.1 *UK Balance of Payments, Annual, 1947–52, £m*

	1947	1948	1949	1950	1951	1952
Exports of goods[1]	1,180	1,639	1,863	2,261	2,735	2,769
Imports of goods[1]	1,541	1,790	2,000	2,312	3,424	3,048
Trade balance	−361	−151	−137	−51	−689	−279
Net invisibles[2]	−20	+177	+136	+358	+320	+442
Current balance excluding grants	−381	+26	−1	+307	−369	+163
Grants	30	138	154	140	43	—
Current account	−351	+164	+153	+447	−326	+162
Intergovernmental loans (net)[3]	+307	+304	−172	−14	−68	0
Net long-term capital flows[4]	−301	−167	−207	−812	−266	−72
Overseas sterling holdings	+250	−336	+169	+341	+83	−357
Change in official reserves[5]	−152	−55	−3	+575	−344	−175

Notes
[1] fob.
[2] Includes private and government transfers *except* major grants of aid.
[3] Includes UK subscriptions to IMF and IBRD.
[4] Includes balancing item.
[5] With respect to reserve figures, + = increase, − = decrease.

Sources
As Table 3.1.

small overall surplus (excluding grants) of £26m in 1948 and approximate balance the following year. After the September 1949 devaluation there was a large surplus of £307m in 1950, but that was followed by an even larger deficit in 1951 of £369m. Including the contribution of Marshall Aid the current account was in surplus in 1948, 1949, and 1950, but in sizeable deficit again in 1951. The improvement in Britain's current account came from sustained, though not steady, export growth—in terms of value at a rate of 39 per cent in 1948, 14 per cent in 1949, and 21 per cent in each of 1950 and 1951—and a strong positive contribution from invisibles, which approximately doubled over 1948–51. In 1948 and 1950 the growth of visible imports was kept below that of exports; the deterioration in the UK current account in 1949 and 1951 largely reflects a failure to keep the growth of imports down below that of exports, especially in 1951 when imports rose by 48 per cent, slightly faster than in 1947.

While the behaviour of the UK's overall balance of payments was encouraging in 1948–9 the balance with the dollar area remained in deficit (Table 5.2). Although the trade and services deficits for 1948 were approximately half those of 1947 the current

TABLE 5.2   *UK Balance of Payments with Dollar Area, Annual, 1947–52, £m*

	1947	1948	1949	1950	1951	1952
Exports of goods[1]	130	196	194	323	392	408
Imports of goods[1]	567	406	442	439	742	606
Trade balance	−437	−210	−248	−226	−350	−198
Net invisibles	−69	−31	−43	+37	−77	+32
Current balance excluding grants	−506	−241	−291	−79	−427	−166
Marshall Aid	—	+144	+244	+239	+54	—
Current balance	−506	−97	−47	+160	−373	−166
Intergovernmental loans (net)[2]	+776	+82	+75	−17	−46	−16
Long-term capital flows (net)	+18	−24	+35	+126	−4	+44
Overseas sterling holdings	−15	+1	+12	+48	−41	−4
Gold and dollar reserves	+152	+55	+3	−575	+344	+175
RSA sales of gold in UK (net)	+77	+55	+68	+98	+77	+71
Other transfers	−502	−72	−146	+160	+43	−104

Notes
[1] fob.
[2] Includes UK subscriptions to IMF and IBRD.

Source
United Kingdom Balance of Payments, 1946–57 (HMSO, 1959), table 4.

account deficit exceeded Britain's share of Marshall Aid and worsened again in 1949. As Cairncross has noted, 'It was this imbalance that provided the rationale for devaluation in 1949 although it was not what led up to it; a short-lived depression in the United States and a consequent sharp drop in the reserves were the proximate causes.'[5] After devaluation there was a considerable improvement in 1950 in the balance with the dollar area, which was wiped out again in 1951–2.

The overseas sterling area remained in deficit in 1948 and 1949, although in smaller deficit than in 1947, managed a surplus in 1950 after sterling's devaluation, and went heavily into deficit again in 1951 (see Table 4.7). Britain's reserves, which had continued to fall in 1948–9, rose very substantially in 1950, by £575m, and fell by almost as much (£519m) in the next two years (Table 4.1).

Table 5.3 shows the steady improvement in the domestic economy in 1948–51. Real gross domestic product grew by 10 per cent, consumers' expenditure by 3 per cent, government current expenditure on goods and services by 14 per cent and gross domestic fixed capital formation by 16 per cent over the four years (all

[5] Cairncross, *Years of Recovery*, 22.

TABLE 5.3 *Gross Domestic Product and Gross National Product, 1948–52, £m at 1958 Market Prices*

	1948	1949	1950	1951	1952
Consumers' expenditure	12,531	12,765	13,116	12,941	12,876
Government current expenditure on goods and services	3,072	3,255	3,255	3,502	3,857
Gross domestic fixed capital formation	2,135	2,333	2,459	2,469	2,479
Value of change in stocks	+250	+90	−275	+615	+65
Exports of goods and services	3,113	3,545	3,947	3,907	3,825
Imports of goods and services	3,228	3,589	3,620	3,873	3,584
Gross domestic product	17,773	18,308	18,882	19,561	19,518
Net property income from abroad	321	292	466	306	230
Gross national product	18,094	18,600	19,348	19,867	19,748

Source
Feinstein, *National Income, Expenditure and Output of the United Kingdom 1855–1965*, table 5.

in real terms). Investment in stocks was usually positive, being negative only in 1950. The government's attempt to prune the overambitious 1947 investment programme did not result in a planned fall in total fixed capital investment in 1948 but it helped to smooth the expansion in 1948–50 and spread it more evenly over the different categories.[6] The government also ran a sizeable current surplus throughout the period (see below). Prices (both retail prices and the GDP deflator) rose by about 7 per cent in 1948 and by 3 per cent or less in each of the next two years, but inflation accelerated in the Korean war period to 7 per cent for the GDP deflator and nearly 10 per cent for retail prices in 1951 (see Table 4.3). A voluntary 'incomes policy' introduced in February 1948 and accepted by the trade unions for a couple of years helped to keep the increase in wage rates down to little over 2 per cent a year in 1948–50.[7] One sign of the easing of inflationary pressures was the gradual dismantling of controls from 1948, although import controls remained extensive. Finally, the rates of growth of the monetary aggregates (M1 and M3) were generally below 3 per cent every year and negative in 1951 (Table 5.4). Hence real

---

[6] *Capital Investment in 1948*, Cmd. 7268, Dec. 1947; Cairncross, *Years of Recovery*, 452–5.
[7] *Statement on Personal Incomes, Costs and Prices*, Cmd. 7321, Feb. 1948; Dow, *Management of the British Economy*, 35; Russell Jones, *Wages and Employment Policy 1936–1985* (London, 1987), 36–40.

TABLE 5.4 *Growth Rates of Monetary Aggregates and Other Variables, Annual, 1948–52, % p.a.*

Year to December	C	R	H	D	M1	M3	P	Money GDP	Real GDP
1948	−5.2	2.1	−3.1	3.4	2.4	2.2	7.3	10.0	2.6
1949	−0.1	5.2	1.5	0.1	−0.6	0.3	3.0	5.6	3.0
1950	2.6	0.5	2.0	2.6	3.7	2.2	0.6	4.2	3.1
1951	5.3	−0.5	3.5	−1.3	−0.3	−0.3	7.4	11.5	3.6
1952	4.9	6.2	5.3	1.8	−0.7	2.0	9.0	8.4	−0.2

Notes
C = currency in circulation outside banks
R = reserves of UK commercial banks
H = C + R
D = net deposits of UK commercial banks
M1 = currency in circulation + demand deposits of UK commercial banks
M3 = C + D
P = GDP deflator

Sources
As Table 3.7.

balances (measured as M3 divided by the GDP deflator) were falling through these years, except in 1950 when inflation was negligibly low.

A good deal has been written elsewhere about the Keynesian budgetary policy pursued under Stafford Cripps and the influence of the government economists advising him in 1948–51.[8] As the minister responsible for economic planning as well as Chancellor of the Exchequer he relied on the advice of his Economic Planning Staff under Sir Edwin Plowden and the Economic Section under Robert Hall as well as his Treasury officials. His budgets were explicitly related to the *Economic Surveys* and the national income and expenditure forecasts. They continued the disinflationary budgetary policy initiated by Dalton in 1947, with large surpluses in each of the financial years 1948/9 to 1950/1 (see Table 5.5). As Dow has remarked, 'The impressiveness of ... Cripps's budgets depended less on the rigour of his measures, than on the uncompromising principles on which they were

[8] Dow, *Management of the British Economy*, 33–40, 46–9, 178–88, 196–201; Cairncross, *Years of Recovery*, ch. 15; Plowden, *An Industrialist in the Treasury*, esp. chs. 3, 5, and 6; *Robert Hall Diaries 1947–53*, esp. 19–25, 47–55, 99–110; Cairncross and Watts, *Economic Section*, esp. chs. 9 and 15; Neil Rollings, 'British budgetary policy 1945–1954: a "Keynesian revolution"?', *EHR* 41 (1988), 283–98.

Table 5.5 *Cripps's Budgets, 1948-50*

	Expected surplus £m	Realized surplus £m	Total change in taxation £m[1]	Major tax changes
1948-9	789	831	+49	*Income tax*: increase in earned income relief; extension of reduced rate relief for small incomes Simplification of *purchase tax*. *Tobacco, beer, wines and spirits, and betting duties increased. Special contribution* on investment incomes.
1949-50	470	549	−92	Limit on *cost-of-living subsidies*. Reduction in *beer duty;* increase in tax on football pools and matches and in Post Office charges. *Depreciation allowances* for new investment doubled. *Death duties*: Amalgamation (and increase) of estate and legacy and succession duties.
1950-1	443	720	−1	*Income tax*: reduction in reduced rates for small incomes. Increase in *petrol tax* and in *purchase tax* on commercial vehicles.

Note
[1] In full financial year.

Sources
Cairncross, *Years of Recovery: British economic policy 1945-51*, 421; Dow, *The Management of the British Economy 1945-60*, 198-9; budget speeches of 6 Apr. 1948, 6 Apr. 1949, and 18 Apr. 1950.

based and the tenacity with which he held to them',[9] since his tax changes were fairly modest. Here I outline the main decisions involved in the preparation of the budgets introduced by Cripps in 1948–51 in order to indicate the context in which the monetary policy discussions of those years took place. Table 5.5 lists the main points of the three budgets.

Cripps opened his first budget, on 6 April 1948, by discussing the *Economic Survey for 1948*, published a month earlier. He explained:

[9] *Management of the British Economy*, 36.

Government expenditure and revenue ought not to be considered in isolation from their effects upon the general economic prospects of the country, nor can any survey of the economic position of the country be complete without a knowledge of the Government's Budget proposals. . . . The new task of the Chancellor of the Exchequer is not merely to balance the Budget; it is a much wider one—to match our resources against our needs so that the main features of our economy may be worked out for the benefit of the community as a whole.[10]

The preparation of this budget had begun as soon as the new Chancellor had dealt with the Parliamentary debates on Dalton's last budget and Finance Bill. The decisions taken by the Chancellor and the Budget Committee on 3 December 1947 included what became the main features of the 1948 budget. The first was to try out an alternative presentation of the 1947/8 budget, to distinguish accurately between revenue and capital items on both sides. This produced an estimate of the 'true' surplus, that is, the government contribution to total savings, for 1947/8 of £338m, which was given in the budget speech. The second decision was that the Economic Section should estimate the size of the 1948/9 surplus needed to combat inflation. The estimate was a target surplus of around £500m on the traditional presentation, or a 'genuine' surplus of £300m. On taxation it was decided to simplify purchase tax, to investigate the extension of the new betting duty, to consider raising the tobacco duty again, and to consider whether any changes could be made in income tax to improve incentives for lower income earners. On inheritance taxes there would 'probably [be] nothing further', but the 1945 study of a capital levy should be brought up to date and submitted to the Chancellor. On cost-of-living subsidies, 'no reduction [was] to be contemplated (except in so far as prices may fall) but no increase either'; Cripps had 'no present intention of departing from that policy [of his predecessor]'of a ceiling at the current level.[11]

The Economic Section put the inflationary gap for 1947 at £425m and that for 1948 at £480m, on the basis of the national income and expenditure estimates. The Treasury commented

[10] *House of Commons Debates*, vol. 449, 6 Apr. 1948, col. 37.

[11] Trend, 'Summary of Decisions at a Meeting of the Chancellor and the Budget Committee on Wednesday, 3rd December 1947', BC(48)3, Economic Section, 'Note on Inflation', and BC(48)12, 'Subsidies and Prices, Memorandum by the Chancellor of the Exchequer', 13 Jan. 1948, T171/394, PRO.

that 'the gaps disclosed are of such magnitude as to reinforce other general evidence that there was inflationary pressure in 1947 and will be more in 1948' and agreed with the Section's suggested target of an increase of £200–300m in the budget surplus over that expected on current rates of taxation (£270m). [12] When the Inland Revenue revised upward the 1948/9 estimated revenue on the basis of existing taxation in February 1948, it was decided to aim for £200m in new tax revenue, of which £40m would be used for income tax concessions to lower income earners. By April the surplus for 1948/9 on the basis of existing taxation had reached £778m and the tax changes in the budget were only to produce £11m net in 1948/9 (£51.5m in a full tax year), including the 'special contribution'. The tax changes included increases in the duties on beer, wine, and spirits, on tobacco, and on betting, as well as the simplification of purchase tax and the income tax concessions. [13]

The 'special contribution' was a small substitute for a full-scale capital levy, a once-for-all levy based on individuals' investment incomes in 1947/8. According to Dalton, he had on leaving office told Cripps that he was contemplating a capital levy for the 1948 budget along with some income tax reductions (not very different from those adopted). When Cripps read the Treasury note on the subject that he had asked for in December he commented that 'he was not convinced that as much weight had been given to the "pros" for such a levy as to the "cons"'. While the administrative burdens of a capital levy would be heavy, 'it must not be forgotten that the political pressure for a capital levy would be extremely strong, and he was, therefore, in favour of imposing some sort of non-recurrent anti-inflationary impost'. His officials were set to investigate such a scheme, for instance a special levy on surtax payers. (The Treasury note was largely based on the National Debt Enquiry report, which was also circulated to the Budget Committee, but it laid considerably more stress on the

[12] BC(48)3, 'Note on Inflation', 'Inflation, Treasury comment on BC(48)3', and Trend, 'Budget', 20 Jan. 1948, T171/394.

[13] BC(48)23(Final), 'Special measures to counter inflationary pressure, Memorandum by the Treasury', 5 Feb., and 'Summary of decisions taken at Roffey Park', T171/394; *House of Commons Debates*, vol. 449, 6 Apr. 1948, cols, 63–9, 74–7. Roffey Park, a rehabilitation centre for industrial workers outside Horsham, Sussex, was the location of a weekend-long meeting of the Budget Committee on 14–15 February. For the decisions on income tax, purchase tax and the increases in other duties see T171/395, sects. A, B, C, D, and G.

administrative difficulties and the possibility of a 'severe loss of confidence' and capital flight.)[14] The Inland Revenue considered a special levy on surtax payers and a special contribution charged on investment incomes: both were administratively feasible but the first would bear hardly on a high income earner with a small investment income and would probably have the more serious effects on confidence. The Budget Committee agreed the second scheme was 'the more defensible' but still feared a loss of confidence unless it were presented as one of a series of emergency measures. At the committee's weekend meeting Cripps agreed to the second scheme, but he was not sure that the proposed rates were heavy enough. He also had to be persuaded by Plowden to emphasize the 'once for all' nature of the levy in his budget speech.[15] The special contribution applied to investment incomes over £250 but only when total annual income was over £2,000, at a rate of 10 per cent on investment incomes between £250 and £500 and rising to 50 per cent on investment incomes over £5,000. Expected to yield £105m in a full financial year, it produced more revenue (£80m) in 1948/9 than the £50m anticipated.

The preparation of the 1949 budget also began from the by now usual essay on inflation from the Economic Section. Using the provisional national income estimates for 1948 this argued that the disinflationary budgetary policy in 1948 had improved the current balance of paymemts without a fall in investment by keeping down the growth of consumption. The reduction of aggregate demand was, however, less than hoped for because of the unplanned rise in investment and the larger than anticipated reduction in the current account deficit. Hence the problem of inflation in 1949 was 'to consolidate the gains of 1948, to avoid any renewed increase in inflationary pressure, and to achieve if possible a further, moderate, easing of the pressure of demand'. The surplus should therefore be maintained at its 1948/9 level.

[14] Dalton, *High Tide and After*, 288–90; Trend, 'Budget', 20 Jan. 1948, T171/394; BC(48)18, 'Note on capital levy', 14 Jan. 1948, T171/395. On the National Debt Enquiry see Ch. 1 above.

[15] BC(48)17, Gregg, 'Special contribution payable by sur-tax payers', 23 Jan., BC(48)22, Gregg, 'Special contribution charged on investment income', 2 Feb., BC(48)20 Revise, Bridges, 'Special levy on sur-tax payers or on investment income', 3 Feb., BC(48)20 Final, 'Proposals for a special levy', 5 Feb. 1948, T171/395, sect. I; Report of discussion at Roffey Park on 14–15 Feb. 1948, T171/394; Plowden, *Industrialist in the Treasury*, 38, and Plowden to Cripps. 31 Mar. 1949, T171/395; *House of Commons Debates*, vol. 49, cols. 71–3.

With increasing government expenditure this would require an increase in taxation; in January the Section put this as at least £150m 'as a rough quantitative judgement'.[16]

When the Budget Committee held its weekend meeting in February it agreed on a series of measures designed to produce an addition to the budget surplus of £134m. Hall described the meeting as 'a desperate search for money and we decided on a few more attempts though whether any of them are adopted will depend on whether S.C. can persuade his colleagues'. Some of the tax changes were indeed dropped after the Chancellor discussed his budget proposals with his senior colleagues early in March; by that time there had also been an improvement in the estimates of 1949/50 revenue and expenditure. The proposed measures included: increases in duties on football pools, matches, and petrol; the simplification of death duties with some increase in rates; a doubling of the 'initial' depreciation allowance for new plant and machinery (from 20 to 40 per cent); increases in postal and telephone charges; and a rise in the reduced rates of income tax in order to finance expenditure on the new and expensive National Health Service. The most notable proposal was on subsidies, which in spite of the 'ceiling' introduced by Dalton had risen to £485m in 1948/9. They were now to be limited to £465m and the prices of the subsidized items allowed to rise, although the effect on the cost of living would be mitigated by lowering the duties on tea, sugar and beer.[17] When his senior colleagues objected to the details of the subsidy proposals and proposed a smaller income tax increase, Cripps stuck to his subsidy proposals and abandoned the tax increase as too small to be worthwhile. A couple of weeks later, in light of a 'last look' at the budget figures the petrol tax increase was dropped—or rather

[16] *Robert Hall Diaries*, 44, 46–7; Hall to Bridges, 'Budget prospects 1949', and 'The problem of inflation in 1949', 6 Dec. 1948, BC(49)10(Revise), 'The Problem of Inflation in 1949', 20 Jan. 1949, T171/397, PRO; see also Cairncross and Watts, *Economic Section*, 247–8. There had been a 'preliminary Budget discussion' with the Chancellor in September 1948, following the preparation during the summer of a lengthy memorandum by Dow and Hall on the budgetary prospects for the next four years: see *Robert Hall Diaries*, 24, 32; Economic Section, 'Budgetary prospects and policy, 1948–1952', 17 July, and Trend, 'Budget—1949', 15 Sept. 1948, T171/397; Cairncross and Watts, 246.

[17] *Robert Hall Diaries*, 52; BC(49) 22, 'Budget Committee, Summary of Decisions taken at Roffey Park February 5–6th, 1949', T171/397; for the preceding official discussions see earlier papers on the same file, and, on the detailed proposals, T171/398.

postponed since it was adopted a year later. The net effect of the tax changes was to leave revenue almost unchanged in 1949/50 and to reduce it by £27m in a full financial year.[18]

By 1950 Cripps's ministerial colleagues were growing restive at the restraints on expenditure and on tax concessions implied by the budget surpluses. In the Treasury Robert Hall and other senior officials worried about the disincentive effects on work and saving of the high taxation needed to maintain the surpluses, while government expenditure, especially on the National Health Service, was threatening to increase, further complicating the budget problem. The final decisions on the 1950 budget were also delayed by the February 1950 general election which returned the Labour government with a severely reduced majority of only five MPs.

To the Economic Section, considering the problem of inflation in 1950 for the Budget Committee, the 'moral to be drawn from 1949 is that we want no increase in the pressure of demand in 1950, and would welcome some further reduction'. Aggregate demand in 1949 had been 'uncomfortably high' with domestic investment and government expenditure on goods and services both higher than anticipated. The devaluation of the pound in September 1949 also required a reduction in absorption in order to release resources for exports. The Section suggested a target reduction in domestic demand of £250m for 1950, £150m of this on account of devaluation. Allowing for cuts in the investment programme after the devaluation and some increase in private saving due to the increased depreciation allowances, the budget surplus should probably be increased by £50–150m. The Budget Committee decided to aim for a higher figure of £200m, in case the voluntary incomes policy broke down. As for raising the extra revenue, however, direct taxes could not be raised because of their disincentive effects, and an increase in the major indirect taxes, on beer and tobacco, would probably produce less rather than more revenue because of the elasticity of demand, leaving only an increase in the petrol tax. There ought, therefore, to be some expenditure cuts, in addition to those made the previous autumn after devaluation, to fall especially on the National

[18] Note by Trend, 16 Mar., Trend to Bamford, 16 Mar., and Trend to Croft, 15 and 30 Mar. 1949, T171/397; *House of Commons Debates*, vol. 463, 6 Apr. 1949, cols. 2087–99.

Health Service, for instance by introducing charges for some services.[19]

The Budget Committee prepared its submission to the Chancellor during the election campaign. When it came to discuss this with the Chancellor after the election, the Cabinet had decided that the Chancellor should 'give his colleagues a broad picture of the financial position of the country and of the main factors which he would take into account in framing his Budget'. Cripps gave an oral report on 3 March and had to defend his budgetary policy again at another Cabinet meeting on 17 March. The Lord Privy Seal, Lord Addison, had raised a point on which the Prime Minister thought 'there is doubt . . . in the minds of a good many of our colleagues', namely, as Attlee put it to Cripps, 'the somewhat theoretical basis for the Capital Investment Programme and the need for the very large Budget surplus'. Cripps used some of the defence produced for him by Hall and Gaitskell again in his budget speech, when he stressed the need, 'our unquestionable duty', to avoid the 'twin evils of inflation and deflation' by maintaining aggregate demand approximately equal to the output produced by a fully employed labour force.[20] In the meantime the two junior Treasury ministers, Douglas Jay (now Financial Secretary) and Hugh Gaitskell (Minister of State for Economic Affairs), settled the details of the budget proposals with the senior officials, before Cripps discussed them with Attlee, Bevin and Morrison. It was finally decided to increase the petrol tax, to lower the reduced rates of income tax, to apply purchase tax to commercial vehicles, in order to reduce domestic demand for these vehicles,

[19] BC(50)3 (Revise), 'The problem of inflation in 1950', 9 Feb., and BC(50)15, 'The Budget position 1950/51, Memorandum by the Budget Committee', 22 February 1950, T171/400; Cairncross and Watts, *Economic Section*, 250–1.
An increase in petrol tax had been strongly pressed by Douglas Jay. One reason for dropping it the previous year had been the difficulty of providing exemptions for deserving users, for instance, of agricultural tractors; the solution found in 1950 was to promise a subsidy to farmers with petrol-driven tractors: Croft to Chancellor, 22 Feb. 1949, T171/398; PB(49)6, 'Minute by Economic Secretary to the Treasury', 9 Dec., and Note by Cripps. 10 Dec. 1949, T171/400; memoranda in section 3(a), T171/401. The yield from doubling the duty was estimated in the budget as £73m in a full financial year (£68.5m in 1950/1).
[20] Extracts from Cabinets 5(50) and 7(50), 25 Feb. and 3 Mar. 1950, Addison to Cripps, 10 Mar., and Attlee to Cripps, 11 Mar., CP(50)35, 'Budget Policy, Note by the Chancellor of the Exchequer', 15 Mar. 1950, T171/400; *House of Commons Debates*, vol. 474, 18 Apr. 1950, cols. 61–3. The Chancellor's note to the Cabinet was written by Hall and rewritten by Gaitskell: *Robert Hall Diaries*, 106–8.

while reducing purchase tax on larger and more expensive private cars which were in demand overseas, in order to encourage their production, and to adjust beer duty so that the alcoholic strength of beer, which had been reduced by 20 per cent during the war, could be raised without an increase in the price of a pint. The cost of the reduction in income tax was estimated to be covered almost exactly by the revenue from the petrol tax increase and purchase tax on commercial vehicles, making this a 'no change' budget, instead of the original official intentions.[21]

The Chancellor had not been able to persuade his colleagues to accept any significant further reductions in government expenditure. In his budget speech he warned there could be no further increase in expenditure on the National Health Service and that the government might be obliged to introduce charges for prescriptions. Food subsidies would be limited to the 1949/50 ceiling which had, however, been reduced by the autumn expenditure cuts to £410m. In face of the political pressures it was, as Dow emphasized, a major achievement to have pursued a tough fiscal stance for three years.[22] Against this background there was growing official consideration, initiated by Douglas Jay in the winter of 1947/8, of the possibility of using monetary policy to support the disinflationary budgets.

Jay's campaign

In 1947 monetary growth was much slower than in 1946, with M3 growing at about 5 per cent rather than nearly 15 per cent. This was observed by contemporaries in the similar behaviour of the deposits of the London clearing banks (see Table 5.6). Nominal interest rates were nearly 2½ per cent for short-term government bonds and 3 per cent for long-term bonds. Douglas Jay was none the less worried about the inflationary consequences of the monetary expansion during the war and under Dalton's now failed cheaper money experiment, while also concerned to prevent any further rise in interest rates. As Dalton's PPS he submitted a memorandum to the Chancellor on 'Interest rates, credit inflation

---

[21] Notes of meetings on 8 and 11 Mar., and 'Budget 1950, Decisions on the main proposals', 21 Mar. 1950, T171/400; *House of Commons Debates*, vol. 474, 18 Apr. 1950, cols. 71–9.

[22] Ibid., cols. 59–61; Dow, *Management of the British Economy*, 48.

TABLE 5.6 *London Clearing Banks Assets and Liabilities, 31 December 1945–52, £m*

	1945	1946	1947	1948	1949	1950	1951	1952
Total deposits	4,850	5,685	5,934	6,200	6,202	6,368	6,333	6,460
Net deposits	4,660	5,438	5,682	5,914	5,964	6,100	6,036	6,155
Change from previous year	6.6%	16.7%	4.5%	4.1%	0.8%	2.3%	−1.0%	2.0%
Cash	536	499	502	501	532	540	531	549
	(11.1)[1]	(8.8)	(8.5)	(8.1)	(8.6)	(8.5)	(8.4)	(8.5)
Money at call and short notice	252	432	480	485	571	592	598	529
	(5.2)	(7.6)	(8.1)	(7.8)	(9.2)	(9.3)	(9.4)	(8.2)
Bills discounted	369	610	793	741	1,109	1,408	972	1,248
	(7.6)	(10.7)	(13.3)	(12.0)	(17.9)	(22.1)	(15.4)	(19.3)
Treasury deposit receipts	1,523	1,560	1,288	1,397	793	456	102	—
	(31.4)	(27.4)	(21.7)	(22.5)	(12.8)	(7.2)	(1.6)	(0)
Investments	1,234	1,427	1,483	1,478	1,512	1,528	1,965	2,148
	(25.4)	(25.1)	(25.0)	(23.8)	(24.4)	(24.0)	(31.0)	(33.3)
Advances	815	980	1,206	1,378	1,523	1,644	1,931	1,749
	(16.8)	(17.2)	(20.3)	(22.2)	(24.6)	(25.8)	(30.5)	(27.1)

Note
[1] Figures in parentheses = percentage of total deposits.

Source
Monthly Digest of Statistics

and the budget surplus', which received little attention in the run-up to Dalton's fourth and last budget. After Dalton resigned, Jay tried again with the new Chancellor. (Jay was also promoted to Economic Secretary in December.) This time the officials responded once they had dealt with the issue of the first transport nationalization stock (on which see Chapter 4).

Jay pointed out that clearing bank deposits had increased during the war from around £2,200m to £4,800m and had further increased during 1946 to £5,600m. The cause of the further increase was 'fairly evidently' a budget deficit and the attempt to finance it at lower interest rates. He was also clear that the monetary expansion was increasing domestic absorption:

(*a*) Though it cannot increase imports, it makes it profitable all along the line for the less public-spirited businessmen to divert goods from export to the home market.

(*b*) It maintains the pressure for labour to go into inessential industries ...

(c) It prolongs a queue situation in practically all markets, because there is too much money still pursuing quite a high quantity of goods.

(d) It, therefore, makes all controls rather more difficult to hold . . .

(e) For these reasons, it stimulates a tendency towards more wage demands.

He believed that the authorities should take the opportunity about to be provided by a budget surplus to reduce bank deposits by the same amount, namely £600m. It was necessary first to issue the transport stock (with no more than a 2¾ per cent yield) but then, in the new year, government departments with surplus funds should buy up securities from the market while at the same time the Bank of England should sell securities so as to induce the banks to sell some of their large holdings of government securities, 'to such an extent as will lead to a sale over the year of about £600,000,000 of Government securities by the Bank and the clearing banks together'. Jay thought that if the public departments were buying up the same amount of securities this would prevent a fall in gilt-edged prices and hence a rise in interest rates, while the banks' holdings of gilts and their deposits would both be reduced by £600m. If, instead, the authorities used the budget surplus to retire floating debt the banks' reserves would be unchanged and there would be no reduction in bank deposits.[23]

Jay's curious proposal was thus for a combination of the use of the surplus to retire government debt and of deflationary open-market operations by the Bank to bring about a fall in bank reserves by the amount necessary to induce the banks to reduce their deposits by £600m. Although one can work out what quantity of government securities the Bank would in principle have to sell to reduce bank reserves it is difficult to see how the Bank could have conducted these operations without raising interest rates. After all, if the whole manœuvre were to succeed in its objective of reducing bank deposits by the amount of the budget surplus the non-bank public would have to be persuaded to hold a smaller amount of money, which would require a rise in interest rates (except in the unlikely event that the demand for money were to fall by exactly the amount of the budget surplus). It was

[23] Jay, 'Interest rates, credit inflation and the budget surplus', 5 and 24 Nov. 1947, T233/481, PRO. In order to finance the transport nationalization at 2½ or 2¾ per cent he suggested the authorities take up Davenport's suggestion of issuing two transport stocks, on which see Appendix to Ch. 4.

also quite unrealistic for Jay to assume that the banks would react to a shortage of reserves by selling gilts. The banks could always replenish their reserves by reducing their Treasury bill holdings since the authorities were in the 1940s committed to buying in Treasury bills in order to maintain the fixed Treasury bill rate. This 'open back door' to the Bank of England was not closed until the abandonment of the wartime ½ per cent Treasury bill rate in November 1951.[24] In these circumstances the overall effect on bank deposits of the budget surplus plus the operations recommended by Jay would have been nil. But Jay was correct to suspect that the use of the surplus to retire floating debt held mainly by the banks would by itself counteract the effect of the surplus on bank reserves.

The Treasury officials were puzzled by Jay's proposal. They told him that the budget surplus was already being used as it accrued to reduce floating debt, and, after consulting the Bank, that the banks would not usually react to a shortage of cash by selling gilts but would reduce call money or Treasury bills or TDRs. They pointed out that the whole of the published budget surplus was not necessarily available for debt redemption because of 'below the line' expenditure. They also followed the Bank's advice in arguing that reducing floating debt was the way of reducing 'the most "inflationary" part of the National Debt', that the Bank's 'normal practice' was to adjust the banks' reserves so as to maintain them at 8 per cent of their deposits (so that if bank deposits fell as the budget surplus accrued bank reserves would be reduced to match), and that the authorities could not issue a funding loan, 'one of the orthodox methods of countering inflation', while they had to issue nationalization compensation. They also made it clear that they did not think a reduction of bank deposits could be pursued if it meant a rise in nominal interest rates which would increase the cost of the national debt. Hence 'we should not abandon the cheap money policy, based on the accepted rate of 3% long term, though for the

[24] As R. S. Sayers pointed out, 'the only difference (and it is an important one) between the traditional system and the [1940s] one is that traditionally the operation of the Bank as lender of last resort caused a movement in short interest rates, whereas the new system guarantees cash at the fixed interest rate': *Modern Banking* (3rd edn., 1951), 118–19. It should be noted, however, especially in fairness to Jay, that Sayers did not mention the 'open back door' in the previous (1947) edition of his textbook where he described the traditional system.

time being at least we must abandon the pursuit of 2½% long term.'[25]

Jay was not inclined to believe that this was all that could be done. When he asked to discuss with the Bank 'the technical aspects of the argument', the Governor invited him to lunch and to talk with the Chief Cashier, Sir Kenneth Peppiatt, who became an Executive Director a year later, and Humphrey Mynors, an adviser who became a Director in 1949 and Deputy Governor in 1954. According to Fforde,

The Chief Cashier appears to have been a little perplexed by this about-turn and somewhat at a loss to know how to respond to questions requiring a prolonged excursion into monetary economics and central banking techniques. Two years previously one group of politicians, officials, and economists, had not thought it worthwhile consulting the Bank on these fundamentals of monetary policy.[26]

Mynors and Peppiatt 'agree[d with Jay] that a reduction in the level of bank deposits is desirable. It would be a sign that inflationary pressure is under control and would be helpful abroad in giving confidence in sterling'. But the high level of bank deposits was 'a symptom rather than a cause of inflation', which was due to wartime deficit finance. It would disappear with a real budget surplus as the floating debt was reduced, since the Bank would keep the banks' cash reserves at a constant 8 per cent ratio to their deposits by means of open-market operations in Treasury bills. The Bank men saw no need to employ Bank rate, which was ineffective with a ½ per cent Treasury bill rate, since the authorities were not trying to attract money from abroad or to check a stock exchange boom at home.[27]

[25] Campion, 'Mr Jay and Cheap Money', 19 Dec. 1947, and 'Bank deposits and inflation, Notes on Mr. Jay's memorandum', 21 Jan. 1948, T233/481, PRO; Bamford to Peppiatt, 24 Dec. 1947, and Peppiatt to Bamford, 1 Jan. 1948, C40/685, BOE.

[26] Ibid.; Fforde, *Bank*, 361. Fforde also remarks (p. 318) that 'it was well known that Peppiatt disliked attending meetings at the Treasury, preferring to deal with his customer by correspondence or over lunch in Threadneedle Street'. Mynors had been a fellow in economics of Corpus Christi College, Cambridge, before he joined the Bank in 1933.

[27] Bamford, 'Bank deposits, Note of Mr. Jay's talk at the Bank of England with Sir Kenneth Peppiatt and Mr. Mynors', 31 Jan., and Bank of England, 'Bank deposits and inflation', 28 Jan. 1948, T233/481. Jay's visit to the Bank is the starting point of the chronicle, 'Discussions preceding the change in monetary policy in November 1951', prepared by Maurice Allen in the Bank in 1953: W. M. Allen to Secretary, 12 Nov. 1953, G15/13, BOE.

The Bank also claimed the banks were 'co-operating effectively' in the 'voluntary restriction of advances' which had been requested in the Chancellor's letter to the Governor on 2 December. When the government had taken steps to reduce investment after the summer crisis the Treasury had issued a new Memorandum of Guidance to the Capital Issues Committee. As in 1939 and 1945 the Chancellor of the Exchequer had at the same time asked the Governor of the Bank to ask the London clearing banks to follow the same principles in their lending policy—essentially to favour projects which would help the balance of payments. He also repeated the earlier request not to give large personal loans or loans for speculative purposes.[28] The weakness of the Bank's argument was that this arrangement put no limit on the total of bank advances *at the same time that the Bank placed no reserve constraint on bank deposits.* The banks could, therefore, expand their advances, and hence their deposits, since the Bank of England would provide them with the reserves necessary to maintain their 8 per cent reserve-deposit ratio. If the banks did expand their advances the contractionary effect of the budget surplus on deposits could easily be counteracted.

After his visit to the Bank Jay wanted to formalize the current 'policy' in a memorandum for Cripps. With reluctance, for as Bamford told Jay, 'the Bank don't much like written statements on the exercise of their technique', the Bank and Treasury produced an agreed version of Jay's draft, which Jay sent to Cripps at the end of February.[29] At this point Bridges, the Permanent Secretary, consulted his predecessor and, on Hopkins's advice, D. H. Robertson, as well as asking Robert Hall what he thought of the Bank's policy. Bridges told Hopkins: 'All this is to me very unfamiliar and difficult. . . . I do not feel by any means certain that we have got the bottom of this.' The Chancellor also consulted Hilary Marquand (the Paymaster-General and a professional economist), Hall and Plowden.[30]

---

[28] *Capital Issues Control,* Cmd. 7281, Dec. 1947; Cripps to Governor, 2 Dec. 1947, C40/685, BOE. On the 1939 and 1945 requests see Ch. 1.

[29] Jay to Bamford, 3 Feb., Bamford to Peppiatt, 'Bank deposits and inflation', 13 Feb., Bamford to Jay, 23 Feb., and Jay to Chancellor, 26 Feb. 1948, T233/481, PRO; see also the comments by Peppiatt and Mynors on the draft on C40/685, BOE, and Fforde, *Bank,* 362.

[30] Bridges to Hopkins, 27 Feb. and 15 Mar., Marquand to Chancellor, 19 Mar., and Note by Trend, 25 Mar. 1948, T233/481; *Robert Hall Diaries,* 21.

Hopkins and Robertson both supplied written comments to Bridges on Jay's memorandum. Hopkins was not sure that the growth of bank deposits was inflationary and thought it was 'more important . . . to keep a reasonably stable level of interest rates'. Robertson, on the other hand, was doubtful whether the Bank of England could be relied upon to control monetary expansion without the discipline of the gold standard and noted the rapid increase in bank advances since the war.[31] Marquand shared Jay's concern that a budget surplus might not be translated into a decrease in bank deposits and supported his initiative, as did Bridges. Cripps and his advisers therefore agreed that after the budget he would send Jay's memorandum to the Governor and ask him for 'a formal assurance that the action suggested in that document would, in fact, be taken by the Bank'.[32]

The Chancellor's letter was sent on 7 April, the day after the budget. According to Mynors, the Governor was not pleased to receive it but 'felt that he could not refuse to accept' it. He returned a non-committal reply, which Trend, the Chancellor's private secretary, thought was 'just about good enough' as long as it was followed up.[33] The outcome was the preparation of regular reports by Bank of England and Treasury officials on the use of the budget surplus for debt reduction and on the behaviour of bank assets and liabilities shown by the London clearing banks' monthly statements. What these reports showed can be seen in Tables 5.8 and 5.9 below. In the discussions which followed them the original concern with the growth of bank deposits became increasingly focused on the behaviour of bank lending and the apparent inability or unwillingness of the Bank to restrain it. Robert Hall was particularly involved in trying to dis-

[31] Hopkins to Bridges, undated, and Note by Robertson, 11 Mar. 1948, T233/481. Hopkins's comments also referred to a paper sent to the Treasury by W. F. Crick of the Midland Bank, which analysed the causes of the monetary expansion of 1946 essentially as a continuation of the wartime passive monetary policy. For Crick's analysis see also his 'The changing shape of Britain's monetary system, Part I: 1931–45' *Midland Bank Review* (Nov. 1947), 1–6 and ibid., 'Part II: Post-war transition', (Feb. 1948), 1–7.

[32] Marquand to Chancellor, 19 Mar., Jay to Chancellor, 15 Mar., and Note by Trend, 25 Mar. 1948, T233/481.

[33] Note by Mynors, 'For record', 9 Apr. 1948, C40/685, BOE; Cripps to Catto, 7 Apr., Catto to Chancellor, 19 Apr., and Trend to Chancellor, 21 Apr. 1948, T233/482, PRO.

pel the confusion over the question of whether and to what extent the Bank could control the money supply.

In the first quarter of 1948 the 'Jay exercise' was encouraging, showing a fall in TDRs and a similar fall in bank deposits. This was in spite of the repayment of £300m 3% Conversion Loan 1948/53 which Dalton and then Cripps had decided not to try to convert in the autumn of 1947 (see Chapter 4) and a rise in bank advances.[34] At the beginning of the new financial year an increase in bank deposits could be explained away by some abnormal government payments, although there had also been a substantial rise in bank advances. When the results for the second quarter of 1948 were complete it was clear that while the banks' holdings of floating debt were declining their advances and their deposits were continuing to increase. The reduction of floating debt had also only been possible because of the receipt of Marshall Aid.[35] Jay began to agitate for some further action, especially on advances, and, after discussion of the subject in the Budget Committee, Eady consulted Cobbold. The Bank tried to head off criticism by asserting that the budget surplus for 1948/9 had not yet materialized, that they could not reduce the banks' reserves because the banks could replenish them by selling their Treasury bills, and that although the imposition of a quantitative limit on bank advances would be 'unwise', the banks might respond well to a little moral suasion from the Governor. Cobbold also agreed to 'an informal Bank/Treasury body' to monitor the behaviour of bank advances.[36] This was set up in the autumn.

In September there was 'quite a hunt going on against the Bank over the increase in deposits', with Compton and Eady making 'enormous calculations' as Robert Hall put it. The figures, which showed a large rise in bank advances, prompted the Bank to

[34] Compton to Bamford, 29 Apr., and 'Bank deposits and the Exchequer surplus', T233/482. The authorities' efforts did not go unnoticed: see 'Less money at last?', *The Economist*, 6 Mar. 1948, 389, and [Wilfred King], 'The monetary factor in gilt-edged', *The Banker*, (June 1948), 155–63.

[35] Bamford to Gilbert, 'Bank deposits and inflation', 6 May, 'Bank deposits and the exchequer surplus, Period 31st December, 1947 to 19th May, 1948', and 'Exchequer surplus and the floating debt', 10 Aug. 1948, T233/482. On the preparation of these documents which were mainly the responsibility of Chadwick in the Treasury and Mynors in the Bank see also C40/685, BOE.

[36] Jay to Chancellor, 18 Aug. 1948, T233/482; Griffiths, 'Budget Committee, Deflation and the money supply—Current position', 1 Aug. 1948, T171/397; Eady to Cobbold, 19 Aug., [Mynors?] to Governors, 19 Aug. 1948, C40/685; Eady, 'Bank advances policy', 24 Aug. 1948, T233/482; Fforde, *Bank*, 363.

make enquiries of the banks about the reasons for the rise and the setting up of the Working Party on Bank Deposits and Advances, with Jay as chairman, Hall and Compton from the Treasury, and Mynors and Thompson-McCausland from the Bank.[37] Before the working party met, Hall and Plowden 'sent an angry minute to Bridges about the Bank statements', on which Eady called a meeting with Hall, Compton, Chadwick (the Treasury Account-ant), and Mynors. Mynors recorded that 'Hall [was] very reason-able, although very troubled, and admits that his prime difficulty is to understand what is going on.' Hall, on the other hand, thought it was 'hard not to get the impression that the Bank, and the banks generally, do not think at all about credit control as economists do', having already come to suspect that the Bank 'tends to the early 19th century heresy that *because* prices are rising therefore more money is needed'. Hall also 'fortified' himself before the first meeting of Jay's working party by reading some of Keynes's and Sayers's writings.[38]

Hall was not entirely correct in attributing 'Banking School' views to the Bank of England in the 1940s but the Bank officials in their discussions with Hall and in the working party laid them-selves open to this interpretation, largely by failing to clarify the role of interest rates in monetary control. The day after Eady's meeting Mynors wrote to Eady and Hall, 'to have another go at clearing my fuddled brain'. In his 'simple and old-fashioned' view,

The fundamental problem . . . is the equation of current investment with spontaneous applied saving. To suppose that anything can be achieved by pegging the volume of money in circulation is like Canute telling the waves to stand still, *unless* the indirect effects of such an instruction are to reduce investment and/or increase saving to the appropriate extent and in the appropriate quarters.

A restrictive policy on bank advances might have some effect on investment but 'one cannot say where the effect would work out and whether the desirable would suffer more than the undesir-

[37] *Robert Hall Diaries*, 38, 43; Cobbold to Governor, 4 Oct., and Note by Catto, 5 Oct. 1948, C40/685; Eady to Bridges, 'Deposits and advances in October', 10 Nov., Cripps to Jay, 13 Nov., and Cobbold to Eady, 24 Nov. 1948, T233/482.

[38] *Robert Hall Diaries*, 41; Mynors, 'The Exchequer and bank deposits', 9 Nov. 1948, C40/685, BOE. As already mentioned, however, the current edition of Sayers's *Modern Banking* did not mention the Bank's 'open back door' (see n. 24 above).

able'. He also did not think any 'practicable change in [interest] rates will much affect' investment, although it might encourage saving. The 'first thing' needed was to 'reintroduce some measure of flexibility' in interest rates and to fund some of the floating debt, especially TDRs. As for the monetary base the Bank had little control given the needs of the Exchequer for current expenditure and for replacing maturing debt.[39] In a similar vein, and echoing his views in 1945 (Chapter 1 above), Lucius Thompson-McCausland claimed there had been a 'marked qualitative deflation' in 1948 despite the rise in bank deposits because (a) currency in circulation had fallen and (b) within the deposits total there had been a shift from current accounts to deposit accounts. 'All this amounts to a preliminary re-shaping of the qualitative money structure from which deflation can better be carried through to the final stage in which deflation is also quantitative', so that there was no need to increase the existing pressure on borrowers. A quicker way to reduce advances and hence deposits would be to reduce the investment programme. He also claimed that 'it would be quite impossible to administer a ceiling on deposits'. Inside the Bank Thompson-McCausland acknowledged more clearly than to Hall that the UK money supply was demand-determined: a few days earlier he had minuted Cobbold, 'Surely the Treasury, in worrying about advances, are looking at the wrong side of the balance sheet? With interest rates and employment levels fixed, the public can make deposits what they want them.'[40]

Hall disputed Mynors' Canute analogy:

I do not agree at all that to peg the volume of money is like telling the waves to stand still. If those who wish to finance an increased amount of investment are unable to do so by getting additional banking accommodation, they will be forced either to use their own liquid funds, or to borrow from those who already have such funds, or to realise some of their non-liquid assets. In all these cases, the investment can still be financed but the effect is to reduce the liquidity of some-one or other throughout the system; whereas if the investment is financed by an increase in bank deposits, the overall liquidity is increased and . . . they spend the money and thus put pressure on prices.

[39] Mynors to Eady, 12 Nov. 1948, T233/482; see also Note by Mynors, 8 Oct. 1948, marked, 'Original handed by Deputy Governor to Sir Wilfrid Eady, 4/11', C40/685.
[40] Thompson-McCausland to Hall, 26 Nov. 1948, T233/483; Thompson-McCausland to Deputy Governor, 'The rise in deposits', 12 Nov. 1948, C40/685.

Although it might be difficult to predict the effects of a ceiling on bank deposits, including the effects on interest rates, 'it is a risk which we certainly ought to take' in order to discourage new investment. He agreed with Mynors on the need to fund some of the floating debt. While he did not disagree with the facts used by Thompson-McCausland, he thought there was a case for a more restrictive monetary policy. He was 'at a loss to understand why it is impossible to administer' a ceiling on deposits:

As you yourself say, individual accounts are always rising and falling, and I thought it was the first principle of central banking that there should be an effective control over the aggregate of deposits.[41]

These arguments were to be repeated several times in the working party's meetings over the next year.

Before the first meeting of the working party the authorities considered the possibility of a funding operation to reduce the floating debt. Although Eady thought that 'a slightly higher average rate of interest on the debt [might] have less risks than a continuance of monetary inflationary pressure through short money', he also believed that 'the crucial issue of our monetary policy at present should be to keep an effective rate of 3 per cent for Government longs'. Hence the Bank was asked to assess the prospects for a medium-term issue or a long-term issue heavily underwritten by the Issue Department. The Bank and the Government Broker did not think a large issue could be made without disturbing interest rates. Cobbold suggested instead 'a more technical operation', namely that the Issue Department should buy long-term securities from the NDC in order to sell them gradually to the market, while the NDC should cease buying long-term securities from the market and be provided with a non-marketable annuity for the savings bank funds in due course. Jay thought the proposal was 'in the right direction' and the Chancellor gave his approval on 24 November.[42] This

[41] Hall to Thompson-McCausland, 17 Nov. 1948, C40/685; Hall to Thompson-McCausland, 1 Dec. 1948, T233/482.

[42] Eady to Bridges, 'Deposits and advances in October', 10 Nov., and 'Funding issue', 16 Nov., Compton to Eady, 'Market operations in gilt-edged', 16 Nov., Cobbold to Eady, 18 Nov., Compton to Eady, 'Funding', 22 Nov., Eady to Trend, 23 Nov., Jay to Chancellor, 24 Nov., and Eady to Cobbold, 25 Nov. 1948, T233/482; Peppiatt, 'Funding loan', 15 and 16 Nov., C40/686, BOE.

policy was continued until the gilt-edged market began to weaken along with the exchange rate in May 1949 (below).

The Working Party on Bank Deposits and Advances first met on 30 November and 3 December. The mechanics of the 'technical operation' were explained before the group examined the relation between clearing bank deposits and their holdings of floating debt. It was suggested, no doubt by Thompson-McCausland, that there had been a 'qualitative deflation' (because of a switch from current to deposit accounts) but it was also admitted that this had been offset by an increase in advances. Hall thought this 'would have been more convincing' if the Bank had not previously blamed the increase in deposits on the budget surplus. He found Thompson-McCausland's arguments 'ingenious ... I wish I could make up my mind whether they were genuine or a rationalization of what they want'.[43]

The brief by Eady for the working party meetings had followed the Bank line in claiming that it was 'quite impracticable' to set quantitative limits on either bank deposits or bank advances. Eady also took up the earlier suggestion by Cobbold that the Governor should ask the banks to be more selective and cautious in their lending policy. The working party did not come to a decision on the control of advances but recommended that the accruing budget surplus in the first quarter of 1949 should be used to repay floating debt in another attempt to reduce bank deposits by the amount of the surplus. Eady's paper appeared as an appendix in the report to the Chancellor.[44]

As Fforde has noted, 'There is little doubt that the Bank detested the idea of imposing advances ceilings on the banks, though the precise reasons for this were not well articulated at this time.' It partly reflected the Bank's 'deep-seated practical scepticism about direct banking controls'. Although the Governor was ill, he intervened from his sick-bed with a strongly worded protest in a memorandum, which 'included some

[43] 'Working party on bank deposits and advances, 1st report', 3 Dec. 1948, T233/482; *Robert Hall Diaries*, 45.

[44] 'Deposits and advances of London Clearing Banks in 1948', 25 Nov., 'Working party on bank deposits and advances, 1st report', 3 Dec., and Jay to Bridges and Chancellor, 3 Dec. 1948, T233/482; for Eady's views see also Eady to Economic Secretary, 'Bank deposits and advances', 1 Dec. 1948, C40/685.

imaginative exaggeration of the supposed ill-effects of an advances ceiling'.[45] When Cripps read the Working Party report he had picked up Eady's proposal and when he discussed the report with Jay, Bridges, Plowden, Eady, Compton, and Hall on 21 December he decided that he would not only tell the Bank that he endorsed the report's recommendations but also ask the Bank to ask the banks 'to keep down the level of bank advances by being more selective in certain directions'. When he and Jay talked to Cobbold later the same day they 'had a long discussion ranging over most of the old ground' on the control of bank advances. According to Cobbold they eventually agreed:

(a) that the Banks should not be asked, at any rate for the time being, to put any quantitative or qualitative limits on advances

(b) that we should have a talk to the Clearing Banks [and] explain the Chancellor's anxieties. . . .[46]

On 6 January 1949 Cobbold told the chairman and deputy chairman of the Committee of London Clearing Bankers (Lords Linlithgow and Balfour of Burleigh) that he hoped that any net increase in advances in 1949 I could be kept to 'the minimum that is absolutely necessary to avoid disturbance' so as not to offset the effect on deposits of the reduction in floating debt in that quarter. He told the Treasury that the bankers 'expressed themselves as fully in agreement with this objective' although they expected a continuing heavy demand for advances. To quote Fforde again, this 'first such request to be made since the Bank of England Act 1946 . . . had been made in exactly the manner that the Bank preferred. There was no directive, not even a letter'.[47]

The working party met again on 11 January. It further considered advances control, and agreed the Treasury should revise the December 1947 Memorandum of Guidance to the Capital Issues Committee. The Treasury would issue the new version in the spring about the same time as the annual *Economic Survey* and send copies through the Governor to the clearing banks so as to

[45] Fforde, *Bank*, 364, 366–8; Catto to Chancellor, 17 Dec., and 'Memorandum by Lord Catto', 15 Dec. 1948, T233/483, PRO.

[46] Cripps to Economic Secretary, 5 Dec. 1948, T233/482; Notes by Compton and Trend, 21 Dec. 1948, T233/483, PRO; Note by Cobbold, 21 Dec. 1948, C40/685, BOE.

[47] Note by Cobbold, 6 Jan. 1949, C40/686, BOE; Trend to Mitchell, 27 Jan. 1949, T233/483, PRO; Fforde, *Bank*, 369.

stiffen them in their 'cautious' lending policy. At the same meeting the Bank members explained that the Bank did not try to
control the monetary base but since the wartime increase in the
floating debt had supplied the reserves necessary to enable the
banks to take up the amount of Treasury bills and TDRs desired
by the government. Anticipating 'another seminar on monetary
theory', Mynors recorded that 'the atmosphere was more sympathetic and tentative than I expected' and that neither interest
rates nor gilt-edged market intervention were discussed.[48]

The Treasury issued the new Memorandum to the CIC on 14
April and the Chancellor wrote to the Governor (now Cobbold)
the same day. Cobbold had succeeded Lord Catto on 1 March (in
spite of Dalton's efforts to dissuade Cripps from his appointment).[49] Although the Bank officials had been careful to avoid
the topic of interest rates in discussions with the Treasury, the
new Governor had decided that interest rates must be changed
(upwards) but he was well aware that the ending of cheap money
would be politically difficult for the Labour government and
resisted by the Treasury. As Thompson-McCausland had put it
after the first working party meeting:

The real point at issue, surely is the interest rate.
We are getting into the position of constantly telling Whitehall what
cannot be done; which is a weak position unless we are also satisfied that
nothing need be done—apart from the recent decision to sell longer-
dated stocks as opportunity offers.
But what we mean (do we not?) is that none of the things that we have
been pressed to do can be done without a rise in the interest rate.

Cobbold had begun to discuss interest rates with his senior colleagues the previous day, because, as he subsequently told Catto,
'I still believe that the only satisfactory way [of reducing bank

----

[48] 'Working party on bank deposits and advances, 2nd report', 18 Jan. 1949,
T233/483; Mynors to Niemeyer and the Chief Cashier, 5 Jan., and 'Jay Working
Party', 12 Jan. 1949, C40/686.
[49] The Chancellor's letter to Cobbold is on C40/757, BOE. Dalton warned
Cripps that Cobbold was 'reactionary' and that 'we should be landed with him for
10 years'; Cripps, who admitted he had tried to get someone else (John Hanbury-
Williams, chairman of Courtaulds), replied that Cobbold 'wouldn't want to go on
for more than 5 years' and would want to retire to the country at Knebworth:
Dalton Diary, vol. 36, 11 Sept. 1948. Cobbold remained Governor until 1961. Like
Dalton he was educated at Eton and King's College Cambridge; he was, according
to the latter's obituary notice, 'clearly conscious of the dignity and power attached

lending] is the old-fashioned one of making borrowing more expensive.' He anticipated that government expenditure would increase in 1949/50 and that advances would continue to rise. Therefore 'we ought at least seriously to consider the question of firming up short-term money rates'.[50]

Cobbold's colleagues 'generally agreed that higher rates were called for in existing conditions', in order to check bank lending and hence growth in bank deposits, and that the first quarter of 1949 might provide the best opportunity to initiate the process since the floating debt would be declining. The move could be made without raising Bank rate, by using open-market operations to bring short-term money market rates (including Treasury bill rate) nearer Bank rate and to force the market to borrow from time to time from the Bank—in other words, to make the 2 per cent Bank rate effective. This was preferable to raising the fixed rates for Treasury bills and TDRs since that would retain the 'artificiality' of the present rate structure. A small Bank committee, including Niemeyer and Peppiatt, P. S. Beale, who succeeded Peppiatt as Chief Cashier in 1949, Mynors and Thompson-McCausland, further considered the proposal in January. They concentrated on the anticipated objections, their main argument against the main objection, the increased cost of government borrowing, being that this cost was less than that of inflation to the British economy. Although in March Cobbold decided it was not yet 'wise or appropriate' to put the proposal to the Treasury, the Bank now had a scheme for tightening monetary policy ready to be hauled out at a suitable moment.[51]

In the first half of 1949 Jay's working party met regularly to monitor the effects of the accruing budget surplus on the clearing banks' balance sheets. When these showed that clearing bank deposits in February 1949 were only £18m higher than a year earlier, Jay told Cripps that he thought 'we can congratulate

to the office of Governor and was said to play the part even when shaving in his pyjama trousers': King's College, *Annual Report*, (1988), 42–3. Cf. Fforde, *Bank*, 231–2.

[50] Thompson-McCausland to Deputy Governor, 'Deposits', 3 Dec., Cobbold to Governor, 8 Dec. 1948, C40/685. Cobbold also told the Governor: 'Thompson-McCausland has done a lot of good work with the Whitehall economists, etc. . . . The papers [i.e the working party report] still, however, contain a lot of thought which I believe to be dangerous . . . .'

[51] Peppiatt, 'Interest rates', 3 Dec. 1948, and Niemeyer to Deputy Governor, 3 Feb. 1949, C42/1; Governor's Note, 8 Mar. 1949, G1/70; Fforde, *Bank*, 372.

ourselves that the reversal, particularly in January and February, of the inflation of bank deposits is partly due to the deliberate policy that we and the Bank have been pursuing'. Jay was, however, warned that after the end of the financial year a deficit would appear in 1949 II–IV until the next year's surplus materialized.[52] By July, with advances still rising and threatening to rise further because of the weak state of the new issue market, credit restriction was on Jay's agenda again. According to the minutes of the 4 July meeting of his working party, 'the question was whether it should be done by manipulating the interest rate, or by ... applying pressure through the banks', which was 'less undesirable and ineffective'. According to Mynors, he deflected the question by 'reiterating that the Bank would not in present circumstances advocate any such change except in support of a policy of curtailing Government expenditure'. But, as Mynors also recorded, 'the meeting ... wore an air of exceptional unreality' in considering monetary policy without reference to the balance-of-payments crisis.[53]

Devaluation

It was always likely that Britain would have to devalue the pound after the war given the wartime changes in her creditor position and the structure of her balance of payments. The loss of foreign assets and the acquisition of massive external debts meant that she would no longer enjoy a sizeable services surplus and would have to achieve an improvement in the trade balance in the medium and longer run. This would probably require a change in the exchange rate, which had been chosen almost arbitrarily in 1939 (see Chapter 1). In 1945, however, there was no way of knowing what the appropriate post-war exchange rate would turn out to be. The economists in government were also divided on whether devaluation could significantly improve the balance of payments in the circumstances of

[52] 'Working party on bank deposits and advances, 4th report', and Jay to Chancellor, 10 Mar. 1948, T233/483.

[53] 'Working party on bank deposits and advances, 6th report', 8 July, and Eady to Economic Secretary, 9 July 1949, T233/483; Mynors, 'Working party on bank deposits', 5 July 1949, C40/686.

the transition (imports controlled, exports limited by supply shortages, etc.).[54]

During the summer crisis of 1947 the Bank considered devaluation as one of the steps that would have to be taken if there were no Marshall Aid to Britain, not only to prevent 'a possible breakdown of exchange control over capital movements', but also to correct a probable overvaluation of the pound. The proposal was 'kept to the most restricted circle in *Bank and Treasury only*'.[55] Early in August the Bank decided against the proposal, which had by this time taken the form of abandoning support of the pound in New York so as 'to precipitate a new situation' in which to negotiate with the Americans.[56] As the dollar drain continued in 1948 a small group of Bank and Treasury officials continued to talk about exchange rate changes, including the possibility of floating the pound rather than devaluing to a new fixed rate.

In January 1948 the Deputy Governor (Cobbold) was told 'the Chancellor was anxious to have in early preparation a "war book" on the arguments for and against devaluation, the likely effects, and the technical and other measures which it would be necessary to take if we did devalue'. A short note on technicalities was prepared and updated at intervals while discussion continued on the major issue.[57] One contribution came from R. W. B. Clarke of the Overseas Finance Division of the Treasury. He proposed a change in the sterling-dollar rate in order to change the relative prices in sterling of goods from dollar and non-dollar sources (outside the sterling area) since non-dollar goods were often more expensive than dollar goods at the present exchange rate. He noted that purchasing power parity calculations would

[54] See the exchange between R. W. B. Clarke and Keynes in June 1945, reproduced in Clarke, *Anglo-American Economic Collaboration*, 96–125; see also Cairncross, *Years of Recovery*, 165–6, and Pressnell, *External Economic Policy*, 448–50.

[55] Thompson-McCausland, 'If there is no Marshall plan', 24 June, and 'Devaluation of sterling', 28 June 1947, ADM14/20, BOE; Mynors, 'Meeting at the Treasury 2nd July 1947', 3 July, 'Zero—Exchange policy', 18 July, and Cobbold to Governor, 23 July 1947, G1/101, BOE. The quotations are from Mynors' note (emphasis in original).

[56] Siepmann, 'Ante Marshall', 8 Aug., and Rootham, 'Ante-Marshall, Minutes of meeting: 11th August', 11 Aug. 1947, G1/102, BOE; Fforde, *Bank*, 151–3.

[57] Cobbold to Governor, 27 Jan., 'First draft'. 2 Feb., and Rowe-Dutton, 'Revaluation drill', 19 Feb., Bolton to Deputy Governor and Siepmann, 2 June 1948, G1/106, BOE; Playfair to Wilson Smith, 2 June 1948, T236/2398, PRO; Fforde, *Bank*, 279.

give the opposite answer (see Table 5.12), but rejected them because of the obvious disequilibrium. He assumed that if Britain devalued other non-dollar currencies would follow sterling down, reducing the size of the increase in import prices that a devaluation would cause. His argument did not convince his Treasury colleagues. George Bolton of the Bank of England doubted that the benefits of devaluation to Britain's balance of payments would be as large or the costs in terms of higher import prices and inflationary pressure as small as Clarke hoped.[58]

In August 1948 a 'confused discussion' took place on a fixed versus a floating rate between Ernest Rowe-Dutton of the Treasury's Overseas Finance Division, Stephen Holmes of the Board of Trade, Robert Hall and Bolton. Bolton persuaded the others that 'the adoption of a floating rate policy was not an alternative but the only measure available if all other policies failed'. The Treasury note of the conversation suggests they rejected floating as an alternative to devaluation largely because of the uncertainties it would cause for exporters and importers including government departments, but Bolton's note and other memoranda suggest some ambivalence on his part and a reluctance to abandon the existing exchange control and monetary agreements for the time being at least.[59] The Bank continued to argue against floating in discussions with the Treasury for the next year, although without making the basis of its objections any clearer to the Treasury.

In August 1948 Robert Hall agreed that 'there was no case [for devaluation] at that time', when there was the prospect of continuing inflation in the USA which would make UK exports more

[58] Clarke to Rowe-Dutton, Wilson Smith and Eady, 'The future of sterling', 25 Feb., Rowe-Dutton to Eady and Wilson Smith, and Bolton, 'Devaluation of Sterling', 30 Mar. 1948, T236/2398. 'Otto' Clarke had joined the Treasury in 1945 from the Ministry of Production. Before the war he had been a financial journalist on the *Financial News* and a member of the New Fabian Research Bureau since his undergraduate days at Cambridge, where he had read mathematics and economics. On his role in the post-war Treasury see David Hubback, 'Sir Richard Clarke—1910–1975: a most unusual civil servant', *Public Policy and Administration*, 3 (Spring 1988), 19–34. Bolton, an Executive Director of the Bank, had been one of the managers of the EEA in the 1930s; on his views see Fforde, *Bank*, 279–80.

[59] Bolton to Deputy Governor and Siepmann, 'Sterling, Note of a meeting at H.M.T. 24.8.48', 25 Aug. 1948, G1/106, BOE; Rowe-Dutton, 'Methods of devaluation', 3 Sept. 1948, T236/2311, PRO; Bolton, 'Exchange policy', 1 July 1948, and Bolton to Deputy Governor, 11 Jan. 1949, G1/106; Bolton, 'Variable rates', 18 Aug. 1949, G1/110, BOE and T236/2311, PRO.

competitive. But in redrafting a note on the discussion for the Chancellor he wanted 'to leave the way open to argue in the opposite sense if things changed a great deal. They change fast nowadays'.[60] By March 1949 a mild recession in the United States had changed things. Hall called for at least a serious examination of the case for devaluation, on several related grounds. There were widespread expectations outside Whitehall that Britain would devalue sooner or later, so that the issue could not be ignored. It was now probable that UK prices would rise faster than US prices, given the US recession. A devaluation would make UK exports more competitive *vis-à-vis* US goods in world markets. As for increased inflationary pressures in the UK they would need to be damped down anyway (i.e. without a devaluation). A small group (Sir Henry Wilson Smith, head of the Overseas Finance Division of the Treasury, Hall, Clarke, Mynors and Bolton) was 'called together to consider the exchange problem generally' early in April, but discussions were not confined to this group.[61]

Cairncross has emphasized Hall's role, along with that of Plowden and Wilson Smith, two other early converts to the cause, in the persuasion of Bridges and other senior Treasury officials by the summer, in spite of spirited opposition from the Governor of the Bank. (Bridges' underlying suspicion of devaluation was epitomized for Plowden by the fact that he gave it the code name 'Caliban', 'which he told Robert Hall stood for all that was unsavoury and underhand'.)[62] At the end of June Gaitskell thought Cripps was 'obviously torn' but in too poor health to make up his mind. Gaitskell (then Minister of Fuel and Power) and Jay were not then in favour of devaluation but by the middle of July, at the same time that they and Harold Wilson (President

[60] Hall to Rowe-Dutton, 30 Aug. 1948, G1/106, BOE; [Rowe-Dutton and Hall], 'The dollar-sterling rate', (Aug. 1948), T236/2398, PRO. Cairncross claims that 'There is no evidence that ministers took the slightest interest in the argument or were shown any of the papers' (*Years of Recovery*, 168) but it is clear from the Bank file that the Chancellor was kept informed.

[61] Hall to Plowden, 'Sterling-dollar rate', 28 Mar. 1949, T236/2398; Bolton, 'Note of a meeting at the Treasury', 7 Apr. 1949, ADM14/26 and G1/101, BOE. Cobbold also asked Bolton for a paper on the pros and cons of devaluation and set up a small committee within the Bank: Fforde, *Bank*, 282, 285, 288–9.

[62] Cairncross, *Years of Recovery*, 171–81; see also *Robert Hall Diaries*, 54–84. Plowden's comment on Bridges comes from his *Industrialist in the Treasury*, 57. 'Caliban' was renamed 'Rose' in August 1949 (Note by Playfair, 19 Aug. 1949, G1/110, BOE). For the Bank's opposition see below.

of the Board of Trade) were jointly deputed to stand in for Cripps during his absence in Switzerland in an attempt to recover from exhaustion and ill-health, they had changed their minds. Their reasons included recognition that exchange control could not prevent capital outflows, that the prices of sterling goods were too high relative to dollar goods, and that the elasticities of demand and supply for UK exports were probably higher than they had previously believed, as well as the lack of any desirable alternative policies. They persuaded Attlee and other senior ministers of their case while Cripps was away.[63]

Meanwhile the US administration had been putting pressure on the British government to devalue, forcing it to hold talks with US officials in Washington and London in June and early July. Speculative pressure on the pound in the foreign exchange markets was also increasing. So were transactions in 'cheap sterling', that is the use of supposedly inconvertible but transferable sterling to obtain dollar goods or dollars at a discount on the official exchange rate.[64] As two years earlier, the Chancellor had been forced to alert his Cabinet colleagues to the reserve drain and to the need to take 'sharp action'. This time the reserve losses were attributed to leads and lags in payments because of devaluation fears and to the effects of the US recession on sterling area exports. The action proposed and accepted before Cripps' departure for Zurich was cuts in imports of dollar goods into the UK and the rest of the sterling area.[65] When the Cabinet acknowledged at the end of July that devaluation was inevitable, Attlee informed Cripps and sought his view on the timing. Cripps in-

[63] *Diary of Hugh Gaitskell*, 116–17, 126–32. Jay remembered that he and Gaitskell decided on devaluation separately on Sunday 17 July (*Change and Fortune*, 187); Gaitskell's diary confirms that they told each other of their decisions the next day and talked to Harold Wilson on the Thursday. Both accounts leave Wilson's views ambiguous.

[64] These transactions, which took several forms, were a way of getting round sterling area exchange controls: on the problem, which surfaced in 1948 and persisted until sterling became *de facto* convertible in 1955, see Fforde, *Bank*, ch. 4(c) and Tew, *International Monetary Co-operation* (2nd edn., 1954), ch. 11.

[65] EPC(49)61, 'The dollar drain, Memorandum by the Chancellor of the Exchequer', 11 June, and EPC(49)66, 'The dollar situation, Memorandum by the Chancellor of the Exchequer', 22 June 1949, T269/2; see also Dalton Diary, vol. 37, 15 June and 1 July 1949 (only partially reprinted in Pimlott (ed.), *Political Diary of Hugh Dalton*, 450–2). Dalton was at this time against devaluation and more worried about the thinly veiled threats to cheap money coming from the Bank; he changed his mind on devaluation when Gaitskell and Jay told him they had: Dalton, 'Economic Policy Committee, The Dollar Situation' (Marked, 'Note dic-

sisted that it should not be announced before he and the Foreign Secretary went to Washington for the talks with the US administration (and the IMF annual meetings) in September. This gave the economists in Whitehall plenty of time to try to work out an appropriate exchange rate. The actual rate of US$2.80 was settled by Bevin and Cripps in Washington on 12 September.[66]

In June 1947 Thompson-McCausland in the Bank thought that if the authorities were to give up $4.03 the pound would have to fall below its lowest levels in the interwar period, that is, below about $3.20. A year later R. N. Kershaw in the Bank was considering the domestic consequences of a 20 per cent devaluation (and admitting that 'one of the few serious advantages for a voluntary devaluation is the competitive advantage to be secured for exports'!).[67] The Economic Section's careful calculations of the effect of devaluation assumed a devaluation of 25 per cent, which would be followed by other sterling area countries and some European currencies. The estimates made by Dow suggested such a change would raise import prices by 20 per cent, the cost of living by no more than 5 per cent and wages by about 3½ per cent in the first two years. When it came to recommending a rate the Section paper, after suggesting that a floating rate would probably be preferable, pointed out that in order to convince the outside world that a single devaluation would not be repeated, 'no devaluation of less than 20% (i.e. to £1 = $3.20) could possibly be adequate'. Since 'the desirable rate therefore lies considerably below this, and probably below $3.0 to the pound', it recommended $2.80 (that is, 30 per cent) in order to be reasonably certain of producing sufficient effect on UK exports to dollar countries as to yield approximate balance by 1952.[68] When Cobbold talked to Cripps after he returned from Switzerland and

tated before Dollar meeting of Ministers on 1/7/49') and entry for 'The end of July', Dalton Diary, vol. 37. The Bank's proposals on monetary policy are discussed below.

[66] *Diary of Hugh Gaitskell*, 132–8; Cairncross, *Years of Recovery*, 82–7; *Robert Hall Diaries*, 69–83.

[67] Thompson-McCausland to Deputy Governor, 'Devaluation of sterling', 28 June 1947, ADM14/20; Kershaw, 'Devaluation by 20 per cent, The domestic side', 25 May 1949, G1/106, BOE.

[68] 'Effect of devaluation on the cost of living and on wages' (June 1949), and 'Devaluation, The choice of the new exchange rate, Note by the Economic Section', 6 Aug. 1949, T230/254 and T269/1, PRO; Cairncross and Watts, *Economic Section*, 296–7.

just before he went to the United States—when they had both reluctantly accepted the inevitability of devaluation—the Chancellor was 'shocked by the idea of going below $3' but Cobbold argued for a large devaluation if there was going to have to be one at all.[69] The officials who accompanied the Chancellor and the Foreign Secretary to Washington included Hall, Plowden, and Wilson Smith, and Bolton from the Bank. They unanimously advised $2.75 to $2.80, and the two ministers accepted their recommendation.[70]

All the advisers advocating devaluation or depreciation were clear that it would have to be accompanied by deflationary domestic measures to reduce absorption, although they found it difficult to persuade ministers, indeed impossible when it came to monetary policy. Cobbold lost his first opportunity to tighten monetary policy even though the Treasury officials favoured higher interest rates both before and after the decision to devalue. The Bank did, however, manage to take its first steps to regain its freedom of action to raise interest rates later.

After Cripps warned his ministerial colleagues of the reserve losses on 15 June, Bridges told the Bank that the Treasury 'wished to prepare for the Cabinet a document giving reasoned arguments for and against devaluation'. According to the Deputy Governor (D. G. M. Bernard), Bridges 'explained that both the Chancellor and the Cabinet were very firm against devaluation but this might largely be due to dogma rather than reasoned argument'. The Bank contributed an abbreviated version of an internal report on devaluation and Mynors and Peppiatt attended the Treasury meetings. A couple of days later Cobbold asked his senior colleagues to get out their February report on changing interest rates.[71]

The bundle of papers which Bridges put up to Cripps on 18 June included memoranda by Hall, Wilson Smith and Eady

[69] Cobbold to Bolton, 29 Aug. 1949, G1/110; Cobbold to Chancellor, 26 Aug. 1949, G1/70, BOE; Fforde, *Bank*, 297–8. Both Cobbold and Hall (*Robert Hall Diaries*, 70) recorded that Cripps was doubtful whether devaluation would do much good.

[70] Wilson Smith, 'Note for record, Exchange rates: Washington, August/September, 1949', 19 Sept. 1949, T236/2311.

[71] 'Deputy Governor's note', 15 June, Extract from the Governor's diary, 16 June, Bridges to Cobbold, 17 June (returning Niemeyer, Mynors, Kershaw and Beale, 7 June, 'which was most helpful, as indeed were your chaps'), and Cobbold to Deputy Governor, 19 June 1949, G1/107, BOE. For the Bank report see Fforde, *Bank*, 288–9.

giving their views, the Economic Section's estimates of the effect of devaluation on the cost of living and wages, and a note of the Governor's views. Bridges's covering note summarized the current opinion that 'Most of us, with differing degrees of emphasis, are opposed to devaluation *now*' on the grounds that it would not work without supporting deflationary measures and that its effects were uncertain. He admitted that Plowden and Hall and Leslie Rowan of the Overseas Finance Division of the Treasury had come to a different conclusion, namely that devaluation was inevitable and desirable and that 'it would not be practicable to carry through deflationary measures which will be required to correct the situation if we do not devalue at the same time'. He ended by suggesting the deflationary measures that would be needed to avoid devaluation, namely a reduction in government expenditure and 'necessary supporting measures in the credit field'. The latter would include a review of advances control, 'certainly a willingness to allow interest rates to rise', and possibly an increase in Bank rate.[72]

Cobbold opposed devaluation 'in the immediate future'. He claimed there were

three prerequisites to any consideration of a change in the [exchange] rate—

(*a*) *Action on our own cost structure* . . .
(*b*) *Action to deal with overseas holdings of sterling* . . .
(*c*) *A new Agreement with U.S.A. and Canada.*

On (*a*), Bridges had rightly stressed the need to reduce government expenditure and change monetary policy, but, Cobbold added, 'a great deal of thought needs to be given to the degree of interest rates which might be desirable, and to the question whether direct (i.e. other than by the interest rate) restriction of credit might not be dangerous'. (*b*) and (*c*) reflected Cobbold's desire to resume the progress toward the convertibility of sterling that had been interrupted in 1947. This was an important factor in his opposition to devaluation but it received little attention in Whitehall in 1949. Hall appropriately commented that if the authorities had not managed in three and a half years to carry out the blocking of sterling balances they were committed to under

[72] Bridges to Chancellor, 18 June 1949, T269/1; see also Cairncross, *Years of Recovery*, 177–8.

the 1945 loan agreement it 'seem[ed] ... doubtful whether we should be able to do any better' now. He similarly doubted the Bank's willingness to tighten monetary control.[73]

When Cobbold consulted his senior colleagues on domestic monetary policy, they pointed out the alternatives: either making Bank rate effective, as they had recommended earlier in the year, or raising Bank rate to 2½ or 3 per cent (and making the new rate effective). They were inclined to favour the 'more dramatic' move. Action on bank advances or on capital issues would be slow to take effect, as would a deflationary budget. Mynors communicated their ideas to the Treasury, who incorporated them in the draft package of deflationary measures to go to the Cabinet Economic Policy Committee.[74] Cobbold, however, in discussions with Eady and Trend (now an undersecretary), stressed his line that 'any action in the monetary field could only be secondary and supplementary to a cut in Government expenditure' without which it 'would probably be useless'. A few days later the monetary policy proposals were removed from the Treasury memorandum on Cobbold's initiative, ostensibly because gilts prices had fallen so that long-term interest rates had already risen. According to Mynors, 'several of those present [at the Treasury meeting] made no secret of their dismay that one of the few positive recommendations ... had now been removed. ... I reiterated ... that the Bank view had always been that this must be only a supporting factor to a real attack on Government expenditure'. Cobbold then repeatedly attacked the package of measures announced by the Chancellor on 5 July for not including a large enough cut in government expenditure.[75]

[73] Memoradum by Cobbold, 18 June, and Cobbold to Bridges, 23 June 1949, G1/70, BOE; Hall, '"Caliban"', Note on memorandum by the Governor of the Bank', 24 June 1949, T269/1, PRO; Fforde, *Bank*, 290–1, 295–6. On Cobbold's desire for 'some very radical changes' on the external side see also 'Extract from the Governor's diary dated 1st June 1949', Cobbold to Deputy Governor, 19 June, and Cobbold to Bolton, 11 July 1949, G1/107, BOE, and Cobbold to Attlee, 3 Aug. 1949, PREM8/976, PRO.

[74] Peppiatt to Governor, 21 June, Mynors to Eady, and 'Rate policy', 24 June 1949, C42/1, BOE; Bridges to Chancellor, 'Dollar situation', 24 June 1949, T269/1; Eady, Mynors and Bolton, 'Monetary policy', 25 June 1949, G1/108; Bridges to Chancellor, 'Dollar situation, Part I', T269/2.

[75] 'Governor's note', 23 June, Mynors, 'For record', 28 June, 'Telephone message from the Governor to Sir Edward Bridges ... ', 1 July, Cobbold to Bridges, 4 July, 'Governor's note', 5 July, and Cobbold to Bridges, 14 July 1949, G1/70;

The senior Treasury officials also believed in the need for a cutback in government expenditure and in the desirability of tightening monetary policy—to the alarm of at least Hugh Dalton, now back in the Cabinet as Chancellor of the Duchy of Lancaster.[76] When they were told on 22 July that the junior ministers standing in for Cripps were going to recommend devaluation to the Cabinet they pointed out that devaluation would have to be accompanied by an expenditure-reducing policy, including some reduction of government expenditure and 'action in the monetary field'. According to George Bolton, who was also present, the Bank was not in favour of a major change in monetary policy which would raise long-term interest rates and increase government expenditure on interest payments. He said that it 'might be possible, however, that some action might be taken through the discount market, which would not narrow the credit base' although it would raise short-term rates slightly.[77]

During the previous month the Bank had been polishing its February scheme for tightening monetary policy without a rise in Bank rate. Since 'one of the main reasons ... is to introduce some freedom of movement in rates and get away from the present rigidity and artificiality', the Chief Cashier (P. S. Beale) also proposed the proportion of Treasury bills in the floating debt should be increased so as to reduce that of TDRs. This would also reduce the cost to the Exchequer of raising short-term rates, since Treasury bills carried a slightly lower interest rate than TDRs. The Governor agreed and informed the Treasury verbally. Although a letter was drafted it was not sent, because, as Peppiatt remarked, 'Once we go into print ... Jay and Company will try to make a science of the whole thing.'[78]

EPC(49)72, 'The dollar situation, Memorandum by the Chancellor of the Exchequer', 28 June, and Bridges, 'Mr. Cobbold's comments on the draft announcement', 1 July 1949, T269/2; see also Fforde, *Bank*, 374.

[76] Bridges to Chancellor, 6 July 1949, T269/1; Dalton Diary, vol. 37, 'Note dictated before dollar meeting of ministers on 1/7/49'.

[77] 'Note of a meeting held in Sir Edward Bridges' room at 3.30 p.m. on Friday, 22nd July, 1949', 22 July 1949, T269/1; see also Bridges to Prime Minister, 23 July 1949, T269/2, and 'Economic Situation, Note by the Permanent Secretary, H.M. Treasury', 26 July 1949, T269/1.

[78] Beale, 'Money market technique', 28 June, Peppiatt, 'Money market technique (Chief Cashier's memorandum of 28th June)', 29 June, Cobbold to Peppiatt and Chief Cashier, 4 July, Beale to Peppiatt and Governors, 'Money market

At this point Jay's working party held an *ad hoc* meeting to discuss his report to the Chancellor on their 4 July meeting (above). It agreed that there should be another request to the clearing banks 'to exercise particular caution' in their lending policy and confirmed this decision a week later, when Jay complained to Dalton that Eady was being obstructive.[79] At the same time Hall and Eady were working out that 'a deflationary credit policy' should involve a rise in the Treasury bill rate to 1 per cent in order to make Bank rate effective, then a rise in Bank rate to 3 per cent, and a request to the banks for a general reduction in advances. They estimated that if a 3 per cent Bank rate were made effective it would increase the cost of the floating debt by £65m a year and raise long-term gilt-edged yields to 4 per cent. They also argued that there would have to be a significant reduction in government expenditure in order to reduce government borrowing in the non-surplus quarters of the financial year, if the monetary measures were to be 'fully effective'. Eady, influenced by Cobbold, indeed thought a tighter monetary policy without reduced government expenditure would be 'silly'. Cobbold had categorically told him that he 'would refuse to make any attempt to restrict credit or raise interest rates if there were going to be no reduction in Government expenditure'. He was prepared only to accede to the Chancellor's request, following the recommendation of the Jay working party, to ask the banks for more 'caution' in their lending, which he did on 4 August.[80]

Jay, Treasury officials, and the Economic Section were all concerned that another informal request on advances to the bankers

technique', 11 July, and note by Peppiatt, 11 July 1949, C42/1, BOE; also Fforde, *Bank*, 375. By March 1950 the Bank had reduced the amount of TDRs in the floating debt by half of what they had been a year earlier (see below).

[79] Note of a meeting of Jay, Eady, Trend, Hall, Peppiatt, and Thompson-McCausland (22 July), and 'Working party on bank deposits and advances, 7th report', 5 Aug. 1949, T233/483; Dalton Diary, vol. 37, 'The end of July'. At the second working party meeting, on 28 July, it was suggested—presumably by Jay—that 'a policy of sales of investments by Clearing Banks would lead to a contraction of deposits', but it was pointed out that this would push down further already falling gilt-edged prices and significantly raise the cost of long-term government borrowing.

[80] Eady to Gilbert, 'Sub-committee on expenditure and monetary policy', 26 July, Hall and Eady, 'Credit policy', 26 July, and Eady to Hall, 23 July 1949, T233/1400; Eady to Bridges (23 July 1949), T269/1; Note of 22 July 1949, marked 'Handed by Governor to Sir E. Bridges on 23.7.49', and Cobbold to Eady, 4 Aug. 1949, G1/70, BOE.

could hardly be described as a deflationary monetary policy in the Washington talks with the Americans in September.[81] None the less even the vague reference to monetary action in the drafts of the ministerial brief for the talks did not survive to the final version. This was partly because of Cobbold's attitude and partly because of ministers' reluctance to cut government expenditure which led them to postpone their decisions on domestic policies until after the devaluation. Treasury officials therefore planned to put up specific monetary policy proposals on the Chancellor's return from Washington.[82]

Meanwhile money market interest rates began to rise as the supply of Treasury bills was increased. On 5 August Cobbold warned Trend that 'despite any decision reached by H.M.G. on interest rates, it might not prove practicable to maintain much longer the present discount rate on Treasury Bills'. On 14 September Cobbold asked to be able to continue this process by allowing the Treasury bill rate to rise, in order to make Bank rate effective, once the devaluation had been announced. He wrote to Bridges:

Unless the Chancellor sees objection, it would be our intention as soon as the market re-opens to take the necessary steps gradually to make present Bank Rate effective, bringing the Treasury bill rate in the neighbourhood of 1%. Unless anything unforeseen occurs, we should not contemplate any change in the Bank rate in the immediate future.[83]

The Bank was warned that 'Ministers were at present opposed to any rise in interest rates and that if the Chancellor were to be persuaded the Bank would have to make out a very clear and detailed case.' The Bank responded that the move would reinforce the 'control' of advances, that long-term interest rates were rising and that the Treasury bill rate would have to follow them

[81] 'Working party on bank deposits and advances, 7th report', 5 Aug. 1949, T233/483; Bridges to Attlee, 'Economic Situation, Note by the Permanent Secretary, H.M. Treasury', 26 July 1949, T269/1; Fleming to Hitchman, 'Banking policy and the crisis', 24 Aug., and Fleming to Plowden, 29 Aug. 1949, T233/1400.

[82] Drafts of ministerial brief in T269/3; *Diary of Hugh Gaitskell*, 134–5, 138–43; Cabinet papers CP(49)175, 23 Aug., and CP(49)185, 29 Aug. 1949; Mynors to Rowan, 'Draft brief—para.15(b)ii', 13 Aug., and Mynors to Governor, 23 Aug. 1949, G1/70; Eady to Plowden, 26 Aug., and Eady to Trend, 30 Aug. 1949, T233/1400.

[83] Bank of England, *Statistical Abstract No. 1* (1970), table 29; Note by Peppiatt, 5 Aug. 1949, C42/1, BOE; Cobbold to Bridges, 14 Sept. 1949, T233/1400, PRO.

sooner or later even though it would increase the floating debt charge by £25m a year. Hall was 'definitely in favour' but the other officials, although sympathetic were 'doubtful whether the present is the right moment'.[84] The limited nature of the Governor's request militated against its acceptance. Cripps refused it on 22 September on the advice of Gaitskell, Jay and Harold Wilson who were

unanimous in rejecting the suggestion that any increase in the rate should be made at once. They were influenced partly by the obvious political considerations (the probable reactions of the T.U.C., the effect on wages policy, etc., etc.), and partly by their inability to agree that the very moderate increase in short-term rates ... would have any real disinflationary effect ...

Cripps was, therefore, not prepared to try to persuade his Cabinet colleagues to consider a measure which would increase both the cost of the national debt and the profits of the banks.[85]

While the Cabinet wrangled over the size of cuts in public expenditure and in the investment programme, which were eventually settled at £280m in October,[86] the Chancellor and his officials were still concerned about the stance of monetary policy, in the context of the devaluation package of measures and more generally. Bridges was especially worried: according to Robert Hall, he 'fears a clash between the Government and the Bank [which] he says it is our duty to prevent' and he arranged for discussions on monetary policy between Bank and Treasury officials to continue. Cripps asked for the Bank's views on 'what could be done in the credit field ... on the assumption that there would be no change in the Bank Rate or in short money rates' but assuming cuts in government expenditure and investment. Mynors, with Trend 'sitting at his feet' (Trend's words), produced such a note, which not surprisingly concluded that 'there remains only a direct approach to the bankers on the[ir lending]

[84] Note by Radice, 16 Sept., (Bank of England), 'Short-term interest rates', 19 Sept., Trend, 'Short-term interest rates', 20 Sept., and Trend to Wass, 21 Sept. 1949, T233/1400; see also Niemeyer, Peppiatt, Mynors and Beale to Governors, 'Interest rate policy', 16 Sept. 1949, C42/1, BOE.

[85] Trend to Wass, 21 Sept., and Jay to Chancellor, 21 Sept. 1949, T233/1400, PRO; Mynors, 'Meeting at the Treasury on 22nd September 1949', 22 Sept. 1949, G1/70, BOE; see also Fforde, *Bank*, 376.

[86] On which see Dow, *Management of the British Economy*, 45–6, and Cairncross, *Years of Recovery*, 188–95.

TABLE 5.7 *Nominal Yields on British Government Securities, Monthly, 1948–9, %.p.a.*

		Short-dated[1]	Medium-dated[2]	Long-dated[3]	Consols[4]
End of 1948	Jan.	2.35	2.68	2.88	3.08
	Feb.	2.15	2.65	2.86	3.15
	Mar.	2.16	2.62	2.87	3.22
	Apr.	2.97	2.66	2.88	3.28
	May	2.07	2.56	2.90	3.25
	June	1.95	2.50	2.82	3.27
	July	1.86	2.52	2.80	3.28
	Aug.	1.90	2.50	2.76	3.26
	Sept.	1.87	2.47	2.73	3.22
	Oct.	1.83	2.25	2.69	3.18
	Nov.	1.73	2.25	2.60	3.16
	Dec.	1.72	2.28	2.62	3.14
	Jan.	1.93	2.25	2.60	3.12
	Feb.	1.60	2.25	2.61	3.00
	Mar.	1.58	2.25	2.58	3.11
	Apr.	1.76	2.20	2.53	3.10
	May	1.76	2.25	2.59	3.08
	June	2.26	2.65	2.88	3.21
	July	2.44	2.83	3.31	3.36
	Aug.	2.50	2.79	3.20	3.48
	Sept.	2.05	2.62	3.02	3.45
	Oct.	2.22	2.80	3.23	3.56
	Nov.	1.82	2.59	2.94	3.62
	Dec.	1.86	2.77	3.05	3.51

Notes
[1] Gross redemption yields for 2½% National War Bonds 1952/54.
[2] Gross redemption yields for 2½% Funding Loan 1956/61.
[3] Gross redemption yields for 3% Savings Bonds 1960/70.
[4] Gross flat yields on 2½% Consols.   •

Sources
Short-dated, medium-dated and long-dated security yields: Bank of England, *Statistical Abstract*, No. 1 (1970), table 30.
Yield on 2½% Consols: Capie and Webber, *A Monetary History of the United Kingdom 1970–1982*, vol. 1, table III(10).

criteria'.[87] Although Cobbold had told Cripps that without an increase in short-term interest rates 'he could do nothing more . . . with the banks by way of advice or request and he hoped he would not be asked to do so', he did in fact agree, after consulting the clearing bankers, to make another request to them. The Chancellor's letter to the Governor on 24 October was agreed at a

[87] *Robert Hall Diaries*, 88–9; Cobbold, 'Credit policy', 17 Oct. 1949, G1/70, BOE; Trend to Beale, 20 Oct. 1949, C42/1, BOE; Note by Mynors and Trend, 14 Oct. 1949, T233/1400, PRO.

special 'informal talk' between the Governor, the Chancellor and the Chairman and Deputy Chairman of the Committee of London Clearing Bankers. It asked the banks to 'use every endeavour to ensure that inflationary pressures are held in check'. It was announced as part of the government's anti-inflationary package and at the suggestion of the clearing bankers published in the financial press.[88]

During the balance-of-payments crisis nominal long-term gilt-edged interest rates had risen above 3 per cent with the longest stocks over 3½ per cent (Table 5.7). One matter the Treasury officials had therefore expected to tackle after devaluation was the interest rates charged on central government loans to local authorities, which had been set at 3 per cent for long-term loans, 2½ per cent for medium-term (5–15 years) loans and 2 per cent for short-term loans, in January 1948 (above p. 173). When they proposed an increase in the rate for long-term loans to 3½ per cent in October, Jay strongly opposed it because it would increase the cost of local authority housing, and Cripps turned it down. He agreed a few weeks later to put up a proposal to raise the rate for loans other than for housing, in order to reduce local authority borrowing from the Exchequer, but this met strong opposition from Dalton as well as Jay and was turned down in the Cabinet Economic Policy Committee.[89]

The economists in Whitehall, especially Jay and Hall, still wanted stronger monetary control and were not convinced that quantitative controls were impossible. When opposing Cobbold's attempt to raise the Treasury bill rate Jay made a suggestion that was to be repeated several times in the next eighteen months, namely that if the banks were to try to run down their Treasury bill holdings they could be required to hold specific proportions of Treasury bills and TDRs among their assets. He believed (mistakenly but he was not alone in his belief) this could be done under the 'directions' clause of the Bank of England Act (see Chapter 3). He also thought that if short-term interest rates

[88] Mynors, 'Meeting at the Treasury on 22nd September 1949', Cobbold, 'Credit Policy', 17 Oct. and 21 Oct. 1949, G1/70; Note by Bridges, 21 Oct., and Cripps to Governor, 24 Oct. 1949, T233/1400; Fforde, *Bank*, 376–7.
[89] Eady to Plowden, 26 Aug., Eady to Armstrong, 7 Oct., Eady to Bridges, 14 Oct., and 'Government long-term lending rates', 13 Oct., Jay to Chancellor, 18 Oct. and 1 Dec., 'E.P.C.(49) 52nd meeting, Wednesday, 14th December 1949', T233/1400; Dalton Diary, vol. 37, 14 Dec. 1949.

were out of line with longer-term interest rates because of falling gilt-edged prices the latter could be supported. After talking to Hall, and proposing a meeting of his working party in October, Jay wanted it to consider:

(1) Should steps be taken to encourage more confidence in the gilt-edged market?

(2) Is it right that the Bank of England should in effect surrender control over total bank deposits? Is it the fact?

(3) Should there be a more selective direction to the banks on advances . . . ?

(4) Is there any objection to enforcing a ceiling on deposits?[90]

Steps were in fact taken to support the gilt-edged market (see below). On the other questions Jay asked his working party on 24 October to look at the recent clearing bank statements, the possibility, 'in view of intensified disinflationary drive', of further restraint on advances, and the effect of the weakness in the securities markets on advances. The working party (which now included Trend in place of Compton and on this occasion Peppiatt instead of Mynors) noted gloomily that although the recent trend in bank deposits had been 'not unsatisfactory', the floating debt (including TDRs despite the recent efforts of the Bank) was likely to rise again, because of current government expenditure and as external reserves rose following devaluation. At the same time it would be difficult to reduce bank advances because borrowers could not turn to the new issue market in its present weak state.[91]

When Cobbold had enlisted the help of the clearing bankers in his discussions with the Chancellor a few days earlier, Cripps had asked them for their views on a ceiling on advances and they had agreed to produce a memorandum for him. Their memorandum on 'Growth of bank advances since the end of the war' appeared early in November. It claimed that the growth in advances was part of normal post-war readjustment and 'in no sense indicative of an undesirable expansion of borrowing from the banks'; that a

[90] Jay to Chancellor, 21 Sept. 1949, T233/1400; Jay to Hall, 14 Oct. 1949, T233/483.

[91] Wass, 'Working party on deposits and advances', 20 Oct. 1949, C40/686, BOE; 'Working party on bank deposits and advances, 8th report', 21 Oct. 1949, T233/483, PRO. According to Thompson-McCausland, the meeting also discussed market intervention 'which K.O.P. suggested should not go in the minutes!': Thompson-McCausland to Mynors, 'Jay working party', 1 Nov. 1949, C40/686.

ceiling on advances would have 'consequences harmful to the national interest'; and that the present arrangements should continue. The adverse consequences cited included borrowers' attempts to get round controls, complaints of unfairness in rationing borrowers, reduced availability of finance for exports, and a slowdown of the revival of sterling bills of exchange (since the bankers assumed the ceiling would apply to the discounting of commercial bills by banks as well as to advances). It did not claim a ceiling was impossible, which is perhaps why Cobbold and Eady 'agreed that if the economists etc. could be kept quiet we had much better say no more about this for quite a time'.[92]

The Treasury officials had some trouble keeping the economists quiet. Marcus Fleming, the Deputy Director of the Economic Section, commented that the bankers' note 'shows the Bank has learned nothing and forgotten nothing about credit policy over the last hundred years'; Hall agreed with him that it was based on 'the philosophy . . . of "the banking school" . . . which one had hoped was exploded a 100 years ago' and pointed this out to both Jay and Cripps. Cripps volunteered to send a sharp letter to Cobbold which Hall drafted, but the Treasury officials, having shown it to the Governor, dissuaded him from sending it. The letter was to enquire of the Governor:

If . . . the aggregate of advances is left to the discretion of the Clearing Banks, then the total volume of the deposits, and thus of money, is also left to them. In my view it is the primary and indeed the essential function of a Central Bank to determine the total volume of money, and I do not see how I, or you, could accept any other view. . . .

I should be glad to have your views on this question, and, if you agree with me, I should also like to know whether you consider the present powers of control of the Bank of England over the volume of money are adequate.[93]

On 10 January 1950, ending several months of uncertainty, Attlee announced a general election for 23 February. After the election, Jay became Financial Secretary to the Treasury and his

---

[92] Cobbold, 'Credit policy', 21 Oct. 1949, G1/70, BOE, and Note by Bridges, 21 Oct. 1949, T233/1400; 'Growth of bank advances since the end of the war', 4 Nov. 1949, T233/483; Cobbold, 'Conversation with Sir Wilfrid Eady', 18 Nov. 1949, G1/70; Fforde, *Bank*, 337–8.

[93] Fleming to Hall, 12 Nov. 1949, T230/469; Hall to Economic Secretary, 'Bank advances', 16 Nov. 1949, T233/1400; *Robert Hall Diaries*, 97; 'Draft letter from the Chancellor of the Exchequer to the Governor of the Bank of England', 23 Nov.

working party on bank deposits and advances ceased to meet, so that its meeting on 30 January to review the monetary data for 1949 turned out to be its last. The budget season was then at its height and Hall was particularly concerned about the difficulty of maintaining a tight fiscal stance. According to the minutes of the working party meeting, its members were more optimistic than they had been three months earlier. Bank deposits had risen by little more in 1949 than in 1948, in spite of the recent increases in floating debt, and the tax-gathering quarter of 1949/50 had just begun. Advances were continuing to rise but they had risen by less in 1949 than in 1948: 'the advances position was ... not unsatisfactory and indicated that the Chancellor's letter [in October] was having its effect'. Robert Hall was less sanguine:

it is hopeless. D. Jay means well but it is too complex for him; the Bank cover up all the time and Wilfrid Eady is slightly ga-ga. The deposits have risen very little over the year but this conceals a rise in advances and a fall in floating debt. Not good. However we always lose this battle and the only comfort is that if we keep on fighting, there is at least some attempt at moderation.[94]

The monetary policy discussions which resumed in the summer of 1950 are described in Chapter 6.

Before considering the results of Jay's and Cobbold's campaigns on money and prices in 1948–50, I should note the authorities' gilt-edged market intervention in the financial years 1948/9 and 1949/50. As already mentioned, there had been a change in intervention policy in the autumn of 1948, when the National Debt Commissioners stopped buying long-term securities in the market and had subsequently been issued with non-marketable annuities for the savings bank funds. In the spring the authorities had postponed issuing terminable annuities to the NDC because they needed their funds to support nationalization compensation and local authority issues of government-guaranteed securities

1949, and extracts from the Governor's diary, 19 Dec. 1949 and 2 Jan. 1950, G1/70, BOE: Fforde, *Bank*, 378–9. Cobbold told Bridges that if the letter were sent 'I should have to reply rather sharply ... which did not get anybody anywhere.'

[94] 'Working party on bank deposits and advances, 9th report', T233/483; *Robert Hall Diaries*, 102–4. Mynors recorded: 'Robert Hall emphasized that in his view the situation was not now quite so inflationary except for the Budget prospect for 1950/51, which alarmed him considerably': 'Jay Working Party', 30 Jan. 1950, C40/686, BOE.

(above pp. 174–5). In the autumn the gilt-edged market was firm, the Issue Department was selling off its large holding of Daltons and since there were no new gilt-edged issues in which the NDC could invest the accruing surplus on the Unemployment Insurance and other funds, the NDC were buying Daltons in the market. The Bank agreed with the Treasury that it would be preferable to supply the NDC with long-term securities from the Issue Department portfolio, although it also wanted to be able to use NDC funds to support the gilt-edged market from time to time. When the Bank had sold off most of its Daltons and when it was considering at the Treasury's request the (poor) prospects for a funding operation, it asked to take over and sell £50m 3% Savings Bonds from the NDC to the market. The Treasury agreed and instructed the NDC not to invest their funds in the market for the time being.[95]

By March 1949 the Issue Department had sold £45m Savings Bonds taken over from the NDC as well as the last of its Daltons. The authorities agreed 'a reasonable further amount' of Savings Bonds should be made available. In April the 'policy was proving so satisfactory' that a higher limit of £75m was agreed, but sales had to be discontinued when the gilt-edged market deteriorated in May.[96] Two annuities were issued to the NDC, the first on 18 December 1948 for £50m—considerably less than previous issues—for 30 years at 3 per cent, the second on 29 March 1949 for £90m on the same terms.[97]

After devaluation the policy was reconsidered. In September 1949 the Bank asked the Controller of the National Debt Office (Jerry Pinsent) to 'interpret the policy slightly more elastically . . . [because] the Bank have always taken the view that a little intervention by N.D.O. . . . is a tonic for the market and no doubt . . . consider there is need for a tonic in the midst of present un-

[95] Compton, 'Co-ordination of stock purchases and sales between the Bank and N.D.O.', 10 Sept. 1948, T233/1073, PRO; Peppiatt, 'Issue Department/CRND', 15 Sept. 1948, C40/439, BOE; Compton to Chadwick, 25 Oct. 1948, T233/435; and above pp. 233–4 (for the Nov. 1948 decision).

[96] Peppiatt, 'Disinflation/funding', 2 Feb. 1949, and notes by Peppiatt, 26 Nov. 1948, 10 Jan., 3 and 9 Feb. and 4 Mar. 1949, C40/439, BOE; Peppiatt to Compton, 21 Apr., and Eady to Radice, 22 Apr. 1949, T233/435, PRO.

[97] Pinsent to Compton, 1 Dec., and subsequent correspondence in Dec. 1948 and Mar. 1949 on T233/435, PR0; Pember and Boyle, *British Government Securities in the Twentieth Century, Supplement 1950–1976*, 350.

certainties' (which included the prospect of a general election).[98] Gilt-edged prices in fact rose immediately after devaluation but the rise was short-lived. The Bank claimed the subsequent fall was due to investors' 'disappoint[ment] at the small extent, and the delayed action' of the economy cuts announced in October. By early November the Bank thought the fall was 'overdone', with some nominal gilt-edged yields over 4 per cent: in a well-publicized intervention the Government Broker appeared in the market as a buyer just before lunch on Friday, 11 November. This had 'an electrifying effect' according to the *Financial Times*: the bears ran for cover and the recovery on the day's trading was 'spectacular'. The recovery lasted until the end of the month, assisted by the Broker's continued willingness to buy government securities.[99]

Although it was claimed at the time that the amount of intervention in November was small, intervention in 1949 IV as a whole was larger than in any other quarter in 1945–51.[100] The authorities had decided provisionally in December 1948 and definitely in March 1949 to let 2½% National War Bonds 1949/51 run on to their later maturity date. This was not possible with the £787m 1¾% Exchequer Bonds 1950, which had to be converted or repaid on 15 February 1950. In July 1949 the Bank therefore decided to start buying them up even at the cost of increasing the floating debt. The Bank held nearly half the total in issue by the end of the year, some of which were then sold to the NDC when it was decided not to provide another annuity for the time being.[101] The purchases of Exchequer Bonds account for most of the increase in official holdings of marketable securities in 1949 IV (see Table 5.8), but the authorities also bought back some of the 3% Savings Bonds they had sold earlier in the year.

[98] Radice to Trend, 'National Debt Office investment policy', 21 Sept. 1949, T233/435 and 1073, PRO.

[99] Peppiatt, 'Course of gilt-edged prices since devaluation', 13 Dec. 1949, T233/1400, PRO; *FT*, 12 Nov. 1949, and subsequent comments on 15, 17, 17, 18, 29, and 30 Nov. 1949; see also *The Economist*, 19 Nov. 1949, 1144, and Kennedy, 'Monetary policy', 202.

[100] Tew, 'A second look at Exchequer financing under the Labour governments', table 1; Cairncross, *Years of Recovery*, 441.

[101] Eady to Cobbold, 15 Dec. 1948, Cobbold to Eady, 18 Mar., and Eady to Governor, 31 Mar. 1949, C40/486; Beale, '1¾% Exchequer Bonds 1950', 20 July 1949, C40/451, BOE; Eady to Trend, 'Surplus in N.D.O.', 23 Dec., and Beale to Trend, 30 Dec. 1949, T233/1073, PRO.

. When Pinsent asked for a new annuity for the savings bank funds in November, the Treasury and the Bank delayed their response until they had decided the terms and timing of a conversion offer for the Exchequer Bonds, for they did not want to limit their decision by first fixing the interest rate for an annuity or to tie up NDC funds which might be needed for supporting the new issue.[102] The Bank had originally hoped that the offer to the holders of the bonds might be both a short-term (five years) and a medium-term security, the short at either 2 per cent issued at a substantial discount or 2½ per cent at par. The fall of gilts prices put paid to a medium-term issue but the improvement after the Bank's intervention made 2¼ per cent at a discount for the short look possible by 25 November. The Chancellor, like his predecessor, disliked issuing at a discount and was inclined to wait until January in the hope of further market improvement. When the Bank decided 2¼ per cent at par was possible he agreed. Announced on 2 December, the offer was very successful, £734m of the £787m outstanding being converted into 2¼% Exchequer Bonds 1955, thanks to the authorities' intervention.[103]

In March 1950 the government publicly admitted the nominal interest rate on long-term government debt was 3½ per cent by issuing a last terminable annuity to the NDC at that rate. The Treasury floated the idea that the rate might be 3¼ per cent on the argument that this was the current market rate for a bond with a term to maturity of eighteen years, the *average* term of a thirty-year annuity, but the Governor of the Bank was adamant that the savings banks funds should be invested at the market rate for thirty-year marketable government securities 'in accordance with normal orthodox principles', that is, previous practice. The Treasury officials (even Eady) did not think Cobbold was correct to insist on the market rate, but advised their ministers to accept 3½ per cent. A lower rate might invite adverse although baseless comment on the security of saving bank deposits, and the

[102] Pinsent to Radice, 2 Nov., Trend to Eady, 'National Debt Commissioners—Investment policy', 4 Nov., and Trend to Eady, 29 Nov. 1949, T233/1073, PRO; Beale, 'CRND Ways and Means—£90 million', C40/439, BOE.

[103] Beale, 'Government loan operations,' 18 May, '£787 million 1¾% Exchequer Bonds due 15th February 1950', 2 Nov., and '1¾% Exchequer Bonds due 15th February 1950', 7 Nov., Peppiatt, '1¾% Exchequer Bonds 1950', 11 Nov. and '1¾% Exchequer Bonds 1950', 18 Nov. 1949, C40/451, BOE; Bernard to Eady, 25 Nov., Eady to Bridges, 25 Nov., and Note by Eady, 29 Nov. 1949, T233/393, PRO; Fforde, *Bank*, 379.

government would anyway soon have to admit to 3½ per cent with a forthcoming government-guaranteed issue for the Electricity Authority. On this occasion Jay supported Bridges and Eady, and Cripps agreed to 3½ per cent on 29 March for an annuity of £50m.[104]

Money, prices and the exchange rate 1948–51

The effects of Jay's campaign to use the budget surplus to keep down the growth of clearing bank deposits and of the authorities' more prolonged attempts to reduce the floating debt can be seen in Tables 5.8 and 5.9. Table 5.8 presents the details of Exchequer financing in the form they were prepared for the Jay Working Party. Table 5.9 gives the quarterly changes observed in the London clearing banks published statements of their assets and liabilities.

The central government budget in its conventional presentation went into surplus in 1947 I and showed surpluses for each of the next three financial years. When the necessary adjustments are made to arrive at a net overall surplus or deficit, however, the 1947/8 budget shows a deficit; thereafter there were surpluses for the financial years as a whole but deficits in most quarters except the tax-gathering ones. Although this meant that the largest quarterly reductions in floating debt were in the tax-gathering quarters, there were sizeable reductions in floating and gilt-edged debt in other quarters, mainly because external financing reduced the domestic borrowing requirement. Reserve losses and North American aid contributed a total of £1,631m external financing in the 2¾ years before devaluation and subsequent reserve gains removed this source of finance (until the 1951 balance-of-payments crisis). With small net inflows from national insurance contributions and small savings, the Exchequer had totals of £685m, £821m, and £347m available to reduce government debt in the financial years 1947/8, 1948/9, and 1949/50.

[104] Pinsent to Trend, 'Savings banks funds', 17 Mar., Trend to Eady, 23 Mar., Eady to Bridges, 27 Mar., Notes by Bridges, Jay and Cripps, 29 Mar. 1950, T233/435, PRO. The amount of the annuity was only £50m because the NDC would be able to subscribe to the electricity issue, which was fixed at £150m partly so that the NDC could take up £50m and issued at a discount so as to ensure a coupon rate of 3½ per cent: see Trend to Eady, 'B.E.A. issue', 20 Apr., and Eady to Armstrong, 'Electricity issue', 28 Apr. 1950, T233/382.

TABLE 5.8   *Central Government Financing, Quarterly, 1948–51, £m*

	1948				1949				1950				1951			
	I	II	III	IV	I	II	III	IV	I	II	III	IV	I	II	III	IV
Above the line surplus/deficit	402	179	74	89	570	1	–18	–10	576	45	25	–16	666	13	–39	–200
Below the line expenditure[1]	–186	–146	–90	–123	–92	–172	–122	–122	–71	–111	–109	–123	–130	–118	–137	–121
Overall surplus or deficit	216	33	–16	–115	478	–171	–140	–132	505	–66	–84	–139	536	–105	–176	–321
Adjustments[2]	80	–77	–0	–37	90	–20	30	–32	104	–23	44	11	49	–87	–65	16
Changes in TRCs	–116	4	45	44	–163	26	23	64	–152	45	69	77	–123	81	38	62
Net overall surplus/deficit	180	–40	20	–108	410	–165	–87	–100	454	–44	29	–51	462	–111	–203	–243
External financing EEA sterling receipts	–29	76	36	–21	–10	69	22	–124	–108	–161	–154	–163	–135	–51	232	343
North American aid + loans, net sterling receipts	166	16	206	84	41	17	62	69	84	65	26	–103	–36	–6	96	168
Domestic financing National insurance funds	17	15	45	37	19	37	46	41	38	41	47	43	37	44	51	18
Small savings	60	–27	–25	–8	55	5	–16	–20	23	–20	–22	–20	31	–10	–23	–24
Increase/decrease in fiduciary issue	–150	—	—	–25	–25	—	—	50	–50	50	—	25	–25	50	—	50
Exchequer cash available	244	40	282	9	490	–37	27	–84	441	–69	–74	–269	334	–84	153	312

TABLE 5.8 *continued*

	1948				1949				1950				1951			
	I	II	III	IV	I	II	III	IV	I	II	III	IV	I	II	III	IV
Applied:																
Stocks in market[3]	−261	−34	−29	−17	−28	−40	−55	−344	36	59	21	33	−57	24	22	691
Market floating debt:																
TDRs	−112	177	−18	62	−376	108	−332	−39	−407	−115	155	20	−242	61	−55	−171
Treasury bills	129	−183	−235	−54	−142	−31	360	467	−70	243	−60	216	−35	−1	−120	−832
	−244	−40	−282	−9	−490	37	−27	84	−441	69	74	269	−334	84	−153	−312

Notes

[1] Expenditure expected to bring a cash return in subsequent years, e.g. Post Office capital expenditure, advances to local authorities for capital purposes.

[2] Issue Department income plus Department balances *plus* sinking funds.

[3] Deposits in Post Office and Trustee Savings Banks, national savings certificates and defence bonds.

[4] Issue of goverment stocks *less* redemption of government stocks (including sinking funds) *less* increase in holdings of Issue Department and National Debt Commissioners.

Source

Calculated from 'Exchequer financing and national debt, 1945–51', *Economic Trends* (December 1961), table 1, and Committee on the Working of the Monetary System, *Principal Memoranda of Evidence*, vol. 1, p. 57

TABLE 5.9 Quarterly Changes in Assets and Liabilities of London Clearing Banks 1947–51, £m

	1947				1948				1949				1950				1951			
	I	II	III	IV	I	II	III	IV	I	II	III	IV	I	II	III	IV	I	II	III	IV
Deposits (net)	-56	63	11	226	-73	127	35	143	-293	167	1	175	-376	152	117	246	-292	112	15	101
Cash	-33	-2	1	37	-30	20	-2	11	-47	-3	10	48	-47	-3	10	48	-51	12	2	28
Money at call and short notice	7	21	86	8	-13	6	17	-5	-3	18	18	53	-37	10	-1	49	-55	57	-12	16
Bills discounted	-78	13	-137	35	11	-145	47	35	129	-84	185	138	-3	232	20	50	-95	-141	104	-304
TDRs	-243	24	14	95	-135	208	-16	52	-441	186	-239	-110	-349	-147	138	21	-222	56	-71	-114
Investments	28	24	14	-10	3	-8	-6	6	18	6	14	-4	-9	-6	4	27	24	-2	3	412
Advances	42	97	30	57	93	41	2	36	42	28	19	56	71	54	-47	43	110	128	-5	54

Source
Monthly Digest of Statistics

The cash available was usually concentrated on reducing the floating debt. One exception was 1948 I when the authorities repaid the maturing 3% Conversion Loan 1948/53 which they had decided not to try to convert in the autumn of 1947 (Chapter 4) and reduced the fiduciary issue by £150m (see below), with the result that the floating debt increased slightly. Otherwise the usually negative figures in 1947-9 for 'stocks in market', which show the extent of government intervention in the gilt-edged market, were small, *except* during the convertibility crisis (1947 III) and after devaluation (1949 IV). In 1947 and 1948 the reductions in floating debt were fairly even divided between TDRs and market Treasury bills, but the Bank's decision to reduce the former shows up clearly from 1949 III. 'Market' Treasury bills include those held by overseas official holders (and the Banking Department of the Bank of England) which fell considerably in 1948 and the first half of 1949, so that Treasury bills held by the private sector (mainly British banks and discount houses) did not fall as much as market bills. The reduction in the floating debt was a slow and unsteady process, and although the floating debt held by the clearing banks fell in the first quarter of each year, it rose in many other quarters (Table 5.9).

Turning to Table 5.9, the budget surpluses of 1947-51 were also reflected in the first quarter of each year in falls in clearing bank reserves and deposits, which rose in the other quarters. The banks' investments (mainly gilt-edged securities) showed little change until the advent of the new monetary policy in 1951 IV. The most consistent feature of Table 5.9 is the steady rise in advances which fell only in 1950 III and 1951 III. As the Jay working party kept noticing, the growth in advances offset the decline in floating debt holdings, so that while clearing bank deposits grew slowly at an annual average rate of 2.1 per cent their advances grew by 15.3 per cent.

Dow has suggested that the slow growth of bank deposits in 1947-51 may have been due to the 'informal policy of restraint' on bank advances (at a time when the banks did not wish to expand their already large holdings of bonds) and that the upward drift of long-term interest rates can largely be explained by the *'relative* [to income] restraint imposed on the money supply'.[105] But the behaviour of bank lending shows little sign of restraint before

[105] *Management of the British Economy*, 230-1.

TABLE 5.10   *The Money Stock (M3) and its Proximate Determinants, Monthly, 1948–51*

	M3, £m	H, £m	D/C	D/R
1948				
Jan.	8,059.6	1,738.9	5.37	13.75
Feb.	7,876.3	1,680.6	5.43	14.02
Mar.	8,051.6	1,693.0	5.57	14.02
Apr.	8,129.6	1,699.7	5.64	14.00
May	8,121.4	1,710.0	5.60	13.84
June	8,213.3	1,712.7	5.74	13.62
July	8,207.3	1,737.2	5.57	13.74
Aug.	8,192.8	1,733.3	5.56	13.77
Sept.	8,211.6	1,707.7	5.72	13.85
Oct.	8,294.3	1,696.6	5.83	14.10
Nov.	8,294.9	1,703.9	5.82	13.97
Dec.	8,417.4	1,745.2	5.79	13.67
1949				
Jan.	8,294.2	1,724.7	5.81	13.45
Feb.	8,017.6	1,690.2	5.60	13.73
Mar.	8,038.6	1,703.1	5.53	13.87
Apr.	8,134.5	1,734.1	5.51	13.76
May	8,143.5	1,731.0	5.53	13.72
June	8,309.9	1,733.4	5.58	14.39
July	8,305.5	1,750.7	5.57	13.96
Aug.	8,201.6	1,739.5	5.55	13.73
Sept.	8,262.0	1,722.1	5.67	13.95
Oct.	8,328.3	1,722.6	5.74	13.98
Nov.	8,343.0	1,722.4	5.74	14.00
Dec.	8,443.3	1,770.7	5.81	13.01
1950				
Jan.	8,360.5	1,727.9	5.80	13.67
Feb.	8,089.9	1,695.8	5.55	13.89
Mar.	8,002.9	1,707.3	5.49	13.72
Apr.	8,104.5	1,730.9	5.50	13.66
May	8,118.4	1,726.2	5.48	13.92
June	8,326.1	1,787.9	5.31	14.14
July	8,284.4	1,759.4	5.50	13.84
Aug.	8,274.7	1,763.3	5.52	13.63
Sept.	8,322.8	1,734.5	5.65	14.05
Oct.	8,487.4	1,742.7	5.84	13.92
Nov.	8,512.7	1,743.9	5.83	14.08
Dec.	8,630.8	1,805.2	5.81	13.28
1951				
Jan.	8,526.2	1,768.9	5.83	13.58
Feb.	8,285.3	1,740.6	5.63	13.83
Mar.	8,301.7	1,761.8	5.48	14.09
Apr.	8,430.9	1,782.3	5.55	13.70
May	8,414.0	1,785.5	5.51	13.88
June	8,488.1	1,797.3	5.51	14.05
July	8,525.1	1,825.8	5.47	13.72

TABLE 5.10—*continued*

	M3, £m	H, £m	D/C	D/R
1951				
Aug.	8,458.4	1,824.1	5.58	13.60
Sept.	8,448.4	1,798.3	5.48	13.90
Oct.	8,503.3	1,810.5	5.51	13.70
Nov.	8,466.3	1,818.0	5.53	13.26
Dec.	8,607.7	1,868.3	5.44	13.17

Notes

$$M3 = H \cdot \frac{D/R\,(1 + D/C)}{D/R + D/C}$$

where M3 = currency in circulation plus net deposits of UK commercial banks, C = currency in circulation outside banks, R = reserves of UK commercial banks, D = net deposits of UK commercial banks, and H = C + R.

Sources
As for Table 3.8.

1951. During the war advances fell considerably, from over 40 per cent of deposits in the late 1930s to 16.4 per cent in 1945. Their rise in the immediate post-war years took them back to nearly 30 per cent of deposits by 1951.[106] Since the Bank of England was not trying to control the cash reserves of the banking system and was willing to supply cash whenever required to keep the banks' cash-to-deposits ratio fixed, and the banks held large holdings of liquid assets (whose liquidity was enhanced by the replacement of TDRs by Treasury bills), the banks were always willing and able to meet the demand for loans. It was not until the summer of 1951 that they felt any need to raise their interest rates on advances.

There were falls in advances in 1950 III and 1951 III. A large part of the £47m fall in 1950 III came from the repayment of bank loans to nationalized industries out of the proceeds of government-guaranteed bond issues. At the same time large capital inflows were reducing external financing and increasing the government's domestic borrowing requirement. TDRs rose by £155m, an increase not offset by a reduction of Treasury bills in bank portfolios, and deposits rose by £117m.[107] In 1951 III, however,

[106] H. G. Johnson, 'Some implications of secular changes in bank assets and liabilities in Great Britain', *EJ*, 61 (Sept. 1951), 544–61.

[107] Trend to Eady and Littlewood, 22 Nov., Eady to Financial Secretary, 25 Nov., Jay to Hall, 29 Nov. 1950, T233/484, PRO; see also 'Monetary survey 1950–51', *Midland Bank Review*, (May 1951), 2.

the EEA was contributing sterling to the 'Exchequer cash available' which was used to reduce both Treasury bills and TDRs. The rise in deposits was less than in any other quarter except 1947 III and 1949 III. Advances had been rising very rapidly in the first half of 1951; since the banks raised their overdraft rates in the summer of 1951 for the first time in twenty years, the fall of advances in the third quarter may mean that the authorities' 'control' of advances was at last beginning to make an impact on bank lending.

The outcome for nominal monetary aggregates can be seen in Tables 5.4 and 5.10. The money stock grew very slowly in 1947-51 compared with its rapid growth since 1939 and its moderate growth after 1951. The monetary base fell in 1947-8 and then grew steadily, and faster than M3, for the rest of the period. The deposit-reserve ratio was almost constant in 1947-51, between the sharp jump at the end of 1946 caused by the abolition of the London clearing banks' practice of 'window-dressing' their published reserves at half-year ends and the fall prompted by the tightening of monetary policy in the winter of 1951-2. The deposit-currency ratio, which had fallen during the war and begun to rise again in 1946, rose in 1947-8 to around 5.5 compared with its pre-war level of about 6.5, levelled off in 1949-50, and then fell steadily.

This chapter has noted that the Bank of England was not controlling the monetary base in 1948-51 but letting it respond to the demand for bank reserves in order to maintain a constant reserve-deposit ratio and to ensure the banks held on to the floating debt. There was little direct connection between the monetary base and official international reserves, which were declining, despite occasional improvement, from £679m at the beginning of 1947 to £350m by the time of devaluation. In the next eighteen months the reserves more than doubled, only to fall back to £600m by early 1952. The monetary base moved consistently with changes in reserves only in the summer and autumn of 1947 and the autumn of 1948 (see Table 4.9). While the authorities were usually able to sterilize the effects of reserve changes on the monetary base through the EEA, the mechanism of the EEA, whose sterling resources for the purchase of foreign exchange were held as Treasury bills, meant that reserve losses or overseas financial assistance helped to reduce the amount of the floating debt held by the private sector, as in 1947–9 (above).

In 1947–51 the behaviour of the monetary base therefore usually followed that of the money stock. In the second half of 1947 and first half of 1948, however, the monetary base fell. In the first of these two six-month periods currency in circulation declined by 5 per cent, while the deposit-currency ratio was rising, as part of the post-war readjustment of private sector behaviour. The authorities responded to the fall in the demand for currency by first not making the usual short-lived Christmas increase in the fiduciary issue and then reducing it by £50m at the beginning of each of the next three months. As Peppiatt noted, this 'first real decrease for ten years . . . [was] merely a reflection of what has happened over the past few months and . . . in itself not deflationary, although it is, of course, a good sign in these days of suppressed inflation'.[108]

The behaviour of the money stock in 1948–51 was thus determined by the demand for money. The latter in its turn reflected the private sector's adjustment to post-war conditions, which included the pent-up demand for goods and services unavailable during the war, the excessive money balances caused by wartime saving and inflated by the cheaper money policy, and other changes in the composition of the non-bank private sector's portfolio of financial assets produced by the authorities' debt management policies. The ability of the private sector to run down its money balances depended on the rate of increase of the supply of goods and services and the stringency of the controls imposed on consumption and investment expenditures, which remained extensive but were being reduced in the late 1940s. The gradual rundown of money balances after 1947 can be seen in Table 4.4. As already mentioned in Chapter 4, after the boost given to them by the 1946 monetary expansion the ratios of M1 and M3 to money income returned to their 1945 levels by 1949 but remained above their pre-war levels until the early 1950s. UK prices were rising steadily in the later 1940s, as a result of domestic demand and wage pressures and rising import prices, so that real balances were declining in 1948–52.

With declining real balances and rising real incomes one would expect interest rates, real and nominal, to be rising. Long-term

[108] Peppiatt to Rickatson-Hatt, 'The fiduciary issue', 7 Jan. 1948, C40/573, BOE.

TABLE 5.11   *Interest Rates and Inflation, 1945-51, %.p.a.*

	Short-dated government securities[1]	2½% Consols[2]	20-year debenture and loan stocks	Dividend yield on industrial ordinary shares	Change in prices[3] (a)	(b)[4]
1945 June	2.48	3.00	n.a.	n.a.		
					1.8	3.0
Dec.	2.54	2.73	3.70	3.75		
1946 June	2.15	2.57	3.60	3.52		
					4.4	1.9
Dec.	1.73	2.54	3.25	3.57		
1947 June	2.08	2.68	3.36	3.95		
					5.5	9.0
Dec.	2.54	3.01	3.63	4.26		
1948 June	1.95	3.27	3.63	4.81		
					7.6	7.3
Dec.	1.72	3.14	3.60	4.62		
1949 June	2.26	3.21	3.74	5.63		
					2.6	3.0
Dec.	1.86	3.51	4.18	5.49		
1950 June	2.06	3.55	4.11	5.36		
					2.9	0.67
Dec.	1.84	3.52	4.11	5.27		
1951 June	2.00	3.84	4.36	4.97		
					9.9	7.4
Dec.	2.43	4.05	4.91	5.78		

Notes
[1] 1945-9: gross redemption yield for 2½% National War Bonds 1952/54; 1950-1: gross redemption yield for 2¼% Exchequer Stock 1955.
[2] Gross flat yield on 2½% Consols.
[3] From previous year.
[4] (*a*) % change in retail price index; (*b*) % change in GDP deflator.

Sources
Short-dated goverment security yields, debenture yields, and dividend yields: Bank of England, *Statistical Abstract*, No. 1 (1970), table 30.
Yield on 2½% Consols: F. Capie and A. Webber, *A Monetary History of the United Kingdom 1970-1982*, vol. I, tables III(10) and III(11).
Price changes calculated from Feinstein, *National Income, Expenditure and Output of the United Kingdom 1865-1955*, tables 61 and 65.

interest rates were rising, although nominal short-term interest rates were tied down by the fixed interest rates on the government's floating debt (Table 5.11). The attempts of the authorities to reduce floating debt may have made a small contribution to the upward drift of longer-term interest rates since they produced a shift in the maturity composition of the private sector's holdings of government debt in 1948–51 (see Table 3.6). The proportion of floating debt in private sector portfolios fell from 17 per cent in March 1947 to 13 per cent four years later and that of long-term gilt-edged debt rose from 41 to 47 per cent over the same period. The proportion of short- and medium-term gilt-edged debt combined was around 23 per cent at each end of the four-year period. The changes are small—especially compared to those in the opposite direction during the war—so that their impact on the term structure of interest rates is likely to have been small relative to the effect of (persistent) market expectations of rising interest rates.

This section has described the behaviour of the money supply in 1948–51 as a whole, since there are no striking changes in that behaviour within the period; in particular the devaluation of the pound in September 1949 made little impression on it. Before returning to consider the authorities' continued debate on monetary policy in 1950–1 it is appropriate to review the effects of devaluation in the first eighteen months after the exchange-rate change.

The Economic Section estimates of the effects of devaluation on prices and wages in Britain were largely borne out—allowing for the fact that the depreciation was larger than the 25 per cent the Section had assumed in its 1949 calculations (above). Most of the countries expected to devalue their currencies with sterling did so. Although import prices rose by more than predicted—by over 30 per cent rather than the estimated 20 per cent—by the end of 1950 the cost-of-living index had risen by 3½ per cent since September 1949 and wages by under 2 per cent. The change in the overall balance of payments was *more* favourable than anticipated for the short term, but a large part of the improvement in 1950 came from capital inflows replacing the outflows of the previous year (see Table 5.1), as the Section soon realized. On the current account the significant reduction in the rate of growth of imports largely reflected tighter import controls and UK exporters did not appear to have reaped the full benefits of increased competitiveness. The dollar earnings of the rest of the sterling area were also higher than anticipated following the vigorous revival of the USA from the mild 1949 recession and the outbreak of the Korean war which drove up dollar prices. By February 1951 the Economic Section (in the persons of Nita Watts and Robert Hall) were

TABLE 5.12   *UK and US Price Indices 1939-51, 1939 = 100*

	UK			USA			UK prices/US prices		
	(1)	(2)	(3)	(4)	(5)	(6)	(7)	(8)	(9)
1939	100.0	100.0	100.0	100.0	100.0	100.0	1.00	1.00	1.00
1940	108.6	116.6	113.3	101.6	100.9	101.0	1.07	1.16	1.12
1941	118.4	129.2	124.7	109.3	108.0	106.0	1.08	1.20	1.18
1942	126.9	138.6	132.9	122.7	121.5	117.3	1.03	1.14	1.13
1943	132.5	143.2	137.3	131.0	132.8	124.5	1.01	1.08	1.10
1944	140.7	147.0	140.5	134.7	140.1	126.7	1.04	1.05	1.11
1945	144.9	151.2	143.0	138.2	145.0	129.6	1.05	1.04	1.10
1946	147.7	156.0	149.4	154.4	156.3	140.6	0.96	1.00	1.06
1947	161.0	167.1	157.6	172.7	172.7	160.8	0.93	0.97	0.98
1948	172.8	177.4	169.6	184.3	182.5	173.3	0.94	0.97	0.98
1949	177.9	181.5	174.1	183.1	181.2	171.6	0.97	1.00	1.01
1950	179.1	186.2	179.1	185.6	183.8	173.3	0.96	1.01	1.03
1951	192.3	203.7	196.8	198.1	196.5	187.0	0.97	1.04	1.05

Notes
(1) = GDP deflator, (2) and (5) = implicit price deflators for consumers' expenditure, (3) = retail price index, (4) = GNP deflator, (6) = US Bureau of Labour Statistics consumer price index, (7) = (1)/(4), (8) = (2)/(5), (9) = (3)/(6).

Sources
Calculated from Feinstein, *National Income, Expenditure and Output of the United Kingdom 1855-1965*, tables 61 and 65, and *Historical Statistics of the United States, Colonial Times to 1970* (Washington DC, 1975), Series E1-22 and E135-166.

considering whether there was a case for revaluation as an anti-inflationary policy.[109]

In making the case for devaluation in 1948 Otto Clarke had rejected the evidence of purchasing power parity calculations, which appeared to show sterling was *undervalued* in relation to the US dollar. He asked: 'Does anyone seriously suppose . . . that our dollar situation—our balance of payments with the dollar area—could conceivably be *improved* by *appreciating* sterling? (Ask

[109] Untitled paper by Watts on the effects of devaluation, 5 Feb., and Hall to Armstrong, 15 Feb. 1951, T230/388, PRO. On various assumptions about the reactions of other countries Watts calculated that a 25 per cent revaluation of sterling to US$3.50 could cause a 13 per cent fall in import prices and a 2-3 per cent fall in the cost of living after one or two years. In the short term the effect on the balance of payments would depend crucially on capital movements; in the longer term, dollar exports would depend on US demand and might *increase*, but while UK imports were strictly controlled and would not be allowed to rise overseas sterling area dollar imports might well increase substantially. Hall and Watts argued that the UK should wait and see if sterling really was undervalued *vis-à-vis* the dollar and if it were the exchange rate should be floated.

the Canadians and the Swedes [who had revalued their currencies in July 1946]?)' Four months later, R. G. Hawtrey, who had retired from the Treasury in 1945, answered 'Yes'.[110] At that time Hawtrey was a lone voice but after the devaluation in 1949 the argument was made from time to time by Hawtrey and others that the exchange-rate change was too large and that the resulting undervaluation of the pound was causing persistent domestic inflation in the 1950s and early 1960s.[111] The simple purchasing power parity calculations in Table 5.12 support this argument for they suggest that an overvaluation of sterling against the dollar at the end of the war was removed by the more rapid rate of rise of US prices than UK prices in 1946–8 and that after 1949 UK prices rose more rapidly than US prices. It is also true that the exchange-rate change in 1949 *deliberately* undervalued the pound according to the authorities' own estimates (above).

Against the overvaluation argument, however, most calculations of post-war purchasing power parities take as their starting point a time when the pound may well have been overvalued (having regained its pre-1931 nominal value in the later 1930s). Furthermore, even if the pound had not been overvalued before the war, the wartime changes in the structure of Britain's balance of payments implied an equilibrium real exchange rate different from that produced by the arbitrarily chosen wartime nominal exchange rate of US$4.03.[112] It is reasonable to conclude that a sizeable exchange-rate adjustment was necessary in the early post-war period, even though the large change increased the rise in import prices following the devaluation and caused faster UK inflation in the last two years of the Attlee governments than would have occurred without such a large devaluation.

[110] Clarke, 'The future of sterling',25 Feb. 1948, T236/2398, PRO: Hawtrey to the Editor, *The Times*, 7 June 1948, cited in Cairncross, *Years of Recovery*, 168.

[111] See, for instance, Roy F. Harrod, *The Pound Sterling*, Princeton Essays in International Finance, no. 13, Feb. 1952; Hawtrey, *Towards the Rescue of Sterling* (London, 1954); and R. J. Ball and T. Burns, 'The inflationary mechanism in the U.K. economy', *AER* 66 (Sept. 1976), 473–7.

[112] See, for instance, UN Economic Commission for Europe, *Economic Survey of Europe in 1948* (Washington, Apr. 1949), 66–7, and Colin Clark, 'The value of the pound', *EJ* 59 (June 1949), 198–207; see also Lawrence H. Officer, *Purchasing Power Parity and Exchange Rates: Theory, Evidence and Relevance* (1982), 145–6.

6

The End of Cheap Money

> I thought we had got into rather a ludicrous position in that
> the Government was now never supposed to take any open
> responsibility for credit policy at all. I thought this involved
> too much of a swing in the opposite direction from the atti-
> tude taken up in the immediate post-war years.[1]

AFTER the devaluation of the pound in September 1949 the
government had decided to postpone an election, which had to
be held by the summer of 1950, until the new year. At the end of
the old year Attlee decided on a winter election, Cripps having
insisted on its being before the budget. After the general election
of 23 February, Labour remained in power with a precariously
small majority. In a 'half-reshuffle' of his government Attlee
moved Hugh Gaitskell from the Ministry of Fuel and Power to the
Treasury as Minister of State for Economic Affairs to assist the
ailing Chancellor. Douglas Jay became Financial Secretary. Although only a junior minister and initially concentrating on overseas finance, Gaitskell was a full member of the Cabinet
Economic Policy Committee as well as fully involved in Treasury
domestic policy-making. When Cripps left for three months'
leave at the beginning of August Gaitskell took over his duties
(and moved into his office). On 20 October Cripps resigned and
Attlee chose Gaitskell to succeed him.[2] Before he went to the
Treasury Gaitskell was inclined to advocate 'planning' and controls in preference to demand management policies; at the

---

[1] Note by Gaitskell, 3 July 1951, T233/1401, PRO.
[2] On the election see Morgan, *Labour in Power*, 402–6, and Williams, *Diary of
Hugh Gaitskell*, 154–5, 161; on Gaitskell's move and his first months in the
Treasury see Williams, *Hugh Gaitskell*, 152–62, and *Diary of Hugh Gaitskell*, 164,
171–216. When Gaitskell became Chancellor John Edwards became Economic
Secretary.

Treasury he sought rather to supplement budgetary and monetary policy with more 'socialist' measures and, with respect to the latter, to find ways of controlling the money supply without resort to manipulating short-term interest rates.

The Governor of the Bank of England had other ideas. His campaign to restore 'flexibility' to short-term interest rates was intended to restore the Bank's control over the money market and hence its pre-war position in the British financial system (see Chapter 5). At the beginning of 1950 his colleague Sir Kenneth Peppiatt described his predicament:

The Governor rightly dislikes finding himself in a position where, however much a rise in short-term interest rates may be called for on general grounds, he is (almost) precluded from acting in the orthodox manner because of the adverse impact such a move would have on the budgetary position in view of the present size and nature of the Floating Debt. . . .

The ideal situation would be a large funding operation, but the prospects for this are at present remote. . . .

In any event it might be better—as a matter of tactics—to await the result of the Election before making a move . . . if only because the present Government are unlikely to agree to risk making any such change now and because a Government of a different complexion might be willing to agree to action on orthodox lines . . .[3]

Cobbold's hopes were dashed in February 1950 but fulfilled just over a year and a half later, when the general election of 25 October 1951 produced a Conservative government with a majority of 17. In the meantime the Bank 'proceeded with caution' with its policy begun in July 1949 of gradually reducing the proportion of TDRs within the floating debt. At the end of March 1950 TDRs totalled £465m, just under half of what they had been a year earlier; a year later they were down to £284m. The proportion of TDRs in the floating debt had thus been reduced from 20 per cent to 5 per cent in less than two years.[4] The Bank also managed to begin funding the floating debt on a small scale in the summer of 1950. In the autumn Cobbold recommenced his more

[3] Peppiatt, 'Short-term interest rates/Bank Rate', 5 Jan. 1950, C42/1, BOE.

[4] Note by Beale, 14 Mar., and 'Treasury Bill allotments and TDRs in 1950/51', 9 Mar. 1950, C42/1, BOE; Pember and Boyle, *British Government Securities in the Twentieth Century, Supplement 1950–1976*, 352–4.

direct attempts to raise short-term interest rates and persisted in them for the next year.

This chapter describes Cobbold's renewed campaign in 1950–1, especially his struggles with his new economist adversary, Gaitskell, and the development of the views on monetary policy of Gaitskell and his officials in the same period. It includes the debt management operations undertaken during Gaitskell's time at the Treasury, before relating the details of 'the end of the story', the so-called revival of monetary policy under Gaitskell's Conservative successor, R. A. Butler, in the winter of 1951/2. The monetary debate took place against a background of a rapidly improving balance-of-payments and reserve position in 1950, concerted international moves toward trade liberalization and the negotiation of the European Payments Union (EPU), domestic budgetary struggles in 1950 and 1951 over the finance of the National Health Service and of British rearmament following the outbreak of the Korean war in June 1950, the Korean war inflation, and, finally, another major British balance-of-payments crisis in 1951. The events of 1950–1 also dispelled active fears of a serious post-war depression and led the Labour government to abandon an Economic Planning and Full Employment Bill which is also briefly considered in this chapter.

The balance of payments, rearmament and the budget

The improvement in the UK balance of payments and UK official international reserves following the devaluation of sterling was both substantial and short-lived (see Tables 5.1 and 5.2 in the previous chapter). The current account went from approximate balance in 1949 to a £300m surplus in 1950 and then to a £369m deficit in 1951. The current account balance with the dollar area was in deficit throughout these years, improving from −£291m in 1949 to −£79m in 1950 and deteriorating once more to −£427m in 1951. For the rest of the sterling area there was a sizeable deficit (£369m) in 1949, a respectable surplus (£124m) in 1950 and a deficit again in 1951 (£163m) (see Table 4.7). The major culprits in the deterioration from the middle of 1950 were the Korean war inflation and British rearmament.

The war in Korea broke out in June 1950. Between July 1950 and January 1951 the British defence programme was raised from £2,340m over the financial years 1950/1 to 1953/4 to £4,655m (plus £446m for strategic stockpiling) over the same four years, initially in the hope, which was disappointed, of American assistance at least to mitigate the impact on the balance of payments.[5] The defence programme adversely affected both sides of the UK current account, by increasing imports of raw materials and equipment and by diverting manufacturing industry from exports to military goods; the impact was aggravated by the severe deterioration in the terms of trade caused by commodity price inflation. The price of British imports rose some 50 per cent in 1950–1. The commodity price boom, set off by rapid US re-armament and stockpiling of strategic materials and fuelled by American and European fears of shortages and higher prices, at first benefited the rest of the sterling area, which enjoyed sizeable current account surpluses in the second half of 1950 and first half of 1951. The cessation of stockpiling and the weakening of infla-tionary fears reduced the exports of the overseas sterling area at a time when their imports had been increased by the previous increase in incomes.[6] The renewed deficit of the overseas sterling area increased the drain on the UK official international reserves in the second half of 1951 (see Table 6.1).

Before that crisis period was reached, the macroeconomic policy problem faced by the Labour government in 1950–1 was to restrain domestic demand, first to allow devaluation to have its full effect and then to accommodate rearmament without adding domestic inflationary pressure to that coming from abroad.

The 1950 budget, Stafford Cripps's last disinflationary budget, was outlined in Chapter 5. The main lines of Gaitskell's budget of 10 April 1951 are shown in Table 6.2. At the beginning of the 1951 budget season, while the Economic Section was preparing its assessment of the general economic outlook for the Budget Com-mittee, Robert Hall told the committee that he thought the infla-tionary gap for 1951/2 'would be nearer £100 millions than £200 millions' in spite of increased defence expenditure, because real

[5] On the rearmament programme see Cairncross, *Years of Recovery*, ch. 8; Plow-den, *An Industrialist in the Treasury*, chs. 10–12; *Robert Hall Diaries*, 118–67.

[6] Dow, *Management of the British Economy*, 55–6, 63–4; Bank for International Settlements, *The Sterling Area* (Basle, 1953), 43–4.

TABLE 6.1 *Sterling Area Balance of Payments, Current Account, by Halfyears,*
1950-2, £m

	UK	Rest of sterling area	Total
1950			
First half	42	−6	36
Second half	179	130	309
1951			
First half	−71	271	200
Second half	−394	−434	−828
1952			
First half	24	−432	−408

Source
Bank for International Settlements, *The Sterling Area*, 43.

output was increasing rapidly and government expenditure other than on defence was not threatening to increase as much as in previous years. Tax reductions might well have been possible in the absence of rearmament. It was not clear, however, where additional tax revenue to finance rearmament expenditure would come from, so that 'some measure of inflation during the coming year' might have to be accepted. The other members of the committee thought there might be possibilities for increasing revenue in raising petrol tax, in increasing purchase tax on cars, radios and television sets and confectionery, in increasing the standard rate of income tax, and in reducing tax allowances for depreciation, but the last would only produce revenue after a year's delay. The possible expenditure reductions included imposng charges for some items provided by the National Health Service, and cuts in food subsidies.[7]

A few days later the new Chancellor minuted his officials on the work he wished them to undertake in the 'main fields for activity against inflation', including price control, public expenditure, and taxation. He thought that price controls, 'difficult as they are to administer and enforce', had been effective during the war and that the Treasury should encourage the Board of Trade to identify where controls could be reimposed. On public expenditure he wanted a report on the Treasury's review of possible economies as soon as possible, and on taxation he wanted the Budget Committee to be working out the various alternatives for

[7] BC(50) 6th meeting, 'Budget Committee', 18 Oct. 1950, T171/403, PRO.

TABLE 6.2 *Gaitskell's Budget 1951*

	Expected surplus £m	Realized surplus £m	Total change in taxation £m[1]	Major tax changes
1951–2	39	380	+387	*Income tax*: increase in standard rate (to 9s 6d in £) and in reduced rates for small incomes; increase in married persons' and children's allowances; reduction in top rate of surtax (to prevent it exceeding 19s 6d in £). Increase in *petrol tax* and in *purchase tax* on cars and some consumer durables. Increase in *entertainments duty*. *Profits tax* increased on distributed profits. *Depreciation allowances* on new investment suspended (from 6 Apr. 1952).

Note
[1] In full financial year.

Sources
Cairncross, *Years of Recovery: British Economic Policy 1945–51*, 421; Dow, *The Management of the British Economy 1945–60*, 198–9; budget speech of 10 Apr. 1951.

raising an extra £100m of revenue. Gaitskell also saw a need to come to a decision about a more restrictive credit policy which was already under consideration in the Treasury, and to consider ways to increase private saving. As Minister of State he had also asked for a paper on wages policy and put forward a proposal for the statutory limitation of dividends to accompany any measures to control wages.[8]

When the Section produced its paper for the Budget Committee early in November, it first argued that 'by the middle of 1950 disinflation had resulted in a very happy balance between overall supply and demand', by reducing excess demand for consumer goods and improving the current account of the

[8] Notes by Gaitskell, 31 Oct. and 6 Nov. 1950, T171/403; 'Note of a meeting held in Sir Edward Bridges' room at 4.30 p.m. on Monday: 18th September. Wages Policy', T171/418; BC(50) 5th meeting, (27 Sept. 1950), T171/417, PRO. On credit policy see pp. 284–97 below.

balance of payments, and that in 1951 'the maintenance of present policies and present tax rates should enable the inflationary implications of defence expenditure to be avoided'. But this provisional conclusion was based on optimistic assumptions and 'makes no allowance for anything going wrong'. Since national output might increase less, and investment and government expenditure more, than forecast, an addition of at least £100m to the budget surplus should be made to cover these contingencies. After all, 'Since it is easier, in the event of miscalculation, to loosen than to tighten the screw, the first Budget of a new defence programme should if anything err on the austere side.'[9]

The gloomier paragraphs of the Section paper were added after a meeting of the Budget Committee on 17 November and strengthened after the meeting of the Treasury members on 27 November before the paper went to the Chancellor. Given the difficult choices to be made under conditions of considerable uncertainty, very little was settled at the Chancellor's meeting with his officials on 28 November.[10] The major decisions were taken in the new year after the last upward revision of the defence programme in January.

In February 1951 the Section put the extra taxation required to prevent inflation first at £50–100m and then at £100–150m, again on rather optimistic assumptions. Although defence expenditure was to rise by nearly £500m and civil expenditure by over £200m, business savings and government revenue were expected together to rise by nearly £400m because of rising profits, other incomes and prices, and the current surplus on the balance of payments to fall by £175m (and thus to remain positive while helping to finance domestic expenditure).[11] The Budget Committee thought the Section's first estimate of extra taxation too low: according to Robert Hall,

[9] BC(50)25, 'The general economic outlook for the 1951 budget, Note by Economic Section, Cabinet Office', 13 and 27 Nov. 1950, T171/403.

[10] Agenda and notes of meetings on 17 and 27 Nov. 1950 on T171/417; Bridges to Armstrong, 'Budget prospects, Note by Chairman of the Budget Committee', 27 Nov., and 'General economic policy, Summary of conclusions reached at Chancellor of the Exchequer's meeting on Tuesday, 28th November', T171/403; *Robert Hall Diaries*, 135.

[11] BC(51)16 and BC(51)16 Revise, 'The general budgetary problem in 1951, Note by the Economic Section, Cabinet Office', 2 and 16 Feb. 1951, T171/403.

Dow [who had written the Section paper] was there and was much amused by E.B.[Bridges] having a secret ballot on the amount to write up our £75m deficiency. 3 of £100, 3 of £200, 3 of £150, 3 of £125—average about £145—a write-up of £70 mn.

To achieve the higher figure the committee suggested increasing a range of taxes on consumer goods and services, raising the rate of profits tax and suspending the 'initial' depreciation allowances for new plant and machinery. The last two would not bring in extra revenue in 1951/2, but they would increase company savings and reduce investment. As for income tax, an increase in the rates on higher incomes would tend to reduce savings, and the committee was reluctant to recommend an increase in the standard rate of income tax unless and until it became necessary to raise a large amount of extra revenue. It preferred to recommend reductions in expenditure, even though 'savings to the requisite amount can only be secured by another big policy decision', such as a reduction in the £410m food subsidies.[12]

The question of government expenditure reduction was discussed at length on 17 and 18 February 1951. The new Economic Secretary, John Edwards, thought the time had come to reduce the food subsidies by, say, £200m of which £150m could be used to increase family allowances, national insurance benefits and income tax allowances. But to Douglas Jay the subsidies were

part of the long-term policy of the government for the permanent redistribution of current income, and ... desirable in themselves. ... If the reduction in food subsidies were put forward on the grounds of reducing government expenditure, he would oppose it à l'outrance.

He would, however, accept the present ceiling on food subsidies, and a resulting rise in food prices in 1951/2. Bridges, Plowden and Hall clearly supported Edwards, while other officials were doubtful about making such a major policy change in 1951/2. Gaitskell supported Jay, for he did not like the distributional consequences of cutting the subsidies in order to reduce taxes or avoid increasing them. He also feared a sharp rise in food prices would quickly lead to increased wage demands. He did not rule out any change but he wanted an analysis of the redistributive

[12] *Robert Hall Diaries*, 147; BC(51) 4th, 5th and 6th meetings, 2, 6, and 9 Feb. 1951, T171/417; 'The general budgetary problem, 1951, Note by the Chairman of the Budget Committee' (Feb. 1951), T171/403, PRO.

impact of a £50m net reduction in subsidies before any decision was made.[13] Subsidies were maintained at their existing ceiling in Gaitskell's budget and reduced in Butler's first budget.

On taxation the official recommendations to the Chancellor in February included increases in purchase tax on private cars and on some consumer durables, in petrol tax, in entertainments duty, and an increase in profit tax on distributed profits (to 50 per cent, leaving tax on undistributed profits at 10 per cent). An increase in profits tax had earlier been suggested as an alternative to a statutory limitation of dividends, which the Inland Revenue had advised was unworkable in that none of the schemes considered could freeze dividends (to complement a wage freeze) while allowing small increases in profits to encourage efficiency. Since the proposals would only raise an estimated £67m extra revenue in 1951/2, the Budget Committee agreed in late February 1951 to recommend increases in income tax to raise £50–100m more.[14]

When Gaitskell discussed his budget with the Prime Minister and senior ministers on 6 March he explained that the 'main problem' arose from the increase in 'above the line' expenditure of £810m, half of which was on defence. In the previous three budgets the size of the target surplus had been determined by the need to finance domestic investment while improving the balance of payments; in 1951/2 the situation was different because of rising private savings and the expected movement of the current account balance from surplus to deficit. This reduced the amount of government savings needed to make total savings equal planned investments by about £240m (since private savings were forecast to rise by £140m, the current balance to decline by £150m and investment to rise by £80m). £150m would, therefore, be needed in extra revenue or reduced expenditure in 1951/2, a figure that could be nearer £200m if the forecast's assumptions about productivity growth were too optimistic. In addition to

[13] 'Government expenditure—Note of discussion at Roffey on Saturday and Sunday, Feb. 17/18, 1951', T171/417.

[14] BC(51) 7th meeting, 'Minutes of Meetings held at Roffey Park on Saturday and Sunday, 17th and 18th February 1951', and BC(51) 8th meeting, 'Minutes of a meeting held in Sir Edward Bridges' room on Wednesday, 28th February, at 3.0 p.m.', T171/403; on dividend limitation see the papers in T171/403, sect. 4, and BC(51) 2nd meeting, 'Minutes of a Meeting held in Sir Edward Bridges' room at 3.30 p.m. on Friday, 12th January 1951', T171/417.

defence the increases in expenditure came from the first instal-
ment of interest payments on the US and Canadian loans negotiated in 1945 and 1946, an increase in old age pensions, and the
National Health Service, although the Health Ministers had
agreed to reduce the last by £25m and were currently drawing up
proposals to make these economies. Over the proposals, to impose charges for dentures and spectacles equal to about 50 per
cent of their cost, Aneurin Bevan (Minister of Labour, previously
Minister of Health) and Harold Wilson resigned (as did John
Freeman, a junior minister at the Ministry of Supply) in the
fortnight after the budget.[15]

The tax proposals Gaitskell put to his colleagues were to increase profits tax on distributed profits by 50 per cent; to suspend
the initial depreciation allowances; to raise petrol tax, purchase
tax on private cars and certain consumer durables, entertainments duty, and some postal and telephone charges; and to increase the standard and reduced rates of income tax by 6d. in the
pound while increasing personal allowances. The standard rate
was now 47.5 per cent compared with the wartime 50 per cent. In
the following month there were further revisions in the official
national income forecasts and budget estimates, but they did not
make much difference to the size of the target increase in the
surplus, and Gaitskell's budget on 10 April 1951 closely followed
the arguments and proposals arrived at in February and early
March.[16]

The design of the 1951 budget consciously took risks with the
balance of payments. The deterioration turned out, however, to
be larger than anticipated. The worsening of the terms of trade
had been allowed for but its impact on the UK current account
balance was underestimated and the effect of the end of the commodity price boom on the dollar earnings of the overseas sterling
area not foreseen. According to Douglas Jay, the Treasury saw

[15] 'The Budget 1951, Memorandum by the Chancellor of the Exchequer', T171/
403; on Bevan's resignation see Morgan, *Labour in Power*, 441–61, Williams, *Hugh
Gaitskell*, ch. 8, and *Diary of Hugh Gaitskell*, 239–59.

[16] 'The Budget 1951, Memorandum by the Chancellor of the Exchequer', T171/
403; BC(51)43 and BC(51)43 Revise, 'The general budgetary problem for 1951,
Note by the Economic Section', 13 and 15 Mar., Gilbert to Armstrong, 15 Mar.,
'Note of Meeting held on 19th March, 1951', T171/403; *Robert Hall Diaries*, 149–50,
153–4; *House of Commons Debates*, vol. 486, 10 Apr. 1951, cols. 826–67; see also
Cairncross and Watts, *Economic Section*, 252–7; Dow, *Management of the British
Economy*, 57–60.

TABLE 6.3 *Nominal Yields on British Government Securities, Monthly, 1950–1, %.p.a.*

		Short-dated[1]	Medium-dated[2]	Long-dated[3]	Consols[4]
End of 1950	Jan.	2.23	2.64	3.04	3.59
	Feb.	2.23	2.73	3.23	3.56
	Mar.	2.22	2.68	3.10	3.62
	Apr.	2.18	2.58	3.05	3.62
	May	2.04	2.55	2.91	3.61
	June	2.06	2.68	3.05	3.55
	July	2.09	2.66	3.05	3.61
	Aug.	1.87	2.62	2.95	3.55
	Sept.	1.82	2.54	2.89	3.48
	Oct.	1.74	2.54	2.83	3.40
	Nov.	1.83	2.57	2.94	3.44
	Dec.	1.84	2.58	2.95	3.52
1951	Jan.	1.74	3.05	3.33	3.53
	Feb.	1.73	3.06	3.42	3.64
	Mar.	1.79	3.11	3.43	3.47
	Apr.	1.85	3.14	3.50	3.73
	May	1.95	3.28	3.62	3.81
	June	2.00	3.34	3.69	3.84
	July	1.87	3.24	3.63	3.80
	Aug.	1.76	3.20	3.65	3.81
	Sept.	1.73	3.16	3.68	3.83
	Oct.	1.79	3.34	3.71	3.81
	Nov.	2.16	3.62	3.87	3.95
	Dec.	2.43	3.91	4.16	4.05

Notes
[1] Gross redemption yields for 2½% National War Bonds 1952/54.
[2] Gross redemption yields for 2½% Funding Loan 1956/61.
[3] Gross redemption yields for 3% Savings Bonds 1960/70.
[4] Gross flat yields on 2½% Consols.

Sources
Short-dated, medium-dated and long-dated security yields: Bank of England, *Statistical Abstract*, No. 1, 1970, table 30.
Yield on 2½% Consols: Capie and Webber, *A Monetary History of the United Kingdom 1970–1982*, vol. I, table III(10).

the first signs of a new balance-of-payments crisis in June 1951, when 'the weekly "dollar drain" figures turned again into deficit for the first time since September'. Within a few weeks the strain on the reserves was increased by doubts as to whether the exchange rate could be maintained and the resulting speculation on a new devaluation.[17] The reserves, which were comfortably over

[17] Dow, *Management of the British Economy*, 61–5; Jay, *Change and Fortune*, 208–9; 'Monetary survey 1951–2', *Midland Bank Review*, (May 1952), 1–2.

£1,000m from October 1950 and nearly £1,400m in May and June 1951, fell swiftly to just over £1,000m by the October general election. They continued to fall until April 1952, when they were down to £594m.

Meanwhile medium- and long-term nominal interest rates on government debt were rising gradually in 1950–1 (see Table 6.3). At the end of 1950 long-term rates reached 3½ per cent; by October 1951 they were nearer 4 per cent. Monetary growth remained low. As in the preceding two years this was the resultant of the opposing forces of a reduction in the banks' holdings of floating debt and a sustained rise in their advances. In the second half of 1950 the floating debt increased as large capital inflows increased both UK international reserves and market holdings of Treasury bills. In 1951 the seasonal reduction in the floating debt in the first quarter was smaller than in the previous three years and the increase in advances in this and the next quarter much larger than in any previous post-war quarter (see Tables 5.8 and 5.9). As for the last six months of the Labour government, 'although net bank deposits rose less rapidly ... than in the similar period of 1950, this was solely due to the huge amount of finance that accrued to the Government as a result of Britain's plunge from external surplus into catastrophic deficit'.[18]

Gaitskell versus *Cobbold*

After the general election the first task of the Treasury ministers and their officials was to resume preparation of the 1950 budget (see Chapter 5). During its preparation the Economic Section pointed out that direct controls over fixed investment

should continue to be supplemented by monetary and banking policy to the maximum extent possible, particularly since any additional easing of the pressure of investment made possible by monetary policy would reduce the Budget surplus required, and enable taxes to be reduced by the same amount.

Although 'the most effective and immediate way' to use monetary policy to restrain private investment, a rise in interest rates, would increase the cost of government debt service, it was

[18] *The Economist*, 7 June 1952, 691.

'arguable, on the other hand' that the additional budgetary burden would be 'more than offset by a reduction in the Budget surplus required to finance a lower level of investment, and also by the relief of the general strain upon the economy'.[19] Such considerations underlay the discussions of monetary policy in Whitehall in the summer of 1950; in the autumn they were reinforced by the increase in the defence programme.

In July Sir Wilfrid Eady summoned Humphrey Mynors and Maurice Allen (an adviser and a professional economist) from the Bank to tell them that he 'had two troubles'. One was that Douglas Jay was 'again expressing interest in the level of Bank deposits and advances', the other was a 'more fundamental' concern about the relation between the investment programme and available savings. Mynors also recorded:

Behind all this is a further concern with the lack of direct Government control over the money and capital markets rather than a conviction that existing informal controls have failed in their objective in any specific direction. Eady thinks we are likely to suffer a return to the sort of discussions about controls which we had last year (but fortified by the Minister of State) and Trend [also present at the meeting] adds that he does not think entire stability of rates is likely to be so firmly held as one of the data in the problem.

Trend subsequently told Mynors that they would have to consider 'selective credit policy' again and that Gaitskell was 'likely to want an airing given to "gadgets", e.g. compulsory reserve ratios, etc. etc'.[20] The Bank responded with an assessment of the clearing bank returns for the first quarter of the new financial year and memoranda on 'Selective credit policy' and 'Control of bank credit abroad'. It noted that the rise in advances had accelerated since devaluation and was offsetting the decrease in the floating debt, and expected the rise to continue even without additional defence expenditure. Its memoranda on 'Selective credit policy' and 'Control of bank credit abroad' none the less used the by now familiar arguments (see Chapter 5) to

[19] BC(50)3 (Revise), 'The problem of inflation in 1950', 9 Feb. 1950, T171/400, PRO, para. 11.
[20] Note by Mynors, 26 July 1950, C40/686, and Mynors, 'Note of a conversation with Mr Trend', 9 Aug. 1950, C42/1, BOE. Maurice Allen had recently joined the Bank as an adviser after two years at the IMF; he had previously been a fellow (in economics) of Balliol College, Oxford.

reach 'pretty negative' conclusions on methods to restrain bank lending.[21]

It is interesting to compare the Bank memoranda on 'Selective credit policy' and 'Control of bank credit abroad' with earlier memoranda prepared in the Economic Section initially at Robert Hall's request. The Bank's arguments against selective credit policy were essentially the difficulty of devising criteria for discriminating between borrowers, the existence of approved but unused overdraft facilities, and the possibility of diverting borrowing to non-bank sources of funds rather than reducing it. The Bank stressed the first difficulty in describing the experience with 'qualitative' credit control attempted in other countries such as France. The economists readily admitted that the 'qualitative' credit control practised in France since 1947 had 'proved a complete failure' but noted that the Bank of France had granted almost all the requests put up to it by the commercial banks. Considering a wider range of countries than the Bank of England were prepared to discuss, the Economic Section also noted that moral suasion had had some limited success where too much reliance had not been placed on it, for example in the United States. On more quantitative direct controls on banks, such as requiring them to hold specified amounts or proportions of government debt in their asset portfolios, the Bank claimed that these weapons had proved too 'crude' in France, Belgium, and Italy and had had to be relaxed in order not to restrict investment. The Section, on the other hand, concluded that it was possible to use these controls to help to restrict bank lending when one wished to minimize the movement in short-term interest rates on government debt. The Bank and the Section both emphasized the limited effect of raising central bank discount rates when banks could easily replenish their reserves by running down their holdings of government debt, but the Section was more concerned than the Bank that there should be effective monetary control and hence more willing to contemplate combinations of different instruments to get round the problems posed by post-war government debt.[22]

[21] Mynors, 'Clearing banks' returns: March–June 1950', 26 July 1950, C40/686; Mynors to Eady, 26 Aug. 1950, C42/1, BOE; Fforde, *Bank*, 381–4.

[22] (Bank of England), 'Selective credit policy', 26 Aug., and 'Control of bank credit abroad', 31 Aug. 1950, T233/1400; Abramson to Hall, 'Qualitative credit control in France', 14 Sept., EC(D)(49)5, 'Postwar experience of credit restriction abroad, paper by the Economic Section', 23 Dec. 1949, and EC(S)(50)3, 'The

One way of reducing those problems was to 'fund' the debt, that is to replace some of the floating and short-term debt with longer-term issues. In spite of budget surpluses, funding issues of medium- and long-term government debt had not been poss- ible while the authorities were having to make large issues of government-guaranteed stocks for nationalization compensation in 1948-9. At the beginning of 1950 Cobbold's senior colleagues advised him that 'we must be prepared to fund whenever this can be done at reasonable cost', that is without unduly increasing the cost of debt service. They also raised but rejected the possibil- ity of replacing the banks' holdings of TDRs with 'certificates of indebtedness', fearing that this might be interpreted abroad as '"clever tricks" designed to divert attention from the weakness of our short-term-money policy' and criticized at home as the '"thin end of the wedge"' in forcing the banks to lend to the government.[23] In the summer and autumn of 1950 the Bank managed to begin to fund the debt, when the authorities made their first government bond issues for cash since January 1947.

The two issues were intended to fund some floating debt as well as to convert maturing short-term gilt-edged debt, the £714m 2½% National War Bonds 1949/51 which had been allowed to run on in 1949 (above p. 257). In May Peppiatt suggested a cash and conversion offer, in the first half of June, of a tranche of an existing stock, 2½% Funding Loan 1956/61. The Governor put the proposal to the Treasury on 22 May, since, as the Chief Cashier commented, 'prospects of the gilt-edged market are so uncertain, given the present political situation, that no opportunity of this kind should be lost'.[24] In a return to the pre-war tender method of issuing government bonds, instead of the wartime open-ended tap used for Dalton's two issues, the cash offer was to be limited to £100m, most of which would be taken up by the Issue Depart- ment to be sold gradually later. The authorities did not expect

control of commercial bank credit', 14 Jan. 1950, T230/469, PRO. The Bank used the last of the Section memoranda in preparing its own memorandum on other countries' experience but restricted its discussion to France, Belgium, Italy, and Sweden.

[23] Peppiatt to Governor, 8 Feb., and Beale, 'Impact of short-term interest rates on debt charges', 7 Feb. 1950, C42/1,BOE; see also Fforde, *Bank*, 384-5.

[24] Peppiatt to Governors and Mynors, '2½% National War Bonds 1949/51', 15 May, Beale, 'Possible government loan operation', 18 May, and Cobbold to Eady, 'Government loan operations', 22 May 1950, C40/486, BOE.

large conversions of War Bonds by the public but they had been buying in the bonds for some months and held about £230m between the Issue Department and the NDC. As Eady described it to the Chancellor, 'the operation is not heroic, but it is practical'. Cripps agreed to it, even though it was thought necessary to offer a little more than £100 Funding Loan for each £100 War Bonds (since the former was standing at par and the latter at a premium in the market) and to make the adjustment in cash (£1.690 per cent).[25] When the offer was made on 7 June cash subscriptions and conversions by the public were somewhat larger than expected, with the result that £505m War Bonds were converted, a little over half from official holdings, and the Bank took up £77m of the cash issue.[26]

In October the Bank proposed another medium-term funding loan, for 'mopping up . . . surplus funds' in the money market and for converting the remaining £209m 2½% National War Bonds 1949/51. At this time the balance of payments was strong and the reserves rising, so that the supply of Treasury bills to the market was increasing as the EEA bought foreign exchange. The Bank suggested a new stock, 3% Funding Loan 1966/68, created deliberately for the Issue Department to take up most of it on the day of issue and sell over time.[27] Although the Treasury officials were not at first certain of the need for a new cash issue as well as the conversion offer, they recommended this 'funding operation of a new technique' to Gaitskell, since it would be useful for the Bank to have another stock besides the 2½% Funding Loan available to be sold off as opportunity arose. (The Bank had by now sold the 2½% Funding Loan it had taken up in June and taken over £200m from the NDC for future sale.) Rather to his officials' surprise, the new Chancellor was 'prepared to agree to this without discussion'. He thought the authorities could take the (slight) risk of interest rates rising, for 'We do *not* want any decline in interest rates at present'. Announced on 31 October, £250m of

[25] Cobbold to Eady, 'Government loan operations', 22 May, Eady to Bridges and Armstrong, 23 May, Note by Cripps, 24 May, Eady to Governor, 25 May, and Eady to Trend, 26 May 1950, T233/550, PRO.

[26] Beale to Trend, 9 June, Eady to Trend, 'Conversion operation', 16 June, and Beale to Trend, '2½% National War Bonds 1949/51', 19 June 1950, T233/550.

[27] Beale, 'Government loan operation', 12 Oct. 1950, C40/487, BOE; Beale to Eady, and 'Government loan operation', 20 Oct. 1950, T233/551, PRO; Fforde, *Bank*, 386–7.

the new stock was offered for cash, of which about £200m was bought by the Issue Department and the NDC, and £88m was issued in exchange for National War Bonds. The authorities have continued to use this new 'tap' method of issuing government securities, which the Bank had first contemplated using in the late 1930s, although they experimented briefly with gilt-edged auctions in the 1980s.[28]

During the summer of 1950 the authorities were also considering (at first reluctantly because it would be expensive) whether to raise the interest rates on savings certificates and defence bonds. They decided on a new savings certificate with an increased yield but a low limit on individual holdings and a 3 per cent issue of defence bonds without any premium on maturity or increase in the maximum holding of defence bonds. These were made available from February 1951.[29]

Cobbold seized the opportunity provided him by Gaitskell's willingness to allow long-term nominal interest rates to rise to ask for a rise in *short-term* rates. In September he had asked his usual group of senior colleagues (Niemeyer, Peppiatt, Mynors, and Beale) to bring up to date their views on interest rates. In October they told him they 'found no difficulty in reaching the conclusion that general inflationary pressures and risks are very much greater now' than at the beginning of the year, because of higher world commodity prices, devaluation, rising wages, and rearmament. It would not now be sufficient merely to raise short-term interest rates so as to make Bank rate effective. 'We think that what is needed is a break in the present rate structure which has been rigid far too long.' They advocated the 'mildly spectacular move' of raising Bank rate from 2 to 2½ per cent, possibly only for a brief period, as it was the 'psychological effects' of the signal that would be important. The effects might

[28] Trend to Eady, 20 Oct., Trend to Eady, Bridges and Armstrong, 'Government loan operation', 23 Oct., Bridges to Armstrong, 24 Oct., and Note by Gaitskell (emphasis in original), 24 Oct. 1950, T233/551; Howson, 'Cheap money and debt management in Britain, 1932–51', in P. Cottrell and D. E. Moggridge (eds.), *Money and Power* (London, 1988), 247–8; Jeremy Wormell, *The Gilt-Edged Market* (London, 1985), ch. 6; 'The experimental series of gilt-edged auctions', *BEQB* 28 (1988), 194–7.

[29] Radice, 'Defence Bonds', 5 June, Trend to Eady, 'National savings', 10 July, and Trend to Eady and Armstrong, 'National savings movement', 22 July 1950, T233/507, PRO; Pember and Boyle, *British Government Securities in the Twentieth Century, Supplement 1950–1976*, 302–3, 332.

include 'a moderate slowing down of the increase in the level of bank advances' if banks raised their lending rates, and some reduction in the holding of stocks of commodities and in overseas short-term lending. A rise in short-term interest rates would raise the cost of the floating debt and the interest paid on sterling balances, but would not much affect long-term interest rates, which had already risen significantly in the last two years, and there was no risk of unemployment in present circumstances. Three days later Cobbold put the proposals up to the Treasury, making it clear that he wished at the same time to raise the Treasury bill rate nearer to 1 per cent and stressing that UK money-market interest rates were now considerably lower than those overseas. He added that to follow the recent funding issue with a change in short-term interest rates would 'give the appearance of concerted and consistent policy'.[30]

Cobbold enclosed with his letter to Bridges a revised version of his colleagues' memorandum. The Treasury officials found it a 'very disappointing document' which provided 'only the most vague indication of the justification' for the proposals. As Trend pointed out, the Bank would have to produce a justification 'in far more convincing detail' before the proposals went up to the Chancellor, especially since Gaitskell had just asked for a general review of credit policy. The Treasury therefore asked the Bank for its estimates of the probable consequences for the cost of the floating debt, long-term interest rates and long-term government borrowing, the gilt-edged market and the terms of iron and steel nationalization compensation, the banks' lending policy, the cost of finance in the development areas and for rearmament, and the cost of living. The Bank was also asked to argue for an anti-inflationary monetary step more explicitly and to deal with the counterargument that such a step could take the usual form of stricter instructions to the banks and the Capital Issues Committee.[31]

Before receiving the Bank's reply, Treasury views were divided. According to Eady, the Home Finance division (HF) did not think the move worthwhile, mainly because of the cost to the

[30] Peppiatt to Niemeyer, Chief Cashier and Mynors, 'Interest rates', 22 Sept., Niemeyer, Peppiatt, Mynors, and Beale, 'Interest rates', 30 Oct., and Cobbold to Bridges, 3 Nov. 1950, C42/1, BOE; Fforde, *Bank*, 385–6.

[31] Trend to Eady, 'Bank rate', 8 Nov., and Eady to Peppiatt, 11 Nov. 1950, T233/1401, PRO.

Exchequer; Robert Hall was in favour, even if only as an experiment; the Overseas Finance division was unconcerned at a rise in interest on sterling balances *if* the policy were thought to be useful on domestic grounds; and Eady himself was somewhere in the middle.[32] When the Bank's reply came from Peppiatt on 17 November, Trend (in HF) used it to argue against the move, in the first part of his report to Gaitskell. He was not convinced that on the Bank's own argument it needed to increase short-term rates (i.e. make Bank rate effective) as well as to raise Bank rate. Peppiatt had made it clear that the Bank wanted to restore 'some freedom of manœuvre' so that the change in Bank rate would only be a signal that Bank rate was now variable again. As Trend put it,

the real purpose ... would be to put the economy on notice that the monetary weapon, which has been out of use for a longish time, still existed, and might—but not necessarily would—be brought back into operation again. The monetary system would be given a slight shock; ... lenders and borrowers would not be quite sure where they stood, or—more important—where they were likely to stand in three or six months' time. It is this psychological effect ... rather than any immediate practical consequences which the Bank put forward as the justification for their proposals.

The practical consequences would be small except on the cost of the national debt, 'a serious objection to the proposals' in HF's view. The second part of Trend's report dealt briefly, on the basis of the Bank's earlier memorandum, with the measures of credit control which had been used in other countries. He made four points which are interesting in light of past and future UK monetary experience: that several countries which had raised their central bank rate since the war had found it necessary at the same time to impose direct controls on banks' assets (raising required reserves or holdings of government securities); that in the UK the effect on the gilt-edged market of raising cash or secondary reserve requirements could be 'pretty disastrous' since the banks would try to unload gilts rather than reduce their lending; that the UK monetary authorities could use TDRs to oblige banks to hold specified amounts of government debt; and that if the banks had to hold more cash reserves they would find the extra reserves

[32] Eady to Bridges, 'Interest rates', 14 Nov. 1950, T233/1401; see also Brittain to Wilson Smith, 9 Nov. 1950, on same file, and *Robert Hall Diaries*, 134.

by reducing their holdings of Treasury bills. These 'technical difficulties' were not, however, 'necessarily insurmountable'. Finally, he wondered whether the authorities should not resort again to 'exhortation, advice and control' in order to restrain bank lending: he was not convinced by the Bank's arguments against 'selective credit policy' and thought new instructions to the Capital Issues Committee and the banks could be backed up by controls on hire purchase and a tough 1951 budget.[33]

By the beginning of December, however, 'official opinion ... was slightly on the Bank side'. Eady had been persuaded by the Governor. Robert Hall also supported the Bank and briefed Plowden accordingly. Bridges, Eady, and Plowden agreed to recommend the proposals, putting up to Gaitskell on 12 December a formal request from Cobbold to raise Bank rate 'with corresponding adjustments in short-term bill rates' early in the new year, together with the whole package of Treasury papers on credit policy. The provisionally agreed date for action was Thursday, 11 January 1951.[34]

As in 1949 Douglas Jay was 'strongly opposed' to the Governor's request, mainly because of the cost to the Exchequer and the benefit to the banks' profits. He thought it 'particularly ill-timed' when the government was having to cut back other more socially desirable government expenditure to accommodate re-armament. He also pointed out that it could have little effect on fixed investment, would encourage short-term capital inflows which were helping to increase the money supply, and increase the cost of the iron and steel nationalization. The Treasury officials had also been worried that a rise in Bank rate might send long-term nominal interest rates, which were around 3¼ per cent, back to 3½ per cent or more. Gaitskell, however, did not share this concern. He agreed with Jay that he '[did] not see much point in putting up short term rates', but he '[felt] there is a case for action to push the long term rate up to 3½% & possibly for special

[33] Peppiatt to Eady, 17 Nov., and Trend to Eady, 'Credit policy', 23 Nov. 1950, T233/1401, PRO.
[34] 'Extract from Deputy Governor's note of a conversation with Sir Wilfrid Eady', 1 Dec., and Mynors, 'Meeting in Sir Edward Bridges' room on the 1st December 1950',4 Dec. 1950, G1/70, BOE; Hall to Dow, 24 Nov. 1950, T230/469; Eady to Bridges, 'Credit policy', 24 Nov., Bridges to Eady, 2 Dec., Cobbold to Chancellor, 7 Dec., and Bridges to Chancellor, 'Credit policy', 12 Dec. 1950, T233/1401, PRO.

direction to the Banks on the rate for advances'. The case was essentially that rising long-term nominal interest rates were a normal and necessary part of monetary control, which was needed along with budgetary measures to fight inflation.[35]

When Gaitskell discussed the Bank proposals with his officials, he was against any increase in Bank rate. Hall thought that in talking about directing the banks to put up their lending rates Gaitskell was 'as out of date in his beliefs about how the money system is controlled as I was two years ago' (in the early meetings of the Working Party on Bank Deposits and Advances: see Chapter 5). Hall and Plowden were both 'much in favour of the change [in interest rates]'as a useful addition to the range of weapons that would have to be used to fight inflation during rearmament. Plowden in particular doubted that direct controls over private investment could be made sufficiently stringent without a formidable administrative machinery.[36] They both argued strongly in support of the Bank but did not succeed in persuading Gaitskell to grant the Governor's request.

At this point the Governor himself showed signs of weakening in his determination to restore the pre-war system, by wondering whether it would be possible to persuade the banks to raise their lending rates without raising rates on Treasury bills or TDRs. His colleagues swiftly pointed out that this would 'substitute new fixed rates for the restoration of ... [the] flexibility and movement which we had hoped ... to achieve', and no hint of this suggestion reached the Treasury.[37]

At the beginning of January Gaitskell told Cobbold that he 'certainly did not want to see a long-term rate of interest lower than 3½ [per cent] in the month to come and ... would not be perturbed if it went a little higher'. He was still 'less convinced' of the need to raise short-term interest rates, which would increase interest payments to the banks at the government's expense and

[35] Jay to Chancellor, 13 Dec., Note by Gaitskell, 17 Dec., and Gaitskell's marginal comments on Trend, 'Credit policy', 23 Nov. 1950, T233/1401, PRO; see also Williams, *Hugh Gaitskell*, 165, 186–7.

[36] *Robert Hall Diaries*, 143.

[37] Cobbold to Deputy Governor, 'Interest rates', 28 Dec., Beale, 'Interest rates, Governor's manuscript note of 28/12', 30 Dec. 1950, G1/70, BOE. Cairncross, in his 'Prelude to Radcliffe', *Rivista di Storia Economica* 4 (1987), 9, implies Cobbold's suggestion did reach the Treasury, but there is no evidence for this, which given the reaction of Cobbold's colleagues is most unlikely.

increase his difficulties in trying to persuade his colleagues to reduce government expenditure. 'Against this drawback ... he did not see any advantages which were conclusive', especially since the Bank admitted the 'psychological' effects were uncertain.[38] He made his position clearer at a meeting of all the major participants in the dispute at the Treasury on 5 January. The Governor asked for a change in short-term rates to fight 'a substantial monetary inflation ... in the offing, when the Banks would come under pressure, which they might not be able to resist unless the Authorities strengthened their hands'. The Chancellor responded that 'in so far as the impending inflation could be dealt with by monetary means, there was no dispute that we must all take whatever steps could be taken to this end', but he feared that an allround rise in interest rates would discourage private investment needed for rearmament purposes as well as 'less essential' investment: 'he was not clear how the indiscriminate weapon of an increase in Interest Rates would enable us to deal with this problem'. He also 'could not forget' the increase in interest payments on the floating debt. Jay alone supported Gaitskell. Hall, who like Gaitskell was strongly for rearmament, tried to strengthen the Bank's case by arguing that the attempt to rearm without excessive inflation would sooner or later require a cutback in investment as well as in consumption and that the proposed rise in interest rates would ease the resulting pressure on the controls. Gaitskell admitted that 'leaving on one side the question of the additional cost to the Exchequer, he felt that the other arguments were nicely balanced; and he had not yet finally made up his mind'; but he hoped that investment would not have to be cut back as much as Hall feared and that direct controls would be sufficient. He also hoped that other methods of monetary control not involving increased short-term interest rates could be found. Cobbold replied that he 'was not optimistic about such methods' and that he might ask again to raise Bank rate in due course.[39] A few days later, despite renewed efforts by Hall and Plowden, Gaitskell wrote to Cobbold turning turn down his request to raise Bank

[38] 'Governor's note', 2 Jan. 1951, C42/1, BOE.
[39] Trend, 'Note of a meeting on the 5th January', 23 Jan. 1951, T233/1401, PRO; see also Mynors, 'Meeting at the Treasury: 5th January 1951', 9 Jan. 1951, C42/1, BOE, *Diary of Hugh Gaitskell*, 227, *Robert Hall Diaries*, 143, Fforde, *Bank*, 388.

rate and asking for consideration of further directions to the Capital Issues Committee and to the banks.[40]

Trend had predicted earlier that the outcome of the review of credit policy requested by Gaitskell would be a revised set of instructions to the Capital Issues Committee and a new Chancellor's letter for the Governor to communicate to the London clearing bankers. These were sent out on 17 April 1951, a few days after the budget. The committee and the banks were to 'take into account that the main emphasis' of government policy towards investment was now on rearmament as well as the balance of payments. In his budget speech Gaitskell announced he was about to issue new directions to the CIC and looked for co-operation from the banks in their lending policies, as one of his measures to restrict private investment.[41] The Treasury and the Bank, together with the Board of Trade, also began to consider new direct controls on hire purchase. They decided in the summer that that there was no immediate need for controls, but reconsidered in the autumn (before the election) and the controls came into effect under the Conservative government in February 1952.[42]

Cobbold did not give up. At the beginning of May he warned the Chancellor that he 'was proposing to come to him again fairly soon about short-term interest rates' and at the end of the month he asked to be able to take steps which would raise the Treasury bill rate nearer to 1 per cent.[43] After Trend had told Mynors that the subject of interest rates, possibly even Bank rate, was coming up for discussion again with an official proposal to raise the borrowing rate for local authorities from the central government, Mynors and Beale had considered tactics. As Mynors remarked:

[40] Hall to Chancellor, 'Bank Rate', 5 Jan., Plowden to Chancellor, 'Bank rate', 6 Jan., and Gaitskell to Cobbold, 17 Jan. 1951, T233/1401, PRO; Fforde, *Bank*, 388–9.

[41] Mynors, 'Note of a conversation with Mr Trend', 9 Aug. 1950, C42/1, BOE; *Memorandum to the Capital Issues Committee*, 17 Apr. 1951, and Gaitskell to Governor, 17 April 1951, C40/757, BOE; *House of Commons Debates*, vol. 486, 10 Apr. 1951, cols. 841–2.

[42] Eady to Hall, 7 Mar., and Dow to Hall, 19 Mar. 1951, T230/458, PRO; Beale to Peppiatt and Governors, 12 Apr. 1951, C40/687, BOE; Wiles to Clarke, 'Hire purchase', 31 May, 'Hire purchase', 14 Aug., and Trend to Mynors, 20 Oct. 1951, C40/720, BOE; Dow, *Management of the British Economy*, 246–7.

[43] 'Extracts from the Governor's diary', 4 May 1951, G1/71, BOE; Cobbold to Chancellor, 31 May 1951, T233/1401, PRO.

It is difficult to think of any novel arguments for dearer money. The familiar arguments must be mobilised, after studying where the opposition appears to be concentrated, and bearing in mind any change in the terrain since the last engagement.

Mynors identified three motives for the Labour government's opposition to dearer money: its association with unemployment; the attachment to the idea of the 'planned economy' in which market-oriented policies were redundant; and the belief that money could be also controlled by priorities and rationing. He correctly saw Gaitskell's desire for higher long-term interest rates as a 'crack' in the second belief, but one which would be difficult to exploit. He therefore recommended 'counter-attacking in the last of these sectors' by pointing out that you could not control both quantity and price of any commodity including money. He recommended proposing only to make Bank rate effective, which '(ignoring practical questions for the moment) has the theoretical attractions of appearing not to make money available except (in the last resort) at the planners' own price'. There was no answer to the objection that it would raise interest payments from the government to bankers except that it was unavoidable if one wanted an anti-inflationary monetary policy. More usefully from Cobbold's point of view Mynors pointed out that 'since the last campaign' the yield gap between short- and long-term nominal interest rates had been considerably widened by the rise in the latter to almost 4 per cent. In his submission to the Chancellor Cobbold pointed to the 'out of line and unreal' rate structure, which he claimed would soon 'break down'.[44]

On the 'practical questions' the Chief Cashier suggested that since 'the object is to achieve a breakdown of the present fixity in market rates without unduly loading the cost of Treasury financing', the Bank should introduce a new rate below Bank rate at which the Bank would discount Treasury bills. The existing Treasury bill rate was maintained at ½ per cent by the Bank's willingness to buy in bills at that rate, while the 2 per cent Bank rate was ineffective. A new rediscount rate of say 1 per cent should lead to a rise in the market rate at the weekly tender, to perhaps ⅝ or ¾ per cent, and a corresponding rise in the call money

[44] Mynors to Governor, 'Conversation with Trend—26th April 1951', Mynors, 'Dearer money', 29 May, and Cobbold to Chancellor, 31 May 1951, C42/1, BOE; Fforde, Bank, 390.

rate for bank loans to the discount market.[45] In asking the Chancellor to allow a rise in short-term interest rates Cobbold told him that the Bank had been considering 'some supplementary technique' which would probably involve setting a new rate below Bank rate at which the Bank would in future discount Treasury bills, but he did not elaborate.

In the Treasury Trend thought the criticisms of higher short-term interest rates made six months previously were still valid. The objections were if anything strengthened by the need to borrow for rearmament and for the nationalized industries. After all, 'we financed the war on cheap money . . . basically, on a 3% rate. Must we contemplate for rearmament not merely a 4% rate but something even higher?' It was also still doubtful whether the small step proposed by the Bank would have much effect on bank lending or on inflation especially given the sharp rises in import prices. Bridges and Plowden were more sympathetic to the Bank's approach but knew it would be difficult to persuade the Chancellor.[46] On 2 June Cobbold and Gaitskell 'went over a great deal of the old ground'. According to Cobbold, 'He is not willing to acknowledge the necessity for any rise in interest rates on Government [short-term] borrowing and continues to argue in favour of some arrangement whereby Government short-term finance is assured at present rates and the tightening of credit operates over the rest of the field.' In writing 'to clear his own mind' Gaitskell tackled Cobbold's new argument about the yield gap. It might well be true that the authorities might have difficulty keeping the Treasury bill rate at ½ per cent unless they allowed the monetary base to increase (by reducing the supply of Treasury bills) at a time when they should rather be contracting the monetary base, but a reduction of the monetary base was 'after all only a means to an end', the reduction in the growth of bank deposits. A 'simpler and more effective way' to achieve the end would be to tell the banks to take up an increased quantity of Treasury bills or TDRs at their current interest rates so as to reduce the reserve base of the banking system. Alternatively the authorities could give the banks 'direct instructions about the

---

[45] Beale, 'Short-term rates', 30 May 1951, G1/71, BOE.
[46] Trend to Eady, 'Interest rates', 31 May 1951, T233/1401, PRO; 'Governor's note', 5 June 1951, G1/71, BOE.

level of advances, ... and adjust their cash reserves accordingly'.[47]

Bridges sent Gaitskell's note to Cobbold, who responded in writing. In his view, 'any instructions to the banking system to hold a specified amount of Government debt would, in any circumstances, be a fundamental blow to British Government credit, both at short and at long term' and in present circumstances of rearmament and expected heavy borrowing for the nationalized industries would have 'an immediate and violent adverse effect'. Cobbold also told Bridges that 'his Court [of Directors] would never stand for [such instructions], and that if this policy was pursued it could only be through a first-class row'.[48] Meanwhile the Treasury officials had asked the Treasury Solicitor about the Treasury's powers to give directions to banks under the Bank of England Act 1946 and had learned that they had none. The power to give directions to the banks belonged to the Bank, who could not be forced to issue directions of which they did not approve (see pp. 116–17).

On 3 July the Chancellor and the Governor met again when they 'agreed ... to differ and let the matter stand as it is until the autumn'. Cobbold admitted that he had not expected, and had told the banks not to expect, Gaitskell to agree to a rise in the Treasury bill and TDR rates in the near future; he had therefore been encouraging them to raise their overdraft and commercial bill rates which they were about to do. Gaitskell was still, in his own words, 'most anxious to have a tighter credit policy without the Government paying any more for short term borrowing' but, as Cobbold noted, he did not raise the possibility of 'directions' to the banks—no doubt because of the recent advice of the Treasury Solicitor. Instead he wished to meet the chairmen of the London clearing banks and proposed to include 'something on credit policy' in his forthcoming policy statement on inflation.[49]

Gaitskell reacted calmly to the balance-of-payments crisis. In his House of Commons speech on 26 July he explained that the

[47] Ibid.; Gaitskell, 'Credit policy', 2 June 1951, T233/1401. Fforde (*Bank*, 391–2) quotes Gaitskell's note and Cobbold's reply extensively.

[48] Bridges to Cobbold, 'Credit policy', 19 June, Cobbold, 'Credit policy', 21 June, and Bridges, 'Credit policy', 22 June 1951, T233/1401, PRO.

[49] 'Governor's note', 3 July 1951, C42/1, BOE; Note by Gaitskell, 3 July 1951, T233/1401, PRO; Fforde, *Bank*, 393–4.

balance of payments had deteriorated by more than expected and the sterling area might go into deficit with the dollar area in 1951 III. The government intended to review the dollar import programme and to arrange a meeting of Commonwealth finance ministers. At home some price controls could be reimposed to restrain inflation but to try to offset the effect of rising import prices on the cost of living by increasing subsidies would be both expensive and ineffective. On credit policy he said he thought 'the time has come for a rather tighter check to be imposed' on bank advances which had been rising by about 10 per cent in the past year. Alluding to his exchanges with the Governor, he gave his reasons for not agreeing to a rise in the Treasury bill rate and repeated his hope that the banks would continue to co-operate in advances policy. He also announced that the government would introduce legislation to control dividends in the autumn and hoped that in the meantime the unions would practise 'reasonable' wage restraint, a hope he repeated at the TUC conference in September. He then went to North America to attend the annual IMF/IBRD meetings and a NATO Council meeting and to discuss the financial problems of rearmament with the Americans. While he was away Attlee announced a general election for 25 October and Gaitskell did not meet the bankers because of the election campaign.[50]

Full employment and financial policy

I have already mentioned that Gaitskell's views on macroeconomic policy instruments changed somewhat while he was at the Treasury. By this time there had been changes in the views of other Labour Party economists and other economists working for the government, which are also worth mentioning here. The most important changes followed from acceptance of the openness of the UK economy and recognition that the dreaded post-war slump was not just around the corner.

In January 1950 Gaitskell and Jay argued that the post-war Labour government's use of physical controls along with budgetary policy to restrain consumption and investment had

<hr />

[50] *House of Commons Debates*, vol. 491, 26 July 1951, cols. 657–75; *Control of Dividends*, Cmd. 8318, July 1951; see also *Robert Hall Diaries*, 162, 166, Plowden, *Industrialist in the Treasury*, 122–4.

enabled it to prevent serious inflation and to channel resources into exports while maintaining money incomes at the full employment level. They went so far as to claim that 'it is the use by the Government of direct controls—whether rationing in order to secure fair distribution or industrial controls to expand exports—which has been the distinguishing feature of British socialist policy'. Other countries in Europe that had abandoned controls for 'indirect monetary means' of demand management had more unemployment or a more unequal income distribution. They argued that current proposals for liberalization of trade and payments between the countries of the Organization for European Economic Cooperation (OEEC) risked the loss or at least weakening of controls that the UK needed to maintain full employment and to close the 'dollar gap' in her balance of payments.[51]

As Hall commented (to Plowden and the Chancellor), this paper was 'a real attempt ... to state the economic policy of H.M.G. and it deserves full consideration', especially since it admitted that inflation might be inevitable with full employment. He thought it needed to distinguish between the controls needed to cope with current balance-of-payments difficulties and those that should be permanent and emphasized its underlying untested presumption that the alternative to using controls for balance-of-payments reasons would be severe deflation. (He also criticized the paper, which was circulated to the Economic Policy Committee, for its simplistic distinction between essential and inessential imports.)[52]

Although Gaitskell and Jay had long believed in the necessity for a Labour government to introduce exchange and import controls their position at the beginning of 1950 represented something of a retreat from the multilateralism Gaitskell had espoused in the early 1940s when he persuaded Dalton to support the clearing union and commercial union proposals of Keynes and Meade (see Chapter 2). The experiences of 1947 and 1949 had weakened their faith in relying on exchange controls on capital movements to prevent balance-of-payments crises—one of the

[51] Gaitskell to Cripps, 3 Jan. 1951, and Gaitskell and Jay, 'Controls and economic policy', T230/319, PRO.

[52] Hall to Plowden, 'Controls and economic policy', 4 Jan., and Hall, 'Economic planning and liberalisation, E.P.C.(50)9', 16 Jan. 1950, T230/319; see also *Robert Hall Diaries*, 101, and Cairncross, *Years of Recovery*, 329–32.

reasons they both became converts to the devaluation cause—and they were now suspicious of any moves back towards current account convertibility of sterling.[53]

Within three months Gaitskell found himself negotiating the European Payments Union (EPU) with representatives of the other OEEC countries and the American administration. Under the European Recovery Programme an Agreement on Multilateral Monetary Compensation in November 1947 and two Intra-European Payments Schemes (IEPS) operating October 1948-June 1949 and July 1949-June 1950 had attempted successively to make intra-European payments less bilateral. The IEPS provided increased liquidity as well as indirect Marshall Aid to OEEC member countries: they provided for countries expected to be in surplus with other OEEC countries to extend bilateral (in some cases multilateral) drawing rights to anticipated deficit countries; and the US Economic Cooperation Administration (ECA) provided extra Marshall Aid to the expected surplus countries on condition that they extended such drawing rights to their expected debtors. The more ambitious European Payments Union (EPU) negotiated in 1950 provided pooled and fully multilateral drawing rights between members of OEEC. This further increased liquidity for OEEC members since it reduced the likelihood of paying out gold or US dollars when a country's deficit with another OEEC country exceeded its drawing rights from that country.[54]

Gaitskell was at first very doubtful of the desirability of moves towards convertibility, at least until, according to Hall, 'it is proved that there won't be a US slump'. At the same time Hall and Plowden thought that in prolonged discussions with him 'we made some progress and that if we had time we could convert him to all our ways of thought'. He was indeed prepared to allow provisions for convertibility within EPU as long as there were also safeguards to prevent excessive demands on Britain's exiguous gold and dollar reserves in case of an American recession which would impinge on the UK as another dollar crisis.[55] In

[53] Above, Ch. 5; *Diary of Hugh Gaitskell*, 129–30, 143–50.

[54] On the EPU and its predecessors see Tew, *International Monetary Co-operation*, ch. 8; Kaplan and Schleiminger, *The European Payments Union*; Hogan, *Marshall Plan*, ch. 7; Milward, *Reconstruction of Western Europe*, ch. 10; and Fforde, *Bank*, ch. 4(*b*).

[55] *Robert Hall Diaries*, 109–110; *Diary of Hugh Gaitskell*, 178–82.

the negotiations he succeeded in achieving a European payments scheme which reduced potential gold losses as compared with the previous more limited intra-European payments schemes and also permitted European quantitative restrictions on dollar imports if necessary. He was helped by concessions from the US European Cooperation Administration to accommodate British insistence on maintaining existing arrangements for the use of sterling and by a compromise agreement on the relative use of gold and credit to settle payments imbalances worked out between himself and Milton Katz, deputy US special representative in Europe. As Gaitskell's biographer points out the negotiations 'undermined his deep suspicion of the Americans on economic policy'. The negotiations also increased the amount of intra-European trade to be 'liberalized' from the 50 per cent of each country's imports already agreed in October 1949 and agreed to make intra-European trade non-discriminatory (as between OEEC members).[56]

In the summer of 1950 the Labour government was also for a mixture of reasons working on an Economic Planning and Full Employment bill which it abandoned a few months later. The bill was the last of several attempts at preparing 'anti-slump precautions'. It was also the last attempt made to put the principles and proposals of the party's 1944 policy report on *Full Employment and Financial Policy* into legislation.

In June 1946 ministers had asked for a study of 'the means by which the United Kingdom might maintain its balance of trade in the event of a world slump' and 'the [policy] instruments . . . for maintaining domestic demand' in the same circumstances. This was not regarded as a matter of urgency and it was the end of the year before the Economic Section and the Treasury jointly considered how to proceed (although the Section had prepared a paper on the possible magnitude of a post-war depression and was working on another on the control of consumers' expenditure).[57] In January 1947 a meeting of officials from the Section and the Treasury agreed that 'the most likely contingencies' were

[56] On the negotiations see ibid. 186, 189–91, Kaplan and Schleiminger, *The European Payments Union*, ch. 4 (esp. 70–1, 76–9 for Gaitskell's contribution), and Hogan, *Marshall Plan*, 320–6. The quotation is from Williams, *Hugh Gaitskell*, 157.

[57] MEP(46) 3rd meeting, 17 June 1946, CAB134/187, PRO; Meade, *Cabinet Office Diary*, 284–5, 299, 309, 321; Meade to Gilbert, 22 Nov., and Meade to Bridges, 18 Dec. 1946, T230/214.

a mild recession beginning in the USA in late 1947 or 1948 and 'a major slump rather later—say 1949-50'. The officials agreed to make a study of the effects of a US recession on the UK economy and to delegate the tasks involved to various working parties.[58]

When Meade left the Economic Section in the summer of 1947 he briefed Hall on the (slow) progress of the study since Herbert Morrison, the Lord President, was still anxious for its completion. When Morrison tackled Hall about it in the autumn, Hall replied that 'a great deal of work has already been done on this, but it seems to me to be quite out of touch with present realities' because of the high level of demand on both sides of the Atlantic. By January 1949 Hall thought that 'compared to our present difficulties ... it would be a pleasure to have to deal with a depression'.[59] He none the less agreed to Jay's suggestion a few weeks later for a 'more detailed examination' of anti-slump measures since he thought there could be a fall off in UK exports to non-dollar countries, and the Section prepared a memorandum for the Chancellor to circulate to the Economic Policy Committee just before the devaluation crisis broke. The memorandum did not rate the probabilities of a serious US recession or a decline in domestic demand for any other reason very highly. There were 'some difficult problems of policy regarding exports' but if these became acute a change in the exchange rate or in quantitative trade restrictions should be considered.[60] Meanwhile the various committees and working parties dealing with investment had become more concerned with restraining investment in the present than planning how to encourage it in the future.[61]

By 1950 there was the additional consideration that the Supplies and Services (Transitional Powers) Act 1945, under which the Labour governments had continued wartime controls, would expire in December. An official committee reported in March

[58] EC(S)(47)2, Note by Meade, 22 Jan., T230/24, PRO.

[59] Meade to Hall, 12 June, Hall to Plowden, 4 July, Hall to Lord President, 29 Sept. 1947, Hall to Dow, 'Future depressions', 27 Jan. 1949, T230/214. Morrison responded briefly to Hall: 'Seen; not yet satisfied. H.M. 2/10', but the next paper on the file is Hall's of January 1949.

[60] Hall to Dow, 18 Mar., Hall to Bridges, 'Future unemployment', 21 Mar., and Hitchman to Gilbert, 'Paper for E.P.C. on anti-slump measures', 11 May 1949, T230/214; EC(S)(49)17 (Revise), 'Economic policy in a recession', 20 May 1949, T230/143, PRO.

[61] Cairncross, *Years of Recovery*, ch. 17; Tomlinson, *Employment Policy*, ch. 5.

that there should be an 'Economic Powers Bill' to make permanent the powers to impose some of the controls. After the general election ministers decided that the bill should include 'more positive powers' to promote domestic economic activity in a depression as well as 'negative' powers to control inflation. This would also be a way of implementing some of the recommendations of the recent United Nations Economic and Social Council report on *National and international measures for full employment*, which was itself the result of a British government initiative in 1949.[62] The draft bill was renamed the 'Economic Planning and Full Employment' bill, while ministers and officials considered what 'positive powers' could usefully be included.

Treasury officials and their ministers agreed that fiscal instruments such as variations in rates of taxation and national insurance contributions and repayment of post-war income-tax credits, would be the major weapons used in a depression, but that as budgetary matters these were not eligible for the bill.[63] Over the two other types of measures considered for inclusion at this stage, government financial assistance to public or private industry and government purchase, sale or manufacture of goods in order somehow to maintain employment, there was a difference of opinion between ministers and officials. The 'old guard' in the Treasury, the Joint Second Secretaries Sir Bernard Gilbert (who was in charge of the official preparation of the bill) and Sir Wilfrid Eady, saw both as unnecessary at best. Gaitskell and Jay, on the other hand, thought that there was a case for a bill to provide for measures to supplement budgetary policy if they were needed in a depression. As Chancellor Gaitskell argued that the bill should be converted to a 'Full Employment Bill' whose

[62] LP(50)16, 'Lord President's Committee, Economic controls—long-term powers, Memorandum by the Lord President of the Council', 27 Mar. 1950, T230/319; Tomlinson, *Employment Policy*, 126–31; *Robert Hall Diaries*, 104, 120, 123. On the UN report see also Nicholas Kaldor, 'Recollections of an economist', *Banca Nazionale del Lavoro Quarterly Review*, no. 156 (Mar. 1986), 15–16.

[63] Jay to Bevan, 31 July, Gilbert to Eady, 14 Aug., Trend to Eady, 'Economic planning and full employment bill', 29 Sept., and PC(GE)(50)12, 'Cabinet Production Committee Sub-committee on manufacture in government-controlled establishments of goods for civilian use, Financial powers in connection with employment policy, Memorandum by the Financial Secretary to the Treasury', 10 Oct. 1950, T233/819, PRO. The Economic Section in its 1949 memorandum had also seen fiscal policy as the main instrument for maintaining domestic demand in a slump: EC(S)(49)17 (Revise), 'Economic policy in a recession', 20 May 1949, T230/143.

'starting point should be not the Supplies and Services Act, but our Full Employment Policy'. It should provide for controls needed to combat inflation when aggregate demand was high as well as for direct measures to stimulate demand nationally or locally in a severe slump. He also agreed with Robert Hall that a 'full employment' white paper would accompany the bill and cover the government's policy on inflation instead of issuing a separate white paper on wages policy which had been under consideration since the 'voluntary incomes policy' agreed with the TUC in 1948 had broken down earlier in 1950.[64]

The drafting of the 'Full Employment Bill' continued into the 1950/1 winter. The Treasury considered, in consultation with the Bank of England and without enthusiasm, such 'positive financial powers' as providing loans, guarantees or underwriting of loans to private industry.[65] The final draft of the bill included these suggestions as well as proposals for government purchase of capital goods and for financial incentives to local authorities to prepare a 'reserve of works' ready to be undertaken as soon as a slump threatened. But the progress of rearmament was producing a need for the wide range of wartime and immediate post-war controls which could be continued by renewing the Supplies and Services Act rather than the more limited peacetime controls envisaged in the full employment bill; it was also pushing the feared depression into a distant future. The bill went to the Cabinet with the recommendation from the Lord President and the Chancellor of the Exchequer that for these two reasons it should not be introduced.[66]

[64] Note by Eady, undated, Gilbert to Bridges and Littlewood, 'CP(50)230, Economic planning and full employment bill', 18 Oct., Gilbert to Armstrong, 'CP(50)230, Economic planning and full employment bill', 26 Oct., Jay to Chancellor, 27 Oct., and GEN343/2, 'Cabinet Economic Planning and Full Employment Bill Committee, Economic planning and full employment bill, Memorandum by the Chancellor of the Exchequer', 9 Nov. 1950, T233/819: *Robert Hall Diaries*, 129. 134; Tomlinson, *Employment Policy*, 132–3.

[65] Trend to Eady, 'Economic planning and full employment bill', 22 Nov., A. T. K. Grant, 'Full employment and positive financial powers', 22 Nov., H. S. Kent to Grant, 'Full employment bill', 15 Dec. 1950, T233/819; Mynors to Governor, 'Full employment', 8 and 18 Dec., Mynors to Trend, 13 and 20 Dec. 1950, and Mynors, 'Full employment bill', 11 and 26 Jan. 1951, G1/49, BOE.

[66] Report by the Official Committee on the Economic Planning and Full Employment Bill, Feb. 1951, T233/820; Compton to Dow, 'Full employment bill', 5 Feb., Alec Johnston to Compton, 'Full employment bill', 10 Feb., and Compton to Johnston, 12 Feb. 1951, T228/242; Tomlinson, *Employment Policy*, 132–7.

Economists within the government had started to reconsider the post-war cheap money orthodoxy in 1948. (Meade had questioned it in 1947 before he left government service; in 1948 he published his *Planning and the Price Mechanism: the Liberal-Socialist Solution*, arguing for less reliance on direct controls and more use of interest rates in economic management.) While Robert Hall was trying to discover from the Bank how the authorities could pursue a tighter monetary stance to back up the disinflationary budgetary policy (Chapter 5), his colleagues were looking more theoretically at the possibility of using interest rates in the control of investment. On Keynesian liquidity preference grounds they were still doubtful about the desirability of varying long-term nominal interest rates.[67] In 1949 Hall was not alone in the Economic Section in favouring higher interest rates during and after the balance-of-payments crisis. In their studies of monetary measures in other countries the economists emphasized the successes as well as the failures.[68]

In 1948 the Labour economists in XYZ had been more concerned with reforming the financial system and with the control of investment, which they saw as a task for direct controls rather than use of the price mechanism (see Chapter 3). In March 1951, however, Bill Piercy opened a discussion on credit policy. According to Dalton,

[he] proposed to restrict credit by raising rate of interest—though he thought we needn't on short-term debt. He was opposed by me, and half opposed by Radomysler. He was supported by Tony [Crosland], Berry & Meade [who had recently joined XYZ]—the latter wanting to combine higher interest rates with capital levy. Douglas Jay sat a bit on the fence, but was inclined to oppose. I was rather shocked . . . Tony said that the great argument for a rise in interest rate was that it would depreciate capital values, & to improve distribution of wealth, hit rentiers, & check living on capital, which was bad for income distribution. . . . This is a new argument, not to be found in Keynes, which must be studied.[69]

[67] Meade, 'Annex II' to EC(S)(47)9, Dow, 'The control of private investment', Mar. 1947, T230/24; EC(S)(48)9, Shackle, 'Money, interest and expenditure', 17 Feb., and EC(S)(48)12, Dow, 'Reconsideration of interest rate policy, Some notes on Mr. Shackle's paper', 20 Apr. 1948, T230/27, PRO.

[68] Fleming to Hitchman, 'Banking policy and the crisis', 24 Aug. 1949, T233/1400; EC(S)(49)40, Atkinson, 'Some remarks on monetary policy', 17 Dec. 1949, T230/143; Cairncross and Watts, *Economic Section*, 215–16; above, p. 285.

[69] Dalton Diary, vol. 39, 21 Mar. 1951, BLPES.

Dalton reread the *General Theory* over Easter to produce a paper for the next XYZ discussion. He was sympathetic to the concern for distribution but thought it could be better addressed by 'combining a lower—or, at least for the moment, not a higher rate of interest with a capital levy, or some other form of heavy property tax'. He 'wouldn't fall for' Meade's suggestion of a higher interest rate with a capital levy. As for anti-inflationary control of bank lending, which is what Piercy wanted, he claimed that 'directions' could be given under his Bank of England Act.[70]

At the discussion of Dalton's paper on 30 May Piercy made it clear that he wished to see the banks raise their interest rates on advances, which he thought could be induced by a rise in Bank rate without a rise in Treasury bill or TDR rates. Gaitskell attended the meeting and heard Crosland and Meade argue for higher interest rates before he and Dalton had to leave early for a Cabinet meeting. Four weeks later Dalton lunched with Gaitskell at the Treasury, when he told him that Crosland had now persuaded him that 'it was all right to let gilt-edged prices fall, & not to intervene either by word or deed' in the market. Dalton still, however, thought that interest rates on the floating debt should not go up.[71]

Crosland elaborated his views in *The Future of Socialism* (1956), where he argued for the use of monetary policy as a supplement to budgetary policy in controlling aggregate demand, emphasizing the effects of monetary policy on stockholding and consumption rather than on fixed investment. He implicitly criticized the post-war Labour governments for allowing monetary policy to pull in the opposite direction from budgetary policy, although he also thought they were 'right to resist the orthodox City views'. A Labour government should not rely too much on conventional monetary policy such as Bank rate changes and should try to work through funding operations to reduce bank liquidity and hence bank lending, if necessary resorting also to direct controls. He admitted that 'a rise in Bank rate

[70] Dalton to Piercy, 22 May 1951, Dalton, 'Note on rate of interest, etc.', and 'Rate of interest, Postscript', Dalton Papers 9/19, BLPES. Dalton sent his note to James Lawrie, John Diamond, Jay, Berry, Meade, Radomysler, Gaitskell, and Mayhew as well as to Piercy and Crosland, 'the principal proponents of the dear money heresy': Dalton to Diamond, 22 May 1951, on same file.

[71] [Piercy], 'The relation between last meeting's discussion and this', Piercy Papers 15/117; Dalton Diary, vol. 41, 30 May, 26 June 1951.

might still be necessary in certain circumstances to influence transactions in the foreign exchange market'.[72]

In his budget speech in April 1951 Gaitskell accorded fiscal and monetary policy a larger role in combating inflation than he had allowed a year earlier. Although physical controls were needed to help channel resources into defence expenditure and exports, they 'will not be nearly so effective if they are working against the tide, and . . . must therefore be accompanied by a strict fiscal and monetary policy to restrain civilian expenditure'. Since he had decided not to allow short-term interest rates to rise, he had to rely on a new request to the banks to restrain their lending, new instructions to the Capital Issues Committee, on the recent rise in long-term nominal interest rates, and on suspending tax allowances for depreciation on new plant and machinery. He again stressed the need to reinforce budgetary policy with a tighter monetary stance in his Commons statement on the economic and financial situation in July. He was castigated in the financial press for none the less resorting to exhortation to the banks (as well as for reimposing price control and proposing a statutory limitation of dividends) but he had admitted that he had refused to allow a rise in the Treasury bill rate because he could not see how a small rise would sufficiently influence the banks' behaviour. Hence, 'I could only agree to a step of this kind . . . [which will increase government expenditure] if it were the *only* way to check an increase in bank credit.'[73]

The revival of monetary policy

Gaitskell's reluctance to allow a rise in short-term interest rates meant that Britain was a latecomer in the general 'revival' of monetary policy in the early 1950s. By the time of the fall of the Labour government the inflationary pressures of the Korean war period had prompted several countries to raise their central bank discount rates, including the US and Canada, the Netherlands, Belgium, and the Nordic countries, beginning with Denmark

[72] C. A. R. Crosland, *The Future of Socialism* (London, 1956), 409–14.
[73] *House of Commons Debates*, vol. 486, 10 Apr. 1951, cols. 828, 841–2, and vol. 491, 26 July 1951, cols. 667–70 (emphasis added). For the reaction of the financial press to his July speech see, for instance, 'The eclipse of Hugh Gaitskell', *The Banker*, (Sept. 1951), 143–9.

TABLE 6.4　*Increases in Central Bank Discount Rates*
July 1950–November 1951

		Country	Change
1950	July	Denmark	3½ to 4 per cent
	Aug.	USA	1½ to 1¾ per cent
	Sept.	Belgium	3¼ to 3¾ per cent
		Netherlands	2½ to 3 per cent
	Oct.	Canada	1½ to 2 per cent
	Nov.	Denmark	4 to 5 per cent
		Finland	5¾ to 7¾ per cent
	Dec.	Sweden	2½ to 3 per cent
1951	Jan.		
	Feb.		
	Mar.		
	Apr.	Netherlands	3 to 4 per cent
	May		
	June		
	July	Belgium	3¾ to 3½ per cent
	Aug.		
	Sept.	Belgium	3½ to 3¼ per cent
	Oct.	France	2½ to 3 per cent
	Nov.	UK	2 to 2½ per cent
		France	3 to 4 per cent

Source
Bank for International Settlements, *Twenty-Second Annual Report*, June 1952.
　　chs. 1 and 7.

in July and the US in August 1950 (see Table 6.4). In some cases a first small increase was followed in a few months by a larger one and in most cases the interest rate changes were accompanied or followed by other measures to restrict credit to private borrowers. And in those countries still adhering to the wartime practice of supporting the government securities market the support policy was finally abandoned, for instance in Sweden in July 1950 and in the United States by the famous Treasury-Federal Reserve Accord of 3 March 1951.

In the slow approach to the revival of monetary policy in the US and the UK several similar factors were involved, including prolonged dispute between the Treasury and the central bank over the desirability of raising nominal interest rates on government securities, and attempts to find means of restricting bank lending without raising the cost of government borrowing. The Federal Reserve Bank of New York wanted to restore 'flexibility' in interest rates in order to re-establish the ability of the Federal Reserve to restrain monetary expansion; the Federal Reserve Board in Washington and many outside economists proposed a new kind of reserve requirement to require investors to hold government securities; and the US Treasury was inclined 'to stand fast and not rock the boat' for cheap government borrowing. In the Treasury's view, as described by Herbert Stein, an increase in interest rates would increase the debt burden

for no good purpose. A small rise in interest rates would not deter private spending and therefore would not restrain inflation. A large rise in interest rates would cause a depression. Between an increase too small to be useful and an increase too big to be safe there was no middle ground.[74]

The Federal Reserve managed to end the pegging of the Treasury bill rate at ⅜ per cent in July 1947. It indicated publicly its unwillingness to maintain a fixed pattern of rates on longer-term government securities in June 1949—the so-called 'false accord'—but it took a showdown among the authorities, including President Truman, in the winter of 1950/1 over the terms of Korean war borrowing for the bank to regain, and be acknowledged to have regained, freedom to vary interest rates as a weapon of macroeconomic management.

In light of these developments it is not surprisng that in the early 1950s a return to 'traditional' monetary policy became the intellectual fashion in economic and financial opinion in North America and Western Europe. In Britain, many economists outside and inside government had been concerned about the inflationary potential of monetary policy since 1947 or 1948. In early 1951 economists in the Labour Party were also considering how to use monetary policy actively against inflation (above). The changed attitude of economists was, however, nothing like as pronounced as the tide of opinion in favour of a return to traditional monetary policy sweeping the City and the financial press—though even here there were dissenters.[75] In its 'case for

---

[74] Stein, *The Fiscal Revolution in America*, 244–8.

[75] See, for instance, 'The case for monetary policy, I, II and III', *The Economist*, 5, 12, and 19 May 1951, Oscar R. Hobson, 'Debate on monetary policy, I—The case for dearer money', and H. M. O'Connor, 'Debate on monetary policy, II—The case for letting well alone', *The Banker* (August 1951), 71–83. For the varied attitudes of economists see 'Monetary policy: a symposium', *Bulletin of the Oxford Institute of Statistics* 14 (Apr. and May 1952).

monetary policy', *The Economist* fastened on Gaitskell's admission in his budget speech that 'The recent rise in interest rates may also exercise some check on investment'. It argued that a tighter monetary policy should be used to reinforce deflationary budgetary policy and the controls on investment, and that for such a purpose a modest rise in interest rates should suffice. Although it was not essential to raise Bank rate it would be necessary to allow short-term interest rates to rise as well as long-term gilt-edged rates by closing the 'back door' whereby the discount market could always sell Treasury bills to the Bank of England at the fixed Treasury bill rate. This would allow the Bank of England to regain its pre-war control over the money market.

When Attlee announced a general election for 25 October the Conservatives were generally expected to win. (In the event, although Labour won more votes, it ended up with 295 seats compared with the Conservatives' 321.) The Bank and the Treasury both expected to make a move in monetary policy as soon as there was a new administration. There was 'almost feverish activity in Whitehall' as the Treasury prepared to brief new ministers on the balance-of-payments crisis and to recommend measures to deal with it.[76] In the Bank Cobbold marshalled his forces early in October to prepare the more technical aspects of a 'new' monetary policy.

In May the Chief Cashier (P. S. Beale) had proposed a new rate below Bank Rate for discounting Treasury bills (above pp. 295–6). When in October he reviewed his proposal along with developments in the money market since Bank Rate had been lowered to 2 per cent in 1932, the Governor told him that he wanted something 'more ambitious and comprehensive' that would not only unpeg the Treasury bill rate but also reduce the quantity of floating debt held by the banks. He suggested a special funding operation to replace Treasury bills with short-term bonds, perhaps funding some other short-term gilt-edged debt at the same time, and new arrangements regarding the remaining floating debt with the banks and the discount houses. His objective was to overcome the obstacle to raising short-term interest rates posed by the large post-war floating debt. In his own words,

[76] *Robert Hall Diaries*, 168–9, 173–5.

The first two months of a new Government (particularly if it is Conservative) seems to me to give a chance, and perhaps last chance, of drastic measures to clear up this position and free our hands on rates. . . .

Please consider whether we could try out, for agreement with Clearing Banks, Market and our Central Bank customers as appropriate, something on following lines—

1. Fund large bulk of existing T[reasury] B[ill]s into short bonds, say 50% into 2 year and 50% into 3 year (to give a maturity spread)—? interest 1%–1¼%.

2. Clearing Banks to agree informally to hold initial amounts subject to an undertaking from us to rediscount/buy in event of their deposits decreasing by more than × from present level. Some agreement on similar lines related to liquidity requirements with Central Bank customers.

3.? push on 1951/53 [National War Bonds] to 1954/56 to clear the earlier dates.

4. Agreement with Clearing Banks for 3 years to lend on T.D.R. at present rates, such additional lending not to exceed either (a) total increase in floating debt from present level (after funding as above), or (b) increase in their deposits from present level.

5. B. of E. to require mixture of bank bills and T.B.'s for rediscount or security in proportions to be fixed from time to time.

6. Arrangements with Clearing Banks and Market for covering tender at new levels. ? T.B. tender rate up to ⅞ths–1%.

I don't know whether any of this makes sense or is practicable—but *we must do something* to clear this up and *free our* hands to use interest rates—and this is our only chance.[77]

The proposals put to the new Chancellor of the Exchequer, R. A. Butler, the day he arrived in the Treasury incorporated the ideas of both the Governor and the Chief Cashier. The measures were, in Sayers's words, 'a series of technical steps . . . which, though not constituting a revolution of policy, effectively shook the London discount market out of a torpor that had lasted a dozen years or more'.[78]

Under existing arrangements the discount houses could rediscount eligible bills at Bank rate or borrow for seven or fourteen days on the security of such bills at ¼ per cent above Bank rate. In the 1940s they did not do so since they had the alternative of

---

[77] Beale, 'Inflation and Bank Rate', 11 Oct., and Cobbold to Peppiatt, Mynors, and Chief Cashier, 13 Oct. 1951, C42/2, BOE (emphasis in original); Fforde, *Bank*, 401.

[78] *Modern Banking* (corrected 3rd edn., Oxford, 1952), 328.

selling Treasury bills to the Government Broker at the fixed ½ per cent Treasury bill rate. Introducing a new rate for rediscounting or borrowing against Treasury bills would close off the 'back door' access to the Bank and make it easier in the future to make a Bank rate change effective. In May Beale had suggested a 1 per cent rate for rediscounting Treasury bills (and a slightly higher rate for Bank advances against Treasury bills); in October, assuming 'we now contemplate, as it seems we must, a rise in Bank Rate of a minimum of, say, 1%, with a determination to make this effective', Beale at first stayed with a 1 per cent rate for rediscounting Treasury bills and added a requirement that each offer of Treasury bills for rediscount include a certain proportion of commercial bills (to be rediscounted at Bank rate) (cf. Cobbold's point 5). This would pull up the Treasury bill tender rate to, say, ⅝ per cent. After reading the Governor's note, Beale proposed the monetary package comprise a Bank rate increase, a new rate for discount house borrowing from the Bank against Treasury bills, and a funding offer of about £1,000m special short-term bonds of 1, 2, and 3 years' maturity (carrying interest rates of 1¼, 1½, and 1¾ per cent respectively) to reduce the banks' holdings of Treasury bills. Beale criticized Cobbold's suggestions as retaining some of the existing 'artificiality' by relying on special agreements with the banks.[79] In the final version which went to the Treasury the proposals were for Bank rate to go to 2½ per cent, a new 2 per cent rate for market borrowing from the Bank for seven days on the security of Treasury bills, and the offer of the three Funding Stocks to Treasury bill holders. Bank rate would apply to the rediscounting of eligible commercial bills and to advances against such bills (previously available at 1 per cent above Bank rate).

A few days before the election Cobbold warned Bridges that the Bank was likely to recommend a Bank rate change to the new government. He followed this up with an alarmist letter asking Bridges to 'bring to the attention of . . . [the] new Administration . . . the views of the Bank of England on certain aspects of the present financial situation': 'a creeping distrust of the currency' at home, a loss of confidence in sterling abroad on account of the

[79] Beale, 'Short-term rates', 30 May 1951, G1/71, 'Inflation and Bank Rate', 11 Oct., 'Short-term rates, the Governor's note of 13th October', 16 Oct., and 'Interest rates', 25 Oct. 1951, C42/2, BOE.

balance-of-payments deficits of the UK and the rest of the sterling area, and the domestic 'over-spending, over-consumption and over-investment [which were] the prime cause of the threat to both internal and external value of the currency'. He did not fail to point out as in 1949 that he believed government expenditure had to be cut, and that a deflationary monetary policy could only be a supplementary measure.[80] At the same time the Treasury officials were preparing their own document on the economic and financial situation for the post-election Chancellor—which became part of the first Cabinet paper to be discussed by the new Cabinet—and Robert Hall and the Economic Section were preparing papers on the budgetary prospects for 1952/3 and on the role of budgetary policy more generally. The Treasury had proposals on local authority borrowing rates ready in early October, when Bridges reported to the Budget Committee that on expenditure cuts the Treasury would also be 'preparing a list of candidates for scrutiny and summary execution'.[81]

The new Chancellor started his Treasury life by meeting Bridges and William Armstrong (the Chancellor's Private Secretary) over lunch at the Athenaeum Club. According to Butler, 'Both my singularly able advisers stressed the critical state of the economy . . . Their story was of blood draining from the system and a collapse greater than had been foretold in 1931.'[82] At this point the reserves were still over £1,000m although falling fast. The next day Cobbold handed the Bank's proposals to Bridges and went to see Butler to discuss them and his earlier letter to Bridges. Cobbold saw Butler again on 2 November following discussions on technicalities and timing with senior Treasury officials, including Robert Hall, who were generally in favour of the monetary measures. In a judiciously balanced account by Trend of the pros and cons of the measures, the Treasury view was that an all-round rise in interest rates was the best available

[80] Cobbold, 'Governor's note', 17 Oct. 1951, G1/71, BOE; Cobbold to Bridges, 22 Oct. 1951, T233/1684, PRO, reproduced in Fforde, *Bank*, 398–401.

[81] Strath, 'Economic prospects for 1952', 9 Oct., 'Note of meeting . . . on 11th October 1951', 12 Oct., 'The economic position: analysis of current position and outlook for 1952, Note by the Permanent Secretary to the Treasury', 25 Oct. 1951, T273/315; C(51)1, 'The economic position: analysis and remedies, Memorandum by the Chancellor of the Exchequer', 31 Oct. 1951, CAB129/48; BC(51) 11th Minutes, T171/421, PRO.

[82] Butler, *Art of the Possible*, 156–7; see also Anthony Howard, *RAB: The Life of R. A. Butler* (London, 1987), 182–3.

way of both restricting bank advances and supporting the exchange rate. The Bank's recommendations should be accepted in spite of their estimated cost to the budget of about £25m gross, £13m net of income tax. Hall wondered if the Bank rate rise should not be to 3 per cent, which Butler and Bridges discussed with Cobbold on Monday, 5 November. The Governor stuck to 2½ per cent as a first move, largely to facilitate the funding operation, whose terms he also agreed with the Government Broker on 5 November. Cobbold saw the clearing bankers on the 6th and Butler announced the new monetary policy in the House of Commons on Wednesday, 7 November. His crisis package also included £350m import cuts, with reintroduction of import licensing for some goods from continental Europe in which trade had been 'liberalized' only a year earlier, a reduction in the investment programme, a review of government expenditure to search for economies, and the reintroduction of an excess profits tax. He also announced an increase in the interest rate on local authority borrowing from the central government to 3¾ per cent. As Robert Hall remarked, there was 'not much . . . (except Bank Rate) any different from what Labour has done and would have to do'.[83]

On 8 November the authorities offered a total of £1,000m of three Serial Funding Stocks with 1¾ per cent coupons and maturity dates in 1952, 1953, and 1954, in exchange for Treasury bills. £450m, £200m, and £350m of the three stocks were taken up, the two earlier maturities at 100½ and the later one at 100. The clearing bankers decided to raise their deposit interest rates to ¾ per cent and also agreed with the Governor to increase their lending rates, although they pointed out that they had already raised them earlier in the year. They also made an unprecedented public statement, agreed with Cobbold and published as a letter in *The Times* on 30 November, warning borrowers that credit would be harder to obtain and more expensive. The government followed this with a new directive to the Capital Issues Committee to give priority only to projects essential to rearmament or helpful to the current balance of payments. A new Chancellor's letter on 4 December asked the banks not to provide advances for specula-

[83] Cobbold to Bridges, 29 Oct. 1951, T233/1684, PRO; Cobbold, 'Credit policy', 2 and 9 Nov. 1951, C42/2, BOE; Trend, 'Credit policy', 29 Oct., Hall to Eady, 'Credit policy', 31 Oct., and Note by Cobbold, 5 Nov. 1951, T233/1684, PRO; *Robert Hall Diaries*, 177–9; *House of Commons Debates*, vol. 493, 7 Nov. 1951, cols. 191–209; see also Fforde, *Bank*, 402–6.

tion in securities, real property or stocks of goods, to limit finance for hire purchase, and in general not to make advances for capital expenditure.[84]

In the first week of November the *Financial Times* and *The Economist* had both been predicting a rise in Bank rate on Thursday the 8th, although there was uncertainty about the new level of the rate and a 'pervasive rumour' that it would be 4 per cent. In a spate of articles on the workings of monetary policy in both newspapers after the announcement there was also uncertainty about the effects of the changes, mainly because of the small move in Bank rate which would not be made effective because of the new rediscount rate for Treasury bills.[85] The uncertainty was reduced by the results of the offer of the funding stocks, of which the banks were rumoured to have taken £500m, and by the London clearing bankers' letter to *The Times*. Within two weeks of the Bank rate increase the discount market was forced to borrow from the Bank for the first time since December 1938. When the November clearing bank statements were published, they showed that the banks' holdings of liquid assets had fallen from 39 per cent to 32 per cent of their deposits and also suggested that some banks had been selling gilt-edged securities. There was further selling of gilt-edged in December.[86]

The UK monetary authorities also reopened the foreign exchange market in December 1951. This allowed the banks to buy and sell foreign currencies forward at market rates instead of fixed rates set by the Bank of England and to deal in spot foreign currency within limits set by the buying and selling prices of the Bank and widened to roughly ¾ per cent either side of parity for several currencies (and within the complicated exchange control

[84] Cobbold, 'Credit policy', 9 and 19 Nov., L. H. Ensor (Chairman of Chief Executive Officers Committee of London Clearing Bankers), 'Bankers' advances and interest rates', Nov. 1951, and Balfour of Burleigh to Governor, 26 Nov. 1951, G1/71, BOE; FT, 30 Nov. and 8 Dec. 1951; Butler to Governor, 4 Dec. 1951, C40/757, BOE; see also Fforde, *Bank*, 409–10.

[85] 'The Bank rate: old and new', *FT*, 1 Nov.; 'Back to Bank rate?', *The Economist*, 3 Nov. 1055; 'Government and interest rates . . . Lead expected from Chancellor', *FT*, 6 Nov.; Wilfred King, 'Use of monetary weapons', ibid., 6 and 7 Nov.; 'How the new monetary technique will work', ibid., 8 Nov.; 'Towards monetary orthodoxy', *The Economist*, 10 Nov. 1124–6; 'The new monetary structure', ibid., 17 Nov. 1951, 1219–21.

[86] FT, 20 Nov., 4; 'Funding and the banks', *The Economist*, 8 Dec. 1951, 1417–19; 'The new monetary orthodoxy' and 'Seven months of monetary discipline', ibid., 7 June 1952, 689, 703; see also Fforde, *Bank*, 408–10.

restrictions). For example, the official spot quotation for the US dollar became $2.78–$2.82 instead of just ⅛ of a cent either side of $2.80. The immediate impact in London was to provoke fears of higher short-term interest rates and a further slide in gilt-edged prices.[87]

Meanwhile the reserve losses caused by the large balance-of-payments deficits of Britain and the rest of the sterling area continued at a rate of around £100m a month. Butler announced further imports cuts on 29 January, when the reserve figures for 1951 IV were announced, and in his early first budget on 11 March 1952, taking the total to £600m.[88] In the middle of January he asked the Governor of the Bank whether he should include another rise in Bank rate in his second crisis package. Cobbold replied that an immediate rise to 3 per cent would merely signal another increase was in the offing and advised a rise to a 'crisis' rate of 4 per cent but not before the budget. He repeated this advice to Bridges and Butler in February, because 'if we wish to keep up the disinflationary pressure [at home], we shall need a further turn of the screw sometime in March or April' and because short-term interest rates in London were still below those in New York. He preferred 4 per cent to 3½ per cent because 'the exchange situation is so dangerous'.[89]

From the middle of February until the budget and for several months afterwards official discussion of economic policy was dominated by the controversial ROBOT plan produced by the Bank of England and the Overseas Finance Division of the Treasury. This would have made 'overseas' sterling (mainly current sterling earnings of nonresidents) convertible into dollars at a floating exchange rate, while blocking most of the old sterling balances. Its ardent advocates were Leslie Rowan and Otto Clarke in OF and George Bolton in the Bank; its determined opponents Robert Hall, Edwin Plowden, and Donald Mac-Dougall, who was adviser to Lord Cherwell, the Paymaster

[87] 'Reopening the exchange market', *The Economist*, 7 June 1952, 696–9; 'Exchange control and the foreign exchange market', *Midland Bank Review*, (Aug. 1952), 1–4; *The Economist*, 22 Dec. 1951, 1539–9, 1542. On the decision see Fforde, *Bank*, 412–17.

[88] Dow, *Management of the British Economy*, 71–2, 156–8.

[89] Cobbold to Chancellor, 17 Jan., and 'Credit policy', 13 Feb. 1952, T171/409; Bridges, 'Notes of a discussion with the Governor of the Bank of England', 7 Feb. 1952, T171/409, PRO; Fforde, *Bank*, 445.

General and Churchill's chief adviser on economic matters. The government economists eventually won the bitter dispute. The whole episode goes well beyond my concern with the end of the monetary policy of the post-war Labour governments and it has recently been thoroughly discussed by others.[90] It reveals, however, the hitherto obscure reasons behind the Bank's objections to a floating exchange rate in 1948 and 1949 (Chapter 5 above). ROBOT was in effect the general plan without which Cobbold was opposed to devaluation or depreciation of sterling in July 1949 and demonstrated the Bank's long-standing desire for convertibility at (almost) all costs. The earlier objection to floating the pound had really been a reluctance to abandon the goal of early convertibility and the restoration of the Bank's traditional role of preserving the value of sterling.

The economists' main objections to ROBOT were on two levels. One concern was the likely adverse effect on the balance of payments. A floating pound would depreciate and worsen the terms of trade without improving the current account since the elasticities of demand for UK imports and exports were low. An Economic Section analysis in February 1952 of the effects of the 1949 devaluation of sterling was doubtful whether devaluation by itself had made a major contribution to the improvement in the UK current balance in 1950: the reduction in UK dollar expenditure on imports in 1950 probably owed more to import controls and the increase in UK dollar export earnings to increased activity in the USA, increased European restrictions on imports from the dollar area and the liberalization of intra-European trade. The blocking of sterling balances essential to the ROBOT plan would also *reduce* UK exports to the countries holding the balances and cause unemployment in Britain. The second concern was that full employment would be sacrificed, both because of the immediate impact on employment and because the instruments of fiscal and monetary policy would have to be directed towards external balance in order to prevent the floating convertible pound from falling too far. The postponement of convertibility meant that the Labour

[90] In order of publication: Cairncross, *Years of Recovery*, ch. 9; Donald MacDougall, *Don and Mandarin: Memoirs of an Economist* (London, 1987), ch. 5; Plowden, *Industrialist in the Treasury*, ch. 14; *Robert Hall Diaries*, 202–34; and Fforde, *Bank*, 417–73.

government's policy of aiming for both external balance and full employment was not (yet) abandoned.[91]

Butler's first budget was only mildly deflationary, with cuts in income tax offsetting increases in indirect taxes and a large reduction in food subsidies. It included the 'crisis' Bank rate rise to 4 per cent suggested by Cobbold, mainly for its external effects. The Treasury officials were doubtful whether a higher Bank rate was necessary to reduce bank lending and found the Bank's arguments unconvincing on this point. They were reluctant to quantify the effects of the Bank rate rise on the budget or on long-term interest rates, partly because they were uncertain about the effect on other short-term rates. The increased cost of the floating debt could be £75m, £95m, or £115m depending on whether the Treasury bill rate went to 2, 2½, or 3 per cent. Since it was also uncertain how long the higher Bank rate would last— one of Cobbold's arguments for 4 per cent had been that it would be 'the top' and might come down again soon—the Treasury officials decided the Chancellor could be silent on the budgetary effects of the measures, although they did feel obliged to include in his speech an estimate of a £100m fall in investment as the result of the budget as a whole.[92] After Butler made the announcement of the rise in Bank rate Cobbold agreed with the clearing banks that they would raise their deposit interest rates to 2 per cent (from the ¾ per cent they had been paying since November).[93]

Bank rate was to remain at 4 per cent until 17 September 1953. After the 1952 budget short-term money market rates and medium- and long-term gilt-edged nominal yields jumped immediately, though not to the 6 per cent Treasury pessimists feared. The Treasury bill rate went to just under 2½ per cent and nominal long-term gilt-edged yields to a little over 4½ per cent. In

[91] Hall, 'External financial policy', 22 Feb., Watts, 'The consequences of the 30 per cent devaluation of sterling against the United States dollar in September 1949', 25 Feb., Hall, 'The future of sterling', 25 Mar. 1952, T230/455: Dow, 'Budgetary prospects in the light of the new external measures', 28 Feb. 1952, T171/423, PRO; and *Robert Hall Diaries*, 203–4.

[92] Fforde, *Bank*, 446–7; Trend to Eady, 'Credit policy', 15 Feb., and 'Budget and Bank rate', 3 Mar., Eady to Armstrong, 5 Mar. 1952, T171/409, PRO; Eady to Cobbold, 8 Mar. 1952, G1/72, BOE; *House of Commons Debates*, vol. 497, 11 Mar. 1952, cols. 1282–3.

[93] 'Minutes of a special meeting of the Committee of London Clearing Bankers ... Tuesday, 11th March 1952', G1/72, BOE.

the foreign exchange market the pound rose immediately over US$2.80, having been very close to its lower limit of $2.78 since December, while the forward premium on dollars diminished, but the pound weakened again in May 1952. At the same time clearing bank deposits showed their largest fall for the time of year and clearing bank advances their smallest rise since the end of the war.[94] Prompted by rumours in the City the Bank gave cursory consideration to a further rise in Bank rate. Cobbold's senior advisers (Beale, Allen, Mynors, Niemeyer, and Bolton) were unanimous in seeing no domestic or external reason for a change. At home the minimum rate on bank advances was now 4½ per cent and many borrowers were paying over 5 per cent. London interest rates were now above New York and Swiss rates and there were also signs of deflation at home and in the rest of the sterling area. In Mynors' words, 'The present policy seems to be working well, and not yet exhausted.'[95] In fact the UK economy was going into a recession, which reduced the demand for bank advances. The balance of payments also turned round dramatically in the second half of 1952, thanks to falling import prices, improving terms of trade, and the recession.[96]

Cobbold asked his advisers to consider the possibility of a reduction in Bank rate just over a year later and discussed it at length with the Chancellor and his officials in July. The Bank's main arguments were the need to show 'flexibility' in the use of Bank rate and the fact that money market rates were falling well below Bank rate. The Treasury preferred to wait until the autumn. When the change was made the special rediscount rate for Treasury bills introduced in November 1951 was merged

[94] *The Economist*, 15 Mar. 668-9, 'Elevating Bank rate', 22 Mar. 742-3, 'Sterling since the budget', 29 Mar., 809, and 'Reopening the exchange market', 7 June 1952, 699; 'Monetary survey 1951-2', *Midland Bank Review*, (May 1952), 1; EC(S)(52)14, 'The monetary situation, Review for May 1952', 23 May 1952, T230/ 245, PRO; Bank of England, 'Some features of monetary history, 1951 to 1957', paras. 22-30, in Committee on the Working of Monetary System, *Memoranda of Evidence*, vol. 1.

[95] Notes by Cobbold and Mynors, 27 May, Beale, 'Bank rate (Governor's note of 27th May . . .)', 27 May, Niemeyer to Peppiatt, 28 May, Peppiatt to Governor, 'Bank rate', 28 May, Bolton, 'The Bank rate and sterling', 28 May 1952, G1/72, BOE; Fforde, *Bank*, 614-16.

[96] Dow, *Management of the British Economy*, 71-3; Cairncross, *Years of Recovery*, 255-6, 266-7.

with Bank rate, which thus became again the effective rate for last resort lending to the discount market.[97]

The wartime system of Treasury deposit receipts had also come to an end in 1952. From their peak of nearly £2,000m in March 1945, TDRs were down to £284m by March 1951. In February 1952 they were paid off.[98] There was some further reduction in the banks' holdings of floating debt in October 1952. The authorities offered the holders of the shortest of the three Serial Funding Stocks issued the previous November cash or conversion into the two longer Funding Stocks or a new 3% Serial Funding Stock 1955. They also offered the new funding stock for cash and in conversion of the £522m 2½% National War Bonds 1951/53. The intention had been simply to replace the existing maturities but the banks subscribed unexpectedly heavily to the new issue and cashed in Treasury bills to do so.[99] The clearing banks' balance sheets assumed a more 'normal' aspect, with floating debt accounting for 17 per cent of assets (compared with 38 per cent in 1945), investments 33 per cent, and advances 27 per cent (see Table 5.6).

In Gaitskell's nineteen months at the Treasury, the international and domestic economic situation had dramatically changed, putting paid to fears of an imminent post-war slump. Academic and official views on the role of monetary policy in the post-war world had also changed, among Labour Party economists as others. Gaitskell was not an exception, but what actually happened to UK macroeconomic policy under his brief Chancellorship depended on other factors. One was rearmament, which slowed down and to some extent reversed the gradual movement from reliance on wartime controls to prevent inflation. The party's wartime plans for post-war policy had envis-

[97] Cobbold to Peppiatt, 30 June, Note by Niemeyer, 8 July, Allen to Governor, 'Flexible rate', 14 July, Cobbold to Chancellor, 16 July, and Cobbold, 'Credit policy', 31 July, Mynors to Peppiatt and Chief Cashier, 12 Sept., and Cobbold to Chancellor, 14 Sept. 1953, G1/72, BOE; Fforde, *Bank*, 618–21; see also M. M. Gowing, 'Bank rate changes', 15 Aug. 1957, T230/385, PRO, paras. 15–16.

[98] Pember and Boyle, *British Government Securities in the Twentieth Century, Supplement 1950–1976*, 354; *The Economist*, 1 Mar. 1952, 552. TDRs were formally only suspended, but they have not been revived.

[99] 'Summary of proposals for government loan operation', 16 Sept., Compton, 'Government loan operation', 18 Sept., and Compton to Gilbert, 'The Governor's letter of 17th October', 20 Oct. 1952, T233/842, PRO; Fforde, *Bank*, 416–17.

aged that as the transitional period came to an end there would be less reliance on wartime controls and more active use of macro-economic weapons of economic policy. Another was the unresolved dispute between Bank and Treasury over methods of monetary control which was also an increasingly less disguised conflict over the *aims* of monetary policy. While Gaitskell accepted the need for higher medium- and long-term interest rates in an inflationary environment, he was not willing to abandon the wartime expedients which had kept down short-term interest rates on floating debt and hence the cost to the Exchequer. While Cobbold tried to convince the Chancellor that a small increase in these rates would not have any serious deflationary effect, thus weakening his own case in Gaitskell's eyes, he hoped eventually to achieve the interest-rate flexibility needed to use monetary policy to defend the exchange rate for the pound sterling. When a Conservative government was elected in the midst of a balance-of-payments crisis he had little difficulty in getting his way. The measures taken in the winter of 1951/2 effectively reoriented monetary policy towards external balance as well as dismantling the wartime monetary arrangements the Labour economists had earlier wished to preserve.

Conclusions

'What's Cheap Money?'
'The idea is to avoid a superfluity of the circulating medium concentrated on an insufficiency of what you swop it for.'[1]

IN starting on this study of the monetary policies of the first post-war Labour governments 1945–51 my intention was to answer a series of monetary-historical questions:

> Why were particular monetary policies adopted by the three Labour Chancellors of the Exchequer and their advisers?
> How were these policies put into effect?
> Were they appropriate given the authorities' goals, the rest of their economic policy and the state of the economy at the time?
> What were the effects of monetary policy on interest rates, monetary growth, the exchange rate, and other economic variables?

The first set of questions is about policy targets. The second mainly concerns instruments of policy. The last two seek to assess on different criteria the conduct of monetary policy under the Labour governments of 1945–51—a policy that can be summed up as cheaper (than wartime) money under Dalton, cheap money under Cripps, and 'not quite so cheap' money under Gaitskell.

At the end of the Second World War 'cheap money was an unquestioned, bipartisan, orthodoxy'.[2] Chapter 1 explained how this had come about in Britain, following developments in monetary theory in the 1930s and subsequent wartime monetary practice. Keynes's liquidity preference theory implied that a cheap

---

[1] Anthony Powell, *Books do Furnish a Room* (London, 1971), 88.
[2] Dow, *Management of the British Economy*, 21.

money policy—that is the deliberate pursuit by the monetary authorities of historically low nominal long-term interest rates— was possible and probably desirable in peace as well as in war. It was possible because the interest rates on securities of different maturities depended on both the supplies of the different maturities and on assetholders' expectations of future interest rates and security prices. The authorities could thus determine the level and structure of nominal interest rates by varying the supply of the different maturities as long as they did not try to go too much against the grain of market expectations. Given the importance of assetholders' expectations in determining long-term interest rates, if the authorities allowed nominal long-term interest rates to move up in a boom, they could find it hard to produce low long-term interest rates quickly in a slump. A cheap money policy should therefore be one of *stable* nominal long-term interest rates, which were desirable to encourage private investment in long-term assets such as housing, and to reduce rentier incomes. Wartime experience, when the government and Bank of England successfully pursued a '3 per cent war', seemed to confirm the feasibility of a cheap money policy, while the prospect of a severe post-war slump after a short inflationary 'transitional' period added force to the argument that dear money should be avoided in the transition. Dear money would increase the cost of reconstruction investment and of the large short-term government debt, and would make really cheap money harder to achieve when it came to be needed. These considerations informed the report of the National Debt Enquiry by which the Treasury and the Economic Section gave their advice on immediate post-war monetary policy and debt management to Sir John Anderson, the last wartime Chancellor of the Exchequer.

The National Debt Enquiry, following Keynes's proposals, advocated the lowering of the administered interest rates on short-term government debt in 1945, to be followed by some lowering of rates on medium-term securities, but the retention for the time being of the wartime 3 per cent on long-term gilt-edged debt. The first active monetary policy step that Hugh Dalton took as the first Labour Chancellor, to halve the Treasury bill and TDR interest rates in October 1945, bringing the former back to its later 1930s level, was fully in line with the policy contemplated for the autumn of 1945 under the coalition and caretaker governments earlier in the year. Where Dalton diverged from the consensus policy was in his assault on interest rates on long-term government debt in the new year.

Chapter 3 examined at considerable length the aims and methods of Dalton's cheaper money policy as well as other aspects of his financial policy in his first eighteen months of office. Besides his cheaper money policy, to which I shall return shortly, he wanted to put into practice the financial policy outlined in the Labour Party policy document, *Full Employment and Financial Policy*, which he and his favourite 'young economists' in the party (Durbin, Gaitskell, and Jay) had written in 1944. He also had strong views on what he wanted to achieve with his budgets, which like his cheaper money policy reflected his long-standing professional concern with the distribution of income and wealth.

The origins of the party proposals for post-war monetary and fiscal policy can be traced back to the planning in the 1930s for the third Labour government and to the extensive discussions then and during the war by XYZ and the 'young economists' advising Dalton (Chapter 2). In the late 1930s and early 1940s the anticipation and then the reality of the war changed the details of the plans for monetary and debt policy. The final version was dominated by two factors: apprehension that Britain would soon be faced with a post-war slump like that which had followed the First World War; and belief that the monetary and financial arrangements of 1939–45 could be continued and used effectively in peacetime to control inflation and encourage domestic investment without worrying about external balance. The policy instruments introduced in wartime—exchange control, price control, controls over investment, raw materials, and capital issues, plus the tap bond issues and TDRs designed to facilitate large-scale government borrowing at low nominal interest rates—were envisaged by Dalton and his advisers as means to further Labour objectives such as full employment and a planned economy. As Dalton put it in *Full Employment and Financial Policy*:

How . . . is full employment to be had and held? Clearly by learning the lessons of two wars and following in peace the same principles which have served us well in war. These principles must, of course, be applied differently in peace time. But they must not be thrown aside or forgotten. Particularly in the next few years, in the transition period between war and peace, we must stand firm against backsliding into pre-war ways. (p. 2)

Dalton by and large succeeded in carrying out the proposals of *Full Employment and Financial Policy*, though not in all cases by the methods recommended by his party advisers. He was assisted by the fact that several of the proposals were part of the wartime consensus on post-war economic policy. First of all, *Full Employment and Financial Policy* insisted on the retention of wartime financial controls after the war. The post-war government continued these and made exchange control permanent in the Exchange Control Act, 1947, which is still on the statute book. The Borrowing (Control and Guarantees) Act continued the control of capital issues through the Capital Issues Committee. The other legislative measures envisaged were the nationalization of the Bank of England, which 'must remain no more than a section of the Treasury subject to the direction of the Chancellor of the Exchequer and the Cabinet', and the establishment of a National Investment Board to plan, control, and finance capital investment. The nationalization of the Bank was accomplished with little fuss but with little actual transfer of power or responsibility for monetary policy from the Bank, which managed to retain its traditional semi-independence from the government. The limits to the Treasury's powers were not immediately obvious to ministers and their officials. This was not only the result of the care taken by the Bank and its Governor, Lord Catto in the drafting of the 'directions' clause (see Chapter 3) but also because the Chancellor and his officials did not *want* to change significantly the relationship, as it had developed since the 1930s, between Bank and Treasury. As in other areas of policy the post-war Labour government was here probably not ambitious enough rather than too radical. It was partly for political reasons—to keep the legislation simple and uncontroversial—and partly because Dalton and his party advisers overestimated the power of the monetary authorities to control the banks.[3] Similarly, on TDRs and on the National Investment Board the Treasury officials could persuade their minister in the autumn of 1945 that the

[3] See, for instance, the remarks by Berry quoted above (p. 77); see also Fforde (*Bank*, 12–16), who considers why the Bank accepted such a limited and in certain respects ambiguous Bank of England Act that was 'eccentrically devoid of any reference to the wider purposes and responsibilities of central banking'.

present arrangements for government borrowing from the banks and for the planning of investment were sufficient for Dalton's purposes.

With respect to the conduct of financial policy, the Labour Party document advocated the maintenance of cheap money, the prevention of inflation in the immediate post-war transitional period, and the use of countercyclical budgetary policy to maintain full employment when the transition was over and the expected post-war depression threatened. It also wanted 'no return to the gold standard or any other automatic and rigid foreign exchange system' but welcomed international monetary co-operation to allow stable exchange rates without compromising the objective of full employment. Similarly, while wanting to keep state control of imports it recommended the lowering of tariffs and other trade barriers by international agreement. The Attlee government was generally in favour of joining the Bretton Woods institutions, the IMF and IBRD, and the proposed ITO, even while strongly disliking the American attempts to force the pace towards multilateralism in the Anglo-American loan negotiations in 1945 and the GATT negotiations in 1947.

In his cheaper money policy Dalton went considerably further than *Full Employment and Financial Policy* which had said very little on domestic monetary policy. It had only stated:

The continued control of exports of financial capital is vital if we are to maintain cheap money, as we must, and prevent rates of interest rising here through an outflow of money to take advantage of higher rates elsewhere. (p. 3)

His policy also went beyond the advice of most of the younger economists who had advised him in the previous ten years, including Durbin, Gaitskell, Jay, and Meade. It reflected, I have argued (Chapter 3), the more Keynesian advice of Joan Robinson and of Keynes himself. They both argued—Robinson in the party's Post-war Finance Sub-committee and Keynes in the National Debt Enquiry—that the authorities could and should fix long-term as well as short-term interest rates on government debt at levels which fitted with wider economic and social objectives (wider than the objectives the Treasury and the Bank of England usually had in mind), and that in the immediate post-war period at least monetary policy need not be used to fight inflation,

because physical controls would be needed to restrain investment anyway. Whereas Keynes advocated lowering short-term
interest rates in 1945 and keeping long-term rates around 3 per
cent to encourage saving, Robinson advocated the progressive
lowering of long-term rates below 3 per cent in order to reduce
the rewards to investors. Both saw permanently low long-term
interest rates as a means to increase the rate of growth of the
capital stock in the medium to long run. In other words, monetary policy could be used in the 'comprehensive socialization of
investment' and for the 'euthanasia of the rentier' advocated in
Keynes's *General Theory*.

Dalton thus saw himself as using Keynesian monetary policy to
pursue socialist objectives. His objectives included a reduction in
the cost of government borrowing to finance socially desirable
expenditure by central government and local authorities, and the
inexpensive financing of the nationalization programme. He
hoped to issue long-term government-guaranteed debt yielding
only 2½ per cent (nominal) in compensation to the expropriated
owners of the railways, the fuel and power industries, and the
iron and steel industry. Since these issues were not made until
1948 or later he did not achieve this objective but he did succeed
in reducing the cost of local authority borrowing from the central
government and the market.

Dalton's monetary policy was thus part of a particular assignment of economic policy instruments to targets, similar but not
identical to the wartime assignment. The short-run problem of
external balance was thought to be taken care of by borrowing
from the American and Canadian governments and by import
and exchange controls. Internal balance, the maintenance of full
employment without serious inflation, was to be achieved by a
mixture of budgetary policy and wide-ranging controls, which
should ensure that the high level of private sector liquidity could
not drive up the prices of scarce goods and services. Monetary
policy was apparently freed to pursue other, distributional ends.

Dalton's macroeconomic policy soon proved inadequate to the
tasks he had set it. This was partly because he underestimated the
extent of inflationary pressures, in Britain and overseas, in the
first two years after the war—although, fearing unemployment
rather than inflation, he was prepared to take the risk of pursuing
too inflationary a policy in order to maintain a high level of

aggregate demand. More seriously, he overestimated the power of the physical and price controls to curb aggregate demand and inflation at home and of the sterling area exchange controls to insulate the domestic economy from external influences on the current and capital accounts of the balance of payments. He embarked on his domestic financial policy as though he could treat the UK economy as the approximation to a closed economy that it had been in wartime. His monetary policy was inappropriate because it was likely to increase the already high degree of private sector liquidity left over from the war and could therefore aggravate the existing pent-up demand for goods and services that had been unavailable during the war. (I argue in Chapter 4 above that this is in fact what it did.)

In putting Dalton's policy into effect, the Treasury and the Bank of England used the instruments of monetary policy adopted in 1939–45: fixed interest rates on floating debt, open-ended tap issues for longer-term government securities, official support of the gilt-edged market, and some direct control of private borrowing in the form of new capital issues and bank advances. After reducing the fixed short-term interest rates in the autumn of 1945, the government offered on tap two long-term bond issues in the spring and autumn of 1946, each yielding 2½ per cent at the time of issue, the first with a twenty-year maturity, the second an 'irredeemable'. The Bank of England and the National Debt Commissioners supported the market by buying up long-term gilt-edged securities from the market before and after each issue, especially for the second. The large-scale intervention produced a rapid expansion in bank deposits, which temporarily resumed their high wartime growth rates, in the second half of 1946.

The first bond issue was quite successful but by the time of the second market expectations were changing—at least partly because it could be seen in the behaviour of bank deposits that the money supply was increasing rapidly as the authorities tried to maintain the 2½ per cent yield on long-term gilt-edged. Widely read financial commentators were warning investors that the authorities might get cold feet and that interest rates would sooner or later rise. Investors did not rush to buy the new government stock and the authorities bought most of it themselves. After the issue was closed in January 1947, the authorities ceased to support the gilt-edged market and the prices of long-term government bonds fell. Although Dalton continued to talk about continuing cheaper money during 1947, nothing was being done actively to promote it. His cheaper money policy thus effectively ended at the beginning of 1947.

In preparing to act on the National Debt Enquiry proposals the Treasury officials had accepted the Keynes–Hopkins arguments that full employment policy required low long-term interest rates and that high interest rates would not be needed to combat post-war inflation. A cheap money policy, and even more a cheaper money policy, would also further the traditional aim of reducing the cost of borrowing. The Bank of England, on the other hand, was not enthusiastic about Keynes's or Dalton's ideas. It thought the Treasury was being over-optimistic about future interest rates; but it was prepared to try to issue low interest bonds because any success would ease the problems of managing the post-war national debt. With its senior officials 'looking towards the evolution of a flexible monetary policy involving the discretionary adjustment of short-term interest rates, up or down, and the maintenance of an orthodox funding policy in the gilt-edged market',[4] it wanted to follow wartime debt policy to its logical conclusion and issue irredeemable debt at 3 per cent in 1946. It reluctantly acquiesced in Dalton's aims on *rates* but not the National Debt Enquiry's or Keynes's later proposals on the *techniques* of debt management. Uncertain that cheap money could be maintained indefinitely and concerned about the number of existing stocks maturing within ten years, it wished to maximize the length of new issues, preferring 3 per cent for at least forty years to 3 per cent with an early optional redemption date and 2½ per cent for twenty years to 2 per cent for ten. Although Keynes argued against funding, the Treasury accepted the Bank's advice—and Dalton himself, although he raised Keynes's suggestions on several occasions, was well aware of the advantages to the Chancellor of funding at low nominal interest rates. The Bank assisted the drive for cheaper money in 1946 by buying up government stocks from the market when market demand for them threatened to fall off, but once the second 2½ per cent long-term bond issue had been made, it ended its intervention.

Although the cheaper money policy was not ended by the

[4] Fforde, *Bank*, 325.

balance-of-payments crisis in 1947, it is unlikely that it could have survived it. The signs of changing expectations about future interest rates towards the end of 1946 and the reluctance of the Bank of England to intervene to support the gilt-edged market in the first quarter of 1947 suggest that the amount of intervention that would have been necessary to hold interest rates down to the levels desired by Dalton would have exceeded the intervention the authorities would have been prepared to undertake. More fundamentally, the inflationary forces engendered by lowering interest rates in an inflationary situation probably made cheaper money unsustainable.

Keynesian liquidity preference theory implies that unless the monetary authorities' intentions are in line with assetholders' expectations of future interest rates or unless the authorities can change expectations in the direction they desire, an attempt to lower long-term nominal interest rates will require increasing amounts of official intervention to bring about and sustain the low rates. The further implication is usually drawn that if the authorities persist long enough, assetholders will change their minds about future interest rates and the authorities will win out. As Joan Robinson put it in a frequently quoted passage:

All goes smoothly so long as the authorities are working with the grain of market opinion. But if they embark on the policy and begin to buy bonds at a time when the long rate is generally expected to rise, they come sharply into conflict with market opinion. So long as the expected rate remains high, they have to go on holding bonds and supplying money for bear hoards. If they persist resolutely, a moment will come when the bears are convinced that the new low rate has come to stay. Money then moves out of bear hoards into bonds, and the authorities can gradually sell off to ex-bears the bonds they have been holding, retire bills, and reduce the quantity of money to the level which will just hold the bill rate at its bottom stop.

But if the authorities' nerves are shaken by the ferocious growls with which the bears have been deafening them all this time, and once allow bond prices to relapse, the growling of the bears turns to joyous yelps of 'I told you so' and the expected future bond rate is so much the higher for ever after.[5]

However, as Robinson herself points out, the authorities can only sustain a cheap money policy as long as the 'full-employment

[5] 'The rate of interest', *Econometrica* 19 (Apr. 1951), 110.

interest rate is below the actual level of rates or is held below it by a budget surplus or other means'. Otherwise inflation would set in and nominal interest rates would rise. In the circumstances of 1945–7 with high employment and rising prices the real rates of interest produced by cheaper money would certainly have been below the equilibrium rate corresponding to full employment.

More 'monetarist' theories lead, of course, to the same conclusion and strengthen it, since they envisage a stronger and swifter effect of expansionary monetary policy on expenditure. The lowered interest rates (nominal and real) and larger real money balances in the hands of the public will increase expenditure on both consumption and investment goods and services, tending to push up prices and nominal interest rates. Inflation will accelerate (or the balance of payments continually worsen) as long as real rates of interest are being held below the equilibrium rates determined by the 'real forces of productivity and thrift'. The expectational factors stressed in the Keynesian theory will also speed up the process insofar as expectations of future interest rates depend on some conception of the equilibrium real interest rate based on historical experience.[6]

The evidence relating to the effects of cheaper money on private expenditure in 1946 and 1947 is ambiguous: there were significant increases in investment and consumption expenditures, but there were several other factors involved such as the overambitious investment programme and the release of pent-up demand for consumer goods and services unavailable during the war as they began to become available again. There was already a high degree of private sector liquidity left over from the war. Similarly, the behaviour of prices can be mostly explained in terms of continued price controls, cost-of-living subsidies, and rising import prices. But the size of the monetary shock in 1946, large by any measure, is such as to lead one to suspect at least a serious aggravation of the existing excess demand for goods and services in 1946–7, increasing the pressure on the controls and spilling over on to the balance of payments. Certainly the observable facts are consistent with the modern portfolio approach to the theory of monetary policy, which emphasizes wealth effects

[6] 'The rate of interest', 93. Keynes had warned the National Debt Enquiry in 1945, 'the game is . . . up when the public believe that the Treasury understands it': 'National Debt Enquiry: Lord Keynes' notes', *JMK*, vol. 27, 396.

on consumption of changes in interest rates. Real money balances, in terms of both M1 and M3, increased by no less than 12 per cent in 1946. This was considerably higher than the increases in the war years, which had averaged 7 per cent and only reached double digits in 1941. After 1946 real balances fell for the rest of the decade and in most years of the 1950s. The ratios of money balances (M1 and M3) to income, which had risen substantially during the war (from 33 and 55 per cent to 50 and 70 per cent respectively), jumped up again in 1946. Having reached 57 and 79 per cent, they steadily declined to their pre-war levels by 1952. By increasing the already sizeable 'monetary overhang' from the war, Dalton's cheaper money would have increased domestic absorption in 1946 and 1947, helped to worsen the balance-of-payments deficit, and increased the size of the policy adjustments that had to be made to cope with the balance-of-payments problem in 1947—and probably for the rest of the Attlee governments' period of office.

What might have happened if the authorities had stuck with cheap money, i.e. 3 per cent for nominal interest rates on long-term government debt, in 1945-7, rather than trying to get down to 2½ per cent? They would not have had to expand the money supply deliberately in 1946, which would have avoided one source of inflationary pressure and one source of a change in interest-rate expectations. There were, however, other factors relevant to the breakdown of cheaper money in late 1946: there is evidence of dissaving—a fall in the demand for money and a rise in desired expenditure—which would tend to push up prices and interest rates anyway. But if there had been less inflationary pressure investors might have been less fearful of a rise in interest rates and more willing to believe the authorities could stick to the 3 per cent they had managed to maintain throughout the war.

When the Treasury began to recognize the urgency of the balance-of-payments problem early in 1947 and acknowledged the need for an anti-inflationary macroeconomic policy, it opted for a disinflationary *budgetary* policy, which it staunchly maintained for four years. The budget-making process under the three Labour Chancellors has been described in this book mainly as background to monetary policy deliberations and to illustrate some of the concerns of ministers and officials in their financial policy. It also sheds light on the timing of the major reorientation of macroeconomic policy in 1947—and hence on the so-called Keynesian revolution in British economic policy.

The post-convertibility crisis budget of November 1947 has often been seen as 'the major milestone ... when the Treasury finally turned in peacetime and out of choice to Keynesian analysis to help control inflation'.[7] The strongest evidence for this dating is probably that some of the major participants, notably Plowden and Hall, saw it this way at the time. (It is also, of course, the case that the size of the tax increases and of the resulting surplus were dramatically large.) But, as they themselves acknowledge, Plowden and Hall were not involved in budgetary policy-making before the late summer and early autumn of 1947.[8] The planning for the April 1947 budget, which started from Meade's paper on the inflationary pressure and the need for a surplus, shows that that budget was deliberately an *anti-inflationary surplus* budget, in Dalton's mind no less than that of his official advisers (pp. 163-4 above). Some economic historians who have claimed that November 1947 was the milestone have failed to notice Meade's presence on the Budget Committee in 1945 and 1946 or Dalton's expressed intentions to his officials at the end of 1946. Also, although Dalton did not agree to a ceiling on the cost-of-living subsidies until the autumn, it seems ironic (to say the least) to take reduction of the subsidies as the test of 'Keynesian' intentions given that they had been introduced in the 1941 stabilization budget for the very purposes for which Dalton would have liked to retain them.[9]

One can go further. The first post-war budget was explicitly an interim budget, for which Keynesian calculations were not thought to be feasible and in which some relief from high wartime taxation should be given as a harbinger of peacetime normality. The second and third budgets both reflected a mixture of objectives—and the immediate post-war assignment of macroeconomic weapons to targets mentioned above (p. 327). With inflation and the balance-of-payments problem apparently fairly well under control for the time being, the budget in 1946 (for which Keynes was an adviser) should 'hold the line': there could

[7] Booth, 'The 'Keynesian Revolution' in economic policy-making', *EHR* 36 (Feb. 1983), 123.

[8] Plowden, *Industrialist in the Treasury*, 14-15; *Robert Hall Diaries*, 19-22.

[9] Booth, 'The "Keynesian Revoluton"', 121-2; see also Rollings, 'British budgetary policy 1945-1954: a 'Keynesian revolution'?', *EHR* 41 (1988), 286-91.

be some further tax reductions and some increase in social expenditure as long as they allowed the deficit to be reduced from its wartime level. The budget could also, therefore, be used, like monetary policy, for more socialist, redistributive purposes. In the third post-war budget, when controls were obviously not sufficing to combat inflation, the Keynesian element came to dominate over the socialist one.

In 1948–50 Stafford Cripps maintained the large disinflationary budget surpluses initiated under Dalton, although without having to resort to large tax increases as Dalton had in 1947. There was increasing concern in the Treasury that the high tax rates needed to produce the surpluses could reduce incentives to work and save, and increasing awareness that a tighter monetary stance might allow smaller surpluses and hence lower taxation. None the less the disinflationary budgetary policy was accompanied by an apparently passive monetary policy, with short-term interest rates fixed at the levels to which Dalton had reduced them, longer-term interest rates allowed to move gradually upwards, and occasional requests to the clearing banks to restrain their lending to particular sorts of customers. The authorities gave up trying to sell long-term bonds with nominal yields of less than 3 per cent and paid nationalization compensation in government-guaranteed stocks with 3 per cent coupons in 1948 and 1949. The rate of nominal monetary growth was modest (around 2 per cent a year) so that real money balances declined steadily. There was no change in monetary stance to accompany devaluation in 1949, essentially because the government and the Bank could not agree on what could and should be done to tighten monetary policy. The often confused and inconclusive discussions on the use of monetary weapons, which I described in Chapters 5 and 6, began early in 1948 and continued through the next three and a half years.

Although most of the plans drawn up by Labour Party economists in the 1930s had been concerned to deal with unemployment in a depression, the younger Labour economists had also been concerned to avoid inflation in boom conditions and had assumed that countercyclical monetary and fiscal policy would be used to reduce excess demand. Several were critical of Dalton's monetary policy and some by 1947 were proposing a tighter monetary stance to accompany the anti-inflationary budgetary measures. When Douglas Jay became a junior Treasury minister in October 1947 his first attempt to influence Treasury policy was to argue for tighter monetary control. He weakened his case by wanting to reduce bank deposits without raising interest rates, but his agitation did lead to a Treasury-Bank Working Party on Bank Deposits and Advances, which met regularly until the February 1950 general election.

In the Working Party discussions the Bank of England made it clear that it did not, and did not want to, directly control the money supply. During the war its policy had been accommodating, supplying currency and bank reserves to the banks so as to keep their reserves a more or less constant proportion of their rapidly growing deposits. The Bank continued the practice throughout the 1940s. It was, however, in favour of devoting some of the budget surplus to redeeming floating debt and also of converting short-term government debt to longer-term debt whenever market conditions allowed. The behaviour of the money supply was the resultant of the opposing forces of reduction in the banks' holdings of floating debt and persistent increase in their lending to the private sector. During 1948 the Bank gave no indication of wishing to see any rise in its ineffective 2 per cent Bank rate or in other short-term interest rates. In the Treasury the officials were also concerned with debt management. This made them reluctant to raise nominal interest rates, especially the short-term rates on floating debt, because this would immediately increase the interest burden of the debt. The reluctance to raise short-term interest rates was shared by senior ministers, including Cripps, because it would increase the interest paid by the government to the banks and increase bank profits.

The authorities had thus boxed themselves in, having ruled out both control of bank reserves and the use of interest rates for monetary control. Not surprisingly the Treasury, including Douglas Jay and Robert Hall, tried to find a way out in quantitative direct controls on the assets or liabilities of the clearing banks. The Bank initially took the line that quantitative controls on bank assets or liabilities were impossible or at least impracticable. All that could be done was to ask the banks to be 'selective' and 'cautious' in their lending—requests that were made by the Chancellor through the Governor on several occasions in 1948–51 but without conspicuous success and without satisfying the more concerned people in the Treasury (Douglas Jay and Robert Hall in particular). By the beginning of 1949, however, the Bank had decided that what it really wanted was a rise in short-term nominal interest rates, at the least in the Treasury bill and other money-market rates, if not (yet) in Bank rate. From the time he became Governor in March 1949, Cobbold campaigned for higher short-term interest rates, for a reduction in the floating debt, and for the restoration of control of the money market to the Bank. Since he succeeded only when a Conservative government replaced the Labour administration in the autumn of 1951, it might be thought that the reason it took him so long was the Labour government's reluctance to increase the cost of the debt. But Cobbold's tactics were not well chosen: during the 1949 balance-of-payments crisis he campaigned for government expenditure cuts, first as a substitute for devaluation, and then to accompany it, and thus lost a possible chance to tighten monetary stance which the Treasury people then favoured. When he did ask to raise interest rates, after the devaluation decision and then again in December 1950 and June 1951, he failed to explain how the small interest rate rise he was asking for would significantly reduce the growth of the money supply and hence failed to persuade Cripps and Gaitskell to overcome their distaste for raising the interest rates on Treasury bills and TDRs.

As Fforde puts it from the Bank of England point of view, Cripps and Gaitskell 'when pressed into a corner ... both pleaded political impossibility [in raising short-term interest rates]. But they were also inclined to make use of the debating fork that while a large rise in money rates seemed to be in nobody's mind, a small one was unlikely to achieve anything worthwhile to justify its budgetary and external cost.' With this I largely agree, and also with his remark that 'The effects of interest-rate policy in the heyday of Cripps' Treasury seemed either nebulous or malign, and their exposition [by the Bank] seemed beset with mystique or "mumbo-jumbo".' But it is going on too far to state, as Fforde also does, that 'The truth was that a disinflationary interest-rate policy was unwelcome to the political and economic Left, while Dalton's gilt-edged experiment must have further dulled Ministerial appetites for any adventures in that direction. ... There was a strong element of irrationality or even hysteria about this opposition to any use of the interest-rate weapon', which was regarded as outdated and dangerous.[10] Leaving aside the question of whether one would wish to attribute irrationality or hysteria to the brilliant Cripps or the intellectual Gaitskell, whose advisers invariably record their willingness to respond positively to good arguments, this runs together several separate strands in ministerial attitudes to monetary policy. Although Cripps on taking office as Chancellor would have preferred to be able to issue nationalization compensation stocks at 2½ rather than 3 per cent, there is no evidence that he (or Gaitskell) would have wanted to pursue a monetary policy like Dalton's. With his official advisers, he could see a need for a tighter monetary policy in 1948–9 and, again like them, would have preferred it not to involve paying higher interest charges on the floating debt. Gaitskell positively wanted higher *long-term* interest rates in 1950–1. He also wanted tighter monetary control and, with his background in the party economists' discussions of 'socialist' financial policy in the late 1930s and early 1940s, could raise more sophisticated, academic objections to claims that this could *only* be achieved with a higher Treasury bill rate.

The conventional description of monetary policy in 1948–51 as a 'neutral' policy thus does not accurately reflect the authorities' objectives or intentions in these years. They were in fact anxious to curb monetary growth, specifically to reduce or at least to prevent further increases in bank deposits as part of an anti-inflationary policy. It is true that the Labour government did not want short-term interest rates to rise, because that would increase the cost of the national debt and the profits of the banks. The obvious 'solution', to try to resort to quantitative control of bank assets or liabilities, was ruled out by the Bank. The authorities' inaction reflected this dilemma and the dispute was not resolved under the Labour governments. As a result the episode throws little light on the perennial question of whether and to what extent a central bank can control the growth of commercial bank lending and hence of the money supply.[11] The outcome of the authorities' deliberations and disagreements, and of the

[10] *Bank*, 371.
[11] For a recent discussion of this question from a central bank point of view see J. C. R. Dow and I. D. Saville, *A Critique of Monetary Policy: Theory and British Experience* (Oxford, 1988).

Bank's actions with respect to the monetary base, was an endogenously determined money supply. The Treasury hoped to
reduce monetary growth by using budget surpluses to reduce
bank assets, but the slowdown in monetary growth that was
observed after 1947 owed more to the external financing of the
government's borrowing needs and to the private sector's adjustment to peacetime conditions. Although direct 'controls' on
bank advances continued in the 1950s and 1960s, they probably
had little impact in 1948–51, except in the summer of 1951 when
the banks raised the interest rates they charged on their lending.

By 1951 the combined pressures of rearmament and the
deteriorating balance-of-payments position of the UK and the
rest of the sterling area had renewed the need for domestic 'disinflation' in Britain. It was met mainly by tightening the fiscal
stance once more, with total tax increases almost double those of
Dalton's last budget. Both Bank and Treasury renewed their
efforts to find an appropriate monetary policy, and failed yet
again to reach full agreement on the instruments to be used.
However, in addition to the usual request to the bankers to restrain their advances, the Governor managed to persuade them
to raise their lending rates, *without* a change in the fixed interest
rates on the floating debt.

Gaitskell's attitude to monetary policy in his nineteen months
in the Treasury, first as Minister of State and then as Chancellor,
is particularly interesting. Although he was in many respects an
enthusiastic supporter of 'planning' during the Attlee governments' period of office (for instance, in being reluctant to give up
physical controls entirely and to rely on financial controls instead), he surprised his officials on becoming Chancellor by
admitting he wanted to see at least long-term interest rates rise in
1950. He had already as Minister of State asked for a review of the
weapons of monetary and credit control used in other countries,
in order to find out what alternative methods of monetary control
might be available. When the Governor of the Bank asked him to
permit a rise in short-term interest rates, he took some time and
considerable thought to make up his mind. As he put it to his
officials, 'leaving on one side the question of the additional cost
to the Exchequer, he felt that the other arguments [for and against
a rise in short-term interest rates] were nicely balanced'. His
officials were then divided with some strongly in favour of the

proposal and others doubtful. Douglas Jay as Financial Secretary was against, partly because it might raise the cost of the next nationalization—the iron and steel industry in 1951—and partly because the Bank had still not explained exactly how a small rise in short-term interest rates would have a major impact on bank lending and hence the money supply. Gaitskell was irritated by the Governor's refusal to produce good arguments, turning down his request in January 1951 and then delaying a decision on his next request in the summer until the autumn.

I have speculated elsewhere that Gaitskell would have allowed a rise in short-term interest rates if he had remained Chancellor after the general election in October 1951.[12] There were discussions earlier that year among economists in the Labour Party, which concluded that it would not be inappropriate (or 'unsocialist') to pursue an anti-inflationary policy involving higher short- and long-term interest rates. Tony Crosland even managed to persuade Hugh Dalton that a rise in interest rates was not wicked, and would not necessarily have undesirable redistributive consequences. It was also in 1951 that the government, and economists in and out of the Party, stopped worrying about the imminence of a post-war slump like that of the 1920s. Several of the Labour arguments for preserving cheap money had thus disappeared. A rise in interest rates could be justified on domestic economic grounds (internal balance). On the other hand, there was suspicion—not unjustified as the ROBOT episode was soon to show—that if the Bank was allowed to restore interest-rate flexibility it would wish to use it to defend the reserves and the exchange rate (external balance).

The 'revival' of monetary policy in the UK in the winter of 1951/2 finally ended the stalemate over monetary policy, largely in the Bank's favour. The Bank reasserted its traditional semi-independence from the government in the conduct of monetary policy and—helped by the balance-of-payments crisis—its traditional concern with external balance. But although some of the distinctive features of 1940s cheap money went (notably the fixed Treasury bill rate and TDRs), the technical aspects of monetary practice remained—for nearly two decades—in essentials similar to that adopted under Cripps and Gaitskell. The instruments of

[12] '"Socialist" monetary policy', *HOPE* 20 (1988), 562–3; see also Fforde, *Bank*, 387.

monetary policy used in the 1950s and 1960s included, beside the variation of short-term interest rates—'administered cautiously and in large part with an eye on the performance of sterling' as Fforde puts it—and the newly introduced hire purchase controls, continued use of 'requests' on bank advances to try to reduce bank lending, and funding operations in gilt-edged securities to reduce bank liquidity. At the same time the dominant objective of debt management was to maximize the demand for government debt, especially long-dated securities by the non-bank public. Believing that the gilt-edged market was dominated by investors' expectations and that stocks could not be sold on a falling market, the Bank sought to sell long-term debt only when gilts prices were tending to rise. In the 1960s it moved to stabilize gilt-edged prices by 'leaning into the wind' in both directions. In both decades the fact that long-term nominal interest rates could not be varied enough to assist in short-run monetary control meant increased reliance on direct controls on bank crdit. The immediate post-war experience goes a long way to explain the curious and idiosyncratic British monetary arrangements of the following twenty years. [13]

I draw several final conclusions from the story of monetary policy in 1945–51 reported here. First, the policy espoused by the Labour Party as well as by the authors of the wartime coalition government's *Employment Policy* white paper, of maintaining wartime controls and wartime cheap money into the post-war transitional period was understandable, given the desire not to repeat the 1919–23 experience when dear money imposed to fight uncontrolled post-war inflation had preceded a severe and prolonged slump. Secondly, Dalton's cheaper money policy went beyond that limited objective and was inappropriate in the post-war monetary situation. It was inappropriate because it exacerbated the existing 'excess' (by normal peacetime standards) liquidity of the private sector, which in itself threatened serious

[13] On UK domestic monetary policy and debt management in the 1950s and 1960s see Committee on the Working of the Monetary System, *Report*, chs. 6 and 7; Fforde, *Bank*, 398–412 and ch. 10 (quotation from 407); Bank of England, 'Official transactions in the gilt-edged market', *BEQB* 6 (June 1966), 141–8; Brian Tew, 'Monetary policy, part I', in F. T. Blackaby (ed.), *British Economic Policy 1960–74* (Cambridge, 1978), 218–57; and Donald R. Hodgman, 'British techniques of monetary policy: a critical review', *Journal of Money, Credit and Banking* 3 (Nov. 1971), 760–79.

inflation unless the feared slump arrived soon. Dalton was not alone in his undue pessimism about the timing of the depression, but he was also excessively optimistic about the ability of controls to prevent open inflation. He therefore took an unwarranted risk in trying to use nominal interest rates as an instrument to influence income distribution and ruling out its use as a weapon of macroeconomic policy. Thirdly, when the inflationary consequences of Dalton's monetary policy were recognized (even if not fully understood), the authorities failed to use monetary means to undo them because of disagreement between the Treasury and the Bank of England over the role of monetary policy in the postwar world. This had at least two consequences. The adjustment to lower, more 'normal' levels of real balances during the later 1940s came about slowly and indirectly, since the supply of money was endogenously determined. And the Labour government was obliged to place greater reliance on other macroeconomic policy instruments (including budgetary policy, incomes policy, and devaluation) in order to contain inflation and improve the balance of payments.

Bibliography

Archives

Bank of England Archives, Bank of England, London.
Butler Papers, Trinity College, Cambridge.
Cabinet Office Records, Public Record Office, London.
Colin Clark Papers, Brasenose College, Oxford.
Cripps Papers, Nuffield College, Oxford.
Crosland Papers, British Library of Political and Economic Science.
Dalton Papers, British Library of Political and Economic Science.
Durbin Papers, British Library of Political and Economic Science.
Fabian Society Papers, Nuffield College, Oxford.
Labour Party Archives, National Museum of Labour History, Manchester (previously at Labour Party Headquarters, London).
Meade Papers, British Library of Political and Economic Science.
Pethick–Lawrence Papers, Trinity College, Cambridge.
Piercy Papers, British Library of Political and Economic Science.
Joan Robinson Papers, King's College, Cambridge (Unpublished writings of Joan Robinson copyright The Provost and Scholars of King's College, Cambridge, 1993).
Treasury Records, Public Record Office, London.

Books and articles

'The evolution of exchange control in the United Kingdom—1939–49', *Midland Bank Review* (Feb. 1949), 6–13.
'Exchange control and the foreign exchange market', *Midland Bank Review* (Aug. 1952), 1–4.
'Government control over the use of capital resources', *Midland Bank Review* (Aug. 1950), 1–7.
'Monetary survey 1950–51', *Midland Bank Review* (May 1951), 1–6.
'Monetary survey 1951–2', *Midland Bank Review* (May 1952), 1–7.
'"National savings": Types and trends', *Midland Bank Review* (Oct. 1949), 3–7.
'Sir Richard Hopkins', *Public Administration* 34 (Summer 1956), 115–23.
A Citizen, *The City Today*, NFRB pamphlet no. 38 (London: Gollancz and New Fabian Research Bureau, 1938).

ABREU, MARCELO DE PAIVA, 'Brazil as a creditor: sterling balances, 1940–1952', *Economic History Review* 43 (Aug. 1990), 450–69.

ADDISON, PAUL, *The Road to 1945: British Politics and the Second World War* (London: Jonathan Cape, 1975).

ALLEN, J. E., 'Railway compensation examined', *Economic Journal* 58 (Mar. 1948), 125–8.

ANDREWS, P. W. S., 'A further inquiry into the effects of rates of interest', *Oxford Economic Papers* no. 3 (Mar. 1940), 33–73.

BALL, R. J., and BURNS, T., 'The inflationary mechanism in the U.K. economy', *American Economic Review* 66 (Sept. 1976), 467–84.

BEVERIDGE, WILLIAM H., *Full Employment in a Free Society* (London: Allen and Unwin, 1944).

BOOTH, ALAN, 'The "Keynesian Revolution" in economic policy-making', *Economic History Review* 36 (Feb. 1983), 103–23.

——*British Economic Policy, 1931–49: Was There a Keynesian Revolution?* (Hemel Hempstead: Harvester Wheatsheaf, 1989).

BROWN, A. J., 'The liquidity-preference schedules of the London Clearing Banks', *Oxford Economic Papers* no. 1 (Oct. 1938), 49–82.

——'Interest, prices and the demand schedule for idle money', *Oxford Economic Papers* no. 2 (May 1939), 46–69.

——'A worm's eye view of the Keynesian Revolution', in John Hillard (ed.), *J. M. Keynes in Retrospect, The Legacy of the Keynesian Revolution* (Aldershot: Edward Elgar, 1988), 18–44.

BULLOCK, ALAN, *Ernest Bevin, Foreign Secretary* (Oxford: Oxford University Press, 1985).

BURK, KATHLEEN, *The First Privatisation: The Politicians, the City and the Denationalisation of Steel* (London: The Historians' Press, 1988).

BUTLER, R. A., *The Art of the Possible* (London: Hamish Hamilton, 1971).

CAIRNCROSS, ALEC, *Years of Recovery: British Economic Policy 1945–51* (London: Methuen, 1985).

——'Prelude to Radcliffe: Monetary policy in the United Kingdom 1948–57', *Rivista di Storia Economica* 4 (International issue 1987), 1–20.

——(ed.), *The Robert Hall Diaries 1947–53* (London: Unwin Hyman, 1989).

——and WATTS, NITA, *The Economic Section 1939–1961: A Study in Economic Advising* (London: Routledge, 1989).

CAPIE, FORREST, and WEBBER, ALAN, *A Monetary History of the United Kingdom 1870–1982, Volume I: Data, Sources, Methods* (London: Allen and Unwin, 1985).

CHESTER, D. N. (ed.), *Lessons of the British War Economy* (Cambridge: Cambridge University Press, 1951).

CHESTER, SIR NORMAN, *The Nationalisation of British Industry, 1945–51* (London: HMSO, 1975).

CLARK, COLIN, *The Control of Investment*, NFRB pamphlet no. 8 (London: Gollancz and New Fabian Research Bureau, 1933).

——*A Socialist Budget*, NFRB pamphlet no. 22 (London: Gollancz and New Fabian Research Bureau, 1935).

——'The value of the pound', *Economic Journal* 59 (June 1949), 198–207.

CLARKE, SIR RICHARD, *Anglo-American Economic Collaboration in War and Peace 1942–1949*, ed. Sir Alec Cairncross (Oxford: Clarendon Press, 1982).

CLAYTON, G., 'The role of the British life assurance companies in the capital market', *Economic Journal* 61 (Mar. 1951), 83–101.

CLEAVER, GEORGE, and CLEAVER, PAMELA, *The Union Discount: A Centenary Album* (London: Union Discount Co., 1985).

COLE, G. D. H. (ed.), *What Everybody Wants to Know About Money: A Planned Outline of Monetary Problems* (London: Gollancz, 1933).

Conservative Party, *Work: the Future of British Industry* (London: Conservative Party, Jan. 1944).

CORDEN, W. M., 'Australian economic policy discussion in the post-war period: a survey', *American Economic Review* 58 (Supplement June 1968), 88–138.

[CRICK, W. F.], 'The changing shape of Britain's monetary system, Part I: 1931–45', *Midland Bank Review*, Nov. 1947, 1–6.

——'The changing shape of Britain's monetary system, Part II: Post-war transition', *Midland Bank Review*, Feb. 1948, 1–7.

CROSLAND, C. A. R., *The Future of Socialism* (London: Jonathan Cape, 1956).

DACEY, W. MANNING, 'The cheap money technique', *Lloyds Bank Review* no. 3 (Jan. 1947), 49–63.

DALTON, HUGH, 'The measurement of the inequality of incomes', *Economic Journal* 30 (Sept. 1920), 348–61.

——*Some Aspects of the Inequality of Incomes in Modern Communities* (London: Routledge, 1920).

——*Principles of Public Finance* (London: Routledge, 1922; 2nd edn., 1929; 3rd edn., 1936; 4th edn., 1954).

——*The Capital Levy Explained* (London: Labour Publishing Co. Ltd., 1923).

——*Practical Socialism for Britain* (London: Routledge, 1935; New York, Garland Publishing Inc., 1985).

——'Our financial plan', in Fabian Society, *Forward from Victory! Labour's Plan* (London: Gollancz, 1946), 38–51.

——*Call Back Yesterday: Memoirs 1887–1931* (London: Frederick Muller, 1953).

——*The Fateful Years: Memoirs 1931–1945* (London: Frederick Muller, 1957).

——*High Tide and After: Memoirs 1945–1960* (London: Frederick Muller, 1962).

DAVENPORT, NICHOLAS, *Memoirs of a City Radical* (London: Weidenfeld & Nicolson, 1974).

Dow, J. C. R., 'The economic effect of monetary policy 1945–47', in Committee on the Working of the Monetary System, *Principal Memoranda of Evidence*, vol. 3 (London: HMSO, 1960), 76–106.

——*The Management of the British Economy 1945–60* (Cambridge: Cambridge University Press, 1964).

—— and SAVILLE, I. D., *A Critique of Monetary Policy: Theory and British Experience* (Oxford: Clarendon Press, 1988).

DURBIN, ELIZABETH, *New Jerusalems: The Labour Party and the Economics of Democratic Socialism* (London: Routledge, 1985).

——'Keynes, the British Labour Party and the economics of democratic socialism', in O. F. Hamouda and J. N. Smithin (eds.), *Keynes and Public Policy after Fifty Years* (Aldershot: Edward Elgar, 1988), vol. 1, 29–42.

DURBIN, EVAN F. M., *Purchasing Power and Trade Depression: A Critique of Under-Consumption Theories* (London: Jonathan Cape, 1933).

——*Socialist Credit Policy*, NFRB pamphlet no. 15 (London: New Fabian Research Bureau, Dec. 1933).

——*The Problem of Credit Policy* (London: Chapman and Hall, 1935).

——*How to Pay for the War: An Essay on the Financing of War* (London: Routledge, 1939).

——'The economic problems facing the Labour government', in Donald Munro (ed.), *Socialism: the British Way* (London: Essential Books Limited, 1948), 3–29.

EBERSOLE, J. F., 'The influence of interest rates upon entrepreneurial decisions in business—a case study', *Harvard Business Review* 17 (Autumn 1938), 35–9.

ELLIS, HOWARD S. (ed.), *A Survey of Contemporary Economics* (Philadephia: Blakiston, 1948), 314–51.

FEINSTEIN, C. H., *National Income, Expenditure and Output of the United Kingdom 1955–1965* (Cambridge: Cambridge University Press, 1972).

FFORDE, J. S., *The Federal Reserve System 1945–1949* (Oxford: Clarendon Press, 1954).

——*The Bank of England and Public Policy, 1941–1958* (Cambridge: Cambridge University Press, 1992).

FRIEDMAN, MILTON, and SCHWARTZ, ANNA J., *A Monetary History of the United States 1867–1960* (Princeton NJ: Princeton University Press, 1963).

—— ——*Monetary Trends in the United States and the United Kingdom:*

Their Relation to Income, Prices and Interest Rates, 1867–1975 (Chicago: University of Chicago Press, 1982).

GAITSKELL, HUGH, 'Financial policy in the transition period', in G. E. G. Catlin (ed.), *New Trends in Socialism* (London: Lovat Dickson and Thompson, 1935), 169–200.

GARDNER, RICHARD N., *Sterling-Dollar Diplomacy* (London: Oxford University Press, 1956).

GORDON, H. SCOTT, 'A twenty year perspective: some reflections on the Keynesian revolution in Canada', in S. F. Kaliski (ed.), *Canadian Economic Policy since the War* (Ottawa: Canadian Trade Committee, 1965), 23–46.

HANCOCK, W. K., and GOWING, M. M., *British War Economy* (London: HMSO, 1949).

HARGREAVES, E. L., *The National Debt* (London: Edward Arnold, 1930).

HARROD, R. F., *Are these Hardships Necessary?* (London: Rupert Hart-Davis, 1947).

——*The Pound Sterling*, Princeton Essays in International Finance no. 13, Feb. 1952.

HAWTREY, R. G., *Towards the Rescue of Sterling* (London: Longmans, 1954).

HENDERSON, H. D, 'The significance of the rate of interest', *Oxford Economic Papers* no. 1 (Oct. 1938), 1–13.

——'Cheap money and the budget', *Economic Journal* 57 (Sept. 1947), 265–71.

HICKS, J. R., *Value and Capital* (Oxford: Clarendon Press, 1939).

——'The empty economy', *Lloyds Bank Review* no. 5 (July 1947), 1–13.

HIGGINS, BENJAMIN, 'Concepts and criteria of secular stagnation', in *Income, Employment and Public Policy: Essays in honor of Alvin H. Hansen* (New York: Norton, 1948), 82–107.

HOBSON, OSCAR, 'Debate on monetary policy, I—The case for dearer money', *The Banker* 47 (Aug. 1951), 71–7.

HODGMAN, DONALD R., 'British techniques of monetary policy, a critical review', *Journal of Money, Credit and Banking* 3 (Nov. 1971), 760–79.

HOGAN, MICHAEL J., *The Marshall Plan: America, Britain and the Reconstruction of Western Europe, 1947–52* (Cambridge: Cambridge University Press, 1987).

HOWARD, ANTHONY, *RAB: The Life of R. A. Butler* (London: Jonathan Cape, 1987).

HOWSON, SUSAN, '"A dear money man'?: Keynes on monetary policy, 1920', *Economic Journal* 83 (June 1973), 456–64.

——*Domestic Monetary Management in Britain 1919–38* (Cambridge: Cambridge University Press, 1975).

——*Sterling's Managed Float: The Operations of the Exchange Equalisation Account, 1932-39*, Princeton Studies in International Finance No. 46 (Nov. 1980).

——'The origins of cheaper money, 1945-7', *Economic History Review* 40 (Aug. 1987), 433-52.

——'Cheap money and debt management in Britain, 1932-51', in P. L. Cottrell and D. E. Moggridge (eds.), *Money and Power: Essays in Honour of L. S. Pressnell* (London: Macmillan, 1988), 227-89.

——' "Socialist" monetary policy: monetary thought in the Labour Party in the 1940s', *History of Political Economy* 20 (Winter 1988), 543-64.

——'Cheap money versus cheaper money: a reply to Professor Wood', *Economic History Review* 42 (Aug. 1989), 401-5.

——'The problem of monetary control in Britain, 1948-51', *Journal of European Economic History* 20 (Spring 1991), 59-92.

——(ed.), *The Collected Papers of James Meade, Volume I: Employment and Inflation* (London: Unwin Hyman, 1988).

——(ed.), *The Collected Papers of James Meade, Volume II: Value, Distribution and Growth* (London: Unwin Hyman, 1988).

——(ed.), *The Collected Papers of James Meade, Volume III: International Economics* (London: Unwin Hyman, 1988).

—— and MOGGRIDGE, DONALD (eds.), *The Collected Papers of James Meade, Volume IV: The Cabinet Office Diary 1944-46* (London: Unwin Hyman, 1990).

—— ——, *The Wartime Diaries of Lionel Robbins and James Meade, 1943-45* (London: Macmillan, 1990).

—— and WINCH, DONALD, *The Economic Advisory Council: A Study in Economic Advice during Depression and Recovery* (Cambridge: Cambridge University Press, 1977).

HUBBACK, DAVID, 'Sir Richard Clarke—1910-1975: a most unusual civil servant', *Public Policy and Administration* 3 (Spring 1988), 19-33.

JAY, DOUGLAS, *The Socialist Case* (London: Faber and Faber, 1937).

——*Change and Fortune: A Political Record* (London: Hutchinson, 1980).

JOHNSON, H. G., 'Some implications of secular changes in bank assets and liabilities in Great Britain', *Economic Journal*, 61 (Sept. 1951), 544-61.

JOHNSON, H. G., KENNEDY, C. M., *et al.*, 'Monetary policy: a symposium', *Bulletin of the Oxford Institute of Statistics* 14 (April and May 1952), 117-76.

JONES, RUSSELL, *Wages and Employment Policy 1936-1985* (London: Allen and Unwin, 1987).

KALDOR, NICHOLAS, 'Recollections of an economist', *Banca Nazionale del Lavoro Quarterly Review* no. 156 (Mar. 1986).

KALECKI, M., 'The short-term rate and the long-term rate', *Oxford Economic Papers* no. 4 (Sept. 1940), 15–22.

KAPLAN, JACOB J., and SCHLEIMINGER, GÜNTHER, *The European Payments Union: Financial Diplomacy in the 1950s* (Oxford: Clarendon Press, 1989).

KENNEDY, C. M., 'Monetary policy', in G. D. N. Worswick and P. H. Ady (eds.), *The British Economy 1945–1960* (Oxford: Clarendon Press, 1952), 188–206.

KEYNES, JOHN MAYNARD, *The General Theory of Employment, Interest and Money* (London: Macmillan, 1936).

——*How to Pay for the War: A Radical Plan for the Chancellor of the Exchequer* (London: Macmillan, 1940).

KINDLEBERGER, CHARLES P., *A Financial History of Western Europe* (London: Allen and Unwin, 1984).

KING, W. T. C., 'Gilt-edged and the volume of money', *The Banker* 80 (Oct. 1946), 7–16.

——'The monetary factor in gilt-edged', *The Banker* 82 (June 1948), 155–63.

KINROSS, JOHN, *Fifty Years in the City: Financing Small Business* (London: John Murray, 1982).

—— and PLANT, ARNOLD, 'Rt. Hon. the Lord Piercy, C.B.E.', *Journal of the Royal Statistical Society*, ser. A, 1967, pt. 2, 274–6.

KYNASTON, DAVID, *The Financial Times: A Centenary History* (London: 1988).

Labour Party, *Currency, Banking and Finance* (London: Labour Party, July 1932).

——*Labour's Immediate Programme* (London: Labour Party, Mar. 1937).

——*Full Employment and Financial Policy* (London: Labour Party, Apr. 1944).

——*Report of the 43rd Annual Conference held in Central Hall, Westminster, December 11th to December 15th, 1944* (London: Labour Party, 1944).

——*Let Us Face the Future, A Declaration of Labour Policy for the Consideration of the Nation* (London: Labour Party, 1945).

Liberal Industrial Inquiry, *Britain's Industrial Future* (London: Ernest Benn, 1928).

LINDBECK, ASSAR, 'Theories and problems in Swedish economic policy in the post-war period', *American Economic Review* 58 (Supplement, June 1968), 1–87.

LITTLE, I. M. D., 'Fiscal policy', in G. D. N. Worswick and P. H. Ady (eds.), *The British Economy in the Nineteen-Fifties* (Oxford: Clarendon Press, 1962), 231–91.

LITTLE, LEO T. 'Insurance companies and industrial capital', *The Banker* 95 (Aug. 1950), 80–7.

LUNDBERG, E. 'The rise and fall of the Swedish model', *Journal of Economic Literature* 23 (Mar. 1985), 1–36.

LUTZ, FRIEDRICH A., 'The interest rate and investment in a dynamic economy', *American Economic Review* 35 (Dec. 1945), 811–30.

MACDOUGALL, DONALD, *Don and Mandarin: Memoirs of an Economist* (London: John Murray, 1987).

MCKINNON, R. I., 'The exchange rate and macroeconomic policy: changing postwar perspectives', *Journal of Economic Literature* 19 (1981), 531–57.

MAYHEW, CHRISTOPHER, *Planned Investment: The Case for a National Investment Board* (London: Fabian Publications, 1939).

——*Socialist Economic Planning: The Overall Picture*, Discussion Series no. 1 (London: Fabian Publications, 1946).

MEADE, JAMES, *Public Works in their International Aspect*, NFRB pamphlet no. 4 (London: New Fabian Research Bureau, 1933).

——*An Introduction to Economic Analysis and Policy* (Oxford: Clarendon Press, 1936; 2nd edn., London: Oxford University Press, 1937).

——*Planning and the Price Mechanism: The Liberal-Socialist Solution* (London: Allen and Unwin, 1948).

—— and ANDREWS, P. W. S., 'Summary of replies to questions on effects of interest rates', *Oxford Economic Papers* no. 1 (Oct. 1938), 14–31.

MIDDLETON, ROGER, *Towards the Managed Economy: Keynes, the Treasury and the Fiscal Policy Debate of the 1930s* (London: Methuen, 1985).

MILWARD, ALAN S., *The Reconstruction of Western Europe 1945–51* (London: Methuen, 1984).

MOGGRIDGE, D. E., *British Monetary Policy 1924–1931* (Cambridge: Cambridge University Press, 1971).

——(ed.), *The Collected Writings of John Maynard Keynes, Volume XXI, Activities 1931–1939, World Crises and Policies in Britain and America* (London: Macmillan, 1982).

——*The Collected Writings of John Maynard Keynes, Volume XXII, Activities 1939–1945, Internal War Finance* (London: Macmillan, 1978).

——*The Collected Writings of John Maynard Keynes, Volume XXV, Activities 1940–1944, Shaping the Post-war World: The Clearing Union* (London: Macmillan, 1980).

——*The Collected Writings of John Maynard Keynes, Volume XXVII, Activities 1940–1946, Shaping the Post-war World: Employment and Commodities* (London: Macmillan, 1980).

—— and HOWSON, SUSAN, 'Keynes on monetary policy, 1910–1946', *Oxford Economic Papers* 26 (1974), 226–47.

MOORCOCK, MICHAEL, *Mother London* (Harmondsworth: Penguin, 1989).

MORGAN, E. VICTOR, 'The future of interest rates', *Economic Journal* 54 (Dec. 1944), 340–51.

MORGAN, KENNETH O., *Labour in Power* (Oxford: Clarendon Press, 1984).

MUNDELL, ROBERT A., 'The appropriate use of monetary and fiscal policy for internal and external stability', *IMF Staff Papers* 9 (1962), 70–7.

O'CONNOR, H. M., 'Debate on monetary policy, II—The case for letting well alone', *The Banker* 47 (Aug. 1951), 78–83.

OFFICER, LAWRENCE H., *Purchasing Power Parity and Exchange Rates: Theory, Evidence and Relevance* (Greenwich, CT: JAI Press, 1982).

OHLIN, BERTIL, 'Some notes on the Stockholm theory of savings and investment', *Economic Journal* 47 (June and Sept. 1937), 53–69, 221–40.

PAISH, F. W., 'Cheap money policy', *Economica* 14 (Aug. 1947), 26–33.

PEDEN, G. C., *British Rearmament and the Treasury, 1932–1939* (Edinburgh: Scottish Academic Press, 1979).

——'Sir Richard Hopkins and the "Keynesian revolution" in employment policy, 1929–1945', *Economic History Review* 36 (1983), 281–96.

PEMBER AND BOYLE, *British Government Securities in the Twentieth Century, The First Fifty Years* (2nd edn., London, 1950).

——*British Government Securities in the Twentieth Century (First Supplement, March, 1948)* (London, 1948).

——*British Government Securities in the Twentieth Century, Supplement 1950–1976* (London, 1976).

PIERCY, LORD, 'The Macmillan gap and the shortage of risk capital', *Journal of the Royal Statistical Society*, ser. A, 118 (1955), 1–7.

PIMLOTT, BEN, *Labour and the Left in the 1930s* (Cambridge: Cambridge University Press, 1977).

——*Hugh Dalton* (London: Jonathan Cape, 1985).

——*The Second World War Diary of Hugh Dalton, 1940–45* (London: Jonathan Cape, 1986).

——*The Political Diary of Hugh Dalton 1918–40, 1945–60* (London: Jonathan Cape, 1986).

PLOWDEN, EDWIN, *An Industrialist in the Treasury: The Post-War Years* (London: André Deutsch, 1989).

POWELL, ANTHONY, *Books do Furnish a Room* (London: Heinemann, 1971).

PRESSNELL, L. S., *External Economic Policy since the War, Volume I: The Post-war Financial Settlement* (London: HMSO, 1987).

ROBBINS, LIONEL, 'Economic prospects', *Lloyds Bank Review* no. 3 (Jan. 1947), 21–32.

——'Inquest on the crisis', *Lloyds Bank Review* no. 6 (Oct. 1947), 1–27.

——*The Economic Problem in Peace and War* (London: Macmillan, 1947).

——*Autobiography of an Economist* (London: Macmillan, 1971).

ROBERTSON, ALEX J., *The Bleak Midwinter 1947* (Manchester: Manchester University Press, 1987).

ROBERTSON, D. H., 'Some notes on Mr Keynes' general theory of employment', *Quarterly Journal of Economics* 51 (Nov. 1936), 188–91.

——*Essays in Monetary Theory* (London: P. S. King, 1940).

ROBINSON, AUSTIN, 'The economic problems of the transition from war to peace: 1945–49', *Cambridge Journal of Economics* 10 (1986), 165–85.

ROBINSON, JOAN, 'The rate of interest', *Econometrica* 19 (Apr. 1951), 92–111.

RODGERS, W. T. (ed.), *Hugh Gaitskell* (London: Thames and Hudson, 1964).

ROLLINGS, NEIL, 'British budgetary policy 1945–1954: a "Keynesian revolution"?', *Economic History Review* 41 (1988), 283–98.

SABINE, B. E. V., *British Budgets in Peace and War 1932–1945* (London: Allen and Unwin, 1970).

SAYERS, R. S., 'The rate of interest as a weapon of economic policy', in T. Wilson and P. W. S. Andrews (eds.), *Oxford Studies in the Price Mechanism* (Oxford: Clarendon Press, 1951), 1–16.

——*Modern Banking* (London: Oxford University Press, 1938; 2nd edn., Oxford: Clarendon Press, 1947; corrected 3rd edn., 1952).

——*Financial Policy 1939–45* (London: HMSO and Longmans, 1956).

——*The Bank of England 1891–1944* (Cambridge: Cambridge University Press, 1976).

SELTZER, LAWRENCE H., 'Is a rise in interest rates desirable or inevitable?', *American Economic Review* 35 (Dec. 1945), 831–50.

SHEPPARD, DAVID K., *The Growth and Role of UK Financial Institutions 1880–1962* (London: Methuen, 1971).

SPARKS, GORDON R., 'The theory and practice of monetary policy in Canada: 1945–83', in John Sargent (ed.), *Fiscal and Monetary Policy* (Toronto: University of Toronto Press, 1986), 119–49.

STEIN, HERBERT, *The Fiscal Revolution in America* (Chicago: University of Chicago Press, 1969).

STONE, RICHARD, 'The use and development of national income and expenditure estimates', in D. N. Chester (ed.), *Lessons of the British War Economy* (Cambridge: Cambridge University Press, 1951), 83–101.

SUPPLE, BARRY, *The Royal Exchange Assurance: A History of British Insurance 1720–1970* (Cambridge: Cambridge University Press, 1970).

TEW, BRIAN, *International Monetary Co-operation 1945–52* (London: Hutchinson, 1952; 2nd edn., 1954).

——'Monetary policy, part I', in F. T. Blackaby (ed.), *British Economic Policy 1960–74* (Cambridge: Cambridge University Press, 1978), 218–57.

TOMLINSON, JIM, *Employment Policy: The Crucial Years 1939–1955* (Oxford: Clarendon Press, 1987).

TOWERS, GRAHAM F., 'Review of post-war monetary policy', in E. P. Neufeld (ed.), *Money and Banking in Canada* (Toronto: McClelland and Stewart, 1964), 259–74.

Trades Union Congress, *Interim Report on Post-War Reconstruction* (London, 1944).

——*Four TUC Documents Approved by the Blackpool Congress 1945* (London: 1945).

WALLICH, HENRY C., 'Debt management as an instrument of economic policy', *American Economic Review* 36 (June 1946), 292–310.

——'The changing significance of the interest rate', *American Economic Review* 36 (Dec. 1946), 761–87.

WILLIAMS, FRANCIS, *Nothing So Strange: An Autobiography* (London: Cassell, 1970).

WILLIAMS, PHILIP M., *Hugh Gaitskell* (Oxford: Oxford University Press, 1982).

——(ed.), *The Diary of Hugh Gaitskell 1945–1956* (London: Jonathan Cape, 1983).

WILMOT, JOHN *Labour's Way to Control Banking and Finance* (London: Methuen, 1935; 2nd edn., 1946).

WILSON, T. and ANDREWS, P. W. S. (eds.), *Oxford Studies in the Price Mechanism* (Oxford: Clarendon Press, 1951).

WORMELL, JEREMY, *The Gilt-Edged Market* (London: Allen and Unwin, 1985).

WORSWICK, G. D. N., and ADY, P. H. (eds)., *The British Economy 1945–1950* (Oxford: Clarendon Press, 1952).

————*The British Economy in the Nineteen-Fifties* (Oxford: Clarendon Press, 1962).

WRIGHT, KENNETH M., 'Dollar pooling in the sterling area, 1939–1952', *American Economic Review* 44 (Sept. 1954), 559–76.

Unpublished papers

PRESSNELL, LESLIE, 'The 1947 crisis', presented to the Postwar Policy Seminar, Oxford, January 1989.

TEW, BRIAN, 'A first look at Exchequer financing under the Labour governments', 24 Oct. 1960 (mimeo.).

——'A second look at Exchequer financing under the Labour governments', 24 Nov. 1960 (mimeo.).

Official publications

'Exchequer financing and national debt 1945–51', *Economic Trends*, Dec. 1961.

Bank for International Settlements, *Twenty-Second Annual Report* (Basle, June 1952).

——*The Sterling Area*, Basle, Jan. 1953.

Bank of England, *Statistical Abstract*, No. 1, 1970.

'Official transactions in the gilt-edged market', *Bank of England Quarterly Bulletin* 6 (June 1966), 141–8.

'The U.K. exchange control: a short history', *Bank of England Quarterly Bulletin* 7 (Sept. 1967), 245–60.

'The monetary base—a statistical note', *Bank of England Quarterly Bulletin* 21 (Mar. 1981), 59–65.

'The experimental series of gilt-edged auctions', *Bank of England Quarterly Bulletin* 28 (1988), 194–7.

Capital Investment in 1948, Cmd. 7268, Dec. 1947.

Capital Issues Control, Cmd. 7281, Dec. 1947.

Committee on Finance and Industry [Macmillan Committee], *Report*, Cmd. 3897, 1931.

Committee on National Debt and Taxation [Colwyn Committee], *Report*, Cmd. 2800, 1927.

Committee on the Working of the Monetary System [Radcliffe Committee], *Report*, Cmnd. 827, 1959.

——*Principal Memoranda of Evidence* (London: HMSO, 1960).

Control of Dividends, Cmd. 8318, July 1951.

Economic Survey for 1947, Cmd. 7046, Feb. 1947.

Economic Survey for 1948, Cmd. 7344, Mar. 1948.

Employment Policy, Cmd. 6527, May 1944.

Financial Agreement between the Governments of the United States and the United Kingdom, Cmd. 6708, Dec. 1945.

House of Commons Debates.

House of Lords Debates.

Investment (Control and Guarantees) Bill, Memorandum and Draft Order to be made under Clause 1 of the Bill, Cmd. 6726, Jan. 1946.

League of Nations, *Economic Stability in the Post-War World: Report of the Delegation on Economic Depressions, Part II* (Geneva, 1945).

Monthly Digest of Statistics.

Reserves and Liabilities 1931 to 1945, Cmd. 8534, 1951.

Statement on Personal Incomes, Costs and Prices, Cmd. 7321, Feb. 1948.

United Kingdom Balance of Payments, 1946–1957 (London: HMSO, 1959).

UN Economic Commission for Europe, *Economic Survey of Europe in 1948* (Washington DC: US Government Printing Office, 1949).

US Bureau of the Census, *Historical Statistics of the United States, Colonial Times to 1970* (Washington DC: US Government Printing Office, 1975).

Newspapers

The Banker
The Economist
Financial Times
The Times

Index